W9-ABQ-646

Date: 2/13/13

641.651 MOR
Morgan, Diane,
Roots : the definitive
compendium with more than

PALM BEACH COUNTY
LIBRARY SYSTEM
3650 Summit Boulevard
West Palm Beach, FL 33406-4198

ROOTS

ROOTS

The **DEFINITIVE COMPENDIUM** *with more than* **225 RECIPES**

DIANE MORGAN

FOREWORD BY **DEBORAH MADISON**
PHOTOGRAPHS BY **ANTONIS ACHILLEOS**

CHRONICLE BOOKS
SAN FRANCISCO

IN LOVING MEMORY OF MY PARENTS,
Julius Ronald LevKoy and Irene Miller LevKoy

Text copyright © 2012 by Diane Morgan.
Foreword copyright © 2012 by Deborah Madison.
Photographs copyright © 2012 by Antonis Achilleos.

All rights reserved. No part of this book may be reproduced
in any form without written permission from the publisher.

Library of Congress Cataloging-in-Publication Data available.
ISBN 978-0-8118-7837-1

Manufactured in China

Designed by SARAH PULVER
Prop styling by PAIGE HICKS
Food styling by JAMIE KIMM
Typesetting by KATE KAMINSKI
The photographer wishes to thank Jamie and Paige, for the great collaboration,
hard work, and beautiful vision that made this project a lot of fun. Also I would
like to thank the creative team at Chronicle for their great attentiveness and for
promptly answering our countless questions about all the different types of roots.

Some of the roots described in this cookbook can be toxic if eaten uncooked.
Please purchase roots only from trusted sources and read and follow recipe
instructions carefully. While every effort has been made to present the information
in this book in a clear, complete, and accurate manner, every reader is different,
experts differ in their opinions of proper preparation, not every situation can be
anticipated, and the reader uses the information contained herein at his or her
own risk. The author and Chronicle Books disclaim any and all liability for
injuries suffered while consuming any of the roots described in this book.

10 9 8 7 6 5 4 3 2

Chronicle Books LLC
680 Second Street
San Francisco, California 94107
www.chroniclebooks.com

CONTENTS

FOREWORD

GOOD ROOTS ALL THE WAY DOWN

by Deborah Madison

Diane Morgan has written a masterful book about root vegetables, and I'm honored to have been asked to write this foreword for *Roots*, her truly worthy volume. The challenge of doing so got me to thinking about roots, not just the ones we cook, which are so thoroughly covered in this book, but roots in a more human, less vegetable realm and the vital role they play in both our culinary and our psychological worlds. Curiously, they overlap in some ways.

It's difficult to imagine the human world without the idea of roots. What are our roots? To whom and to where do we return for our most rooted essence? Do our roots run deep in a culture, history, or spot on this earth, or are we mere transplants, people who embrace a new place of residence and its culture but who aren't from that locale? The sense of the transplant is keenly felt in the warm regions that attract those from the cold climate. New Mexico has its strong native cultures that you might feel you've disrupted by adding your presence. You're not recognized as being from Vermont if your family hasn't lived there for many generations. Those who have deep roots in a place are respected and proud of them, whether they can trace their people back to the *Mayflower* or can claim to be a seventh-generation Californian, New Mexican, New Yorker—it matters not the place, only the time spent there, preferably measured in generations. We humans have an abiding interest in family trees, and trees, of course, have roots as well as trunks and branches. Sometimes in life we decide to go back to our roots as a way of reestablishing ourselves in attitude or approach to the world. When my Southern husband tasted pork after being a vegetarian for twelve years, he definitely went back to his roots. Culinarily speaking, he was home. He wasn't a Southerner for nothing.

A literary woman I once worked for had an odd but clearly scathing phrase that she used to describe an acquaintance of hers. She would say, "She is very nice, but she has no roots all the way down." All the way down. She must have had the idea of a taproot somewhere in her mind, a single, strong root that goes down deep to find its nourishment or, in this case, its character. It was a peculiar thing to say, but somehow I knew exactly what she meant. A rootless person is lacking in substance, is not firmly attached or committed, be it to a place, a person, or an idea. Those who are rootless might skittle across the surface of their lives like a tumbleweed whose shallow roots have lost their grip on the earth come winter. Once you start to think about the importance of roots, you see them mentioned in all kinds of places, including advertisements. "We know our roots," brags the founder of Bob's Red Mill, speaking of grains and where they come from.

Indeed, a special regard is given to the roots of plants that is not always given to stems and leaves. Plants are extolled for their root systems, and the deeper, larger, more complex they are, the more likely they are to impress. Take the tall prairie grasses of the Great Plains. Wes Jackson, founder of The Land Institute, often brings the root system of a single plant with him when he gives his talks on the perennial crops he is developing in Kansas. The roots of this grass go over his considerably high shoulder, cascade down his back, and trail along the floor, the whole thing resembling an intricately woven mantle. It's easy to see how roots such as these would knit the soil of the prairie into a rich and stable home. The prairies didn't blow away until those long grass roots were destroyed to make room for the more shallow-rooted wheat.

The roots of other plants are small and delicate. They spread out and hover near the surface where their chances of capturing nourishment are best. Pine trees in the Adirondacks may grow tall, but their shallow roots leave them vulnerable to high winds and storms. When you see them fallen, you can scarcely believe those roots were able to support such a tall tree for as long as they did. In contrast, the roots of other plants, notably those in dry places, go deep indeed, plunging 50 feet/15 meters into the earth. These are strong, well-rooted beings that intend to stay put for a while. It's hard work to dig up the deep-rooted junipers and salt cedars that dot the Colorado Plateau, but when one succeeds, water suddenly becomes available to other plants, which begin to flourish.

Roots, with the exception of aerial roots, are the plant's organs that grow beneath the soil's surface. They are what survive once the ground has closed up for winter and the leafy matter and stems have frozen and died. Roots don't bear leaves or fruits. They don't have nodes. They aren't stems, although swollen stems are often treated as roots. Taproots may be tapered, round, flat, lumpy, smooth, dull, or brightly colored. Regardless of their looks, their work is to absorb and store water and nutrients, all the while holding the plant fast to the ground so that it doesn't blow away, which in turn prevents the erosion of the soil in which it lives and that nourishes it—in other words, its home.

The underground world of edible roots, tubers, corms, and rhizomes is vast and extremely useful both in and out of the kitchen. Many herbal medicines and teas are derived from the roots of plants. I'm thinking of angelica, sassafras, licorice, sarsaparilla, ginger, osha, turmeric, and ginseng, for starters. Sugar is pulled from sugar beets; the diosgenin in wild yams is converted to estrogen. Eyes water and the nose stings when (happily) confronted with horseradish and wasabi. In the kitchen, roots find their way into every course of the meal, from pickles to soups, salads to entrées, and breakfast, from hash browns to parsnip muffins. They even show up in desserts, lending their good sweetness to carrot cake, beet-enhanced chocolate cake, and ginger ice cream.

Roots are a storehouse of nutrients that feed life itself. Even if you do nothing, sprouts leap forth from potatoes whether they've been stashed in a dark drawer or suspended in water. Sweet potatoes left on the counter eventually put forth their purple sprouts. Beets held in a jar of water with toothpicks will produce a virtual garden of green leaves in winter. Turnips, too, will eventually start to sprout leaves. What a goldmine of energy all of these edibles harbor. One can't help but think it's a good thing if some of that energy is transferred to our bodies, and indeed, edible roots carry many benefits: vitamins, minerals, antioxidants, plenty of fiber, and few calories.

And yet, so many people think of roots as dull and brown and stodgy. They're not, of course. If you don't already know this, you'll find out in reading *Roots* that color abounds, from scarlet radishes to golden, striped, and burgundy beets. We have pale gold rutabagas and snowy white–fleshed turnips; orange, purple, and yellow carrots; and red-skinned and orange- and even lavender-fleshed sweet potatoes. Roots can be brilliant and they can brighten the dark skies of winter at the table with ease.

Given the importance of roots for one's sense of self in the world and for the physical well-being and pleasure

that esculent roots provide, roots deserve special attention in the kitchen, which they have been given in heaps in Diane's work. Impressive in its scope, she definitely gives roots their due and then some. Not content to rest with the familiar roots of the supermarket, her broader scope includes roots of the Andes (ullucos and yellow potatoes), rhizomes (ginger and turmeric), and an odd collection of tuberous roots (kudzu and prairie turnips), of which the sweet potato is the most familiar. Corms, those swollen underground or underwater plant stems, include taro and water chestnuts, as well as arrowhead, konjac, and malanga—strangers to many, no doubt. They were to me until I opened this book. But many of the plants we now eat were also strangers not that long ago. I can remember when jicama was something of a novelty. Yuca is still new to many, as are Chioggia and golden beets and deep purple-skinned carrots, even though the earliest carrots were likely purple. Some roots were once familiar but no longer are, and I'm glad to see that Diane has thought to rescue them. Salsify, scorzonera, Hamburg parsley, and turnip-rooted chervil have come and gone from our tables before. In *Gardening for Good Eating*, written in 1939, Helen Morgenthau Fox sets out to rescue these same plants from threatened oblivion, and their rescue is still needed today as we turn our attention to other foods of the now global table.

Obviously, one of the best ways to introduce new roots and to keep older ones from disappearing is to have someone in the kitchen who knows what she's doing to make them enticing to the point of being addictive. That's how we can go from "What's this?" to "I've got to have it again!" Aren't you curious about a ragout of wild mushrooms and scorzonera, an oyster stew with salsify, or a chicken soup with Hamburg parsley? I am, and I'm glad I planted an entire bed of salsify, for I look forward to cooking these dishes and a great many more of the very appealing recipes in *Roots*.

There is something mysterious about growing root vegetables, for you judge their growth by looking at their tops. The leaves are the signpost for what's happening below. You might see the broad shoulder of a beet or daikon revealed at the junction between earth and sky, but you don't know until you give it a tug what exactly you've got. And when you've got it, take a whiff and inhale its earthy depth and sweetness, its promise. Then head to the kitchen, open this book, and further unlock the secrets of these all-important vegetables, for *Roots* is the definitive guide to the charmers that grow hidden from our sight.

INTRODUCTION

ON A CRISP FALL SATURDAY MORNING, AS I SHOPPED AT THE PORTLAND FARMERS' MARKET—A WEEKLY RITUAL—A WOMAN TURNED TO ME AND ASKED, "WHAT IS THAT?" I WAS REACHING FOR A CELERY ROOT, A CREAMY-SKINNED, GRAPEFRUIT-SIZE GNARLY ROOT WITH DRIED DIRT STUCK BETWEEN ITS HAIRY TENDRILS.

"Oh, this? It's celery root. Scary looking isn't it?"

"What do you do with it?" she asked.

"Well, you can cube it and use it in soup, mash it like you would potatoes, or toss chunks of it with olive oil, salt, and pepper and high-heat roast it. I love it, almost more than potatoes."

As I paid for my celery root, I held up a long, brown, hairy sticklike root and asked the farmer, "What is this?"

"Oh, that's burdock root. Have you ever tried it?" I hadn't. He proceeded to tell me how to cook it. It struck me as an amusingly circular story.

Weighed down with a market basket full of roots, squashes, and winter greens, I walked back to my car wondering why we don't know more about this underworld of roots. Sure, the popular roots stand out: the rosy beets, the glowing carrots, the always agreeable potato, and the smooth-skinned radishes. But so much more grows deep in the dirt. Lurking on the sidelines, waiting to get noticed, are hearty, healthful, nutrition-packed, budget-friendly root vegetables that deserve the spotlight.

Beyond the locavore movement of shopping at farmers' markets and joining community-supported agriculture organizations (CSAs), we are global eaters, excited to explore the tables of Thailand, China, Japan, Peru, India, Ethiopia, and more at ethnic restaurants. Adventuresome cooks buy cookbooks focused on a particular cuisine and hunt down ingredients in Asian or Latin American markets so they can make a hot pot, simmer a curry, or madly stir-fry. If you're like me, you wander through the produce section of an ethnic market selecting the ingredients you know—lemongrass, ginger, Thai chiles—all the while wondering, what the heck is this hairy potato-like tuber? or what do I do with galangal?

I have written this book for selfish reasons. I wanted a go-to volume that was both a comprehensive reference book and a cookbook of simple yet creative ways to prepare dozens of different root vegetables, the local ones and the global ones. Beyond that, I wanted a guide to vegetable varieties so that I could figure out how best to use, say, Chioggia or golden beets or even malanga. Plus, I needed answers to seasonal availability and information on the best way to buy and store all of these interesting vegetables. The recipes had to be numerous, accessible, and varied—from basic to sublime, savory to sweet. (As I've discovered, not all roots have a sweet side but many do!) So I decided to write the book I wanted to own.

As I began assembling the material, I realized that I wanted to include nutritional information for each root. Vegetables are our new best friends. Packed with antioxidants, these nutritionally dense, diet-friendly, cancer-fighting, immune-boosting, heart-healthy, easily digestible healers are "superfoods." When Michael Pollan says, "Eat food, not too much, mostly plants," he means the green and leafy vegetables that grow above the ground and the vast underworld of roots. They deliver a healthy diet that nourishes the body and the soul and preserves our farmland. So, in the course of writing the book, I happily learned that sweet potatoes score at the top of their class in seven nutrients, vitamins A and C, folate, iron, copper, calcium, and fiber, according to the Center for Science in the Public Interest, which conducted a study of fifty-eight vegetables. Now, I no longer think of sweet potatoes as just a Thanksgiving side dish. In fact, I often eat one for breakfast. When time permits, I roast sweet potatoes in the oven. But if I'm in a hurry, I poke one with a fork, pop it into the microwave, and in less than five minutes I have a hot, tender sweet potato that I drizzle with maple syrup—a nutrient-loaded package to start my day.

I know a sweet potato when I see one, but I'll admit that I sometimes got confused when researching roots that were new to me. For example, I might be in a Chinese market and see a long, creamy white root dotted with little hairy dimples labeled *yamaimo*. On another day, I might be shopping in the large local Japanese market and see a similar-looking root labeled *nagaimo*. Are they the same root? Are they different roots? I go home, pull my books on Asian vegetables off the shelf, and eventually figure out that the roots are two closely related types of yam and that both names are Japanese, despite the use of one of them in a Chinese market. Then, further sleuthing in other plant books provides corroborating evidence based on the botanical name. Jicama presents a similar knot of confusion. Head to a supermarket or a Latin American market and you will find jicama labeled just that. But walk into a Chinatown grocery and the same rotund root with the cappuccino-colored skin will be labeled yam bean. It convinced me that providing common names for these worldly root vegetables was not enough. I knew that I had to include the botanical name as well, so I have.

As I began exploring these edible roots, I discovered intriguing tales of a vegetable diaspora from the New World to the Old World and the reverse. Curious lore and odd stories from antiquity relate how some roots were used medicinally as aphrodisiacs and others to treat scurvy. Did you know that the first carrots were purple, not orange, were native to Afghanistan, and can be traced back three thousand years? Or that over forty thousand years ago, aboriginal Australians, who cultivated large crops of yams, were the first people to develop the technique of burying their produce to preserve it for future use? Could this have been the primitive beginnings of a root cellar? Learning the history of these roots was fascinating, and I felt a story for each root needed to be told.

The book is organized simply. At the beginning, I share the history and lore of the root cellar. How amazing it is to think that early hunter-gatherers figured out a way to preserve roots and, though modernized, many of those ancient methods translate to the root-storing techniques we still use today. In a separate section, I provide basic botanical information on roots. In fact, roots aren't just roots. They may be true roots or modified plant stems, and those classifications are further subdivided into rhizomes and corms. It's fascinating, especially for those of us who both cook and garden.

When you really dig in to the book, you'll find twenty-eight chapters arranged alphabetically by vegetable. The building blocks that help you learn about and work with each root vegetable are presented at the beginning of each chapter. You will discover its history and lore, names and descriptions of some popular varieties, details on its nutritional value; tips on how to recognize what's seasonally available and how to select the best; and information on storage to keep it fresh. In addition, I provide basic use and preparation techniques for each root, helping you appreciate the different ways it can be cooked and how to go about preparing it. Some roots have character traits (or flaws) the unsuspecting cook should know. I've added cautionary notes, where needed, to alert the cook. For instance, taro and malanga should never be eaten raw, turmeric stains like nobody's business and needs a quick cleanup as soon as it is chopped or grated, salsify must be submerged in acidulated water the moment it is peeled or it will discolor, and Jerusalem artichokes will produce gastric distress in some diners. Finally, I provide yields for each root so the cook will know how much to buy or harvest for a recipe.

The recipes themselves form the heart of the book. I wanted to let these fascinating, nutritious, and amazingly delicious subterranean beauties shine, highlighting each root with a variety of recipes that exploits its goodness and versatility. This is neither a vegetarian nor vegan cookbook (though many recipes fit these categories), but it will appeal to anyone who is eating less meat and increasingly putting vegetables at the center of a meal. Root vegetables such as celery root, turnips, sweet potatoes, and even rutabagas are nutritious and filling and can replace bread and pasta if you are trying to reduce carbohydrates in your diet. In the following pages, roots turn up in many wonderful guises: in appetizers, soups and chowders, side dishes, braises, vegetarian main courses; as breakfast fare; pickled and preserved; snuck into desserts; and even exploited in cocktails. It's an inspiring collection, whether you are a novice or an experienced cook.

The last chapter in the book, Other Roots, features just that. In the spirit of both global interest and comprehensiveness, I have provided limited information on a number of roots that you may never see in your local markets but are nonetheless important and essential food sources for millions of people around the world. As cultures and customs meld, opportunities for travel expand, and foreign cuisines are explored, you are sure to encounter roots new to you, and you will want to understand and appreciate them. Many of those valued roots are described here.

Finally, I want to explain a deliberate decision I made regarding the scope of this book. The focus is roots, that is, vegetables that have fleshy, edible underground parts that originate from roots, stems, or leaf bases. Within this category of plants we have taproots, tuberous roots, rhizomes, corms, stem tubers, and bulbs. The large genus of subterranean buds (*Allium*), which includes onions of various types, shallots, garlic, chives, ramps, and so on, is not included in this book. Space considerations meant one of two things: either I had to constrain the number of recipes I could include for each root so that all could be squeezed in, or I had to consider the wonderful family of edible bulbs for another project. I chose the latter.

I began this introduction with an amusingly circular story at the farmers' market, and I have a final one to share. I was young when the back-to-the-earth natural foods movement of the 1960s started. When Frances Moore Lappe's seminal book, *Diet for a Small Planet*, was published in 1971, I bought it and read it cover to cover. To my mother's dismay, I declared myself a vegetarian who ate fish—what is labeled a pescatarian today. It was a valiant effort that didn't last once I went to college. I look back on those beginnings and think about where

we are now thanks to victory gardens, CSAs, a growing network of farmers' markets, and ever-expanding national chains of natural foods stores. When a store like Walmart embraces organics and promotes them on billboards, you know the message has trickled down. And the push toward healthier eating continues today, with schoolyard gardens and with educational initiatives coming directly from the White House.

We are currently going back to our roots, to generations not so long ago when our grandparents and great-grandparents ate seasonally and shopped locally because that was their only option. They ate roots because they were cheap, stored well, and were nutritious. They planted backyard gardens and pickled and preserved out of necessity and economy. I delight in all of that and remember fondly the tomatoes my father grew and the sinus-clearing horseradish my grandfather uprooted from his garden in preparation for Passover. This book takes me back to my roots and yet it goes further, allowing me to embrace this subterranean world from both a local and global perspective. Researching and developing these recipes has deepened my understanding and appreciation of root vegetables. I hope the next time you see a gnarly root in a market that you'll buy it, and you'll then turn to this book to discover how to prepare it. I have packed these pages with back-to-basics home cooking at its finest, which is my favorite way to cook.

ROOTS, TUBERS, RHIZOMES, AND CORMS

LONG BEFORE I STARTED WRITING THIS BOOK—BUT WHEN I WAS ALREADY ON THE GARDEN PATH, SO TO SPEAK, OF RESEARCHING ROOT VEGETABLES—I ASKED A FARMER FRIEND OF MINE WHAT DEFINED A ROOT VEGETABLE. IT SEEMED LIKE A SIMPLE QUESTION THAT WOULD DELIVER A STRAIGHTFORWARD RESPONSE.

Without waiting for an answer, I began to rattle off a long list of common roots: potatoes, carrots, parsnips, turnips, beets, sweet potatoes, radishes, kohlrabi. Sheldon stopped me at kohlrabi and said, "Actually, kohlrabi isn't a root. It is an above-ground swollen stem, and it's in the Brassicaceae family. Turnips are in the same family, and *they* are true roots."

For a culinarian without a botany background, but with a keen interest in understanding classifications and categories for all of the roots I have eaten or seen in ethnic markets, I went to the library and studied, bought an armful of books on food plants, and searched Web sites. While my goal for this book is to provide a broad collection of terrific recipes that highlights the attributes of each root, I think it's helpful and fun for the interested cook to have some botanical context. Many cooks garden, frequent farmers' markets, belong to a CSA (community-supported agricultural organization), explore ethnic cuisines, or engage in all of these activities. Giving common and uncommon roots a botanical context, albeit a rudimentary one, is useful and sometimes even necessary. For instance, a close friend of mine has a son who is allergic to potatoes, so knowing that potatoes are in the nightshade family (Solanaceae) would lead her to question

whether he can tolerate eggplant and tomatoes, which are in the same family.

Botanically, vegetables, including salad plants, are edible food products that can have many different edible parts: flowers (broccoli and cauliflower); seeds (corn, beans); leaves (spinach, kale, cabbage); leaf sheaths (leeks); buds (capers, Brussels sprouts); stems or swollen stems (kohlrabi); stems of leaves (celery, rhubarb, lemongrass); stem shoots (asparagus, bamboo shoots); whole-plant sprouts (alfalfa, mung beans); tubers (potatoes, yams, Jerusalem artichokes); roots (carrots, parsnips, beets, radishes); bulbs (onions, shallots, garlic); legumes (green beans, soybeans); and fruits (tomatoes, eggplant, zucchini, peppers).

This book's focus is roots, or vegetables that have fleshy, edible underground parts that originate from roots, stems, or leaf bases. In general, they are storage organs enlarged to hold energy in the form of carbohydrates. Within this category, root crops are botanically distinguished as true roots, which include taproots and tuberous roots, and as modified plant stems, which include rhizomes, corms, stem tubers, and bulbs.

I'd like to remind the reader again that the large genus of subterranean buds (*Allium*), which includes onions, shallots, garlic, and the like, is not included in this book. With twenty-eight chapters focused on a global collection of common and uncommon roots available in most markets today, scope management was an issue, and edible bulbs, though culinarily significant, are left to another project. Of course, they appear throughout the recipes in this book as flavor enhancers and decorative garnishes.

TRUE ROOTS

TAPROOTS A taproot is the main root of a plant that absorbs nutrients and moisture as it grows vertically downward, often bearing smaller lateral roots. Taproots vary in shape and are categorized as conical (widest at the top, tapering gradually to the bottom; carrots and parsnips are examples), fusiform (widest in the middle, tapering at both the top and bottom; radishes are an example), and napiform (shaped like a spinning top, broad at the top, tapering to a tail at the bottom; turnips and beets are examples).

Beets	Peruvian parsnips
Burdock root	Radishes
Carrots	Rutabagas
Celery root	Salsify
Chicory root	Scorzonera
Jicama	Skirret
Maca	Turnip-rooted chervil
Parsley root	Turnips
Parsnips	

TUBEROUS ROOTS These enlarged modified lateral roots function as storage organs. Yuca and sweet potatoes resemble stem tubers in their high starch content but are tuberous roots rather than tubers.

Earthnut	Sweet potatoes
Kudzu	Yacón
Mauka	Yuca
Prairie turnips	

MODIFIED PLANT STEMS

RHIZOMES A rhizome is a fleshy horizontal plant stem that spreads below the soil surface and forms leaves above and thin roots below. Often referred to as creeping rootstalks, these stems characteristically send out roots or shoots from their nodes. This secondary sprouting stem is called a stolon. If a rhizome is separated into pieces, each piece should be able to produce a new plant. This is known as vegetative reproduction.

Arrowroot	Licorice
Galangal	Lotus root
Ginger	Turmeric
Ginseng	Wasabi

CORMS A corm is a short, swollen underground or underwater plant stem whose inner structure is made up of solid tissue. From the vertical top of the corm, one or a few buds grow into shoots that produce leaves and flowers. What distinguishes corms from true bulbs is the inner structure. A halved corm reveals a solid interior, while a halved bulb exposes fleshy layers. Compare the tissue layers of a shallot (a bulb) with the solid heart of a water chestnut.

Arrowhead	Malanga
Enset	Taro
Konjac	Water chestnuts

STEM TUBERS A stem tuber is a swollen underground storage organ that forms from a thickened rhizome or stolon. The top or sides of the tuber produce shoots that grow into stems and leaves, and the underside produces roots. Stem tubers have a vertical orientation with one or a few vegetative buds on top and fibrous roots extending from the bottom. (Think back to grade-school science when you stuck wooden toothpicks into a sprouting potato and elevated it in a jar with the bottom of the potato immersed in water. Placed in a sunny window, the potato sent out roots from the bottom and buds from the top.) Tubers typically store large amounts of starch, a valuable food source with a high-energy value.

Andean potatoes	Oca
Crosnes	Potatoes
Groundnut	Tigernut
Jerusalem artichokes	Ullucos
Mausha	Yams

THE ROOT CELLAR

I DUG MY CELLAR IN THE SIDE OF A HILL SLOPING TO THE SOUTH, WHERE A WOODCHUCK HAD FORMERLY DUG HIS BURROW, DOWN THROUGH SUMACH AND BLACKBERRY ROOTS AND THE LOWEST STAIN OF VEGETATION, SIX FEET SQUARE BY SEVEN DEEP, TO A FINE SAND WHERE POTATOES WOULD NOT FREEZE IN ANY WINTER. . . . I TOOK PARTICULAR PLEASURE IN THIS BREAKING OF GROUND.

—Henry David Thoreau, Walden, 1854

Fast-forward from Thoreau's time to today and you will find a bumper crop of interest in the decidedly low-tech cold-storage system of root cellaring. Whatever the reason—rising food costs, food insecurity, concern over unsafe commercial production methods, living off the grid—root cellars are enjoying a twenty-first-century revival.

Forty thousand years ago, the indigenous people of Australia harnessed the cooling and insulating properties of underground storage to preserve their bountiful yam harvest. They also discovered its value for fermentation, an early precursor of the wine cellar.

The emergence of the walk-in root cellar occurred much later, in seventeenth-century England. Other great civilizations had perfected techniques for preserving fruits and vegetables—the Chinese mastered salting, pickling, and spicing; the Egyptians were experts at drying foods—but cool, dank winters and motivated Englishmen gave rise to the root cellar, which the colonists brought with them to North America (thousands of old root cellars exist in the eastern United States and Canada).

The American root cellar of the early 1800s was usually a pantrylike room with a dirt floor, deeply excavated and typically sited on the northern side of a house. Farm families often used cellars not only to preserve their own food but also to store food for their livestock and to keep their crops until winter when they would fetch better prices. In the mid-nineteenth century, cellars sometimes literally preserved life, serving as hiding places or "stations" for fugitive slaves traveling north along the Underground Railroad.

By the early decades of the twentieth century, with the arrival of modern refrigeration and the change in the diet of livestock from vegetables to grain, root cellars began to go out of fashion. In time, only survivalists and back-to-the-landers continued to rely on them.

Today, you can design a root cellar to accommodate almost any storage need and living situation, including townhouses and condominiums. Choose a portable bin system, permanently installed bins, wooden boxes with lids, or alternate your vegetables "parfait style" between layers of damp sand, sawdust, or peat moss in garbage cans. You can build a cellar or you can adapt a "found" space (under the front porch, on the basement steps) to create the perfect microclimate for beets, carrots, celery root, ginger, parsnips, potatoes, rutabagas, and turnips. All you need are three conditions: a cold temperature (a year-round, above-freezing temperature ranging from 32° to 40°F/0° to 5°C), high humidity (between 70 and 90 percent), and good ventilation.

How far to burrow? A root cellar 12 inches/30.5 centimeters deep can create a temperature 20°F/7°C cooler than the aboveground summertime temperature. Some 3 or 4 feet/90 or 120 centimeters of soil will do nicely in most cases, but 10 feet/3 meters of soil above and alongside is optimal to ensure maximum insulation and minimize temperature variability. Also, whether you are building a walk-in basement root cellar or a stand-alone one, check first into any possible legal or permit issues.

Thermometers (to measure temperature) and hygrometers (to measure humidity) are critical pieces of equipment to monitor the climate in a root cellar. It is desirable to have multiple gauges at various locations to record the microclimates at different heights, especially since one size does not fit all when it comes to optimizing conditions for storing different fruits and vegetables.

Many root vegetables require cold, very moist conditions. In contrast, sweet potatoes, for example, require moderately warm and dry conditions. Since the temperature in a root cellar is never uniform (it is typically a few degrees warmer near the ceiling), it's important to place produce that tolerates warmer temperatures closer to the top. Most root vegetables are "good keepers," meaning they will last four to six months if properly stored.

Seek out the seminal, decades-old book on the art and science of root cellars, *Root Cellaring: Natural Cold Storage of Fruits and Vegetables* by Mike and Nancy Bubel, and *The Complete Root Cellar Book* by Steve Maxwell and Jennifer MacKenzie for a wealth of information on building and using root cellars. In the meantime, here are a few tidbits of conventional wisdom—and a smattering of molecular gastronomy—on preparing your root vegetables for storage.

- Never wash root vegetables before putting them in storage. Washing damages the skin and greatly reduces storage life.

- Use cut, blemished, or runt produce first.

- Dip rutabagas in melted food-grade wax, preferably beeswax, to reduce moisture loss and extend storage life.

- Radishes, which store well for five to eight weeks, will shrivel unless wrapped in damp sand, sawdust, or peat moss.

- The cellular life of some vegetables, including potatoes and sweet potatoes, can be prolonged by "curing" them in a dry, warm, well-ventilated space for a couple of weeks before storage. This process toughens the skin and helps retard spoilage.

- Protect against "flavor transfer" by strategic placement of foodstuffs (keep potatoes away from onions, for example).

- Don't place vegetables directly on a concrete floor.

- Beware of plants behaving badly when exposed to ethylene. This colorless, odorless gas, which is present in many ripening fruits, accelerates the ripening and spoilage of nearby produce. Potatoes and sweet potatoes will sprout prematurely unless stored away from apples. Other good candidates for the root cellar, such as broccoli and cabbage, respond by dropping their leaves in a process called abscission. One way to prevent ethylene contamination from apples is to wrap them individually in newspaper or store them in sealed plastic bags and puncture the bags with pinholes.

- Keep an inventory of what you have stored and check your cache often for possible spoilage.

So make a list of your favorite fruits and vegetables and picture your winter's table laden with harvest-fresh produce, including pan-roasted pork tenderloin with salsify, carrots, chickpeas, and cranberries; thyme-infused roasted beets; and apple and rutabaga tart—all made with recipes from this cookbook, of course!

ANDEAN TUBERS

For centuries, many root vegetables common to the Andean region have been cultivated as food staples. Among them are jicama, sweet potato, yam, yuca (cassava), and (especially) the potato, all of which have global importance today and each of which has been given its own chapter. A number of other indigenous Andean roots deserving attention are, to the best of my knowledge, available only in the markets of the Andean countries. Because these intriguing roots, including maca, mashua, mauka, oca, Peruvian parsnips, and yacón, are not seen fresh in North American markets, they have been briefly profiled in Other Roots on page 399.

This chapter focuses on two tubers, ullucos and Andean potatoes. Although both are somewhat exotic, they are available in North American markets. I have concentrated on two popular Andean potato varieties, yellow potatoes (*papas criollas*) and blue or purple potatoes (*papas moradas*). For thousands of years, the Andeans have been preserving potatoes at high altitudes by freeze-drying them, either whole or broken, and these are discussed here, as well.

ULLUCOS *Ullucus tuberosus*

HISTORY AND LORE A member of the family Basellaceae, ullucos, commonly known as *papalisas*, are indigenous to the Andean region and were cultivated by the Inca. They are the second most economically important tuber crop in the area, after the potato. In Peru alone, some thirty thousand tons are sold annually in local markets.

VARIETIES The ulluco is a stem tuber with edible leaves similar to spinach and a root with an earthy flavor that tastes like a cross between a potato and a beet. Its flesh is white or pale yellow, and the skin, which is thin and soft and, like the skin of a potato, does not need to be removed before eating, comes in striking colors of tan, pink, white, red, or purple. These tubers tend to be 6 to 8 inches/15 to 20 centimeters long and variously shaped: some roundish, others a little crooked and sausagelike.

NUTRITION Ullucos are a major source of carbohydrates for the Andeans, and contain high levels of protein, calcium, carotene, and vitamin C.

AVAILABILITY AND SELECTION In the United States, ullucos are available canned and sometimes frozen in Latin American markets. I found them packed in brine in cans.

STORAGE Store as you would any frozen or canned vegetables.

BASIC USE AND PREPARATION Ullucos keep their crisp texture even when cooked. They can be boiled, simmered, roasted, added to soups and stews, and even sliced and used in salads. If using canned ullucos, drain them, discarding the brine, rinse well, and blot dry.

YIELDS

One 20-oz/570-g can ullucos packed in brine, drained and sliced = about 2 cups/400 g

---

ANDEAN POTATOES *Solanum tuberosum*

The greatest diversity in wild potato species occurs in the Lake Titicaca region of Peru and Boliva, where it is speculated potatoes were domesticated between seven and ten thousand years ago. From a single botanical species, *Solanum tuberosum*, thousands of varieties have been cultivated. Of interest in this chapter are the Peruvian yellow potatoes commonly known as *papas criollas* and the blue or purple potatoes known as *papas moradas*. These two unique varieties are still found in Peru and are available in North American markets. Specialty distributors, such as Frieda's or Melissa's (see Sources), supply the U.S. markets. On occasion, potato growers at farmers' markets have unique Peruvian varieties.

VARIETIES Many different varieties of Peruvian yellow potatoes are cultivated. One popular cultivar, the Criolla, is small and round and typically grown at 6,500 feet/2,000 meters. It has thin skin and golden yellow flesh and is almost always roasted or boiled in its jacket. The Criolla is often used in Latin American soups, where it imparts a characteristic dark yellow color and is cooked until it falls apart and thickens the broth.

Blue or purple potatoes are small to medium size and have thin, dark blue to black-violet skin and bright purple flesh. They get their vivid interior color from certain minerals in the soil. The showy purple color mellows with cooking, but refrigerating the potatoes before cooking will heighten their color once they are cooked. Stirring freshly squeezed lime juice into the cooked and mashed potatoes will also brighten the color.

NUTRITION Potatoes have a reputation for being fattening, but they aren't. With 75 calories per 14-ounce/400-gram serving, they are actually a boon for the weight-conscious eater. Potatoes are about 80 percent water, 18 percent carbohydrate (most of which is starch), and 2 percent protein and are rich in lysine (an amino acid essential to good health). They also carry a fair amount of mineral salts (calcium, potassium, and iron) and are a good source of vitamin C.

AVAILABILITY AND SELECTION Harvesting times depend on the particular variety, but some fresh purple or yellow potatoes will be available year-round. Select firm potatoes with taut skin free of blemishes or sprouts. On occasion, a potato grower at the farmers' market I frequent has Peruvian potatoes. When I don't find them, I substitute small Yukon Gold potatoes. I have found frozen whole Peruvian yellow potatoes in Latin American markets.

STORAGE Store potatoes in a cool, dark spot with good air circulation. Protect them from both daylight and artificial light, which can cause them to develop green patches (evidence of the toxic compound solanine), and from frost. They will keep for up to a month. During the cool months of the year, I store potatoes in my basement, in a loose brown-paper sack with the top crumpled over but not tightly sealed. In the warmer months, I buy only what I need for a recipe and use them right away.

BASIC USE AND PREPARATION Potatoes are always cooked and are among the most versatile of all vegetables for preparation. They can be boiled, baked, roasted, steamed, simmered, sautéed, grill-roasted, and deep-fried. Scrub potatoes under cool running water with a vegetable brush to rid them of dirt. These small potatoes are typically cooked in their skins and then peeled or not peeled, depending on the recipe. If buying frozen Peruvian yellow potatoes, partially thaw them before using

---

YIELDS

1 very small potato = 1½ to 2 oz/40 to 55 g

1 small potato = about 3 oz/85 g

1 medium potato = 7 to 8 oz/200 to 225 g

1 large potato = 9 to 10 oz/255 to 280 g

1 cup cooked and sliced small potatoes = 8 oz/ 225 g

2 cups peeled, cooked, and mashed potatoes = 1 lb/455 g

FREEZE-DRIED PERUVIAN POTATOES

Natives of the highlands of Peru and Bolivia have long preserved potatoes by freeze-drying them. One method results in dehydrated potatoes known as *chuño*, which last indefinitely. Once the nighttime temperature drops below freezing, the potatoes are left whole on the ground overnight to freeze. The next day, the potatoes thaw in the warmth of the sun, are squeezed dry, and then left out to freeze again that evening. This process is repeated for several weeks until all of the moisture has evaporated and the potatoes are completely dehydrated, leaving them white and very light. They are then stored for use in months when no potatoes are harvested. To use them, they are rehydrated over the course of several days by soaking them in warm water until the flesh is chalky and the skin can be easily removed. Cooked *chuño* can be found in cans at some Latin American markets.

Peru's Quecha Indians use a different method to dehydrate potatoes, yielding what are known as *papa seca*. They cook them, leave them to freeze overnight, and then warm them in the sun the next day and squeeze them dry. They repeat the freezing and thawing steps until the potatoes are fully dehydrated. As the moisture evaporates, they break the potatoes into irregular pieces. When it is time to use the pieces, they first toast them in a dry frying pan and then soak them in water to rehydrate them. I found *papa seca* packed in bags on the grocery shelf of a well-stocked Latin American market in Portland, Oregon.

YIELDS

9¼ oz/260 g *papa seca* = 2 cups dried potato pieces

CAUSA TRUCHA AHUMADO
(POTATO CAKE WITH SMOKED TROUT)

Causa is a savory cake made from mashed yellow potatoes typically seasoned with lime juice, onion, oil, and, sometimes, puréed chiles. It is often formed into a dumpling shape and served cold along with hard-boiled eggs and olives. I learned some of the finer points of cooking Peruvian potatoes and making *causa* from the executive chef of Adina, the award-winning Peruvian restaurant in Portland, Oregon. For this recipe, Peruvian purple potatoes are used. To retain the regal purple of the potatoes, you need to cook them whole in their skins, and to achieve their delicate texture, they must be riced while they are hot. The addition of the lime juice turns them an even more vivid color. Using a pair of molds to shape the potatoes and salad into a tower is very chef-y, of course, but it is also quite easy to do at home and makes a spectacular presentation. See the Cook's Note that follows for information on where to find the molds and for suggestions for suitable substitutes.

SERVES 6 AS AN APPETIZER OR LIGHT LUNCH WITH ACCOMPANIMENTS

2 lb/910 g Peruvian purple potatoes

1 tbsp plus 1 tsp kosher or fine sea salt

½ cup/120 ml canola or other neutral oil

¼ cup/60 ml fresh Key lime or regular lime juice

½ tsp freshly ground pepper

SMOKED TROUT SALAD
12 oz/340 g smoked trout, skin and bones removed

⅔ cup/165 ml mayonnaise

½ cup/70 g finely diced celery

½ cup/70 g finely diced red onion

GARNISH
2 large Hass avocados, halved, pitted, peeled, and thinly sliced

Radish sprouts or microgreens

1 In a large pot, combine the potatoes with water to cover, cover partially, and bring to a boil over high heat. Uncover, add the 1 tbsp salt, and reduce the heat so the water boils gently. Cook until the potatoes are tender when pierced with a fork, 20 to 30 minutes, depending on the size of the potatoes.

2 Drain the potatoes in a colander and let cool for 10 minutes. Peel the potatoes. (To make peeling them easier, wear disposable surgical gloves, available at any pharmacy.) Pass the warm potatoes through a ricer or a food mill into a large bowl. Using a rubber spatula, slowly work in the oil. Add the lime juice, the remaining 1 tsp salt, and the pepper. Use the spatula to fold over the potatoes until they are completely smooth and almost like a soft, smooth dough. Cover and refrigerate until cold and firm, about 2 hours.

3 Meanwhile, make the trout salad. In a medium bowl, use a fork to flake the trout. Stir in the mayonnaise, celery, and onion. Cover and refrigerate until ready to serve.

4 Have ready two round presentation molds, each 3 in/7.5 cm in diameter and 3 in/7.5 cm deep. Cut parchment paper into two 3-by-12-in/7.5-by-30.5-cm rectangles, and then line each mold with a rectangle. Place each lined mold in the center of a salad plate. For each tower, scoop up ⅓ cup/75 ml of the potato and use a spoon to pack it into the bottom of a mold. Smooth the top of the potato, packing it down a bit more to release any air pockets. Add ⅓ cup/75 ml of the trout salad to the mold, again smoothing the top and gently packing it down. To complete the tower, scoop up another ⅓ cup/ 75 ml of potato and spoon it into the mold, pressing it down gently. Repeat to fill the second lined mold the same way. Carefully lift each mold straight up to remove it, and then unwrap the parchment paper from around each tower. Repeat to form four more towers, each on its own salad plate.

5 To garnish each plate, fan an equal number of avocado slices to one side of each tower, then mound a small amount of sprouts on top of each tower. Serve immediately.

COOK'S NOTE

The presentation molds, also known as stack rings or cake rings, are simple tubes made from stainless steel or aluminum. Using molds that are 3 in/ 7.5 cm tall brings drama to these potato towers. Look for the molds in gourmet kitchen shops or order them online from www.fantes.com, Philadelphia's oldest cookware shop. For an inexpensive alternative, head to a hardware store and buy 3-in/7.5-cm PVC pipe and either cut it into 3-in/7.5 cm lengths or ask the store clerk to do it for you. In a pinch, a tall biscuit cutter or a soup can with both ends removed will work.

CAUSA VEGETARIANO
(POTATO CAKE WITH VEGETABLES AND CHEESE)

You might find it hard to imagine that cold mashed potatoes can be both delicious and beautifully presented; *Causa* is often served at weddings and other celebrations, proving that it meets both descriptions.

Ají amarillo, the most common Peruvian chile, is known as yellow Peruvian chile in the United States. It delivers moderate heat with fruity, citrusy accents. Look for jars of prepared *amarillo* chile paste; otherwise, buy either whole dried chiles or jarred water-packed chiles and make an easy homemade paste (see page 31).

SERVES 6 AS AN APPETIZER OR LIGHT LUNCH

2 lb/910 g Peruvian yellow potatoes or Yukon Gold potatoes

1 tbsp plus 1 tsp kosher or fine sea salt

½ cup/120 ml canola or other neutral oil

¼ cup/60 ml fresh Key lime or regular lime juice

1 tbsp *amarillo* chile paste (see page 31 or store-bought)

TOPPING

6 to 8 green beans, stem end trimmed and cut into ¼-in/ 6-mm dice

¼ cup/35 g fresh corn kernels

¼ cup/35 g diced red onion (¼-in/ 6-mm dice)

¼ cup/40 g pitted Botija or Kalamata olives, cut into ¼-in/ 6-mm dice

¼ cup/15 g lightly packed fresh cilantro leaves, coarsely chopped

¼ cup/40 g diced, seeded Roma tomato (¼-in/6-mm dice)

1½ oz/40 g *queso Oaxaca* or *queso fresco*, cut into ¼-in/6-mm dice

1 tbsp canola or other neutral oil

2 tsp fresh Key lime or regular lime juice

6 fresh cilantro sprigs for garnish

1 In a large pot, combine the potatoes with water to cover, cover partially, and bring to a boil over high heat. Uncover, add the 1 tbsp salt, and reduce the heat so the water boils gently. Cook until the potatoes are tender when pierced with a fork, 20 to 30 minutes, depending on the size of the potatoes.

2 Drain the potatoes in a colander and let cool for 10 minutes. Peel the potatoes. (To make peeling them easier, wear disposable surgical gloves, available at any pharmacy.) Pass the potatoes through a ricer or a food mill into a large bowl. Using a rubber spatula, slowly work in the oil. Add the lime juice, the remaining 1 tsp salt, and the chile paste. Use the spatula to fold over the potatoes until they are completely smooth and almost like a soft, smooth dough. Cover and refrigerate until cold and firm, about 2 hours.

3 Meanwhile, make the topping. Bring a small pot of salted water to a boil. Add the green beans and corn and simmer until crisp-tender, about 2 minutes. Using a slotted spoon, transfer to a bowl of ice water. Let cool for 2 minutes, then drain and blot dry with paper towels.

4 In a medium bowl, combine the green beans, corn, onion, olives, cilantro, tomato, and *queso*. Stir in the oil and lime juice. Cover and refrigerate until ready to serve.

5 Have ready two round presentation molds (see Cook's Note, page 25), each 3 in/7.5 cm in diameter and 3 in/7.5 cm deep. Cut parchment paper into two 3-by-12-in/7.5-by-30.5-cm rectangles, and then line each mold with a rectangle. Place each lined mold in the center of a salad plate. For each tower, scoop up ⅔ cup/165 ml of the potato and use a spoon to pack it into the bottom of a mold. Smooth the top of the potato, packing it down a bit more to release any air pockets. Repeat to fill the second lined mold the same way. Carefully lift each mold straight up to remove it, and then unwrap the parchment paper from around each tower. Repeat to form four more towers, each on its own salad plate. Spoon an equal amount of the topping on top of each potato tower. Garnish each plate with a cilantro sprig. Serve immediately.

PAPAS A LA HUANCAÍNA
(POTATOES WITH CHEESE AND CHILE SAUCE)

This humble potato dish, with its creamy, vibrant yellow sauce, is from Huancayo, a mountain town some six hours by car from Lima. The region claims to be home to more than three thousand potato varieties, and the distinctive sauce was created to celebrate the prolific tuber. In some areas, the sauce is made from the *rocoto* chile; in others, the *amarillo* chile is used. The sauce is reasonably easy to make and can also be served as a dip with crudités. Markets selling Latin American and Peruvian foods will carry *amarillo* chiles fresh, frozen, or sold in jars packed in either brine or water. You'll find Botija olives there, too. See Sources for online sites selling Peruvian foods.

SERVES 8 AS AN APPETIZER OR LIGHT LUNCH; MAKES ABOUT 3 CUPS/720 ML SAUCE

HUANCAÍNA SAUCE

4 fresh or jarred *amarillo* chiles (⅔ cup/80 g)

3 tbsp canola or other neutral oil

¾ cup/105 g coarsely chopped red onion

3 garlic cloves, thinly sliced

Kosher or fine sea salt

Freshly ground pepper

4 saltine crackers, crushed

2 cups/225 g crumbled *queso Oaxaca* or *queso fresco*

1 cup/240 ml milk

½ tsp granulated sugar

1½ lb/680 g petite Peruvian purple potatoes

1 tbsp kosher or fine sea salt

4 hard-boiled eggs, peeled and quartered lengthwise

1 First make the sauce. If using fresh chiles, halve them lengthwise, remove the seeds, and then coarsely chop. If using chiles packed in brine or water, rinse them under cold water, blot dry, halve them lengthwise, remove the seeds, and coarsely chop.

2 In a medium sauté pan, heat the oil over medium heat and swirl to coat the pan bottom. Add the chiles, onion, and garlic and sauté, stirring frequently, until the onion is soft but not brown, about 4 minutes. Season lightly with salt and pepper and remove from the heat.

3 While the onion mixture is still hot, transfer it to a blender and process for 2 minutes to yield a smooth purée. Add the crackers, *queso*, milk, and sugar and process again until smooth. Transfer the mixture to a covered container and refrigerate until ready to use. (The sauce can be made up to 3 days in advance. Remove from the refrigerator 30 minutes before serving.)

4 In a large pot, combine the potatoes with water to cover, cover partially, and bring to a boil over high heat. Uncover, add the salt, and reduce the heat so the water boils gently. Cook until the potatoes are tender when pierced with a fork, 12 to 15 minutes, depending on the size of the potatoes.

5 Drain the potatoes in a colander, and let cool. Peel the potatoes. (To make peeling them easier, wear disposable surgical gloves, available at any pharmacy.) Cut the potatoes into fans by slicing them thinly but leaving one end uncut. This way, you can fan out the slices without them separating.

6 Spoon about ⅓ cup/75 ml of the sauce in the center of each plate, forming a circle. Put two egg quarters at the top of each circle. Place three or four potatoes, depending on their size, on each plate, fanning the slices and arranging the potatoes in a circular pattern on the sauce. Serve immediately.

OCOPA LIMEA
(PERUVIAN YELLOW POTATOES WITH OCOPA SAUCE)

Incredibly popular in Peru, *ocopa* is an ancient cold potato dish from Arequipa, in the Andes. The divinely rich, nutty sauce is made from dried chiles, which are rehydrated and then sautéed with red onions, garlic, and a very fragrant herb called *huacatay*, known in English as black mint. Thinking it would be hard to find, I was surprised to see it sold as a paste in jars at my local Latin American market. Alternatively, you might also find the whole leaves frozen. Use a mortar and pestle to crush them into a paste with a tiny bit of oil. The rest of the ingredients are a curiosity but authentic. Peanuts are no surprise, but the traditional thickener, a mixture of saltines and sweet vanilla-flavored cookies, is. Some chefs use animal crackers! I bought a box, crushed up the gorilla for the sauce, and munched on the other animals as I cooked. I hadn't had a box since I was a child.

SERVES 6 AS AN APPETIZER; MAKES ABOUT 2 CUPS/480 ML SAUCE

SAUCE

2 dried *amarillo* chiles (sometimes labeled *ají mirasol*)

2 tbsp canola or other neutral oil

¾ cup/105 g coarsely chopped red onion

3 garlic cloves, thinly sliced

2 tsp *huacatay* (see headnote)

Kosher or fine sea salt

Freshly ground pepper

½ cup/70 g dry-roasted peanuts

1½ tsp crushed animal crackers

1 saltine cracker, crushed

1 cup/115 g crumbled *queso Oaxaca* or *queso fresco*

½ cup/120 ml milk

1¼ lb/570 g petite Peruvian yellow potatoes or Yukon Gold potatoes

2 tsp Kosher or fine sea salt

6 large butter lettuce leaves

3 hard-boiled eggs, peeled and quartered lengthwise

12 Botija or Kalamata olives

1 First make the sauce. Remove and discard the stems and seeds from the dried chiles, then tear the chiles into small pieces. Place the pieces in a small bowl, add hot water to cover, and let soak while you chop and assemble the other ingredients. When the pieces have softened, drain and blot dry.

2 In a medium sauté pan, heat the oil over medium heat and swirl to coat the pan bottom. Add the chiles, onion, garlic, and *huacatay* and sauté, stirring frequently, until the onion is soft but not brown, about 4 minutes. Season lightly with salt and pepper, then set aside to cool for 3 minutes.

3 Transfer the onion mixture to a blender and process for 2 minutes to yield a smooth purée. Add the peanuts, both types of crackers, *queso*, and milk and process again until smooth. Transfer the mixture to a covered container and refrigerate until ready to use. (The sauce can be made up to 3 days in advance. Remove from the refrigerator 30 minutes before serving.)

4 Scrub the potatoes but do not peel them. Put the potatoes in a large pot, add cold water to cover, partially cover the pot, and bring the water to a boil over high heat. Uncover, add the salt, and reduce the heat so the water boils gently. Cook until the potatoes are tender when pierced with a fork, 12 to 15 minutes, depending on the size of the potatoes.

5 Drain the potatoes in a colander and let cool. Peel the potatoes. (To make peeling them easier, wear disposable surgical gloves, available at any pharmacy.) Cut them into thick slices just before serving.

6 Place a lettuce leaf on each plate. Divide the potato slices evenly among the plates, mounding them toward the bottom of each lettuce leaf and artfully overlapping the slices. Spoon about ⅓ cup/75 ml of the sauce at the bottom of the plate and on the potatoes. Garnish each plate with two egg quarters and two olives. Serve immediately.

PICANTE DE ULLUCOS
(ULLUCOS IN HOT SAUCE)

When I was researching Peruvian roots and came across ulluco, a tuber from the highlands of Peru (as well as Colombia, Ecuador, and Bolivia), I didn't expect to find it in Portland, but there it was, in cans, at my local Latin American market. It is accurately described as earthy, tasting like a cross between a potato and a beet. I found even canned ullucos appealing and love them in this classic Peruvian recipe, adapted from Maria Baez Kijac's cookbook, *The South American Table*. Admittedly, this recipe has two subrecipes, but they are quick and easy to make and well worth the effort because both the annatto lard and the chile paste can be used in other recipes.

SERVES 4

One 20-oz/570-g can ullucos packed in brine

1 tbsp creamy natural peanut butter

½ cup/120 ml milk

3 tbsp *manteca de color* (facing page)

¾ cup/105 g finely chopped yellow onion

1 tbsp *amarillo* chile paste, (facing page or store-bought)

1 tsp kosher or fine sea salt

½ tsp ground cumin

¼ tsp freshly ground pepper

1 Drain the ullucos in a colander and rinse well. Blot dry. Cut the ullucos crosswise into slices ¼ in/6 mm thick. In a small bowl, whisk together the peanut butter and milk until smooth. Set aside.

2 In a deep sauté pan, warm the *manteca* over medium heat and swirl to coat the pan bottom. Add the onion and chile paste and sauté, stirring frequently, until the onion is soft but not brown, about 5 minutes. Add the salt, cumin, and pepper and cook, stirring often, for 2 minutes longer. Add the milk mixture, stir to combine, and bring to a simmer. Add the ullucos and cook until the sauce has thickened, about 3 minutes. Transfer to a warmed serving bowl and serve immediately or keep warm until ready to serve.

MANTECA DE COLOR
(ANNATTO LARD)

This flavored fat is used in Peruvian cooking and other Latin American cuisines to add color and rich flavor to foods. You can substitute canola or another neutral oil for the lard. Leaf lard is available from high-quality butcher shops selling pork. Annatto seeds are available at Latin American markets or online from www.penzeys.com.

MAKES ½ CUP/120 ML

½ cup/115 g leaf lard

½ cup/45 g annatto seeds

In a small sauté pan, melt the lard over low heat. Add the annatto seeds and cook until the melted fat colors and takes on flavor, about 5 minutes. Remove from the heat, let cool slightly, and strain through a fine-mesh sieve into a container with a tight-fitting lid. Discard the seeds. (Some cooks reuse the seeds to make a second batch.) Let the lard cool completely, then cover and refrigerate. It will keep for several months.

AMARILLO CHILE PASTE

This paste is simple and satisfying to make. It's brilliantly colored and enticingly hot—my new favorite condiment to have on hand.

MAKES ½ CUP/120 ML

1¼ oz/35 g dried *amarillo* chiles (sometimes labeled *ají mirasol*)

1½ cups/360 ml water

1 Remove and discard the stems and seeds from the dried chiles, then tear the chiles into small pieces. Place the pieces in a small saucepan, add the water, and bring to a boil over high heat. Reduce the heat so the water simmers, cover, and cook until the pieces are soft enough to purée, 10 to 15 minutes.

2 Remove from the heat and drain the chiles, reserving both the chiles and the cooking liquid. Transfer the chiles to a blender and process until a smooth paste forms, adding up to 6 tbsp/90 ml of the cooking liquid to achieve the consistency of a thick purée. Transfer to a covered container and refrigerate. The paste will keep for up to 2 months.

CARAPULCRA
(PORK AND FREEZE-DRIED POTATOES)

The culinary wizardry of Peru's Quecha Indians is extraordinary. During the growing season, they cultivate potatoes, a staple of their diet, eat some of them, and then freeze-dry the balance for eating during the long winters (see page 23). Called *papa seca*, these freeze-dried potatoes are available at Latin American markets or through online sites (see Sources) selling Peruvian foods. In Peru, you see this stew served with rice or small boiled potatoes.

SERVES 6

2 cups/260 g *papa seca* (see headnote)

2 lb/910 g boneless pork shoulder, fat trimmed and cut into 2-in/5-cm chunks

Kosher or fine sea salt

Freshly ground pepper

3 tbsp canola or other neutral oil

1½ cups/215 g diced yellow onion

5 garlic cloves, minced

2 tbsp *amarillo* chile paste (page 31 or store-bought)

1-in/2.5-cm piece cinnamon stick

1 tsp ground cumin

9 cups/2.1 L water

½ cup/70 g dry-roasted peanuts

1 tsp dried oregano

2 tbsp fresh lime juice

1 cup/240 ml *Salsa Criolla* (recipe follows)

1 In a dry, heavy frying pan, toast the *papa seca* over medium-low heat, stirring and tossing constantly, until brown, about 5 minutes. Do not allow the pieces to burn. Transfer to a colander and rinse under cool running water to cool slightly. Put the potatoes in a medium bowl, add cold water to cover, and set aside to soften while you prepare the stew.

2 Season the pork lightly on all sides with salt and pepper. In a large Dutch oven or other heavy pot with a tight-fitting lid, warm the oil over medium heat and swirl to coat the pot bottom. Working in batches so as not to crowd the pot, add the pork and cook, stirring frequently, until browned on both sides, about 5 minutes. Add the onion, garlic, chile paste, cinnamon, and cumin and sauté for 2 minutes longer. Add the water, increase the heat to medium-high, and bring the water to a simmer. Reduce the heat so the liquid barely simmers, cover, and cook, stirring occasionally, for 1 hour.

3 Drain the potatoes and stir them into the stew. Re-cover and cook until the pork is nearly falling apart, 1 to 1¼ hours longer.

4 Meanwhile, using a mini-chop or food processor, pulse the peanuts until they are ground but not a paste, about 15 pulses.

5 Stir the ground peanuts, oregano, and lime juice into the stew. Cover and cook for 5 minutes longer. Taste and adjust the seasoning. Spoon into warmed shallow, wide bowls. Garnish with the sauce and serve immediately.

SALSA CRIOLLA (PERUVIAN ONION, PEPPER, AND LIME SALSA)

MAKES ABOUT 1 CUP/240 ML

1 cup/115 g thinly sliced red onion

2 tbsp fresh lime juice

2 tsp finely minced fresh cilantro

½ tsp finely minced fresh or jarred *amarillo* chile

½ tsp kosher or fine sea salt

In a medium bowl, toss together the onion, lime juice, cilantro, chile, and salt. Cover and set aside at room temperature until ready to serve. The salsa can be made up to 8 hours in advance.

CAZUELA DE GALLINA
(CHICKEN POT WITH VEGETABLES)

Filled with vegetables, Peruvian potatoes, rice, and corn, this restorative stew comes from the region of Tacna, in the far south of Peru. While the traditional recipe would use a whole hen, I chose bone-in chicken thighs. The dark meat delivers rich flavors and a succulent texture. If you prefer, you can cut up a whole chicken.

SERVES 8

3 lb/1.4 kg chicken thighs

4 tsp kosher or fine sea salt

3 tbsp canola or other neutral oil

1 medium red onion, 10 oz/ 280 g, diced

1 red bell pepper, 6 oz/170 g, seeded and diced

2 tbsp minced garlic

1 tbsp peeled and finely minced fresh ginger

1 tsp ground turmeric

2½ qt/2.4 L water

8 oz/225 g daikon radish, peeled and diced (about 1½ cups/200 g)

1 large carrot, trimmed, peeled, and thinly sliced (½ cup/85 g)

1 celery rib, thinly sliced (½ cup/55 g)

1 small leek, about 3½ oz/100 g, white and light green part only, thinly sliced

12 petite Peruvian yellow potatoes or fingerling potatoes, halved lengthwise

1 cup/200 g long-grain white rice

10 oz/280 g butternut squash, peeled and cut into ¾-in/2-cm dice

2 ears yellow corn, husks and silk removed and cut crosswise into wheels 1 in/2.5 cm thick

1 cup/140 g frozen green peas, partially thawed

½ cup/120 ml *Salsa Criolla* (facing page)

1 Remove any excess lumps of fat and trim any dangling skin from the chicken thighs. Pat dry. Season on both sides with 2 tsp of the salt. Set aside on a plate.

2 In a large Dutch oven or a deep 12-in/30.5-cm sauté pan with a tight-fitting lid, warm the oil over medium heat and swirl to coat the pan bottom. Working in batches so as not to crowd the pan, add the chicken thighs, skin side down, and brown, turning once, on both sides, about 10 minutes total. Transfer to a clean plate or baking sheet.

3 Pour off all but 2 tbsp of the fat from the pan. Return the pan to medium heat, add the onion and bell pepper, and sauté, stirring frequently, until soft and just beginning to brown, about 6 minutes. Add the garlic, ginger, and turmeric and sauté for 1 minute longer. Return the chicken, skin side down, to the pan, nestling it in the onion mixture. Add the water, daikon, carrot, celery, leek, and the remaining 2 tsp salt. Increase the heat to medium-high and bring the water to a simmer. Reduce the heat so the liquid barely simmers, cover, and cook, stirring occasionally, for 15 minutes.

4 Add the potatoes and cook for 5 minutes. Stir in the rice, cover, and cook for 5 minutes longer. Add the squash and corn and cook until the squash and potatoes are fork-tender and the rice is fully cooked, about 10 minutes longer. Stir in the peas and cook just until heated through, about 1 minute. Taste and adjust the seasoning.

5 Spoon into warmed individual *cazuelas* or shallow, wide bowls. Garnish with the sauce and serve immediately.

ARROWHEAD

Sagittaria sagittifolia

CHINESE ARROWHEAD / CHINESE POTATO / SWAMP POTATO / DUCK POTATO / INDIAN POTATO / WAPATO *(CHINOOK INDIAN)* **/ TSE GOO** *(CANTONESE)* **/ CIGU** *(MANDARIN CHINESE)* **/ KUWAI** *(JAPANESE)*

HISTORY AND LORE A member of the water-plantain family (Alismataceae), arrowhead is a hardy perennial water or marsh plant of Europe, Asia, and America. The egg-size tuberous root—technically a corm—has a little shoot, smooth, thin beige skin, and a few modest, scaly-layered leaves covering the bottom. Prepared in ways similar to those used for potatoes, it has a bland, slightly sweet taste, though it can have a bitter finish if not cooked properly. Cultivated extensively in China and Japan, it is typically braised, especially with pork, in Chinese cooking, where it is known as *cigu*, and is a favorite New Year's food in Japan, where it is called *kuwai*. Some 80 percent of Japan's commercial crop is cultivated in the area around Hiroshima.

In North America, arrowhead was traditionally harvested in the wild by Native Americans who observed geese, ducks, beavers, and muskrats chomping on the small corms with gusto. Considered the most valuable of the available edible roots, it was gathered in the late fall by women who, holding on to a canoe, waded into the water and located the corms with their toes. They then boiled their harvest in wooden kettles with hot stones, or roasted them on sticks stuck in the ground near the fire. The Chinook use the word *wapato* (or *wapatoo*) for the arrowhead,

their general term for potato. Members of the Chinook tribe of the lower Columbia River in the Pacific Northwest reportedly sold the tuberous roots to Lewis and Clark when they wintered in Oregon.

VARIETIES Arrowhead, in China and Japan, was botanically classified as *Sagittaria sinensis*, and the North American species was known as *S. latifolia*. Now both are classified as a single species, *S. sagittifolia*. (Do not confuse arrowhead with arrowroot, which is a different root. See page 399 for information on arrowroot.)

NUTRITION According to *A Cook's Guide to Chinese Vegetables* by Martha Dahlen, the arrowhead is a highly nutritious, starchy vegetable with significantly higher levels of protein, minerals (particularly phosphorus), and fiber than either potato or taro. The Chinese warn that those with constipation issues should not overindulge.

AVAILABILITY AND SELECTION Arrowhead is typically planted in the spring and harvested about 6 months later, making its appearance in Chinese and Japanese markets during the winter, especially around their respective New Year's celebrations. Look for these bulb-shaped, ivory-colored tubers in the produce section, kept dry and away from the misting machines. They should have a small sprout at the top and feel firm and solid, except for the very center of the base, which will give a little when pressed. Buy larger ones, which will be easier to peel.

STORAGE Wrap the corms loosely in paper towels and place them in a plastic bag. Leave the bag partially open so as not to trap moisture. Store them in the refrigerator for up to 1 week.

BASIC USE AND PREPARATION Rinse the corms and blot them dry with paper towels. Using a paring knife, trim off the shoot and the soft base. Then, use either a swivel peeler or a paring knife to remove the outer skin, paring down to the creamy white flesh. Prepare arrowhead as you would potatoes. The corms can be cooked whole in salted boiling water until fork-tender and then sliced or cubed. They can be chopped and fried, mashed, creamed, or braised.

A CAUTIONARY NOTE The biggest challenge for the cook is to overcome the inherent bitterness of these roots. It is mellowed when they are marinated, simmered, stir-fried, or braised in a flavorful liquid.

YIELDS

1 arrowhead = about 1¾ oz/45 g

9 to 10 arrowhead = about 1 lb/455 g

PERSIMMON AND ARROWHEAD

My colleague and friend Elizabeth Andoh was very helpful with the research on arrowhead. During Japanese New Year's celebrations, arrowhead (*kuwai* in Japanese) is colored yellow and cut to look like temple bells or pinecones. This holiday dish, which combines arrowhead with persimmons and dried plums or raisins, is a condiment or chutney. I consider Fuyu persimmons my wintertime tomato, often using them raw in salads. Slice, dice, or wedge them, peeling only if the skin is thick. The process of soaking, simmering, cooling, and then soaking the arrowhead again removes its natural bitterness.

SERVES 4 AS A CONDIMENT

7 oz/200 g arrowhead

½ Fuyu persimmon, calyx and core removed and cut into thin wedges

4 dried plums (prunes), diced, or ¼ cup/85 g golden raisins

2 tbsp unseasoned rice vinegar

1 tsp granulated sugar

⅛ tsp kosher or fine sea salt

1 Soak the arrowhead in a bowl of cool water for 20 minutes and then drain. Bring a small pot of water to a boil over high heat, add the arrowhead, reduce the heat so the water simmers, and cook, skimming any scum that comes to the surface, for 20 minutes. Drain in a colander and let cool to room temperature. When cool, use a paring knife to trim off the shoot and soft base and then peel them. Place in a bowl of fresh cool water and soak for an additional 30 minutes. Drain, blot dry, and cut in half to form half-moons. Cut crosswise into slices ¼ in/6 mm thick.

2 In a medium bowl, combine the arrowhead slices, persimmon wedges, and dried plums. In a small bowl, stir together the vinegar, sugar, and salt until the sugar and salt are dissolved. Drizzle the mixture over the arrowhead mixture, toss well, and set aside to macerate for 1 hour before serving. (This condiment can be made up to 6 hours in advance. Cover and set aside at room temperature.)

ARROWHEAD LEEK SOUP

Think of this as arrowhead vichyssoise. I find this soup to be equally delicious hot or cold. Its silky texture, from the puréed arrowhead, and its underlying sweetness, from the apples and butter-cooked leeks, deliver a subtle, delectable complexity. One spoonful and I immediately wanted a bowlful. After blending, the soup is frothy on top, almost as if it has been foamed. The result is a wonderful mouthfeel, especially when served cold.

SERVES 4 TO 6

2 tbsp unsalted butter

2 medium leeks, white part only, thinly sliced (about ¾ cup/65 g)

¾ cup/105 g diced yellow onion

9 oz/255 g arrowhead, trimmed, peeled, and cut into small chunks

2 cups/480 ml homemade chicken stock or canned low-sodium chicken broth

1 tsp kosher or fine sea salt

¼ tsp freshly ground white pepper

1 large Granny Smith apple, about 10 oz/280 g, peeled, halved, cored, and cut into ½-in/12-mm dice

1½ cups/360 ml milk

2 tbsp finely snipped fresh chives

1 In a medium saucepan, melt the butter over medium-low heat and swirl to coat the pan bottom. Add the leeks and onion, and cook slowly, stirring occasionally, until they are translucent and very soft with no browning, about 10 minutes. (Reduce the heat to low if the onion begins to brown.)

2 Add the arrowhead, stock, salt, and pepper, raise the heat to medium-high, and bring to a boil. Reduce the heat so the liquid just simmers and cook until the arrowhead chunks are fork-tender, about 20 minutes. Remove from the heat and let cool slightly.

3 Transfer the arrowhead mixture to a blender, add the apple, and process until smooth. Add the milk and process until incorporated. Taste and adjust the seasoning. (The soup can be prepared up to 2 days in advance. Let cool, transfer to a covered container, and refrigerate.)

4 To serve the soup hot, return it to the saucepan and reheat over low heat until steaming. Keep the soup below a simmer so the milk doesn't curdle. Ladle into warmed soup bowls, garnish with the chives, and serve immediately. To serve the soup cold, let cool completely, transfer to a covered container, and refrigerate until well chilled. Taste and adjust the seasoning before serving (cold dulls flavors), then ladle into chilled bowls and garnish with the chives.

ROASTED LEMONGRASS CHICKEN WITH ARROWHEAD

A deeply rich and fragrant sauce slicks this Vietnamese pan-roasted chicken, which has the added crunch of arrowhead. I like to cut up my chicken in the French style, separating the legs and thighs, splitting the breasts, leaving the wings attached to the breasts, and then cutting each breast on the diagonal into two pieces. I remove the wing tips, which leaves the two wing joints tucked in close to the breast. Alternatively, you can buy an equivalent amount of chicken parts. Buy just the hindquarters, for example, and enjoy this aromatic sauce on dark meat only. This dish reheats well. Accompany with Yellow Rice (page 323).

SERVES 4 TO 6

MARINADE

3 lemongrass stalks

¼ cup/60 ml canola or other neutral oil

3 tbsp Asian fish sauce, preferably Vietnamese *nuoc mam*

2 tbsp oyster sauce

1 tbsp granulated sugar

2 tsp Chinese chili-garlic sauce

½ tsp coarsely ground pepper

2 tbsp finely chopped shallot

1 large garlic clove, minced

One 4 lb/1.8 kg chicken, cut up

2 tbsp canola or other neutral oil

12 oz/340 g arrowhead, ends trimmed, peeled, and quartered

FINISHING SAUCE

½ cup/120 ml water

2 tbsp fresh lime juice

2 tbsp Asian fish sauce, preferably Vietnamese *nuoc mam*

1 tbsp granulated sugar

⅓ cup/20 g firmly packed fresh cilantro leaves

1 To make the marinade, trim off the root end from each lemongrass stalk, then cut off and discard the tough green tops. You should have a bulb about 4 in/10 cm long. Peel away the tough outer leaves and then finely chop the bulb. In a large bowl, whisk together the oil, fish sauce, oyster sauce, sugar, chili-garlic sauce, and pepper. Add the lemongrass, shallot, and garlic and stir to combine.

2 Add the chicken pieces to the marinade and turn to coat all sides. Set aside at room temperature for 1 hour, or cover and refrigerate for up to 8 hours.

3 Position a rack in the center of the oven and preheat to 400°F/200°C/gas 6.

4 In a large ovenproof sauté pan that will comfortably accommodate the chicken in a single layer, heat the oil over medium-high heat and swirl to coat the pan bottom. Remove the chicken pieces from the bowl and reserve the marinade in the bowl. Add the chicken pieces, skin-side down, to the pan and cook until lightly browned, about 5 minutes. Turn the chicken skin-side up and add the reserved marinade to the pan, distributing it evenly. Nestle the arrowhead pieces between and around the chicken pieces. As soon as the liquid begins to simmer, transfer the pan to the oven.

5 Roast the chicken, uncovered, until an instant-read thermometer inserted into the thickest part of a thigh away from bone registers 170°F/77°C, about 25 minutes. Remove from the oven and transfer the chicken and arrowhead pieces to a warmed serving platter, leaving any liquid in the pan. Keep them warm while you make the sauce.

6 To make the sauce, place the pan over medium-high heat and add the water, lime juice, fish sauce, and sugar, stirring well. Bring to a boil and cook, stirring occasionally, until slightly thickened, about 3 minutes. Tilt the pan slightly and use a broad metal spoon to skim off any fat from the surface of the sauce. Strain the sauce into a gravy boat, small pitcher, or bowl.

7 Sprinkle the cilantro leaves over the chicken and serve immediately. Pass the sauce at the table.

CLAY POT–CARAMELIZED PORK BELLY AND ARROWHEAD STEW

Inspired by a pork clay-pot dish I enjoyed at Slanted Door, Charles Phan's celebrated Vietnamese restaurant in San Francisco, I decided to combine slices of rolled pork belly with arrowhead and braise them in a rich Vietnamese-style stew. Arrowhead is naturally bitter, and in a braised dish, it needs a rounded, rich, sweet flavor to balance it. Caramelizing the sugar and then stirring in the aromatics—shallots, garlic, ginger, and chiles—delivers flavors that enhance both the pork and arrowhead. Serve with steamed rice to sop up every bit of the sauce—it's that good.

SERVES 4 AS A MAIN COURSE

2 tbsp canola or other neutral oil

¼ cup/50 g granulated sugar

¼ cup/30 g minced shallot

1 tbsp minced garlic

1 tbsp peeled and minced fresh ginger

1 small serrano chile, stemmed, halved lengthwise, seeded, and diced (see Cook's Note)

1½ lb/680 g rolled pork belly, thinly sliced across the grain, then cut into 3 in/7.5 cm lengths

1¼ cups/300 ml water

2 tbsp Asian fish sauce, preferably Vietnamese *nuoc mam*

1 tsp freshly ground pepper

14 oz/400 g arrowhead, ends trimmed, peeled, and halved lengthwise

4 hard-boiled eggs, peeled and left whole

4 green onions, including green tops, cut into matchsticks for garnish

1 In a Dutch oven or other heavy pot, heat the oil over medium heat and swirl to coat the pot bottom. Add the sugar and cook, stirring frequently, until dissolved and golden brown, 3 to 4 minutes. (At first, the sugar will form a paste with the oil, but it will eventually melt.)

2 Add the shallot, garlic, ginger, and chile and sauté, stirring frequently, until the aromatics are softened, about 3 minutes. Add the pork, raise the heat to medium-high, and sauté, stirring frequently, until the pork is cooked through and beginning to brown, about 7 minutes. (The edges of the pork will get brown first, with bits sticking to the pot bottom.) Add the water, fish sauce, and pepper and bring to a boil. Nestle the arrowhead halves and the eggs in the liquid. Reduce the heat to maintain a slow simmer, cover, and cook, stirring once or twice, until the pork and arrowhead halves are tender, about 30 minutes. (The pork should be slightly chewy but no longer rubbery and tough. Stirring helps to color the eggs on all sides.)

3 Serve immediately or keep warm until ready to serve. Garnish with the green onions just before serving.

COOK'S NOTE

Keep pairs of disposable surgical gloves (available at any pharmacy and many supermarkets) on hand to wear when working with fresh chiles. They keep the capsaicin, the caustic compound that is naturally present in chiles, from irritating your skin.

BEET

Beta vulgaris

HISTORY AND LORE A member of the goosefoot family (Chenopodiaceae), the beet in some form was probably consumed in prehistoric times. The plant is native to western Europe and the Mediterranean, specifically northern Africa, where it evolved from the wild sea-beet, a common seashore plant. The Romans were the first to cultivate the plants for their roots. Prior to that, they were grown exclusively for their leaves, until spinach cultivation drastically reduced the popularity of the greens. It wasn't until the sixteenth century that the garden, or table, beet, in the color and form that we know it today, was cultivated and consumed in Europe. Another three centuries would pass before it was grown in the United States. Within the last decade or so, beets have transformed from a rather utilitarian winter crop for canning and pickling to a shining star that graces the menus of many fine restaurants.

VARIETIES Beets have succulent green leaves with red or golden veins, depending on the variety. Several species are cultivated, but table beets are the common garden variety. The vibrant red, yellow, and orange hues are due to betalains (nitrogen-containing pigments). Betacyanin is the pigment in red and violet beets, and betaxanthin gives gold and orange beets their lively color. These pigments are water soluble and leak, or "bleed," when beets are cooked, bruised, or pierced.

RED BEETS

Boltardy It is hardy and bolt resistant, which gardeners like.
Bull's Blood A nineteenth-century variety with richly dark red leaves.

Detroit Dark Red A relatively low concentration of geosmin (an organic compound with a distinct earthy flavor and aroma) makes this cultivar a popular commercial beet.
Lutz Green Leaf Especially appreciated for its good storage properties, this unusual variety can grow much larger than most beets, but tastes sweeter when harvested on the small side.
Red Ace This is the principal beet—bright red root, red-veined green foliage—grown in the United States.
Warrior A relatively new hybrid, this cultivar was bred to be deep red both inside and outside and to be tender and deliciously sweet.

CHIOGGIA BEETS

Chioggia Barbabietola (candy stripe) This sweet-tasting Italian heirloom variety boasts distinct and striking concentric rings of red and white flesh. When the raw beets are sliced, the beautiful circles of color remain, but when the beets are cooked, the flesh turns pale pink.

GOLDEN OR YELLOW BEETS

Burpee's Golden Large roots, with orange or rosy red skin and golden yellow flesh.

OTHER BEETS

Albina Aereduna *or* **Blankoma** Two white varieties, both with especially sweet flesh.
Green Top Bunching Although the flattened, globe-shaped red roots are tasty, this cultivar is grown primarily for its full, lush green tops.

NUTRITION Beets are packed with nutrients and low in calories, making them a dieter's delight. The roots are an excellent source of folate, fiber, and beta-carotene. The betalains, or pigments, found in all colored beets add phytonutrients and antioxidants. The greens are a good source of fiber, high in calcium and iron, and packed with vitamins A, C, and K.

AVAILABILITY AND SELECTION Although beets are available in most supermarkets year-round, they are typically planted in the spring and summer and harvested in late summer through fall. They vary in color and shape based on variety but all should be firm with smooth skins and no sign of bruising. In general, the larger the beet, the more fibrous and woody it is. Medium-size beets are ideal for most uses, as they have a silky texture and are easy to peel. Purchase beets of uniform size for even cooking. If the greens are attached and will be consumed, they should be bright colored and appear fresh. Also, the smaller and more tender the leaves, the better. The leaves deteriorate more quickly than the roots, so even if the greens are wilted, the roots may still be firm and full flavored.

STORAGE If beets are purchased with their greens attached, cut the greens off, leaving 1 inch/2.5 centimeters of the stem attached to the root, and store the greens separately. If left attached, the greens draw moisture, flavor, and nutrients from the roots, ultimately leaving the roots shriveled and sad. Store unwashed and untrimmed beets in the refrigerator or in a cool, humid place for up to 4 weeks, or longer if they remain firm and appear fresh. Unwashed greens will keep in the refrigerator for a few days. Loosely wrap them in paper towels to wick moisture, and then place them in a perforated plastic bag.

BASIC USE AND PREPARATION Beets can be consumed raw, pickled, canned, or cooked by a variety of methods. Roasting is my preferred method because it enhances their naturally sweet, earthy flavor and it is the best way to retain their beautiful color and satiny sheen. Beets can also be boiled, steamed, microwaved, or grill-roasted. Young, tender beet greens can be consumed raw; when they are older and heartier, they are best sautéed, steamed, or stewed.

To prepare beets for roasting, trim the stems to ½ inch/ 12 millimeters. Using a vegetable brush, scrub the beets under cool running water to rid them of sand and dirt, especially at the top where the stem meets the root. Pat the beets dry with paper towels. Trim the "tails" if they are long; stubby ones can be left intact. Wait to peel beets until after they are roasted. Their skins will slip right off.

A CAUTIONARY NOTE I always use disposable surgical gloves when working with dark red beets to keep my fingers from being stained red. Look for gloves at a pharmacy or in a supermarket, stocked with the bandages and other first-aid supplies. Beets will stain countertops and cutting boards, so work with care and clean up quickly, using a diluted bleach solution to wash away the water-soluble beet juices.

YIELDS

ROOTS

1 small beet = 2 oz/55 g

1 medium beet = 3 to 5 oz/85 to 140 g

1 large beet = 8 to 10 oz/225 to 280 g

4 or 5 trimmed medium beets = 1 lb/455 g

1 lb/455 g beets, trimmed, peeled, cooked, and puréed = 1 cup/240 ml

⅔ cup peeled and diced beets = 5 oz/140 g

1 cup peeled and grated beets = 6 oz/170 g

GREENS

Greens from 1 bunch beets, stemmed and leaves roughly chopped = 4 to 5 cups/115 to 150 g

ROASTED BEETS

I prefer to roast beets, rather than boil or steam them, for four primary reasons: Roasting is the best method for retaining their bright color and naturally sweet flavor. Boiling and steaming leach more vitamins from the beets than roasting does. Cooking beets in the oven is especially easy because you don't have to keep an eye on the water level in the pot or steamer. And finally and best of all, roasting doesn't make a mess. Here are three easy methods for roasting beets.

SERVES 4 AS A SIDE DISH

METHOD 1: SIMPLE ROASTED BEETS

1 lb/455 g uniformly sized beets, any type, trimmed

1 Position a rack in the center of the oven and preheat to 350°F/180°C/gas 4.

2 Gently scrub the beets under cool running water to remove any dirt. Pat dry. Set each beet in the center of a square of aluminum foil large enough to enclose it and wrap tightly. Arrange the wrapped beets, not touching, on a rimmed baking sheet. Roast the beets until tender, 1 to 1½ hours, depending on their size. The beets are done when a paring knife easily pierces to the center of each beet. (If the beets are not the same size, remove the smaller beets from the oven when tender and continue to roast the larger beets until done.) Remove the pan from the oven and place on a wire rack to cool. (If not using the beets right away, leave them wrapped in the foil, let the packets cool, and refrigerate for up to 5 days.)

3 When the beets are cool enough to handle, unwrap and remove from the foil. Wearing disposable gloves, use a paring knife to trim the stem and root ends. Using paper towels, rub each beet to remove the skin. At this point, the beets can be cut into slices or wedges and served as a side dish, or they can be cooled completely and used in recipes calling for roasted beets.

METHOD 2: THYME-INFUSED ROASTED BEETS

1 lb/455 g uniformly sized beets, any type, trimmed

4 or 5 fresh thyme sprigs

Extra-virgin olive oil

Kosher or fine sea salt

Freshly ground pepper

1 Position a rack in the center of the oven and preheat to 350°F/180°C/gas 4.

2 Gently scrub the beets under cool running water to remove any dirt. Pat dry. Set each beet and a thyme sprig in the center of a square of aluminum foil large enough to enclose the beet. Drizzle a little oil over each beet and roll it around until lightly coated. Sprinkle the beets evenly with a large pinch of salt and a small pinch of pepper. Wrap each beet tightly in the foil. Arrange the wrapped beets, not touching, on a rimmed baking sheet. Roast the beets

...CONTINUED

until tender, 1 to 1½ hours, depending on their size. The beets are done when a paring knife easily pierces to the center of each beet. (If the beets are not the same size, remove the smaller beets from the oven when tender and continue to roast the larger beets until done.) Remove the pan from the oven and place on a wire rack to cool. (If not using the beets right away, leave them wrapped in the foil, let the packets cool, and refrigerate for up to 5 days.)

3 When the beets are cool enough to handle, unwrap and remove from the foil. Discard the thyme. Wearing disposable gloves, use a paring knife to trim the stem and root ends. Using paper towels, rub each beet to remove the skin. At this point, the beets can be cut into slices or wedges and served as a side dish, or they can be cooled completely and used in recipes calling for roasted beets.

METHOD 3: AROMATIC ROASTED BEETS

1 lb/455 g uniformly sized beets, any type, trimmed

1 cup/240 ml water

1 medium orange, thinly sliced and cut into half-moons

10 fresh thyme sprigs

1 tsp kosher or fine sea salt

½ tsp freshly ground pepper

1 Position a rack in the center of the oven and preheat to 350°F/180°C/gas 4. Line the bottom and sides of a medium-size baking pan with aluminum foil. (This makes cleanup much easier!)

2 Gently scrub the beets under cool running water to remove any dirt. Arrange the beets in the prepared pan. Add the water, orange slices, thyme, salt, and pepper. Cover the pan tightly with foil. Roast the beets for 40 minutes. Using oven mitts, shake the pan from side to side to rotate the beets. (This does the trick and is a lot easier than removing the foil and stirring the beets.) Continue to roast the beets until tender, 20 to 50 minutes longer, depending on their size. The beets are done when a paring knife easily pierces to the center of each beet. (If the beets are not the same size, remove the smaller beets from the oven when tender and continue to roast the larger beets until done.) Remove the pan from the oven.

3 Uncover the pan and transfer the beets to a plate to cool. Discard the orange slices, thyme, and roasting liquids. (If not using the beets right away, let the beets cool completely, wrap them tightly in foil, and refrigerate for up to 5 days.) When the beets are cool enough to handle, don disposable gloves and use a paring knife to trim the stem and root ends. Using paper towels, rub each beet to remove the skin. At this point, the beets can be cut into slices or wedges and served as a side dish, or they can be cooled completely and used in recipes calling for roasted beets.

SAUTÉED BEET GREENS

It's like getting a bonus prize, a twofer, when you buy fresh beets with their lovely beet greens attached. Not only do you have the rosy subterranean beauties to enjoy but you also have the striking green tops with their bold red veins to savor. I find a simple sauté to be the best way to cook these greens.

SERVES 2

1 bunch beets (about 4 beets), with lush green tops attached

1 tbsp olive oil

1 large garlic clove, thinly sliced

1 tsp fresh lemon juice

Kosher or fine sea salt

Freshly ground pepper

1   Trim off the greens, leaving 1 in/2.5 cm of the stem attached to each root. Reserve the roots for another use. Trim and discard the thick, fibrous stems from the greens and remove any wilted or spotted leaves. Stack the leaves, then cut the stack in half lengthwise through the center vein. Chop the greens crosswise into large pieces, about 2 in/5 cm wide. Rinse the greens in several changes of cold water until they are clean and the water is clear. Dry them in a salad spinner or blot dry with paper towels.

2   In a large sauté pan, heat the oil over medium heat and swirl to coat the pan bottom. Add the garlic and sauté until soft but not brown, about 1 minute. Add the greens and toss with tongs until wilted but still crisp-tender and bright green, about 3 minutes. Add the lemon juice, season lightly with salt and pepper, and then give the greens a final toss in the pan. Serve immediately.

PICKLED BEETS WITH STAR ANISE AND CINNAMON

Without the bother of a water bath or of pressure canning, you can easily make aromatic and deeply spiced pickled beets that keep for a month in the refrigerator. In the springtime, when I see baby beets at the farmers' market, I'm inspired to keep the dainty orbs whole and pickle them. At other times, slicing, or even cutting wedges, of small- or medium-size beets is the best bet for packing beets comfortably into jars.

MAKES TWO 1-PT/480-ML JARS

1 lb/455 g Simple Roasted Beets (page 45), prepared with red beets, cooled, peeled, and cut into ¼-in/6-mm-thick slices

⅓ cup/35 g thinly sliced shallots

2 cups/480 ml cider vinegar

½ cup/120 ml water

½ cup/100 g firmly packed light brown sugar

1 tbsp kosher or fine sea salt

1½-in/4-cm piece cinnamon stick, broken in half

10 whole cloves

2 star anise pods

1 tsp whole allspice

1 Wash two 1-pt/480-ml heatproof jars with tight-fitting lids in hot, soapy water and dry thoroughly. Alternatively, run the jars through the regular cycle of your dishwasher and wash the lids by hand.

2 In a large bowl, toss together the beets and shallots. Pack the jars evenly with the beet mixture; set aside.

3 In a medium saucepan, combine the vinegar, water, brown sugar, salt, cinnamon, cloves, star anise, and allspice. Bring to a boil over high heat, stirring constantly until the sugar dissolves. Boil the pickling liquid for 1 minute, then remove from the heat.

4 Using a widemouthed funnel, ladle the hot pickling liquid into the prepared jars, covering the beet mixture completely and leaving ½-in/12-mm head space. Distribute the whole spices that sink to the bottom of the saucepan evenly between the jars, making sure each jar of beets has a piece of cinnamon, a star anise pod, and an equal amount of cloves and allspice. Wipe the rims clean and attach the lids.

5 Let the beets steep at room temperature until cool, then store in the refrigerator for at least 3 days before serving to allow the flavors to permeate the beets. They will keep in the refrigerator for up to 1 month.

BEET SALSA WITH AVOCADO AND BLOOD ORANGE

This is a fabulous salsa for serving with chips, but think about using it as an accompaniment to seared salmon or scallops, grilled shrimp skewers, or just about any fish preparation, too. It also makes a good wintertime condiment to brighten a main course, such as roast chicken, sliced skirt steak, or seared pork tenderloin.

MAKES ABOUT 2 CUPS/480 ML

2 medium blood oranges

2 medium Aromatic Roasted Beets (page 46), prepared with red beets, cooled, peeled, and cut into ¼-in/6-mm dice

1 large Hass avocado, halved, pitted, peeled, and cut into ¼-in/6-mm dice

¼ cup/15 g chopped fresh cilantro

2 green onions, including green tops, thinly sliced on the diagonal

1 jalapeño chile, stemmed, halved lengthwise, seeded, deribbed, and minced (see Cook's Note, page 40)

1 tbsp minced, seeded Anaheim or other mild chile

2 tsp fresh lime juice

½ tsp kosher or fine sea salt

⅛ tsp freshly ground pepper

1 Working with one orange at a time, cut a slice from the top and bottom to reveal the flesh. Stand the orange upright and slice away the peel from the sides in wide strips, cutting downward, following the contour of the fruit, and removing all of the white pith. Holding the orange over a bowl, use a sharp paring knife to cut along both sides of each segment, releasing the segments and allowing the juice and segments to drop into the bowl. Discard any seeds that might adhere to the fruit or drop into the bowl. Repeat with the other orange. (This technique is called supreming.)

2 Strain the orange juice into a large bowl. Cut the orange segments into ¼-in/6-mm pieces and add to the bowl with the juice. Add the beets, avocado, cilantro, green onions, both chiles, the lime juice, salt, and pepper to the bowl. Using a rubber spatula, gently fold the ingredients together, being careful not to mash the avocado. Taste and adjust the seasoning.

3 Cover and set aside for at least 1 hour to allow the flavors to meld before serving. (The salsa can be prepared up to 8 hours in advance, covered, and refrigerated. Remove from the refrigerator 45 minutes before serving.)

RAW BEET SLAW WITH FENNEL, TART APPLE, AND PARSLEY

Beets are terrific raw! Serve this slaw as an alternative to coleslaw for a summer barbecue, a beautiful accompaniment to cured salmon for a brunch or appetizer, or a condiment to cured meats or alongside a slice of country pâté. I like to use a mandoline to cut the beets into matchsticks. A sharp chef's knife works well, too. With all this fine cutting, you'll have rosy red hands if you don't wear disposable surgical gloves (see the Cautionary Note on page 44).

SERVES 4 TO 6

DRESSING

3 tbsp extra-virgin olive oil

1 tbsp fresh lemon juice

1 tbsp freshly grated orange zest

½ tsp honey

½ tsp kosher or fine sea salt

⅛ tsp freshly ground pepper

1 medium red beet, 3 to 5 oz/ 85 to 140 g, peeled and cut into matchsticks

½ fennel bulb, trimmed, halved lengthwise, cored, and cut into matchsticks

½ medium crisp tart apple such as Granny Smith, cored and cut into matchsticks

½ cup/30 g firmly packed chopped fresh flat-leaf parsley

1 To make the dressing, in a small bowl, whisk together the oil, lemon juice, orange zest, honey, salt, and pepper.

2 In a medium bowl, toss together the beet, fennel, apple, and parsley. Add the dressing and mix gently to coat all of the ingredients evenly. Serve immediately, or cover and refrigerate until ready to serve, then remove from the refrigerator 30 minutes before serving. (The slaw can be made up to 8 hours in advance.)

FRISÉE SALAD WITH GOLDEN BEETS, POACHED EGGS, AND BACON-SHERRY VINAIGRETTE

Whether served for brunch, lunch, or supper, these tempting ingredients meld together when the creamy, runny yolk is broken, creating a luscious sauce over the greens, bacon, and beets. For me, this is salad perfection.

SERVES 4 AS A MAIN COURSE

2 tsp distilled white vinegar or fresh lemon juice

Kosher or fine sea salt

4 large eggs

1 small head frisée, about 8 oz/ 225 g, torn into bite-size pieces

5 oz/140 g thick-cut bacon, cut crosswise into strips ¼ in/6 mm wide

1 tbsp sherry vinegar

Freshly ground pepper

2 medium Thyme-Infused Roasted Beets (page 45), prepared with golden beets, cooled, peeled, and each cut into 8 wedges

Fleur de sel for sprinkling

1 Have ready a dinner plate lined with a double thickness of paper towels. Pour water to a depth of 2 in/5 cm into a large sauté pan. When the water boils, add the white vinegar and 1 tsp kosher salt. Adjust the heat so the water is at a simmer, not a rolling boil. Crack each egg into a separate small bowl and slip them one at a time into the water. After 2 or 3 minutes, use a slotted spoon to lift an egg to see if the white has completely set. When it has, remove the eggs with a slotted spoon. Use kitchen shears or a paring knife to trim any ragged edges or "tails" from the whites of the eggs. Carefully set the eggs on the towel-lined dinner plate and cover to keep warm. (The eggs may be poached in advance; see the Cook's Note.)

2 Meanwhile, place the frisée in a large bowl and set aside. In a 10-in/25-cm sauté pan, cook the bacon over medium heat until crisp, about 5 minutes. Pour the bacon fat and bits of bacon over the frisée, and then drizzle the sherry vinegar over the top. Toss to coat. Season with kosher salt and pepper.

3 Divide the frisée salad evenly among four warmed shallow salad bowls. Place a poached egg on top of each serving, in the center of the greens. Arrange four beet wedges around the edges of each salad. Top the egg and beets in each salad with a pinch of fleur de sel. Serve immediately.

COOK'S NOTE
Poached eggs can easily be made up to 1 day in advance and then reheated. As soon as the eggs are cooked, immediately slip them into a bowl filled with cold water. Cover the bowl and refrigerate the eggs. To reheat, slip the eggs back into a pan filled with simmering water until heated through, less than 1 minute. (This is a great trick for entertaining.)

CHIOGGIA BEET CARPACCIO WITH ARUGULA AND PANKO-CRUSTED PANFRIED GOAT CHEESE

Consider this a vegetarian alternative to traditional carpaccio. Chioggia beets, the candy-striped beauties of the beet family, line the plate, standing in for the beef slices. A fluffy green mound of baby arugula brings focus back to the center, and a topknot of crunchy fried panko-coated, creamy goat cheese completes the picture.

SERVES 4 AS A FIRST COURSE OR AS A MAIN-COURSE SALAD

DRESSING

¼ cup/60 ml extra-virgin olive oil

1 tbsp balsamic vinegar

1 tsp whole-grain mustard

½ tsp granulated sugar

½ tsp kosher or fine sea salt

Freshly ground pepper

One 8-oz/225-g log fresh goat cheese

Kosher or fine sea salt

Freshly ground pepper

1½ tbsp finely minced fresh herbs such as tarragon or rosemary

½ cup/65 g all-purpose flour

1 large egg

1 cup/55 g *panko* (Japanese bread crumbs) or unseasoned dried bread crumbs

About 1 cup/240 ml canola or other neutral oil for frying

3 medium Aromatic Roasted Beets (page 46), prepared with Chioggia beets, cooled, peeled, and thinly sliced into rounds with a mandoline or chef's knife

4 cups/100 g lightly packed baby arugula

1 To make the dressing, in a small jar, combine the olive oil, vinegar, mustard, sugar, salt, and a few grinds of pepper, cover tightly, and shake vigorously to blend. Taste and adjust the seasoning. Set aside.

2 Slice the goat cheese into four equal rounds and shape each round into a patty 2½ in/6 cm in diameter and ½ in/12 mm thick. Season each patty on both sides with salt and pepper. Gently press the herbs into the cheese, coating the patties evenly on both sides. Put the flour in a small, shallow bowl. Lightly beat the egg in a second small bowl, and put the *panko* in a third bowl. Working with one goat cheese patty at a time, dredge it in the flour, then dip it in the egg, and finally coat it with the *panko*, gently pressing the crumbs to coat thoroughly and evenly on all surfaces.

3 Have ready a dinner plate lined with a double thickness of paper towels. Pour the oil to a depth of ¾ in/2 cm into a frying pan and heat over medium-high until the oil shimmers but is not smoking. Carefully place the goat cheese patties into the hot oil and fry, turning once, until golden brown on both sides, 3 to 5 minutes. Using a slotted spatula, transfer the cheese rounds to the towel-lined plate to drain.

4 Divide the beet slices evenly among four large plates, arranging them in a single layer to cover the bottom of the plate and overlapping them. Place the arugula in a large bowl.

5 Give the dressing a last-minute stir, then drizzle two-thirds of it over the arugula and toss just until coated. Divide the arugula evenly among the plates, mounding it in the center atop the beets. Place a fried goat cheese patty on top of each arugula salad. Drizzle the uncovered beet slices with the remaining dressing, and then sprinkle them with salt and pepper. Serve immediately.

BEETS, PROSCIUTTO-WRAPPED PERSIMMONS, AND BITTER GREENS WITH CREAMY BLUE CHEESE

What a selection of eye candy: beets, persimmons, and radicchio! I've combined them all in a wintertime salad that was inspired by an appetizer of prosciutto-wrapped persimmons that I ate at Metrovino Restaurant in Portland, Oregon.

SERVES 4

1 small head escarole, about 1 lb/455 g, cored

1 small head radicchio, about 8 oz/225 g, cored

DRESSING

½ cup/120 ml buttermilk

¼ cup/60 ml sour cream

¼ cup/55 g packed crumbled good-quality blue cheese such as Roquefort, Gorgonzola, or a domestic blue

2 tbsp finely snipped fresh chives

1 tbsp fresh lemon juice

Kosher or fine sea salt

Freshly ground pepper

4 paper-thin slices prosciutto

2 Fuyu persimmons, cored and cut into 4 wedges

2 medium Aromatic Roasted Beets (page 46), prepared with red beets, cooled, peeled, and cut into thin wedges

1 Tear the escarole and radicchio into large bite-size pieces. Rinse the escarole in several changes of cold water and then dry in a salad spinner. Soak the radicchio in a bowl of cold water for 1 hour to crisp it. Drain and dry in a salad spinner. After drying, spread the greens on large cotton towels (not terry cloth) or on several sheets of paper towels. Roll up like a jelly roll and place in a large plastic bag. Refrigerate the greens until ready to use. (This can be done 2 days in advance of serving.)

2 To make the dressing, in a small bowl, whisk together the buttermilk, sour cream, blue cheese, chives, and lemon juice. Season with salt and pepper. Set aside.

3 Position an oven rack 4 in/10 cm from the heat source and preheat the broiler. Cut each slice of prosciutto in half lengthwise. Wrap each persimmon wedge with a prosciutto strip and secure with a toothpick. Place the wrapped wedges, skin-side up, on a baking sheet. Broil the persimmons, turning once, until the prosciutto is crisp and just beginning to blacken on the edges, about 6 minutes. Remove the toothpicks after broiling.

4 Place the escarole, radicchio, and beet wedges in a large bowl. Give the dressing a last-minute stir, then drizzle it over the greens and beets and toss just until coated. Divide the salad evenly among four dinner plates. Arrange two persimmon wedges on the center of each salad. Serve immediately.

CHILLED BEET SOUP WITH DILL AND CRÈME FRAÎCHE

My taste buds have certainly matured since childhood. My paternal grandmother, Rebecca, would make chilled beet soup in the summertime and bring it for dinner on Friday nights. When she would try to serve me a bowl, I'd say, "It's pretty but no thank you, Grandma." The color was a blushing rosy pink, but beyond that it was completely unappealing. I wish she were alive today to know how much I adore it now. It can be artfully served in small porcelain cups, is quite dramatic in black bowls, or is playful offered as soup shots at cocktail parties.

MAKES 4½ CUPS/1 L; SERVES 6

1 cup/210 g peeled and diced Simple Roasted Beets (page 45), prepared with red beets

1-by-2-in/2.5-by-5-cm strip lemon zest

2 tbsp finely minced shallot

1½ cups/360 ml sour cream

1 cup/240 ml crushed ice cubes

1 cup/240 ml homemade chicken stock or canned low-sodium chicken broth

1 tbsp prepared horseradish

1 tsp kosher or fine sea salt

⅛ tsp freshly ground pepper

2 to 3 tbsp crème fraîche for garnish

1 tbsp minced fresh dill for garnish

1 In a blender, combine the beets, lemon zest, and shallot and process until roughly puréed. Add the sour cream and ice and continue to process until smooth and emulsified. Add the stock, horseradish, salt, and pepper. Blend until completely puréed and smooth. Taste and adjust the seasoning. Transfer to a covered container and refrigerate until cold.

2 Ladle the soup into chilled individual bowls, cups, mugs, or tall glasses. Add a small dollop of crème fraîche and sprinkle with dill before serving.

HOT BEEF BORSCHT

Wintry days make me hungry for comfort foods, and nothing satisfies me more than this hearty eastern European–style soup. Make it when you have a hunk of roast beef or beef brisket to reimagine and stretch into another meal. Sometimes, when I am in the mood for this borscht and the refrigerator isn't offering up any cooked beef, I buy thick-sliced rare roast beef from my local deli.

SERVES 6 TO 8

3 tbsp unsalted butter

1 large yellow onion, cut into ½-in/12-mm dice

2 celery ribs, cut into ½-in/12-mm dice

1 fennel bulb, stalks and bulb cut into ½-in/12-mm dice, feathery fronds chopped and reserved for garnish

1 tsp ground coriander

1 tsp ground cumin

1 tsp caraway seeds

1 tsp freshly ground pepper

3 medium red beets, peeled and cut into ½-in/12-mm dice

½ small green cabbage, cored and cut into ½-in/12-mm dice

7 cups/1.7 L homemade chicken stock or canned low-sodium chicken broth

12 oz/340 g cooked brisket or roast beef, cut into ½-in/12-mm dice

Kosher or fine sea salt

½ cup/120 ml sour cream for garnish

1   In a Dutch oven or other heavy pot, melt the butter over medium heat and swirl to coat the pot bottom. Add the onion, celery, and fennel and sauté, stirring constantly, for 1 minute. Cover, reduce the heat to low, and cook until the vegetables are softened but not brown, about 5 minutes. Add the coriander, cumin, caraway, and pepper and sauté, stirring constantly, until the spices are fragrant, about 1 minute. Add the beets, cabbage, and stock and bring to a simmer. Partially cover the pot and simmer until the beets are tender, about 35 minutes.

2   Add the beef and heat through, then season with salt. Ladle into warmed soup bowls and top each serving with a dollop of sour cream and a sprinkle of fennel fronds before serving.

GOLDEN BEET RISOTTO WITH CRUMBLED RICOTTA SALATA AND SAUTÉED BEET GREENS

A divine dinner in just over a half hour! Creamy white risotto dotted with small cubes of golden beets is topped with sautéed beet greens and garnished with slightly salty *ricotta salata* and Parmesan. The beets are cooked in chicken stock, which is then used to make the risotto. This imparts an earthy sweetness and golden color to the stock, while the beets absorb flavor from the stock. By using both the beets and the beet greens, none of the plant's nutrients is lost.

SERVES 4 AS A MAIN COURSE

2 medium golden beets, trimmed, peeled, and cut into ¼-in/6-mm dice

6 cups/1.4 L homemade chicken stock or canned low-sodium chicken broth

4 tbsp/55 g unsalted butter

1 tbsp olive oil

⅔ cup/90 g diced white onion

1½ cups/300 g Arborio rice

Kosher or fine sea salt

1 cup/240 ml dry white wine

Sautéed Beet Greens (page 47)

¼ cup/30 g freshly grated Parmesan cheese, preferably Parmigiano-Reggiano

3 oz/85 g *ricotta salata* cheese, crumbled

2 tbsp chopped fresh flat-leaf parsley

Freshly ground pepper

1 In a 2-qt/2-L saucepan, combine the beets and stock and bring to a simmer over medium heat. Cook the beets until tender yet still quite firm when pierced with a fork, about 15 minutes. (They should be slightly underdone, as they will finish cooking in the risotto.) Using a slotted spoon, transfer the beets to a bowl and set aside. Adjust the heat so the stock barely simmers.

2 In a heavy 4-qt/3.8-L saucepan over medium heat, melt 2 tbsp of the butter and then add the oil. Add the onion and sauté until translucent but not brown, about 3 minutes. Add the rice and 1 tsp salt and stir until the grains are well coated with the butter and oil, about 1 minute. Add the wine and let it come to a boil. Cook, stirring constantly, until most of the wine is absorbed.

3 Add the beets and 2 cups/480 ml of the stock to the rice and cook, stirring frequently, until the rice has almost completely absorbed the liquid. Adjust the heat so the risotto is kept at a slow simmer. Repeat, adding 1 cup/240 ml of the liquid at a time, stirring until it is almost fully absorbed before adding more. Reserve ¼ cup/60 ml of the liquid for adding at the end.

4 Meanwhile, prepare the sautéed greens as directed and keep warm.

5 After about 18 minutes, the rice will be plump, creamy, and cooked through but still slightly chewy and the beets will be tender when pierced with a fork. Stir in the remaining ¼ cup/60 ml stock. Remove the risotto from the heat and stir in the remaining 2 tbsp butter, the Parmesan cheese, about half of the *ricotta salata*, and the parsley. Season with salt and pepper.

6 Spoon the risotto into warmed shallow bowls. Mound a portion of the beet greens on top. Garnish with the remaining *ricotta salata* and serve immediately.

BEET HASH WITH SPICY CHICKEN SAUSAGE AND SOFT-COOKED EGGS

Consider this as a main course for weekend brunch or even Sunday supper—it's all about comfort food. Adding beets puts a spin on classic potato hash, bringing a shock of color and an earthy sweetness to an otherwise traditional dish. Bring out the hot sauce if your guests want some spice—that's traditional, too.

SERVES 6 AS A MAIN COURSE

4 tbsp/60 ml olive oil

8 oz/225 g spicy Italian chicken sausages (about 2 links)

2 lb/910 g red-skinned, Yukon Gold, or Yellow Finn potatoes, peeled and cut into ½-in/12-mm dice

1 lb/455 g red beets, peeled and cut into ½-in/12-mm dice

Kosher or fine sea salt

1 large yellow onion, cut into ½-in/12-mm dice

1 tbsp fresh thyme leaves

Freshly ground pepper

6 large eggs

1 In a 12-in/30.5-cm frying pan, preferably cast iron, heat 2 tbsp of the oil over medium heat and swirl to coat the pan. Add the sausages and brown on all sides until cooked through, about 8 minutes. Remove the sausages from the pan and set aside to cool.

2 Reduce the heat to medium-low, add the remaining 2 tbsp oil, and swirl to coat the pan. Add the potatoes, beets, and 1 tsp salt and sauté just until coated with the oil, about 1 minute. Cover and steam for 5 minutes, stirring once. Add the onion and stir to incorporate, then re-cover and cook, stirring once or twice, until the onion is softened, about 7 minutes longer.

3 Meanwhile, cut the sausages into rounds ¼ in/6 mm thick. Set aside.

4 Uncover the pan, increase the heat to medium-high, and add the thyme and ½ tsp pepper. Stir to dislodge any bits stuck to the pan bottom, then continue to sauté the potatoes and beets until tender, about 10 minutes longer. Gently fold in the sliced sausages and cook until heated through, about 2 minutes longer. Taste and adjust the seasoning.

5 Using a large spoon, make six shallow depressions in the hash, spacing them evenly around the pan and putting one in the center. Carefully crack an egg into each depression. Cover the pan, reduce the heat to medium, and cook the eggs until the whites are set and the yolks are still runny, about 5 minutes. Serve immediately, topping each egg with a sprinkle of salt and pepper.

RED VELVET CUPCAKES WITH ORANGE BUTTERCREAM

These darling magenta cupcakes are brilliantly colored all the way through. No food coloring is used here. The color comes from puréeing freshly roasted beets. I tested the recipe with canned beets and the color was drab and faded. But roasting beets is easy, and you can measure and prepare the rest of the ingredients for the cupcakes and buttercream while they roast. I finely chop the roasted beets and then purée them in a food processor. Let the machine run for a couple of minutes until the purée is completely smooth.

MAKES 12 CUPCAKES

CUPCAKES

2 cups/200 g sifted cake flour

1 tsp baking powder

¼ tsp kosher or fine sea salt

⅛ tsp ground cinnamon

1½ cups/340 g puréed Simple Roasted Beets (page 45), prepared with red beets (3 medium or 2 large beets)

1 cup plus 2 tbsp/225 g granulated sugar

3 large eggs, beaten

⅔ cup/165 ml canola or other neutral oil

¾ tsp pure vanilla extract

ORANGE BUTTERCREAM

1¼ cups/280 g unsalted butter, at room temperature

2 cups/200 g confectioners' sugar

1 tbsp heavy whipping cream

½ tsp pure orange oil (see Cook's Note)

¼ tsp pure vanilla extract

2 to 3 tbsp fresh orange juice

1 To make the cupcakes, position a rack in the center of the oven and preheat to 350°F/180°C/gas 4. Line a 12-cup standard muffin pan with paper liners.

2 Sift together the flour, baking powder, salt, and cinnamon. Set aside.

3 In a large bowl, stir together the beet purée, granulated sugar, eggs, canola oil, and vanilla. Using a rubber spatula, stir in one-third of the flour mixture, continuing to stir just until the flour disappears. Do not beat or overmix. Repeat, adding the remaining flour mixture in two batches.

4 Spoon the batter into the prepared muffin cups, dividing the batter evenly and filling each cup almost to the top of the liner. Bake until a toothpick inserted into the center of a cupcake comes out clean, 25 to 30 minutes. Let the cupcakes cool in the pan on a wire rack for 10 minutes. Then carefully release the cupcakes from the pan and let cool completely on the rack, about 1 hour.

5 To make the buttercream, in the bowl of a stand mixer fitted with the paddle attachment, or in a medium bowl using a handheld mixer, cream the butter on low speed until creamy and smooth. Add the confectioners' sugar, cream, orange oil, and vanilla and beat on low speed until incorporated, about 2 minutes. Add the orange juice, a little at a time, until the buttercream is fluffy and smooth.

6 Spread a thick layer of buttercream on the top of each cooled cupcake, swirling it to create a decorative finish. Alternatively, transfer the frosting to a pastry bag fitted with a medium star tip and pipe the frosting on the top of each cupcake. The cupcakes can be made in advance; cover and store at room temperature for up to 2 days or freeze for up to 1 month.

COOK'S NOTE

Pure orange oil is an essential oil that is cold pressed from the rind of oranges. Do not confuse it with pure orange extract, which is alcohol flavored with orange oil. Look for pure orange oil in the baking section of natural foods stores, at baking supply stores, or in Middle Eastern grocery stores. Two brands I often see are Boyajian and Frontier.

BURDOCK ROOT

Arctium lappa

BURDOCK ROOT / GREAT BURDOCK / GOBO *(JAPANESE)* / NGAU PONG *(CANTONESE)* / NIUPANGZI *(MANDARIN CHINESE)*

HISTORY AND LORE A member of the family Asteraceae (commonly known as the sunflower, aster, or daisy family), the roots and seeds of this Siberian native have been used in traditional Chinese medicine for centuries. The Chinese introduced burdock to the Japanese, who used it in herbal remedies for sore throats and colds and other maladies. The Japanese are responsible for its use as an edible plant and consider it a delicacy, enjoying its pleasant crunchy texture and earthy, meaty flavor. Edible burdock was introduced to France in the 1870s, and though the plant was admired for its hardiness, it never caught on as a garden crop. It also made its way to North America but was considered a weed until the second half of the twentieth century, when it was promoted by practitioners of the then-popular macrobiotic diet. Nowadays, it is recognized as a diuretic and is used in topical creams to combat chronic skin conditions.

Interestingly, the prickly, thistle-topped heads of burdock plants were the inspiration for a now-common commercial product. In the early 1940s, George de Mestral, a Swiss inventor, was taking his dog for a walk and became curious about the seeds (burrs) of the burdock plant that stuck to his clothes and the dog's hair. When he viewed them under a microscope, he could see the hook-and-loop system that they used to attach themselves to passing animals, which is what ensured their dispersal. Realizing he could use this naturally occurring adhesion system to join other things, he invented Velcro.

VARIETIES In Asia, savvy foragers seek out wild burdock. Only a few cultivated varieties of this hardy biennial grown as an annual are available. The fleshy tapering root can reach 4 feet/120 centimeters in length and 1 inch/ 2.5 centimeters in diameter. The plant is also cultivated for its immature flower stalks, which are harvested in the spring and cooked; their taste resembles that of artichoke. Certain burdock cultivars, mostly developed in Japan, are grown for their young, soft leaves, which are prized and eaten by the Japanese.

NUTRITION Burdock root is low in calories and high in dietary fiber, with 88 calories and 6 grams of fiber in a 3½-ounce/100-gram serving. The roots are also rich in potassium, phosphorus, calcium, and magnesium.

AVAILABILITY AND SELECTION Stocked nearly year-round in Japanese, Korean, and some natural foods stores, burdock root can also be found at farmers' markets in late summer, autumn, and early winter, from plants sown in early spring. Look for long, slender roots no more than 1 inch/2.5 centimeters in diameter. The young roots are less fibrous than the more mature ones. The brownish, sometimes dirt-cloaked skin should be free of bruises and cracks and the root should feel firm and stiff, rather than flabby and flexible. Roots available in Asian markets can be up to 1 yard/1 meter long; roots grown locally and sold at farmers' markets are typically 12 to 14 inches/ 30.5 to 35.5 centimeters long. You will usually see them loose rather than bundled.

STORAGE Wrap the unwashed roots in damp paper towels and place in a long plastic bag in the refrigerator. They should keep for several weeks if you keep the toweling damp. They can also be kept in a shallow pan of water.

BASIC USE AND PREPARATION In Japan, very young roots and tender leaves are eaten raw, but burdock is usually cooked. The roots should be scrubbed with a vegetable brush to remove any clinging dirt and then rinsed under cool running water. Burdock tastes best when left unpeeled, delivering its characteristic nutty, earthy taste. Trim both ends of the root to create a fresh cut, revealing moist root rather than woody ends. The flesh will darken once it is exposed, so have a bowl of acidulated water handy (water with a few drops of vinegar or lemon juice added). Depending on the recipe, burdock may need to be parboiled before it is stir-fried, roasted, braised, marinated, or pickled. See the recipe for Parboiled Burdock Root on the facing page.

YIELDS

1 small (12-in/30.5-cm) root = 3 to 4 oz/85 to 115 g

1 large (24-in/60-cm) root = 7 to 8 oz/200 to 225 g

7 oz/200 g burdock root, trimmed and thinly sliced = about 1¼ cups/185 g

14 oz/400 g burdock, trimmed and cut into matchsticks = about 2 cups/385 g

---

PARBOILED BURDOCK ROOT

The first step for using burdock in recipes in which it will be pickled or marinated is to parboil it. This makes it crisp-tender and ready to absorb flavor-rich sauces and pastes.

MAKES ABOUT 2 CUPS/385 G

8 cups/2 L water

1 tbsp unseasoned rice vinegar or distilled white vinegar

14 oz/400 g burdock root, scrubbed and trimmed

1   Pour the water into a large pot, add the vinegar, and set aside. Have ready a large bowl of ice water and a colander.

2   Cut the unpeeled burdock into slices on the diagonal or into matchsticks, depending on the recipe you will be using. As soon as the burdock is cut, add it to the vinegar water to prevent discoloration.

3   Bring the water to a boil over high heat and cook the burdock until it softens, about 5 minutes. (Burdock flesh is hard and fibrous, so it will tenderize when it is parboiled, but it won't be tender-crisp like a carrot.) Drain the burdock in the colander and transfer to the ice water to cool, about 2 minutes.

4   Wrap the burdock in several thicknesses of paper towels to dry. The burdock is now ready to use in any recipe calling for the parboiled root. To store for up to 1 day, wrap in dry paper towels, slip into a lock-top plastic bag, and refrigerate.

SHREDDED BURDOCK IN TANGY SESAME SAUCE

Served as an appetizing condiment alongside rice or alone with sake, this side dish or salad is called *tataki gobo* in Japanese. The word *tataki* means "to pound" or "to beat" and also means "joy aplenty." Here, the burdock is parboiled and then pounded to prepare this healthful and restorative dish that is traditionally served during the long New Year holiday in Japan.

SERVES 8 TO 10 AS A SIDE DISH OR CONDIMENT

14 oz/400 g burdock root, scrubbed, trimmed, cut into matchsticks 3 in/7.5 cm long and about ¼ in/6 mm wide and thick, and parboiled (see page 63)

3 tbsp Japanese toasted sesame seed paste (*shiro neri goma*) or roasted tahini (see Cook's Note)

2 tbsp unseasoned rice vinegar

1 tbsp soy sauce

1 tbsp granulated sugar

2 tsp water

½ tsp kosher or fine sea salt

2 tsp sesame seeds, toasted (see Cook's Note)

1 Once the matchstick-cut burdock root is parboiled and cooled, pat it dry with paper towels and spread it out on a large cutting board. Using a smooth-bottomed meat pounder, heavy-bottomed saucepan, or sturdy rolling pin, pound the burdock root to flatten it and break up the fibers. Using your fingers, shred the sticks into halves and put in a large bowl.

2 In a small bowl, whisk together the sesame seed paste, vinegar, soy sauce, sugar, water, and salt until smooth.

3 Pour the sauce over the burdock root and use a rubber spatula to coat all of the burdock sticks evenly with the sauce. Transfer to a serving bowl, garnish with the toasted sesame seeds, and serve immediately. Alternatively, cover and refrigerate for up to 1 week. Remove from the refrigerator 1 hour before serving.

COOK'S NOTE

To make this recipe more accessible for most home cooks, I chose to use jarred Japanese sesame seed paste (*shiro neri goma*) rather than make my own from scratch, which begins with toasting hulled sesame seeds. In a traditional Japanese home, the cook uses a *suribachi* (a coarsely textured grinding bowl) and a *surikogi* (a wooden pestle) to laboriously grind warm toasted sesame seeds until they release their oil and become creamy. For an American kitchen, the grinding process is even harder with a smooth-walled mortar and pestle, and that assumes the cook owns these tools. Look for toasted sesame seed paste in a Japanese market or use Middle Eastern roasted tahini.

To toast sesame seeds, spread the seeds in a single layer on a small, rimmed baking sheet and place in a preheated 350°F/180°C/gas 4 oven until fragrant and lightly browned, 5 to 7 minutes. Alternatively, you can brown the sesame seeds in a microwave oven, but you must watch them closely and stir them occasionally. Spread the seeds in a single layer on a microwave-safe plate and microwave on high power, stirring once or twice, until lightly browned, 2 to 3 minutes.

BURDOCK IN SPICY KOCHU JANG SAUCE

Kochu jang, Korean hot bean paste, was easier to find than I thought it would be. Without a Korean market close by, I found this paste at a well-stocked Japanese market and then later saw it at two other Asian markets. (The romanization of Korean varies; another popular spelling for this sauce is *gochujang*.) Considered a must-have ingredient for Korean cuisine, this alluring paste is sweet, sour, and hot but not killer hot like some Chinese bean pastes I have used. Although you can blend together red miso, mirin, and ground dried chile to approximate the flavor of the sauce, I urge you to seek out a jar at a local Asian market or online. It will keep forever in your refrigerator, and I now use it in hearty soups and stews whenever I'm seeking an East-meets-West flavor combination.

These spicy pickles are addictively delicious on their own, or they can be served with grilled foods, steamed vegetables, or rice dishes.

SERVES 8

1 tbsp Korean hot bean paste (*kochu jang*)

1 tbsp white miso paste

1½ tbsp soy sauce

1 tbsp Asian sesame oil

1½ tsp granulated sugar

2 tbsp finely minced green onion, including green tops

1½ tsp finely minced garlic

1 tsp peeled and finely minced fresh ginger

7 oz/200 g burdock root, scrubbed, trimmed, cut on a sharp diagonal into ovals ⅛ in/3 mm thick, and parboiled (see page 63)

1 In a medium bowl, stir together the hot bean paste and miso. Add the soy sauce and stir to thin the mixture. Stir in the sesame oil and sugar until thoroughly combined. Using a rubber spatula, fold in the green onion, garlic, and ginger until evenly distributed. Now fold in the parboiled burdock root.

2 Transfer to a serving dish, cover, and set aside at room temperature for 1 to 2 hours to allow the flavors to meld before serving. The pickles can be stored in an airtight container in the refrigerator for up to 3 weeks.

BURDOCK MISO-ZUKE

When I was researching burdock root, I found two different references to burdock simmered in a soy-mirin-sake broth and then drained and "buried" in red miso paste for several days. Too intrigued not to give it a try, I adapted a recipe I found in Ikuko Hisamatsu's *Tsukemono: Japanese Pickling Recipes*, an obscure cookbook first published in Japan and later translated into English. Referred to as a rich-tasting pickle, this dish is meant to be served as a condiment, one of those little bites or nibbles that accents a rice dish or makes a terrific match with grilled fish, grilled tofu, or satay. It keeps well in the refrigerator, so plucking a few pieces out now and then to eat alongside a sandwich or with steamed vegetables makes the pickle delightful to have on hand.

SERVES 8 TO 10 AS A CONDIMENT

½ cup/120 ml water

1 tbsp soy sauce

1 tbsp mirin (Japanese sweet cooking wine)

1 tbsp sake

7 oz/200 g thin burdock root, scrubbed, trimmed, halved lengthwise, and cut into 5-in/12-cm lengths

¾ cup/180 ml red miso paste (see Cook's Note)

1 In a small saucepan, combine the water, soy sauce, mirin, and sake. Set the pan near your cutting board. As you cut the burdock root, immediately place it in the liquid to keep it from browning.

2 Place the saucepan over medium-high heat and bring to a boil. Cook for 1 minute, remove from the heat, and let steep for 1 hour.

3 Select a nonreactive container with a tight-fitting lid that will hold the burdock root in two layers with little room to spare. Use about ⅓ cup/ 75 ml of the miso paste to cover the bottom of the container with a thick layer. Remove the burdock from the liquid, shaking off any excess moisture, and arrange it in the container, forming two tightly packed layers. Press the burdock into the bottom layer of miso. Spread the remaining miso paste on top, pressing it into any spaces between the lengths of burdock and the layers and making sure it covers the burdock completely. Cover the container and refrigerate for 2 to 3 days to allow the miso flavor to be absorbed.

4 Lift out as many pieces as you wish to serve, scraping off the miso with a table knife or chopstick back into the container, and then respreading the miso evenly. Using a sharp paring knife, cut the burdock on a sharp diagonal into bite-size pieces about 1½ in/4 cm long. The remaining burdock will keep in the refrigerator for up to 1 month.

COOK'S NOTE

Miso, one of Japan's most important ingredients, has an appealing flavor and aroma and is packed with protein. There are many different kinds, with white miso (*shiro miso*) and red miso (*aka miso*) the two best-known types. Red miso, which has a deep, rich saltiness and is a burnished red, is made from a combination of rice, barley, and crushed boiled soybeans, to which a yeastlike mold is added. It comes in smooth and chunky textures. I used Sendai red miso for this recipe.

BURDOCK AND CARROT KINPIRA

Kinpira is the name of a powerful mythical hero of old Japan who was bold and dashing—just like the flavor combination of sake with soy sauce. The same word refers to a Japanese cooking style that combines stir-frying and braising. This basic recipe is commonly used to cook such root vegetables as burdock, carrot, and lotus root, or a combination of roots.

SERVES 4

2 cups/480 ml water, plus 3 tbsp

2 tsp unseasoned rice vinegar or distilled white vinegar

5½ oz/155 g burdock root

2 tbsp canola or other neutral oil

1 medium carrot, 4 oz/115 g, trimmed, peeled, and cut on a sharp diagonal into slices ⅛ in/ 3 mm thick

2 tbsp sake

1 tbsp mirin (Japanese sweet cooking wine)

1 tbsp granulated sugar

1 tbsp soy sauce

2 tsp tamari

¼ tsp *shichimi togarashi* (see Cook's Note, page 71)

1 tbsp sesame seeds, toasted (see Cook's Note, page 64)

1 tbsp very thinly sliced green onion tops

1 In a medium bowl, stir together the 2 cups/480 ml of water and vinegar. Set aside.

2 Scrub and trim the burdock root. Then, using a chef's knife, cut the root on a sharp diagonal into slices ⅛ in/3 mm thick. As the slices are cut, immediately submerge them in the vinegar water to keep them from discoloring. Leave the slices in the vinegar water until you are ready to begin stir-frying, then drain and blot dry with paper towels.

3 In a wok or a large, deep frying pan, heat the oil over high heat and swirl to coat the pan bottom and sides. Add the burdock root and stir-fry until well coated with the oil and beginning to soften, 2 minutes. Add the carrot and stir-fry for 1 minute longer. Add the remaining 3 tbsp water, the sake, mirin, and sugar. Cook, stirring occasionally, until almost all of the liquid is absorbed, about 3 minutes. Add the soy sauce and stir-fry for 30 seconds. Add the tamari and *shichimi togarashi* and toss once or twice to coat the vegetables.

4 Transfer to a warmed serving bowl and garnish with the sesame seeds and green onion. Serve hot or at room temperature.

KALE AND BURDOCK ROOT IN CURRIED CREAM

When I cook kale and other dark leafy greens, I don't bother to blanch them in boiling water first to wilt the leaves. For one, I'm a bit lazy and I don't want another pot to clean up. But more important, blanching leaches the nutrients out of the greens and into the boiling water. So even though it is a bit unwieldy to wilt down handfuls of greens in the sauté pan, it works, and all of the vitamins and minerals remain in the vegetables. Pick a large, deep pan, stir, stir, stir, and be patient as the greens wilt. To make this dish vegetarian, substitute vegetable broth or make the Roasted Root Vegetable Stock on page 267.

SERVES 4

1 tbsp unsalted butter

1 tbsp extra-virgin olive oil

½ medium yellow onion, thinly sliced

4 oz/115 g burdock root, scrubbed, trimmed, and cut on a sharp diagonal into slices ⅛ in/3 mm thick

½ cup/120 ml homemade chicken stock or canned low-sodium chicken broth

2 tsp curry powder

1 tsp granulated sugar

Kosher or fine sea salt

1½ lb/680 g kale, tough stems discarded and roughly chopped

½ cup/120 ml heavy whipping cream

Freshly ground pepper

1 In a large, deep frying pan, melt the butter with the oil over medium-high heat and swirl to coat the pan bottom. Add the onion and sauté, stirring constantly, until the onion is translucent, about 2 minutes. Add the burdock root and continue to sauté, stirring frequently, until the burdock is fork-tender and the onion is just beginning to brown, about 5 minutes. Reduce the heat if the onion is browning too quickly. Stir in the stock, curry powder, sugar, and 1 tsp salt. Bring to a simmer and cook until the liquid is reduced by half, about 2 minutes longer.

2 Grab a handful of kale, add it to the pan, and stir to wilt it. Immediately add another handful and repeat to wilt it. Continue to add handfuls of kale until all of it is in the pan and is wilted. Add the cream, stir to blend, and then cover the pan. Reduce the heat to medium and simmer until the kale is tender, about 5 minutes longer. Add a few grinds of pepper and season with salt. Serve immediately.

ELIZABETH ANDOH'S MISO-THICKENED PORK AND BURDOCK SOUP

This recipe is adapted from one that appears in Elizabeth Andoh's terrific cookbook, *Washoku: Recipes from the Japanese Home Kitchen*. She refers to this hearty soup as "a jumble of pork bits, root vegetables, and diced tofu in a miso-thickened broth." I find this soup soulful and absolutely delightful on a cold winter's night.

SERVES 6 TO 8

½ tsp canola or other neutral oil

8 oz/225 g boneless pork loin, trimmed of fat and cut into small, thin strips

1 large leek, about 8 oz/225 g, white and light green part only, halved lengthwise and thinly sliced cross-wise into half-moons

7 oz/200 g burdock root, scrubbed, trimmed, and cut on a sharp diagonal into slices ⅛ in/3 mm thick

1 small carrot, about 3 oz/85 g, trimmed, peeled, and cut into matchsticks

1-in/2.5-cm chunk daikon radish, about 2 oz/55 g, peeled and cut into matchsticks

1 tsp kosher or fine sea salt

2 tbsp sake

8 cups/2 L water

12-in/30.5-cm square *kombu*, wiped lightly on both sides with a damp paper towel (see Cook's Note)

½ tsp soy sauce

1 block fresh firm tofu, about 15 oz/430 g, drained, pressed to release more moisture, and then blotted dry

1 small bunch *mitsuba* (about 15 stalks), trimmed, stems cut into ½-in/12-mm pieces, and leaves chopped (see Cook's Note)

3 tbsp *mugi miso* (see Cook's Note)

3 tbsp Saikyo miso or white miso (see Cook's Note)

1 In a deep pot, heat the oil over high heat. Add the pork and stir-fry until it begins to color, about 1 minute. Add the leek, burdock root, carrot, and daikon and continue to stir-fry for another minute. Add the salt and sake and continue stir-frying until the burdock root smells fragrant like the woods, about 2 minutes longer.

2 Add the water and *kombu*, reduce the heat to medium-high, and bring to a boil. Using a large spoon or a soup skimmer, skim away any froth, and then reduce the heat to maintain a steady, slow simmer. Continue to cook, skimming any froth that comes to the surface, until the vegetables are tender and the pork is thoroughly cooked, about 5 minutes longer. Using tongs, remove and discard the *kombu*. Add the soy sauce and tofu to the soup and simmer until heated through, about 1 minute longer.

3 Divide the *mitsuba* among warmed soup bowls. Just before serving, place the miso in a medium bowl, ladle in some of the hot stock from the pot, stir to mix, and then add the miso mixture to the soup and stir briefly. Ladle the soup into the warmed bowls and serve immediately.

COOK'S NOTE

Kombu (kelp) is a sea vegetable harvested in the chilly waters around and near the coastline of Hokkaido, Japan. It is dried in long sheets that are then cut and packaged. Look for packages labeled *dashi kombu*.

Mitsuba is a delicate herb that Japanese cooks typically use for garnishing soups. It adds a lovely touch of color. I found it at a well-stocked Japanese market carefully wrapped in a long cellophane bag. If you cannot find *mitsuba*, substitute watercress or even flat-leaf parsley.

Mugi miso is a caramel-colored miso made from barley and soybeans. It is readily available at Japanese markets. Once the container is opened, it can be resealed and stored in the refrigerator for up to six months.

Saikyo miso, a specialty of Kyoto, is a type of *shiro* (white) miso that is very sweet, with caramel overtones. The Japanese use it to make confections and flavor sauces. It will keep in the refrigerator for up to six months.

GRILLED BEEF-WRAPPED BURDOCK ROOT

Here's an appetizer worth talking about—and I promise these meaty grilled rolls will stop the small talk at a cocktail party. With both the beef strips and the burdock marinated, these grilled rollups have a big beefy flavor and a delightful crunch from the strips of burdock root. The accent garnish of *shichimi togarashi*, a spice blend, gives a hint of warm—not fiery—heat that nicely complements the beef. If you can, head to an Asian market and look for boneless short ribs or other well-marbled beef that has been sliced paper-thin for sukiyaki. It will save you a lot of time. Otherwise, ask your butcher to slice it. If you end up doing it yourself, partially freeze the meat and cut it into paper-thin strips when it is firm and ice-cold.

MAKES THIRTY 3-IN/7.5-CM BEEF ROLLS

BURDOCK MARINADE

1½ cups dashi (see Cook's Note)

3 tbsp mirin (Japanese sweet cooking wine)

2 tbsp light soy sauce

14 oz/400 g burdock root, scrubbed, trimmed, cut into matchsticks 3 in/7.5 cm long and about ⅛ in/3 mm wide and thick, and parboiled (see page 63)

BEEF MARINADE

6 tbsp/90 ml dark soy sauce

6 tbsp/90 ml mirin (Japanese sweet cooking wine)

3 tbsp sake

1¼ lb/570 g boneless short ribs, sliced into paper-thin strips 5½ in/14 cm long and 1 in/2.5 cm wide as for sukiyaki

3 green onions, green tops only, cut into pieces 3 in/7.5 cm long and then halved lengthwise

Vegetable oil for brushing the grill grate

Shichimi togarashi for garnish (see Cook's Note)

1 To make the burdock marinade, in a small bowl, stir together the dashi, mirin, and light soy sauce.

2 Place the parboiled burdock in a shallow dish or bowl and pour the marinade over. Cover with a piece of plastic wrap, pressing it directly onto the burdock to keep it submerged in the marinade. Set aside at room temperature for 3 hours.

3 To make the beef marinade, in a large, shallow baking dish, stir together the dark soy sauce, mirin, and sake. When the burdock root has been marinating for 2 hours, arrange the beef in the marinade, making sure the slices are submerged, cover the dish, and set aside at room temperature to marinate for 1 hour. At least 30 minutes before the beef is ready, submerge twenty bamboo skewers, each 6 in/15 cm long, in water.

4 Drain the burdock and discard the marinade. Remove the beef from its marinade and pour the marinade into a small bowl. (The marinade will be used for basting the rolls on the grill.) On a clean work surface, lay two strips of the meat vertically, arranging them side by side with the edges overlapping slightly. (I think it is easiest for rolling if you orient the slices vertically, which will give you enough room to lay out six slices and make three rolls at a time.) Arrange eight burdock strips and one green onion strip in a horizontal bundle about 1 in/2.5 cm from the end of the beef strips nearest you. Working from the end nearest you, roll the beef strips over the vegetables and then continue to roll to form a stuffed cylinder (the burdock and green onion should stick out slightly on both sides). Repeat to make two more beef rolls. Place the rolls together in a flat vertical stack, and thread two skewers equidistance apart through the three rolls. Spread the rolls out so they are about 1 in/2.5 cm apart. Place the skewered rolls on a baking sheet. Repeat to make more rolls and skewer them the same way. (The rolls can be prepared up to 8 hours in advance. Cover and refrigerate the rolls and the basting liquid until ready to grill. Remove the rolls and basting liquid from the refrigerator about 45 minutes before you are ready to begin grilling.)

5 Prepare a hot fire in a charcoal grill or preheat a gas grill to high. When the fire is ready, brush the grill grate with vegetable oil. Place the skewered rolls directly over the hot fire and grill, basting once, until nicely seared on one side, 2 to 3 minutes. Turn and continue to grill, basting once or twice, until seared, about 3 minutes longer. Remove the skewers from the grill and let rest for 2 minutes.

6 Using tongs or your fingers, nimbly slide the rolls off the skewers onto a warmed platter. Garnish with a light sprinkling of *shichimi togarashi* and serve immediately. (The beef rolls can be kept warm in a low oven for up to 20 minutes before serving.)

COOK'S NOTE

Dashi is the Japanese basic soup stock made from *bonito* (tuna) flakes, *kombu* (kelp), and water. You can prepare it from scratch, but most home cooks, even in Japan, buy instant dashi. Available in Asian markets, instant dashi may be labeled *dashi-no-moto* and is sold in granules, as a powder, or as a concentrate. I prefer the granules, which come sealed in small tubes that are sold in either boxes or cellophane packages. Because you open only a tube at a time, the unused granules do not pick up moisture that can cause them to spoil.

Shichimi togarashi is a vibrant Japanese seven-spice seasoning blend used in a variety of dishes, such as soups or sprinkled over udon. Dried chiles are roughly ground and then mixed with six other spices. While spice vendors make their own blends and vary the heat levels from mild to hot, a typical blend includes *sansho* (Sichuan pepper), citrus peel, bits of nori (dried seaweed), black hemp seeds, white poppy seeds, and black sesame seeds.

STEAMED MUSSELS WITH BURDOCK ROOT, SHALLOTS, AND SUN-DRIED TOMATOES

As it turns out, mussels and burdock root are a natural pairing, delivering an incredibly savory, briny flavor to this dish—a true umami taste. Buy fresh, sweet, plump mussels from a trusted fish purveyor. Once home, spread them out in a large, shallow baking dish, cover them with damp papers towels and then loosely with plastic wrap, and refrigerate until ready to use. I always scrub and debeard the mussels right before I steam them. While you are shopping, buy a loaf of crusty bread for sopping up the delicious sauce.

SERVES 3 AS A MAIN COURSE, 4 TO 6 AS A FIRST COURSE

2 tbsp unsalted butter

4 oz/115 g burdock root, scrubbed, trimmed, and cut on a sharp diagonal into slices ⅛ in/3 mm thick

¾ cup/85 g thinly sliced shallots

½ cup/55 g drained oil-packed sun-dried tomatoes, blotted dry and cut lengthwise into thirds

2 fresh thyme springs

1 tsp kosher or fine sea salt

¼ tsp red pepper flakes

2 lb/910 g mussels, scrubbed and debearded

1 cup/240 ml dry white wine

¼ cup/60 ml heavy whipping cream

1 In a large, deep frying pan with a tight-fitting lid, melt the butter over medium heat and swirl to coat the pan bottom. Add the burdock root and shallots and sauté, stirring frequently, until the shallots just begin to turn golden brown, 3 to 5 minutes. Add the sun-dried tomatoes, thyme, salt, and red pepper flakes and sauté for 1 minute longer. Increase the heat to medium-high and add the mussels and wine. Cover and cook until all of the mussels have opened, about 5 minutes.

2 Uncover the pan and add the cream. Give a quick stir to blend it in, then bring the liquid to a simmer and remove from the heat. Divide the mussels and cooking liquid among warmed bowls, discarding any mussels that failed to open. Serve immediately.

CARROT

Daucus carota

HISTORY AND LORE Grown in temperate regions around the world, *Daucus carota* includes a number of both cultivated and wild varieties. Although orange carrots are the most familiar, you can also find white, yellow, purple, and deep violet Asian roots. Most scholars agree that the first carrots, with branched purple roots, originated in Afghanistan and spread eastward to India, China, and Japan, and also westward into Arab-occupied Spain in the twelfth century and then through continental Europe in the fourteenth century. The carrots cultivated in northwestern Europe before and during the sixteenth century were all long, tapered purple or yellow roots. In the seventeenth century, horticulturists in the Netherlands hybridized the bright orange color, which became the favored type.

Soon after the discovery of the New World, European explorers carried the carrot across the Atlantic. By 1565, the roots were grown on Margarita Island, off the coast of Venezuela, and just forty-four years later, colonists in Jamestown, Virginia, were planting them in their gardens.

VARIETIES Many different carrot cultivars are available to gardeners and shoppers. They vary in root shape and in color from white, yellow, orange, and red to deep purple. Go beyond the clip-top carrots in the grocery store and try baby carrots, slender finger-length roots, creamy white specimens, and the shockingly beautiful purple-skinned varieties.

BABY CARROTS

Little Finger Blunt-tipped and extremely bright orange, these finger-size gems are perfect used whole in salads, soups, or stews.

Thumbelina These nearly round carrots, the size of golf balls, are popular with chefs because they are full of flavor, retain their vivid orange color when cooked, and are good keepers. They grow well in clay soil and in containers.

NANTES TYPES

Nantes Scarlet A favorite with home gardeners, these sweet roots grow to about 6 inches/15 centimeters long and are rich tasting and virtually coreless.

CHANTENAY TYPES

Chantenay Royal This group of carrots is stump rooted and tapered, with excellent sweet flavor and texture. Chantenay Royal is a favorite cultivar of home gardeners.

LARGER, LATE-SUMMER CARROTS

Autumn King Large and late maturing, these reddish orange carrots are particularly good eaten raw.

Flyaway Popular with home gardeners, these flavorful carrots grow to 12 inches/30.5 centimeters long and 1½ inches/4 centimeters in diameter.

UNEXPECTED COLOR

Purple Dragon These reddish purple carrots grow to about 9 inches/23 centimeters long and are exceptionally high in vitamin A.

White Satin Crisp and sweet flavored, these beautiful, pure white carrots grow to about 8 inches/20 centimeters long.

NUTRITION Carrots contain the orange pigment beta-carotene, an important antioxidant and major source of provitamin A. Known for decades as the vitamin crucial for eyesight, vitamin A plays a critical role in maintaining the immune system and may help prevent heart disease and slow some cancerous growths. The nutrients in carrots are more bioavailable when cooked. In particular, the absorption rate of beta-carotene in raw carrots is only about 10 percent. But when the carrots are cooked, the rate goes up to about 29 percent. Although some diets suggest avoiding carrots because they are high in sugar, the fiber in carrots prevents the sugar from rushing into the bloodstream and causing insulin spikes.

A 3½-ounce/100-gram portion of steamed carrots contains 45 calories, 1.47 grams of dietary fiber, 227 milligrams potassium, 13 milligrams magnesium, and an astonishing 24,554 IU of vitamin A. Don't throw away the lush green, feathery carrot tops; they are edible and delicious and are high in vitamin K, which carrot roots lack.

AVAILABILITY AND SELECTION Carrots are so common in the supermarket that we hardly think of them as having a season, but they are favorites for gardeners who sow seeds in the spring as soon as the soil is warm and enjoy them throughout the summer and fall. Farmers' markets are the best places to find all of the fun, colorful types. Try to buy carrots with their feathery tops attached, as this assures freshness. These tend to be medium-size carrots that will be sweeter and nearly coreless. Mature carrots should have smooth, unblemished skin; avoid the very large ones, which will have a woody core. Bags of peeled, prewashed baby carrots often aren't baby carrots at all, but rather large carrots that have been machine cut to look like baby ones.

STORAGE If carrots are purchased with their green tops, remove the tops as soon as you get the carrots home, leaving 1 inch/2.5 centimeters of the stem attached. If left attached, the tops draw moisture, flavor, and nutrients from the roots. Store the carrots and tops separately. Put unwashed and untrimmed carrots in a plastic bag lined with a paper towel, which wicks away any trapped moisture and keeps the carrots fresh longer, and refrigerate. They will keep for 3 to 4 weeks. To store the greens, trim off the stem ends and wrap the leafy tops in a paper towel, then seal the towel inside a lock-top plastic bag and put the bag in the refrigerator. For peak freshness, the young green tops should be used within a day or two of purchase.

BASIC USE AND PREPARATION Carrots can be eaten raw, juiced, pickled, canned, or cooked by a variety of methods, including boiling, steaming, microwaving, roasting, stir-frying, and sautéing. The feathery tops can be plucked from their fine stems and used raw in salads, added to soups, or made into fabulous-tasting Carrot Top Pesto (page 79). To prepare the carrots, scrub them with a vegetable brush or peel them using a swivel or serrated peeler. Trim the ends and cut as directed in individual recipes.

YIELDS

ROOTS

1 small carrot = 2 oz/55 g

1 medium carrot = 3 to 5 oz/85 to 140 g

1 large carrot = 6 to 7 oz/170 to 200 g

4 to 6 medium carrots = 1 lb/455 g

1 large carrot = 1 cup/170 g grated

2 large carrots = 2 cups/340 g grated

3 cups sliced or diced carrots = 1 lb/455 g

GREENS

Green tops from 1 bunch small carrots, stems trimmed = 1 cup/20 g lightly packed

SPICY THAI PICKLED CARROTS

Some pickles need several days for their flavor to develop, but these fiery, tart carrots are ready after just one night. They provide a quick fix to plain old sandwiches or basic burgers and will add zest and crunch to any relish tray.

MAKES ONE 1-PT/480-ML JAR

12 oz/340 g carrots, trimmed, peeled, and cut on the diagonal into elongated ovals about ¼ in/ 6 mm thick

1 tsp kosher or fine sea salt

1 cup/240 ml unseasoned rice vinegar

2 tbsp firmly packed light brown sugar

2 green Thai chiles or other spicy green chile, stemmed and thinly sliced (see Cook's Note, page 40)

1 In a small bowl, toss the carrots with the salt and let them stand for 1 hour.

2 Meanwhile, in a small saucepan, combine the vinegar, sugar, and chiles and bring to a boil over high heat, stirring to dissolve the sugar. Boil for 1 minute, then remove from the heat. Let cool to room temperature.

3 Pack the carrots into a clean 1-pt/480-ml glass jar or other storage container. Pour the cooled pickling liquid over the carrots, covering them completely. Seal tightly and refrigerate. Allow the flavors to develop for at least 1 day before serving. The pickled carrots will keep for up to 2 weeks.

CARROT, NAPA CABBAGE, AND APPLE SLAW WITH CREAMY POPPY SEED DRESSING

Simple do-ahead steps make this salad perfect for a summer picnic or backyard barbecue. It's refreshing and brightly colored, with the sweetness of the apples playing off the tang of the creamy lemon dressing. With a sharp knife you can quickly make matchsticks from the carrots and apple. A faster approach, and perfectly satisfactory, would be to use the coarse grating disk of a food processor. The napa cabbage, however, looks best when cut by hand.

SERVES 6

DRESSING

¼ cup/60 ml mayonnaise

3 tbsp extra-virgin olive oil

2 tbsp fresh lemon juice

1¼ tsp kosher or fine sea salt

1 tsp poppy seeds

8 oz/225 g napa cabbage, cored and finely shredded

8 oz/225 g carrots, trimmed, peeled, and cut into matchsticks

1 crisp red apple, cored and cut into matchsticks

2 tbsp finely snipped fresh chives

1 To make the dressing, in a small bowl, whisk together the mayonnaise, oil, lemon juice, salt, and poppy seeds. Set aside while you cut the vegetables, or cover and refrigerate for up to 1 day.

2 In a large bowl, toss together the cabbage, carrots, and apple. Spoon the dressing over the top and toss the slaw to distribute the dressing evenly. Transfer to a serving bowl, garnish with the chives, and serve immediately. (The cabbage and carrots can be cut up to 8 hours in advance. Cover and refrigerate until ready to toss the slaw. It is best to cut the apple right before adding it to the slaw so it doesn't discolor.)

CARROT TOP PESTO

I almost always buy fresh carrots with their feathery green tops attached. In the past, I would invariably cut the tops off and send them to the compost bin. Honestly, it never occurred to me that they were edible. But the tops of other root vegetables are edible, so why wouldn't carrot tops be edible, too? One day I blanched the leaves, puréed them with a little olive oil, and then used the purée as a gorgeous green accent sauce for fish, much in the same way I use basil oil. My next idea was to make pesto, trading out the basil for carrot tops, which proved an amazing alternative. This recipe is an absolute keeper, and it's satisfying to make use of the whole plant. I serve this as a dip with crudités, and often add a dollop on top of bruschetta that has been smeared with fresh goat cheese. It's also perfect simply tossed with pasta.

MAKES ABOUT ⅔ CUP/165 ML

1 cup/20 g lightly packed carrot leaves (stems removed)

6 tbsp/90 ml extra-virgin olive oil

1 large garlic clove

¼ tsp kosher or fine sea salt

3 tbsp pine nuts, toasted (see Cook's Note)

¼ cup/30 g freshly grated Parmesan cheese, preferably Parmigiano-Reggiano

In a food processor, combine the carrot leaves, oil, garlic, and salt and process until finely minced. Add the pine nuts and pulse until finely chopped. Add the Parmesan and pulse just until combined. Taste and adjust the seasoning. Use immediately, or cover and refrigerate for up to 2 days.

COOK'S NOTE

Toasting pine nuts, almonds, walnuts, pecans, hazelnuts, cashews, and pumpkin seeds brings out their flavor. Spread the nuts or seeds in a single layer on a rimmed baking sheet, place in a preheated 350°F/180°C/gas 4 oven and toast until fragrant and lightly browned, 5 to 10 minutes, depending on the nut or seed. Alternatively, nuts and seeds can be browned in a microwave. Spread in a single layer on a microwave-safe plate and microwave on high power, stopping to stir once or twice, until fragrant and lightly browned, 5 to 8 minutes. Watch them closely so they don't burn.

CARROT RIBBONS WITH SORREL PESTO AND CRUMBLED GOAT CHEESE

Knockout gorgeous on the plate—I like to make this salad in the springtime, when freshly dug carrots are abundant at the farmers' market and some farm stands have sorrel for sale. Sorrel isn't always easy to find, so know that baby arugula or even watercress is a suitable substitute. Although basil is usually readily available and would work for the pesto, too, I want a bit of bite, an edge of sharpness to balance the inherent sweetness of the carrots. For the dressing, I adjust my pepper mill for a coarser grind, which delivers a welcome spice note, adding to the complexity of the salad.

SERVES 6 AS A FIRST COURSE

DRESSING

4 tbsp/60 ml extra-virgin olive oil

1 tbsp unseasoned rice vinegar

¾ tsp kosher or fine sea salt

½ tsp freshly cracked pepper

SORREL PESTO

2½ cups/65 g lightly packed roughly chopped sorrel

2 large garlic cloves, chopped

⅓ cup/40 g freshly grated Parmesan cheese, preferably Parmigiano-Reggiano

¼ cup/35 g pine nuts

1½ tsp fresh lemon juice

½ tsp kosher or fine sea salt

⅔ cup/165 ml extra-virgin olive oil

2 large garlic cloves, crushed

2 tbsp kosher or fine sea salt

5 large carrots, about 1½ lb/680 g, trimmed and peeled

4 oz/115 g fresh goat cheese

1 To make the dressing, in a small jar with a tight-fitting lid, combine the oil, vinegar, salt, and pepper. Cover tightly and shake vigorously to blend. Taste and adjust the seasoning. Set aside until ready to serve.

2 To make the pesto, in a food processor, combine the sorrel, garlic, Parmesan, pine nuts, lemon juice, and salt and process until finely chopped. Stop the machine once or twice to scrape down the sides of the bowl with a rubber spatula. With the machine running, pour the oil through the feed tube and process until the sauce is combined. Set aside. (The pesto can be transferred to a jar with a tight-fitting lid and refrigerated for up to 3 days. Remove from the refrigerator 45 minutes before serving.)

3 Fill a large pot three-fourths full of water. Add the garlic and salt and bring to a boil over high heat. Have ready a large bowl of ice water and a pair of tongs to remove the carrots quickly after blanching.

4 Using a vegetable peeler, preferably one that is sharp and serrated, firmly peel each carrot lengthwise to create long ribbons, rotating the carrot so the ribbons are all the same width. Stop peeling when you reach the core, then discard the core. Add the carrot ribbons to the boiling water and cook until crisp-tender, about 1 minute. Using tongs, transfer the carrots to the ice water to cool, about 2 minutes. Drain thoroughly and then wrap the carrots in several thicknesses of paper towels to dry. (The carrot ribbons can be wrapped in dry paper towels, slipped into a lock-top plastic bag, and refrigerated for up to 1 day before continuing.)

5 Place the carrot ribbons in a bowl. Give the dressing a last-minute shake, pour over the carrot ribbons, and toss to coat evenly. Make a pile of carrot ribbons in the center of each salad plate. Drizzle a spoonful or two of the pesto in a circle around each plate. Divide the goat cheese into small dollops and scatter the dollops evenly over the carrot ribbons. Serve immediately.

MOROCCAN CARROT AND CHICKPEA SALAD WITH DRIED PLUMS AND TOASTED CUMIN VINAIGRETTE

Although I don't normally buy prepackaged prepared vegetables such as coleslaw mix or, in this instance, shredded carrots, it does streamline the assembly of this salad. It is a colorful and healthy side dish to a grilled main course, especially if you also serve some grilled zucchini or asparagus and skip a starchy vegetable altogether. This salad is a summertime favorite alongside grilled lamb or chicken, and because it does not need to be refrigerated, it's ideal picnic fare.

SERVES 6

DRESSING

1 tbsp cumin seeds

⅓ cup/75 ml extra-virgin olive oil

2 tbsp fresh lemon juice

1 tbsp honey

¾ tsp kosher or fine sea salt

⅛ tsp cayenne pepper

Freshly ground black pepper

One 10-oz/280-g package shredded carrots

One 15-oz/430-g can chickpeas, drained and rinsed

⅔ cup/100 g dried plums (prunes), chopped into chickpea-size pieces

½ cup/30 g coarsely chopped fresh mint

1 To make the dressing, first toast and grind the cumin seeds. Place a small, heavy frying pan, preferably cast iron, over high heat, add the cumin seeds, and toast, stirring constantly, until fragrant and lightly browned, about 2 minutes. Transfer to a plate to cool. Using a spice grinder or a mortar and pestle, grind the seeds to a powder.

2 In a small bowl, whisk together the oil, lemon juice, honey, ground cumin, salt, and cayenne pepper. Season with black pepper.

3 In a medium bowl, combine the carrots, chickpeas, dried plums, and mint. Add the dressing and toss gently to coat all of the ingredients evenly. Serve immediately, or cover and refrigerate until ready to serve. (The salad can be made up to 8 hours in advance. Remove from the refrigerator 30 minutes before serving.)

BUTTER-BRAISED BABY CARROTS WITH DILL

The simplicity of this braised dish, served with roast chicken or an herb- or dried-fruit-stuffed pork loin, is what I crave in the springtime when it's still damp and chilly. Freshly dug baby carrots, with their bushy green tops, are naturally sweet. Just give them a good scrub with a vegetable brush and skip peeling them. Keep a bit of the green stem attached to give the finished dish a pretty, rustic look. It's easy enough for a weeknight meal, yet special enough for a dinner party.

SERVES 4

3 tbsp unsalted butter

1 bunch baby carrots, green tops removed with ½ in/12 mm of the stem intact

¼ cup/60 ml homemade chicken stock or canned low-sodium chicken broth

1 tbsp sherry vinegar

1 tsp firmly packed light brown sugar

½ tsp kosher or fine sea salt

¼ tsp freshly ground pepper

1 tbsp chopped fresh dill

1 In a large sauté pan, melt the butter over medium heat and swirl to coat the pan. Add the carrots and stir to coat. Add the stock, vinegar, sugar, salt, and pepper and bring to a simmer. Reduce the heat to low, cover, and braise until the carrots are crisp-tender, about 10 minutes.

2 Uncover the pan, increase the heat to medium-high, and cook, stirring frequently, until the sauce thickens to a syrup consistency and the carrots are tender, 3 to 5 minutes. Taste and adjust the seasoning. Remove the pan from the heat and toss in the dill. Serve immediately.

CARAMELIZED SPICED CARROTS WITH HONEY AND ORANGE

Aromatically complex, with toasted Middle Eastern spices, sweet honey, and fragrant orange, these carrots are a bold counterpoint to nearly any main course. Freshly ground spices have more flavor than preground, so I always buy spices whole and grind them when needed in a coffee grinder that I reserve for the task. The carrots can be served hot, warm, or at room temperature, making them perfect for a potluck or holiday dinner.

SERVES 4 TO 6

¼ tsp peppercorns

¼ tsp coriander seeds

¼ tsp cumin seeds

¼ tsp aniseeds

2 lb/910 g carrots, trimmed, peeled, and cut on a severe diagonal into slices ½-in/12-mm thick

1 tbsp extra-virgin olive oil

1 tsp kosher or fine sea salt

⅛ tsp ground Aleppo chile (see Cook's Note)

2 tsp freshly grated orange zest

⅓ cup/75 ml fresh orange juice

3 tbsp honey

1 Position a rack in the center of the oven and preheat to 400°F/200°C/gas 6.

2 Place a small, heavy frying pan, preferably cast iron, over high heat. Add the peppercorns, coriander, cumin, and aniseeds to the pan and toast, stirring constantly, until fragrant and lightly browned, about 2 minutes. Transfer to a plate to cool. Using a spice grinder or a mortar and a pestle, grind the spices to a powder.

3 Line a large roasting pan with aluminum foil. Place the carrots in the pan and toss with the oil, ground spices, salt, Aleppo chile, orange zest, and juice. Cover tightly with another sheet of aluminum foil and roast, stirring once or twice, until the carrots are crisp-tender when pierced with a fork, about 30 minutes.

4 Add the honey and toss to coat. Increase the oven to 450°F/230°C/gas 8 and continue roasting, uncovered, until the carrots are tender and dark brown around the edges, about 25 minutes. Serve immediately, or let cool and serve warm, barely warm, or at room temperature.

COOK'S NOTE
Dark red, sweet, sharp-flavored Aleppo chiles are grown in Syria and Turkey and are named after the town of Aleppo, in northern Syria. They are moderately hot but not overpowering and have a fruity quality, almost a raisinlike flavor with a touch of salt. Dried and ground into flakes, they add complex flavor to fish, vegetables, and meats.

STIR-FRIED CARROTS AND FENNEL WITH GARLIC

The combination of carrots and fennel appeals to me, both flavorwise and visually. Root vegetables are typically thought of as candidates for braising, but when they are cut into thin sticks, they are perfect for stir-frying, and that makes for a quick side dish. I always feel a bit cheated when I see fennel bulbs sold with their stalks trimmed off, because I like the look and taste of the feathery fronds. If the only bulbs you can find are trimmed, substitute flat-leaf parsley for the garnish.

SERVES 4

1 fennel bulb, preferably with stalks and feathery fronds attached, about 14 oz/400 g

5 medium carrots, about 13 oz/370 g

2 tbsp extra-virgin olive oil

2 garlic cloves, minced

¾ tsp kosher or fine sea salt

1 Trim the stalks off the fennel bulb, reserving enough of the feathery fronds to yield 1½ tbsp chopped. Set aside. Trim the bottom of the fennel bulb to remove any brown spots and then cut in half lengthwise. Use a paring knife to notch out the core from both sides. Cut each fennel half into thin wedges and separate any layers attached at the base. Set aside in a large bowl.

2 Trim and peel the carrots, then cut into sticks about 2½ in/6 cm long and about ¼ in/6 mm thick. Toss the carrots with the fennel.

3 In a nonstick wok or a large, deep frying pan, heat the oil over medium-high heat and swirl to coat the pan. Add the garlic and allow it to sizzle in the oil until fragrant but not brown, about 15 seconds. Immediately add the fennel and carrots and, using tongs, stir-fry the vegetables until crisp-tender, about 5 minutes. Add the salt and fennel fronds and toss to distribute evenly. Serve immediately.

FARRO WITH CARROTS, RED GRAPES, AND PEARL ONIONS

Farro, an Italian grain (wheat species) found primarily in Abruzzo, Umbria, and Tuscany, has a sweet, nutty flavor and tender texture. Although it looks a lot like spelt, and some sources indicate the two grains are interchangeable, they are not. The directions on the package may indicate the farro should be soaked, but it is not necessary for this recipe. If you buy *farro perlato*, or pearled (semihulled) farro, it will cook more quickly than farro that is not pearled, which will take about 10 minutes longer. This would be a satisfying and hearty dressing at Thanksgiving. For a vegetarian option at your holiday table, substitute vegetable broth for the chicken stock or broth.

SERVES 8 TO 10

4 cups/960 ml homemade chicken stock or canned low-sodium chicken broth

2 cups/480 ml water

2 cups/370 g farro

3 tbsp extra-virgin olive oil

2½ cups/400 g frozen pearl onions, thawed and halved lengthwise

1½ cups/270 g seedless red grapes, halved lengthwise

1 large garlic clove, minced

4 medium carrots, trimmed, peeled, and thinly sliced

1 tbsp finely minced fresh rosemary

1 tbsp finely minced fresh thyme leaves

½ tsp kosher or fine sea salt

½ tsp freshly ground pepper

¼ cup/15 g chopped fresh flat-leaf parsley

1 In a large saucepan, combine the stock and water and bring to a boil. Add the farro, reduce the heat so the liquid just simmers, cover partially, and cook the farro until soft but still with a bit of firmness at the center, 20 to 45 minutes. (The cooking time for farro can vary widely depending on the type you buy. Taste along the way and go by texture rather than timing.) Drain the farro in a sieve placed over a heatproof bowl, reserving the broth. Transfer the farro to a separate bowl and set aside.

2 In a large nonstick sauté pan, heat 2 tbsp of the oil over medium heat and swirl to coat pan bottom. Add the onions and sauté, stirring constantly, for 2 minutes. Adjust the heat to low and continue to sauté, stirring occasionally, until the onions are browned and caramelized at the edges, 7 to 8 minutes longer. Add the grapes and stir to heat through. Transfer to a plate and set aside.

3 Return the sauté pan to medium heat, add the remaining 1 tbsp oil, and swirl to coat the pan bottom. Add garlic and carrots and sauté, stirring frequently, until soft but not brown, about 3 minutes. Add the rosemary and thyme and sauté for 1 minute longer. Add the reserved farro, ⅔ cup/165 ml of the reserved broth, and the salt and pepper. Stir to combine. Add the parsley, stir to combine, and cook for 1 minute longer. Remove from the heat and serve immediately. (The dressing can be made up to 1 day in advance, covered, and refrigerated. To reheat, let sit at room temperature for 1 hour, then transfer to a covered baking dish and place in a preheated 350°F/180°C/gas 4 oven until heated through, about 25 minutes.)

LAMB AND CARROT CURRY

Inspiration for this dish comes from my talented friend Raghavan Iyer, the king of curry and author of the amazing *660 Curries*. This hearty lamb curry has an assertive kick of heat, but if you desire extra fire, simply double the amount of cayenne suggested in the recipe. If time is short, you can sauté the onions until they are tender and brown around the edges, as instructed in the recipe, and skip the next step, which calls for continuing to cook them until they are caramelized. The finished dish won't have the same depth of flavor, but it will still be delicious and soul satisfying. To round out this Indian feast, prepare the Indian-style Okra Curry on page 324 and basmati rice.

SERVES 4

¼ cup/60 ml plain yogurt

3 tbsp minced garlic

2 tbsp peeled and minced fresh ginger

2 tsp coriander seeds, ground

1½ tsp kosher or fine sea salt

1 tsp cumin seeds, ground

1 tsp sweet paprika

½ tsp ground turmeric

¼ tsp cayenne pepper

1 lb/455 g boneless leg of lamb, trimmed of excess fat and cut into 1½-in/4-cm cubes

3 tbsp canola or other neutral oil

1 yellow onion, halved and thinly sliced

4 black cardamom pods (see Cook's Note)

2 bay leaves

One 14½-oz/415-g can diced tomatoes, with juice

12 oz/340 g carrots, trimmed, peeled, and cut on the diagonal into pieces 1½ in/4 cm thick

1 In a medium bowl, stir together the yogurt, garlic, ginger, coriander, salt, cumin, paprika, turmeric, and cayenne. Add the lamb and toss to coat evenly with the marinade. Cover and refrigerate for at least 30 minutes or up to overnight to infuse the meat with flavor.

2 In a medium sauté pan, heat 1 tbsp of the oil over medium heat. Add the onion and sauté, stirring occasionally, until very soft and beginning to brown, 15 to 20 minutes. Reduce the heat to medium-low and continue to cook, stirring constantly, until the onion is evenly golden brown and caramelized, about 10 minutes more. Remove from the heat and set aside.

3 In a medium sauté or frying pan, heat the remaining 2 tbsp oil over medium-high heat. Add the cardamom pods and bay leaves and toast until the leaves just start to brown, about 20 seconds. Immediately add the yogurt-coated lamb, including any marinade at the bottom of the bowl (this adds to the sauce). Cook the meat, stirring occasionally, until browned, 8 to 10 minutes. (As the juices cook down, the meat will brown and the spices coating the lamb will toast and become fragrant.)

4 Add the tomatoes and their juice and stir well, scraping the pan bottom to release any stuck-on bits. Stir in the carrots and caramelized onions and bring the mixture to a boil. Reduce the heat to maintain a slow simmer, cover, and cook until the lamb is very tender, 1 to 1½ hours. Serve piping hot.

COOK'S NOTE
Black cardamom is distinctly different from the more common green cardamom. The pods taste of camphor and are dried over an open flame, creating a smoky flavor. Look for it at specialty grocers and Asian and Middle Eastern markets.

WHITE CARROT CRAB BISQUE

This recipe is the creation of friend and talented chef Ben Bettinger. Executive chef at Beaker & Flask, he is a star on the Portland, Oregon, food scene. He makes this bisque as an elegant starter when white carrots and crab are in season. The recipe has two parts, both of them easy and straightforward. First you make the crab stock and then you complete the bisque using the flavorful, sweet stock. You don't need to make it all on the same day. To break up the time involved, I suggest you make the stock a day in advance and then finish the bisque the next day. Or, if you have used crabmeat for another purpose and want to make stock for this recipe from the shells, you can keep the stock longer. Transfer it to a freezer container, allowing 1 inch/2.5 centimeters of headspace, and freeze for up to 6 months. (I do the same thing with shrimp shells to make a sweet, light seafood stock that I use for a soup or for a seafood risotto.) If you have crab stock on hand, you can buy fresh crabmeat and quickly make the bisque. You'll need to purchase 12 ounces/340 grams crabmeat.

MAKES ABOUT 7 CUPS/1.7 L; SERVES 6 TO 8

CRAB STOCK

2 cooked Dungeness crabs, 1 lb/455 g each

1 small yellow onion, quartered

2 garlic cloves

1 medium white carrot, trimmed and cut into 2-in/5-cm chunks

1 bay leaf

3 fresh thyme sprigs

5 peppercorns

1 cup/240 ml dry white wine

About 8 cups/2 L water

BISQUE

¼ tsp peppercorns

½ tsp coriander seeds

1 bunch white carrots, about 2 lb/910 g, trimmed, peeled, and thinly sliced

2 tbsp unsalted butter

1½ tbsp granulated sugar

Kosher or fine sea salt

⅓ cup/75 ml heavy whipping cream

1 tbsp pale dry sherry

1 To make the stock, first pick the crabmeat from the shells, reserving all of the shells and cartilage. Place the crabmeat in a bowl, cover, and refrigerate until needed.

2 In a large saucepan, combine the crab shells and cartilage, onion, garlic, carrot, bay leaf, thyme, and peppercorns. Add the wine and just enough of the water to submerge the crab shells. Bring to a boil over medium-high heat and then reduce the heat so the liquid is at a bare simmer. Using a large spoon or skimmer, skim any foam that rises to the top. Partially cover the pan and simmer for 1 hour.

3 Set a large, fine-mesh sieve over a large bowl. Using a large slotted spoon, transfer the crab shells and vegetables to the sieve, capturing all of the juices in the bowl. Do not press on the solids. Discard the solids, then pour the stock through the sieve. (The stock can be transferred to an airtight container and refrigerated for up to 2 days before continuing. Once the stock is chilled, use the edge of a large spoon to skim any congealed fat from the surface.)

4 To make the bisque, remove the crabmeat from the refrigerator and allow it to come to room temperature.

5 Place a small, heavy frying pan, preferably cast iron, over high heat. Add the peppercorns and coriander seeds and toast, stirring constantly, until fragrant and lightly browned, about 2 minutes. Transfer to a plate to cool. Using a spice grinder or a mortar and pestle, grind the spices to a powder.

6 In a large saucepan, combine the carrots, butter, sugar, and toasted spices. Add 1½ tsp salt and just enough of the crab stock (about 5 cups/1.2 L) to barely cover the carrots. Bring the liquid to a boil over medium-high heat and then reduce the heat so the liquid is at a simmer. Partially cover and cook until the carrots are fork-tender, about 10 minutes. Remove from the heat and let cool for a few minutes.

7 Working in batches, purée the soup in a blender or food processor until completely smooth, adding more stock as needed to achieve a soupy consistency. (The soup should be just thick enough to coat the back of a spoon.) Return the puréed soup to the pan, place over low heat, and add the cream and sherry. Cook, stirring occasionally, until piping hot. Do not allow the soup to boil. Taste and adjust the seasoning.

8 Divide the soup among warmed shallow bowls. Garnish each serving with a generous mound of crabmeat, piling it in the center.

HOLIDAY CARROT PUDDING

Here is one vegetable dish that doesn't require any last-minute attention from the busy cook focusing on an elaborate holiday meal such as Thanksgiving. The carrots can be cooked and puréed a couple of days ahead. Assemble the pudding on the day you plan to serve it, refrigerate it for up to several hours, and then remove it from the refrigerator about an hour before baking. Hot from the oven, the carrot pudding is gloriously puffed, beautifully browned, and pretty on the plate.

SERVES 8 TO 10

5 large carrots, about 1½ lb/680 g, trimmed, peeled, and cut into 1-in/2.5-cm chunks

2 tsp fresh lemon juice

5 tbsp/70 g unsalted butter, at room temperature

¼ cup/50 g granulated sugar

1 tbsp all-purpose flour

1 tsp kosher or fine sea salt

¼ tsp freshly ground pepper

¼ tsp ground cinnamon

⅛ tsp freshly grated nutmeg

2 tbsp grated yellow onion

1 cup/240 ml milk

3 large eggs, lightly beaten

1 Put the carrots in a medium saucepan, add cold water to cover by 1 in/2.5 cm, and bring to a boil over high heat. Reduce the heat to a simmer and cook the carrots until tender when pierced with a fork, about 20 minutes. Drain and let cool slightly.

2 Transfer the carrots to a food processor and process until smooth. Add the lemon juice, process to combine, and then transfer to a small bowl. (The carrots can be prepared up to 2 days in advance, covered, and refrigerated. Bring to room temperature before making the pudding.)

3 Position a rack in the center of the oven and preheat to 350°F/180°C/gas 4. Coat a 2-qt/2-L soufflé dish with 1 tbsp of the butter.

4 In a medium bowl, combine the remaining 4 tbsp/55 g butter, the sugar, flour, salt, pepper, cinnamon, and nutmeg and beat with a wooden spoon until smooth. Add the onion and puréed carrots and beat until well blended. Add the milk and eggs and mix until smooth. Spoon the mixture into the prepared dish, smoothing the top.

5 Bake, uncovered, until the pudding is puffed and lightly browned and the center is firm to the touch, 50 minutes to 1 hour. Serve immediately.

CARROT-POPPY SEED BUNDT CAKE WITH MEYER LEMON GLAZE

This recipe is a trusted "keeper"—an amazingly scrumptious, cheerful, moist, delicate-crumbed cake you will make time and again for dessert or as a sweet treat for brunch. It's easy to put together, can be made a day in advance, and even freezes well for up to a month. If you decide to freeze it, wait to make the glaze until the cake is fully thawed. The glaze will look fresh and be free of cracks if you drizzle it over the cake on the day you plan to serve it. Use regular lemon juice if the floral and less acidic Meyer lemons are not available.

SERVES 12

CAKE

Unsalted butter for the pan, at room temperature

3 cups/385 g all-purpose flour, plus more for dusting the pan

2 tsp ground cinnamon

1 tsp baking soda

½ tsp kosher or fine sea salt

½ tsp freshly ground nutmeg

2 cups/400 g granulated sugar

1½ cups/360 ml canola or other neutral oil

2 tsp pure vanilla extract

3 large eggs

3 cups/510 g peeled and finely shredded carrots (3 to 4 large carrots)

¼ cup/35 g poppy seeds

GLAZE

2½ cups/250 g confectioners' sugar

5 tbsp/75 ml fresh Meyer lemon juice

1 To make the cake, position a rack in the center of the oven and preheat to 325°F/165°C/gas 3. Butter a 10-in/25-cm (12-cup/2.8-L) Bundt pan, preferably nonstick. Sprinkle the pan with a big spoonful of flour and then tilt and tap the pan to distribute the flour evenly. Turn the pan upside down over the sink and gently shake out the excess flour.

2 In a large bowl, sift together the flour, cinnamon, baking soda, salt, and nutmeg. Set aside.

3 In a stand mixer fitted with the paddle attachment, or in a large bowl using a handheld mixer, beat together the sugar, oil, and vanilla on medium speed for 2 minutes. Add the eggs, one at a time, beating well after each addition. On low speed, add half of the flour mixture and mix just until the flour disappears. Mix in the remaining flour just until combined, stopping and scraping down the sides of the bowl once with a rubber spatula. Add the carrots and poppy seeds and mix on low speed just until thoroughly combined.

4 Gently pour the batter into the prepared pan, spreading it evenly. Bake until a toothpick inserted near the center of the cake comes out clean, about 1¼ hours. Let cool in the pan on a wire rack for 1 hour. Run a table knife around the inside edge of the pan to loosen the cake sides, then invert the cake onto the rack and let cool completely.

5 To make the glaze, whisk together the confectioners' sugar and lemon juice until the sugar is dissolved.

6 With the cooled cake still on the rack, drizzle the glaze evenly over the top, allowing it to drip down the sides. Transfer the cake to a cake plate and cut into wedges to serve.

CARROT CARDAMOM MARMALADE

I smile every time I open a jar of this marmalade and spread some on warm wheat toast at breakfast. Perhaps it sounds trite and quaint to say so, but I feel like I am adding a spoonful of sunshine to my morning. This marmalade is glowing orange and lively on the palate, with a bright, wake-me-up citrus flavor. The carrot adds color, of course, but also an herbal sweetness. It's a flavor pairing that is unexpectedly delicious.

MAKES THREE ½-PT/240-ML JARS

1 small lemon, about 4 oz/115 g

1 Valencia orange, about 8 oz/225 g

2½ cups/600 ml water

12 oz/340 g carrots, trimmed, peeled, and coarsely grated

2½ cups/500 g granulated sugar

¼ tsp black cardamom seeds (see Cook's Note, page 87)

1 Because you will be using their rinds, scrub the lemon and orange well. Trim off the stem and blossom ends of each fruit, and then cut the fruits in half lengthwise. Cut each half crosswise into very thin slices. Put the sliced fruits in a large pot, including any juices left on the cutting board. Add the water and gently press down on the fruit to make sure it is submerged. Bring to a boil over medium-high heat and boil for 10 minutes to soften the flesh and the rinds.

2 Add the carrots, sugar, and cardamom seeds and stir to dissolve the sugar. Adjust the heat so the mixture boils steadily without splattering and continue cooking until the mixture reaches the gel stage (see Cook's Note) or registers 220°F/105°C on a candy thermometer, about 20 minutes longer. Once the marmalade has reached this setting point, remove from the heat and set aside to cool for 10 minutes.

3 Stir to distribute the carrots and fruits evenly and then ladle into hot sterilized jars and cap tightly. Let cool and store in the refrigerator for up to 3 months. (Alternatively, ladle the marmalade into hot sterilized canning jars, seal closed with sterilized canning-jar lids, and process in a boiling water bath for 10 minutes. Store the jars in a cool, dark place for up to 6 months. Once a jar has been opened, store it in the refrigerator.)

COOK'S NOTE
Here's an easy way to check if the marmalade has reached the gel stage. Put a couple of small saucers in the freezer before you start cooking. When the marmalade looks thickish and a bit gelled, spoon a small amount of it onto a chilled saucer and return it to the freezer. After a couple of minutes, run your finger or a spoon down the center of the marmalade blob. If it stays separated and is a bit wrinkled, it is ready. If not, cook the marmalade a little longer and check again with another chilled saucer.

KEVIN LUDWIG'S CARROT MARGARITA

Kevin Ludwig, owner and bartender extraordinaire of Beaker & Flask in Portland, Oregon, has perfected the craft of the cocktail, and his Zanahorita, as this carrot margarita is known on his cocktail menu, is a fine example. Although a martini or Gibson is typically my cocktail of choice, I completely surrender to this margarita, seduced by its herbal accent of cilantro syrup and by the interplay of citrus and sweet vegetal carrot juice. It's really a health drink, right?

   If you have a juicer, use fresh carrots to make carrot juice. Otherwise, you can buy fresh carrot juice in many supermarkets, natural foods stores, and specialty food stores. For individual drinks, using a cocktail shaker is ideal because citrus juice produces a lovely froth when shaken. If you are hosting a large party, making the margaritas in a pitcher is easier. Just multiply the recipe ingredients according to the number of guests, and count on requests for seconds. Remember to chill the cocktail glasses—always a nice touch.

SERVES 1

CILANTRO SYRUP

½ cup/100 g granulated sugar

½ cup/120 ml water

1 bunch fresh cilantro, stems included

Kosher salt

1 lime wedge

Ice cubes

2 fl oz/60 ml _reposado_ tequila (see Cook's Note)

1 fl oz/30 ml fresh carrot juice

¾ fl oz/20 ml fresh lime juice

¾ fl oz/20 ml triple sec

½ fl oz/15 ml cilantro syrup (recipe above)

¼ fl oz/7.5 ml orange juice

Pinch of freshly ground toasted cumin (see Cook's Note, page 324)

1 Place a cocktail glass in the freezer.

2 To make the cilantro syrup, in a small saucepan, combine the sugar and water and bring to a boil over medium-high heat, stirring to dissolve the sugar. Remove from the heat and add the cilantro. Set aside to cool to room temperature, about 1 hour. Strain the mixture through a fine-mesh sieve into a jar with a tight-fitting lid. Discard the contents of the sieve. Refrigerate until ready to use. The syrup will keep for up to 2 weeks.

3 Spread a little kosher salt on a small plate. Moisten the outside rim of the chilled cocktail glass with the lime wedge, then, holding the glass at an angle, roll the outside rim in the salt. Fill the glass with ice. Fill a cocktail shaker half full with ice and add the tequila, carrot juice, lime juice, triple sec, cilantro syrup, and orange juice. Cover the shaker and shake it vigorously for 15 to 20 seconds. Strain the drink into the glass, garnish with the cumin, and serve immediately.

COOK'S NOTE

Reposado, or "rested," tequila has been aged in oak barrels for between two months and eleven months. The resting period yields a smooth tequila with a deep, rich flavor and mouthfeel and a characteristic golden color.

CELERY ROOT

Apium graveolens var. rapaceum

CELERIAC / KNOB CELERY / TURNIP-ROOTED CELERY

HISTORY AND LORE Cultivated for its starch-storing roots rather than its stalks, celery root was developed from wild celery (*Apium graveolens*), a member of the parsley family. Celery is one of the first vegetables to appear in recorded history, a common plant in Europe, the Middle East, and the temperate parts of Asia. Confucius reports that celery (wild celery) was in use in China before 500 B.C., and Homer comments on it, calling it *selinon*, in the *Odyssey*. The ancient Egyptians gathered the plant for its seeds, which they used as a flavoring; the Greeks championed it for medicinal purposes; and it was associated with funerals in both cultures. Alan Davidson, in his estimable *The Oxford Companion to Food*, notes that in 1536, botanical writer Ruellius (a.k.a. Jean Ruel) mentions that the root of smallage (a term for wild celery) was consumed both cooked and raw. Later, in 1613, Swiss physician and botanist J. Bauhin wrote of a celery plant developed for its large root in his *Historia plantarum univeralis*, a seminal work that remained unpublished until 1650.

Celery root has long been a part of German, Hungarian, Dutch, and Scandinavian cooking, but its popularity is striking in French cooking, especially julienned and served raw in the classic bistro salad *céléri en rémoulade* (celery root in mustard mayonnaise; see page 97). With the rise of the organic movement and the burgeoning number of farmers' markets, this Old World vegetable is gaining in popularity in the United States.

VARIETIES Being more of a cook than a gardener, I wasn't familiar with the different cultivars of celery root until I began researching them. Every one of my avid gardener friends like to grow it, calling it an unfussy plant, happy in almost any conditions, and perfectly content to stay in the ground in winter. Here are four favored cultivars.

Brilliant A good keeper that yields a smooth bulb with white flesh that does not readily discolor.
Giant Prague Produces a 5-inch/12-centimeter round, crisp, white celery-flavored root that stores well.
Iram Another medium-size root, it stays white when cooked and stores well.
Marble Ball A medium-size, globular root with a pronounced celery flavor.

NUTRITION Celery root is a good source of dietary fiber, vitamin B_6, magnesium, potassium, vitamin C, and phosphorus. It has twice the iron of a potato and five times the dietary fiber. It's a favorite with weight-loss specialists— 1 cup/155 grams cooked chunks contains only 42 calories— providing a feeling of fullness with minimal calories.

AVAILABILITY AND SELECTION The best celery root is available in the fall and through the winter. At farmers' markets, in CSA boxes, and at natural foods stores, these roughly round taproots with tough, yellowish white or grayish brown skin look like gnarly, hairy, muddy-bottomed orbs, better left alone than embraced for their culinary possibilities. Don't pass them up. They keep well and are brilliant mashed, raw in salads, turned into a silky soup, or braised in a stew. Buy celery roots that feel heavy for their size and are firm with no soft spots. Overly large specimens are often spongy at the center, and very small ones offer little flesh once the tough outer skin is pared away. Look for softball-size roots, weighing 1 to 1½ pounds/455 to 680 grams.

STORAGE Celery root is a good keeper, whether in a root cellar or in the refrigerator. Remove and discard any stalks and leaves. Do not wash the root or trim the gnarly bottom. Wrap in a dry paper towel and place in a loosely sealed plastic bag in the refrigerator. (The paper towel helps wick away moisture trapped in the bag.) Celery root will keep for at least 2 weeks.

BASIC USE AND PREPARATION Scrub the celery root with a vegetable brush to remove any clinging dirt and then rinse under cool running water. The flesh will darken once cut, so have a bowl of acidulated water handy (water with a few drops of vinegar or lemon juice added).

Use a sharp paring knife rather than a vegetable peeler to remove the tough outer skin. Begin by removing the top leaves and stalks if attached and then cut the celery root in half lengthwise, which makes it easier to pare away the skin. Trim away the gnarled roots, then angle the knife to remove the tough skin. As each half is peeled, drop it into acidulated water to prevent the flesh from discoloring. The peeled celery root can be sliced, diced, chunked, or shredded, as desired. Keep the cut celery root in the acidulated water until ready to use.

YIELDS

1 small untrimmed celery root = 11 oz/310 g

1 medium untrimmed celery root = 12 oz to 1 lb/340 to 455 g

1 large untrimmed celery root = 1¼ to 1½ lb/570 to 680 g

1 cup trimmed, peeled, and matchstick-cut celery root = 12 oz/340 g

1¾ cups trimmed, peeled, and diced celery root = 1 lb/455 g

CELERY ROOT RÉMOULADE

The French adore celery root and chances are at a traditional French-style bistro you'll see this salad on the menu. It's a classic. The root is julienned and served raw, tossed in a mustardy mayonnaise–based dressing, perhaps simply done without any herbs. Delicious enough. But I like to add minced cornichons and capers for flavor and textural interest and fresh minced herbs—a mix of chives, parsley, and tarragon—as accents.

SERVES 8 TO 10 AS A SIDE DISH

½ cup/120 ml mayonnaise

½ cup/120 ml sour cream

1 tbsp whole-grain mustard

1 tbsp cider vinegar

1 tbsp fresh lemon juice

1 tbsp minced cornichons

1 tbsp minced capers

Kosher or fine sea salt

Freshly ground pepper

1 large celery root, about 1½ lb/ 680 g

1 tbsp finely snipped fresh chives

1 tbsp minced fresh flat-leaf parsley

1 tbsp minced fresh tarragon

1 In a large bowl, whisk together the mayonnaise, sour cream, mustard, vinegar, lemon juice, cornichons, and capers. Season with salt and pepper. Set aside.

2 Using a sharp knife, cut off the base and a thin slice from the top of the celery root and then cut the root in half lengthwise. Pare away the tough outer skin from one of the halves. Using a chef's knife, mandoline, or the julienne blade of a food processor, cut the peeled half into matchsticks. Immediately add it to the bowl holding the dressing and toss to coat the celery root thoroughly to prevent browning. Repeat with the second half. Add the chives, parsley, and tarragon and mix well. Taste and adjust seasoning.

3 Cover and refrigerate for at least 1 hour before serving. (The salad can be prepared up to 2 days in advance and stored in a covered container in the refrigerator.) Serve chilled.

CREAM OF CELERY ROOT SOUP

When you remove the tough grayish brown skin from this knobby root, you are left with creamy white flesh that turns silky smooth when cooked and puréed. With its unique flavor reminiscent of celery and parsley, this soup, while a match for potato-leek soup in appearance, outshines it with a more nuanced taste and creamy texture.

MAKES ABOUT 6 CUPS/1.4 L; SERVES 8

10 white peppercorns

1 bay leaf

4 fresh flat-leaf parsley sprigs

4 fresh thyme sprigs

2 tbsp unsalted butter

1 large leek, about 8 oz/225 g, white and light green part only, halved lengthwise and thinly sliced crosswise into half-moons

1 large garlic clove, minced

4 cups/960 ml water

1 large celery root, about 1½ lb/ 680 g, trimmed, peeled, and cut into ½-in/12-mm cubes

2 tsp kosher or fine sea salt

¼ tsp freshly ground white pepper

⅓ cup/75 ml heavy whipping cream

¼ cup/60 ml crème fraîche

2 tbsp finely snipped fresh chives

1 Cut an 8-in/20-cm square of cheesecloth and place the peppercorns, bay leaf, parsley, and thyme in the center. Bring up the edges to form a bag and tie securely with kitchen twine to make a bouquet garni. Set aside.

2 In a 4- to 6-qt/3.8- to 5.7-L saucepan, melt the butter over medium heat and swirl to coat the pan bottom. Add the leek and cook, stirring occasionally, until softened, 6 to 8 minutes. Add the garlic and cook for 1 minute more. Add the water, celery root, salt, pepper, and bouquet garni and bring to a boil. Reduce the heat to a simmer and cook, uncovered, until the celery root is tender when pierced with a knife, about 20 minutes. Remove from the heat and let cool for about 10 minutes.

3 Discard the bouquet garni. Working in batches, purée the soup in a blender or food processor. Return the puréed soup to the saucepan, place over low heat, and add the cream. Warm the soup until steaming hot. Do not allow it to boil. Taste and adjust the seasoning. (The soup can be prepared up to 3 days in advance. Let cool, transfer to a covered container, and refrigerate. Rewarm over low heat just before serving.)

4 Ladle the soup into warmed soup bowls. Garnish each bowl with a dollop of crème fraîche and a pinch of chives. Serve immediately.

CELERY ROOT SOUP WITH ROTISSERIE CHICKEN, KALE, AND CREMINI MUSHROOMS

This is the "cheater's version" for a bowlful of nourishment. I'm not quite starting from scratch in making my own chicken stock, but I want the rich flavors just the same. So, the cheater grabs a ready-made rotisserie chicken from the grocery store, quickly pulls the meat off the bones (it usually falls off the bones all by itself), and dumps the bones into a pot with classic vegetables and aromatics for making stock. Walk away and let it simmer (ideally in a slow cooker), and a couple of hours later you have a rich broth ready for a one-pot meal.

MAKES ABOUT 10 CUPS/2.4 L; SERVES 8

1 rotisserie chicken, about 2 lb/910 g

10 cups/2.4 L canned low-sodium chicken broth

2 medium carrots, about 8 oz/ 225 g, chopped

2 large celery ribs, about 8 oz/ 225 g, sliced

1 large yellow onion, about 8 oz/ 225 g, chopped

1 tsp peppercorns

2 bay leaves

4 fresh flat-leaf parsley sprigs

4 fresh thyme sprigs

1 medium celery root, 1 lb/680 g, trimmed, peeled, and cut into ¼-in/6-mm cubes

2 cups/50 g firmly packed chopped kale, stems and thick ribs removed

4 oz/115 g cremini mushrooms, stems trimmed and sliced

Kosher or fine sea salt

Freshly ground pepper

1 Remove the meat from the chicken and place the bones and skin in a 6- to 8-qt/5.7- to 7.5-L saucepan. Shred the meat into bite-size pieces and refrigerate until needed.

2 Add the broth to the pan and bring to a boil over medium-high heat, then reduce the heat so the liquid simmers steadily. Using a large spoon or soup skimmer, skim off the brown foam that rises to the top. After 5 minutes or so, the foam will become white and no more skimming will be necessary.

3 Add the carrots, celery, onion, peppercorns, bay leaves, parsley, and thyme, cover the pan partially, and adjust the heat so the stock barely simmers. Cook the stock for at least 2 hours, but preferably longer, up to 4 hours.

4 Using a slotted spoon, transfer the bones and vegetables to a large, fine-mesh sieve set over a large bowl to catch all of the juices. Discard the solids. Pour the stock through the sieve into the large bowl.

5 Return the stock to the saucepan, add the chicken meat, celery root, kale, and mushrooms, and season with salt and pepper. Place over medium heat and bring to a simmer. Reduce the heat to maintain a gentle simmer and cook, uncovered, until the celery root is tender when pierced with a knife, about 20 minutes. (The soup can be prepared up to 2 days in advance. Let cool, transfer to a covered container, and refrigerate. Rewarm over medium heat just before serving.)

6 The soup can be kept warm over very low heat for up to 30 minutes. Ladle into warmed soup bowls to serve.

CELERY ROOT, CELERY HEART, AND CELERY LEAF SALAD

This salad is for the celery lover, as it uses the root, heart, and leaves. It's a study in contrasts and colors, with textural crunch from the sliced celery heart and matchstick-cut root playing against the delicate tender leaves. The soft green of celery is layered with the darker tones of plucked whole parsley leaves. Look in a specialty food store or gourmet grocer for Moscatel vinegar, which has a delicate, mildly acidic flavor that complements celery root. Sherry vinegar or white balsamic vinegar is an acceptable substitute.

SERVES 4

DRESSING

3 tbsp extra-virgin olive oil

1½ tbsp Moscatel vinegar

½ tsp kosher or fine sea salt

¼ tsp freshly ground pepper

⅓ cup/50 g golden raisins

1 medium celery root, about 12 oz/340 g, trimmed, peeled, and cut into matchsticks

¾ cup/105 g thinly sliced celery heart (see Cook's Note)

½ cup/25 g lightly packed celery leaves

¼ cup/15 g lightly packed fresh flat-leaf parsley leaves

1 To make the dressing, in a small bowl, whisk together the oil, vinegar, salt, and pepper. Add the raisins and set aside for at least 15 minutes to allow the raisins to plump.

2 In a large bowl, combine the celery root, celery heart, celery leaves, and parsley and toss to mix. Whisk together the dressing briefly, then pour just enough over the salad to coat the ingredients lightly and toss well. You may not need all of the dressing. Taste and adjust seasoning.

3 Set the salad aside at room temperature for 5 to 10 minutes to allow the flavors to meld before serving.

COOK'S NOTE

Use only the lightest green, innermost ribs—the heart—of the celery.

CELERY ROOT PURÉE WITH ANJOU PEAR

When summer fades and the markets fill with fall fruits and roots, make this savory-sweet purée of pears and celery root, a perfect accompaniment to roast pork tenderloin or to pork of any kind.

SERVES 8 AS A SIDE DISH

1 large celery root, about 1½ lb/ 680 g, trimmed, peeled, and cut into 1-in/2.5-cm cubes

Kosher or fine sea salt

4 Anjou pears, about 2 lb/910 g

¼ cup/55 g unsalted butter

½ cup/120 ml dry vermouth

¼ tsp freshly grated nutmeg

½ cup/120 ml heavy whipping cream, warmed

Freshly ground white pepper

1 Fill a 6-qt/5.7-L saucepan two-thirds full of water. Add the celery root and 1 tsp salt, cover partially, and bring to a boil over high heat. Reduce the heat so the water simmers and cook until the celery root is tender when pierced with a knife, about 15 minutes. Drain the celery root in a colander and return it to the pan. Place the pan over low heat for 1 minute to evaporate any excess moisture.

2 Meanwhile, using a vegetable peeler, peel, halve, and core the pears and cut them into 1-in/2.5-cm chunks. In a large frying pan, melt the butter over medium heat. Add the pears and ½ tsp salt and cook, stirring occasionally, until the pears are soft, about 5 minutes. Add the vermouth and nutmeg and continue cooking until the pears are very soft and the sauce thickens, about 5 minutes more. Remove the pan from the heat.

3 In a food processor, combine half each of the celery root, pears, and cream and process until completely smooth. Transfer the purée to a warmed serving bowl. Repeat with the remaining celery root, pears, and cream and add to the bowl. Season with salt and white pepper.

4 Serve immediately or keep warm in the top of a double boiler or cover and rewarm in a microwave oven.

CELERY ROOT GRATIN

Here's an opportunity to change up the same-old, same-old potato gratin. Don't get me wrong, there is nothing unlikable about a bubbly, creamy-rich, cheesy gratin made with sliced potatoes. But wait until you try it with celery root in place of the potatoes. The celery root adds a deep herbal note, and I find that the gratin pairs more deliciously with roasted poultry and pork. Plus, it is also a perfect stand-alone vegetarian option.

SERVES 6 TO 8 AS A SIDE DISH OR 4 AS A MAIN COURSE

1 cup/240 ml heavy whipping cream

1 large garlic clove, finely minced

1½ tbsp unsalted butter, at room temperature

2 medium celery roots, about 1 lb/455 g each, trimmed, peeled, and sliced paper-thin

4 tbsp/30 g freshly grated Parmesan cheese, preferably Parmigiano-Reggiano

1½ tbsp minced fresh thyme leaves

Kosher or fine sea salt

Freshly ground white pepper

Freshly grated nutmeg

¾ cup/85 g shredded Gruyère cheese

1 In a small saucepan, combine the cream and garlic and simmer over medium heat for 5 minutes. Turn off the heat and let the cream steep while you prepare the celery root.

2 Position a rack in the center of the oven, and preheat to 350°F/180°C/gas 4. Generously grease a 3-qt/2.8-L shallow baking or gratin dish with the butter. Set aside.

3 Layer about one-fourth of the celery root slices in the prepared dish, arranging the slices in tight, overlapping rows that cover the bottom of the dish. Sprinkle the layer with 1 tbsp of the Parmesan cheese, a big pinch of the thyme, a pinch of salt, and a smidgen each of pepper and nutmeg. Stir the cream and gently pour about ¼ cup/60 ml over the top. Repeat the layers until all of the celery root is used. You should have four layers total. Cover the dish with aluminum foil. (The gratin can be made up to this point and set aside at room temperature for up to 2 hours before baking.)

4 Bake the gratin until the celery root is almost tender when pierced with a knife and the liquid is mostly absorbed, about 1 hour. Uncover and sprinkle the Gruyère cheese evenly over the top. Continue to bake until the liquid is completely absorbed and the cheese is melted and brown around the edges, about 20 minutes longer. If desired, place the gratin under the broiler (make sure the dish can withstand the direct heat) to brown the top cheese layer lightly.

5 Let the gratin rest for 10 minutes before serving. Cut into wedges or squares and serve directly from the dish.

TRUFFLED CELERY ROOT FLAN WITH BACON GARNISH

These flans are easy, elegant, and do-ahead (see the Cook's Note). Does that get your attention? It should if you like to entertain and hate last-minute fussing in the kitchen. Make these flans as a first course or an accompaniment to a main course. If you have them, use the classic white ¾-cup/180-milliliter ramekins. Heatproof glass custard cups work, too, but, aesthetically, I prefer the squared-off bottom of ramekins, which gives the flans a sharper, more distinct edge once they are unmolded. The recipe can be easily doubled for a larger group.

SERVES 6 AS A FIRST COURSE OR SIDE DISH

3 slices bacon

1 tbsp white truffle oil

1 large or 2 small celery roots, about 1¼ lb/570 g, trimmed, peeled, and cut into ½-in/12-mm cubes

2 tsp kosher or fine sea salt

⅔ cup/165 ml heavy whipping cream

4 egg yolks

1 Position a rack in the center of the oven and preheat to 400°F/200°C/gas 6.

2 Line a plate with paper towels. Halve each bacon slice lengthwise, and cut each strip crosswise into three pieces, each about 2 in/5 cm long. Arrange the bacon on a baking sheet and bake until crisp, about 10 minutes. Transfer the bacon to the towel-lined plate to drain. Set aside for garnish.

3 Lower the oven temperature to 325°F/165°C/gas 3. Generously brush six ¾-cup/180-ml ceramic ramekins with the truffle oil, coating them evenly. Have ready a roasting pan large enough to hold the ramekins without crowding.

4 Fill a 4-qt/3.8-L saucepan two-thirds full of water. Add the celery root and 1 tsp of the salt, cover partially, and bring to a boil over high heat. Reduce the heat so the water simmers and cook until the celery root is tender when pierced with a knife, 10 to 15 minutes. Drain the celery root in a colander and return it to the pan. Place the pan over low heat for 1 minute to evaporate any excess moisture.

5 Meanwhile, in a small saucepan, warm the cream over low heat until it reaches a slow simmer (do not let it boil), about 2 minutes. Remove from the heat. Transfer the celery root to a blender, add the hot cream and the remaining 1 tsp salt, and process until a smooth purée forms, about 2 minutes. The purée should be completely smooth and creamy with no chunks remaining.

6 In a large bowl, lightly beat the egg yolks until blended. While whisking constantly to avoid curdling, slowly add the celery root purée to the beaten yolks, about 1 tbsp at a time. When the ratio of the mixture is about half yolks to half celery root purée, add all of the remaining purée and whisk to combine.

7 Using a ladle, transfer the flan mixture to the prepared ramekins, filling each one to within ½ in/12 mm of the rim. Set the ramekins, not touching, in the roasting pan. Pour hot water into the pan to reach about two-thirds of the way up the sides of the ramekins.

8 Carefully transfer the roasting pan to the oven and bake the flans until they are just set in the center, 20 to 25 minutes. To check for doneness, pierce the center of the flan with a knife tip to see if it is set or gently shake a ramekin to see if the center jiggles. Remove the ramekins from the water bath and place on a wire rack to cool slightly.

9 Run a thin knife around the inside edge of a ramekin to loosen the flan. Invert a warmed small plate over the top of the ramekin and invert the plate and ramekin together. Carefully lift off the ramekin, releasing the flan. Repeat with the remaining flans. Stack three pieces of bacon, crisscrossed, on top of each flan. Serve immediately.

COOK'S NOTE

The flans can be made up to 2 days in advance. Let cool completely, tightly wrap each flan, still in its ramekin, with plastic wrap, and refrigerate. To reheat, return the ramekins to the roasting pan, fill it with hot water to reach two-thirds of the way up the sides of the ramekins, and heat, uncovered, in a preheated 325°F/165°C/gas 3 oven until warm, 5 to 10 minutes.

CROSNE

Stachys affinis

JAPANESE ARTICHOKE / CHINESE ARTICHOKE / SPIRAL/ CHORO-GI *(JAPANESE)* **/ GAN LU ZI** OR **CAO SHI CAN** *(MANDARIN CHINESE)*

HISTORY AND LORE The crosne is a member of the mint family (Lamiaceae), a perennial in the same family as many culinary herbs, such as basil, sage, rosemary, and thyme. Also known as Chinese artichoke or Japanese artichoke (although related to neither the globe artichoke nor the Jerusalem artichoke), it is native to northern China and Japan. Crosnes were introduced to France in 1882, when Dr. Brentschneider, a physician with the Russian Legation in Beijing and an avid plant collector, sent some tubers to Auguste Pailleux, a noted *acclimatiseur*, who planted some on rented land near his garden in the village of Crosne. That handful of tubers multiplied successfully within a couple of years and crosnes became popular in the markets of France. Although their popularity increased throughout Europe, France is the only western country that grows them on a large scale.

In recent years, French chefs living in the United States have encouraged local farmers to begin cultivating crosnes. In California, Weiser Family Farms started growing them at the pleading of chef Alain Giraud, and in Portland, Oregon, Viridian Farms planted tubers from France at the behest of chef Pascal Sauton and myself. Crosnes are a good choice for backyard gardeners, as they flourish in any open, sunny site with fertile, moist soil.

VARIETIES Crosnes are small, creamy white tubers at the ends of underground stems. They are about 2 inches/ 5 centimeters long and ¾ inch/2.5 centimeters in diameter, and often smaller, and they look like a spiral seashell with bulging ridges. Imagine a very tiny Michelin man with ridged, chiseled muscles! Crosnes are deliciously juicy, crunchy, and crisp, with a delicate nutty flavor slightly reminiscent of new potatoes or water chestnuts.

NUTRITION Said to be nutritious, crosnes are also praised for their digestibility due to the presence of the carbohydrate stachyose, which is purported to increase the probiotic activity in the intestinal tract.

AVAILABILITY AND SELECTION Availability is a challenge, so if you see crosnes at the farmers' market, by all means buy them. They are amusing and deliciously fun to cook. Look for pale, pearly, firm tubers from late fall to early winter. Because they begin to deteriorate shortly after they are dug up, they must be used right away. Firmness is key. Even if they are more beige than ivory, they will be fine as long as they are firm.

STORAGE Wrap crosnes loosely in dry paper towels, tuck them inside an open plastic bag or paper sack, and refrigerate them. They will keep for up to 1 week.

BASIC USE AND PREPARATION Pick over the crosnes and remove any soft ones. Trim any long rootlets (stem pieces). Place the crosnes in the center of a thick, clean kitchen towel and sprinkle generously with salt. Roll them up in the towel and twist the ends like a candy wrapper. Vigorously shake the towel from side to side. The agitation and friction from the salt will help to remove some of their thin brown skin. Rinse the crosnes under cool running water to remove the excess salt and blot dry. The crosnes are now ready to use in any recipe that calls for prepared crosnes. They can be parboiled, sautéed, fried, stir-fried, steamed, roasted, or pickled.

YIELDS

3½ oz/100 g prepared crosnes = 1 cup

7 oz/200 g prepared crosnes = 2 cups

1 lb/455 g prepared crosnes = 4½ cups

PARBOILED CROSNES

Parboiling is an easy first step to transforming these delightful tubers into delicate, crunchy, nutty additions to sautés, stir-fries, and braised dishes.

MAKES ABOUT 4½ CUPS/455 G

2 tbsp kosher salt or coarse sea salt

1 lb/455 g prepared crosnes
(see Basic Use and Preparation,
facing page)

1 Have ready a large bowl of ice water and a colander. Fill a large pot three-fourths full of water. Add the salt and bring to a boil over high heat.

2 Add the prepared crosnes to the boiling water and cook until crisp-tender, about 2 minutes. Drain the crosnes in the colander and immediately transfer to the ice water to cool, about 2 minutes. Remove the crosnes from the ice water and wrap in several thicknesses of paper towels to dry. Use immediately in any recipe calling for parboiled crosnes, or wrap in dry paper towels, place in a lock-top plastic bag, and refrigerate for up to 1 week.

PICKLED CROSNES

Serve pickled crosnes with charcuterie or as a snack. They can be added to a salad or any dish that needs a little crunch, or, best of all, make the martini on page 114.

MAKES ONE 1-PT/480-ML JAR

2 cups/200 g prepared crosnes
(see Basic Use and Preparation,
facing page)

¾ cup/180 ml water

6 tbsp/90 ml unseasoned
rice vinegar

4½ tbsp/55 g granulated sugar

1½ tsp kosher or fine sea salt

1 Select a 1-pt/480-ml glass jar with a tight-fitting lid large enough to hold the crosnes snugly, allowing for at least 1-in/2.5-cm headspace. Wash the jar thoroughly in hot, sudsy water or run it through the dishwasher to sterilize it. Pack the crosnes into the jar and set the jar aside while you make the brine.

2 In a small saucepan, combine the water, vinegar, sugar, and salt and bring to a boil over high heat, stirring to dissolve the sugar and salt. Pour the hot brine over the crosnes, cover, and set aside at room temperature until cool, then refrigerate for 8 to 12 hours before using. The pickled crosnes will keep for up to 1 week.

CURRIED CROSNE FRITTERS

The delightful crunch of parboiled crosnes lends itself to making fritters. Thinking I could adapt a recipe for corn fritters and use crosnes, I started researching recipes and hit on the idea of adding curry to the crosne fritters to give them an exotic accent. The creamy tang of the dipping sauce complements the curry. In both the fritters and the sauce, I use *fromage blanc*, a soft, spreadable fresh French cheese with a bright, pleasantly sharp taste and a smooth texture. Traditionally, this was a nonfat cheese reminiscent of yogurt, but that runnier style is not suitable for this recipe. Look for *fromage blanc* that is similar in texture to soft fresh goat cheese. I often see it sold in 8-ounce/225-gram tubs in well-stocked grocery stores or specialty food stores with an extensive cheese section.

MAKES 24 FRITTERS

DIPPING SAUCE

3 oz/85 g *fromage blanc* or soft fresh goat cheese

7 tbsp/105 ml heavy whipping cream

3 tbsp finely minced fresh flat-leaf parsley

1 tbsp cider vinegar

1 tsp Dijon mustard

About 5 cups/1.2 L peanut, grape seed, or vegetable oil for deep-frying

FRITTERS

2 large eggs, lightly beaten

3⅓ cups/340 g Parboiled Crosnes (page 109)

¾ cup/105 g finely diced yellow onion

2 oz/55g *fromage blanc* or fresh soft goat cheese

2 tbsp finely minced fresh flat-leaf parsley

1 large garlic clove, finely minced

1½ tsp curry powder

Kosher or fine sea salt

¼ tsp freshly ground pepper

½ cup/65 g all-purpose flour

1 To make the dipping sauce, in a medium bowl, stir together the *fromage blanc,* cream, parsley, vinegar, and mustard until creamy and thoroughly combined. Transfer to a serving bowl, cover, and set aside for 45 minutes to allow the flavors to meld. (The dipping sauce can be made up to 1 day in advance and refrigerated. Remove from the refrigerator 1 hour before serving.)

2 Preheat the oven to 250°F/120°C/gas ½. Line a baking sheet with a double thickness of paper towels and set near the stove. Set a slotted spoon or a wire-mesh skimmer and two soupspoons near the stove. Pour the oil to a depth of about 3 in/7.5 cm into a deep, heavy pot, a wok, or an electric deep fryer and heat to 325°F/165°C on a deep-frying thermometer. (If using an electric deep fryer, follow the manufacturer's instructions for heating the oil.) While the oil is heating, make the fritter batter.

3 To make the fritters, in a large bowl, combine the eggs, crosnes, onion, *fromage blanc,* parsley, garlic, curry powder, ¾ tsp salt, and the pepper. Mix with a wooden spoon until thoroughly combined. Sprinkle the flour over the top and mix in just until absorbed.

4 Scoop up a rounded soupspoon of batter and use a second spoon to flatten the fritter slightly. Carefully slide the fritter into the hot oil. Repeat to form four or five more fritters. (Frying in small batches of five or six fritters will keep the oil at a steady temperature.) Fry the fritters, flipping them once or twice for even browning, until golden brown all over, about 5 minutes. Using the slotted spoon or skimmer, transfer the fritters to the towel-lined baking sheet to drain. Sprinkle lightly with salt. Keep the fritters warm in the oven. Continue frying until all of the batter has been used. Make sure the oil is at 325°F/165°C before you add a new batch. Otherwise, the fritters will absorb too much oil and be greasy.

5 Transfer the fritters to a warmed serving platter and serve immediately. Pass the dipping sauce at the table.

SAUTÉED CROSNES WITH CRISP PEPPER BACON, GARLIC, AND PARSLEY

Anything tastes better with bacon, of course. But it wasn't a culinary stretch to consider a quick sauté of crosnes and pepper bacon for an even more interesting dish. Minced parsley adds a welcome herbal accent and a touch of garlic broadens the flavor profile. I like to serve this dish alongside roast chicken seasoned with lemon and herbs. It would be equally delicious with roasted duck or pork.

SERVES 4 AS A SIDE DISH

4 slices pepper bacon, 3½ oz/ 100 g, diced

3⅓ cups/340 g Parboiled Crosnes (page 109)

1 garlic clove, finely minced

2 tbsp finely minced fresh flat-leaf parsley

Kosher or fine sea salt

Freshly ground pepper

1 In a 10-in/25-cm nonstick frying pan, fry the bacon over medium heat until it is crisp and all of the fat is rendered, about 5 minutes. Using a slotted spoon, transfer the bacon to a plate lined with a double thickness of paper towels to drain. Set aside.

2 Drain off all but 2 tbsp of the bacon fat from the frying pan. Return the frying pan to medium heat and add the crosnes. Sauté, stirring constantly, until crisp-tender and lightly browned, about 3 minutes. Add the cooked bacon, garlic, and parsley and sauté, stirring constantly, until the garlic is fragrant, about 2 minutes longer. Season with salt and pepper and serve immediately.

CROSNES WITH TRUFFLED CREAM

Pascal Sauton, my wonderful friend and a highly regarded French chef in Portland, Oregon, spent a day with me and my assistant, Andrea, showing us how to clean, parboil, and cook crosnes. With a big smile and jolly laugh, he said, "Crosnes in cream is a classic preparation, but crosnes in truffled cream is even better." He brought along a jar of black truffle tapenade that he likes to use at the restaurant and used it to infuse the sauce with a heady truffle flavor. Look for the tapenade at specialty markets selling imported French and Italian foods or online. La Truffiere is the brand Pascal used and it is imported from Italy by Clover Specialties of Gardena, California.

SERVES 4 AS A SIDE DISH

1 cup/240 ml heavy whipping cream

½ tsp kosher or fine sea salt

¼ tsp freshly ground pepper

1 tbsp black truffle tapenade

2¾ cups/285 g Parboiled Crosnes (page 109)

2 tbsp freshly grated Parmesan cheese, preferably Parmigiano-Reggiano

In a medium saucepan, bring the cream to a boil over medium-high heat and add the salt and pepper. Stir in the black truffle tapenade and then add the crosnes. As soon as the cream comes back to a boil, reduce the heat and simmer the crosnes until the sauce is reduced and thick, about 3 minutes. Stir in the Parmesan until evenly incorporated. Remove from the heat and serve immediately.

RUSSIAN SALAD WITH SHRIMP AND CROSNES

Here's a favorite, old-fashioned main-course salad reinvented with poached shrimp, diced carrots, peas, and crunchy crosnes. *Salade Olivier* is the proper name for the French composed salad that we have come to call Russian salad, or *salade russe*. It was invented in 1860 by Lucien Olivier, the chef of the celebrated Hermitage restaurant in Moscow. The traditional salad is composed of diced potatoes, vegetables, and meats bound with mayonnaise. This much fresher and lighter variation is perfect for a brunch or luncheon.

SERVES 4 AS A MAIN COURSE

DRESSING

⅔ cup/165 ml mayonnaise

1 tbsp Champagne vinegar

1 tbsp finely snipped fresh chives

1 tbsp minced fresh flat-leaf parsley

¾ tsp kosher or fine sea salt

1 tbsp capers, rinsed and drained

½ lemon, cut into thin slices

1 bay leaf

10 peppercorns

2 tsp kosher or fine sea salt

5 cups/1.2 L water

2½ cups/225 g prepared crosnes (see Basic Use and Preparation, page 108)

¾ cup/105 g peeled and diced carrots

½ cup/70 g frozen green peas

12 oz/340 g large (26 to 30 count per 1 lb/455 g) shrimp, peeled, deveined, and tail segments removed

1 large head butter lettuce

2 hard-boiled eggs, peeled and quartered lengthwise

Hungarian paprika for garnish

Finely snipped fresh chives for garnish

Minced fresh flat-leaf parsley for garnish

1 To make the dressing, in a small bowl, whisk together the mayonnaise, vinegar, chives, parsley, and salt. Fold in the capers. Taste and adjust the seasoning. Set aside.

2 Have ready a slotted spoon or a wire-mesh skimmer and a large bowl of ice water. In a 4-qt/3.8-L saucepan, combine the lemon slices, bay leaf, peppercorns, salt, and water and bring to a boil over high heat. Simmer for 10 minutes. Reduce the heat to medium-low, add the crosnes, and simmer until crisp-tender, about 2 minutes. Using the slotted spoon or skimmer, transfer the crosnes to the ice water to cool, about 2 minutes. Remove the crosnes from the ice water and wrap in several thicknesses of paper towels to dry.

3 Cook the carrots until crisp-tender, cool, and dry them following the same method, but simmer the carrots for 3 to 4 minutes. Repeat with the peas, simmering for about 1 minute. Using the same water you simmered the vegetables in, cook the shrimp just until they turn pink and are cooked through, about 3 minutes. Transfer them to the ice water to cool for 1 minute, and then blot dry with paper towels. Set aside 12 of the shrimp in the refrigerator for garnish. Chop the remaining shrimp into ½-in/12-mm pieces.

4 In a medium bowl, combine the chopped shrimp, crosnes, carrots, and peas. Add the dressing and toss to coat thoroughly. Taste and adjust the seasoning. Cover the salad and refrigerate for at least 2 hours before serving to allow the flavors to meld. (The salad can be made up to 1 day in advance, covered, and refrigerated until ready to serve.)

5 Arrange three whole lettuce leaves on each chilled plate, fanning them out with the cupped side facing up. Divide the crosne-shrimp mixture evenly among the lettuce-lined plates, mounding it in the center. Arrange the three whole shrimp and two egg quarters against the side of the crosne-shrimp mixture on each plate. Garnish each salad with a dusting of paprika and sprinkle of chives and parsley. Serve immediately.

SPICY GINGER PORK AND CROSNES IN BEAN SAUCE

Stir-fried crosnes are similar in texture to water chestnuts—delighting the palate with an earthy crunch. In this dish, a dark, rich sauce slicks the meat and coats the dainty crosnes, delivering big flavors along with the strips of red bell pepper and green onion. Serve this stir-fry with steamed rice.

SERVES 4 OR 5 AS A MAIN COURSE

MARINADE

1½ tbsp dark soy sauce

1½ tbsp Chinese rice wine or pale dry sherry

1½ tbsp canola or other neutral oil

1½ tbsp cornstarch

1 lb/455 g boneless pork loin, cut against the grain into strips ¼ in/6 mm thick

SAUCE

2 tbsp Chinese bean paste (see Cook's Note)

2 tbsp Chinese rice wine or pale dry sherry

4 tsp hoisin sauce

4 tsp dark soy sauce

4 tsp Asian sesame oil

1 tsp red pepper flakes

3 tbsp canola or other neutral oil

1½ tsp finely minced garlic

1½ tsp peeled and finely minced fresh ginger

2 cups/200 g Parboiled Crosnes (page 109)

1 medium red bell pepper, seeded, deribbed, and cut into narrow strips about 1 in/2.5 cm long (about 1 cup/115 g)

4 green onions, including green tops, cut into 1-in/2.5-cm pieces (about ¾ cup/40 g)

3 tbsp chopped fresh cilantro

1 To make the marinade, in a medium bowl, whisk together the soy sauce, wine, oil, and cornstarch until smooth. Add the pork and toss to coat on all sides. Cover and set aside at room temperature for 30 minutes. (Alternatively, the pork can be marinated for up to 8 hours in the refrigerator. Remove it from the refrigerator 45 minutes before you plan to begin cooking.)

2 To make the sauce, in a small bowl, whisk together the bean paste, wine, hoisin sauce, soy sauce, sesame oil, and red pepper flakes. Set aside.

3 Fill a medium saucepan two-thirds full of water and bring to a boil over high heat. Using a slotted spoon, carefully scatter the meat in the water and cook, stirring occasionally, for 2 minutes. The meat should be only partially cooked. Drain the meat in a colander, discarding the liquid, and then set aside on a plate.

4 In a wok or a large, deep frying pan, heat the oil over high heat and swirl to coat the pan bottom and sides. Add the garlic and ginger and stir-fry just until fragrant but not brown, about 15 seconds. Add the crosnes and bell pepper and stir-fry until crisp-tender, about 3 minutes. Add the pork and stir-fry for 1 minute. Give the sauce a quick stir and add it to the wok. Stir-fry the pork and vegetables until evenly coated with the sauce, about 30 seconds. Add the green onions and stir-fry for 30 seconds longer.

5 Transfer to a warmed serving dish, garnish with the cilantro, and serve immediately.

COOK'S NOTE

Chinese bean paste, sometimes labeled sauce, is a thick brown paste made from fermented soybeans, flour, and salt. It is used widely in northern Chinese cooking and the hot version is used in Sichuan cooking. It comes in two forms: made with whole beans and ground, or puréed. I mostly see the puréed type in the Asian section of my local supermarket, so that is what I am using here. It is sold in glass jars or cans, and once it is opened, it keeps indefinitely in the refrigerator. If you buy it in a can, transfer the unused portion to a covered jar for storage. If it becomes too thick over time, stir in a little canola oil to smooth it out.

DR. GIBSON MEET MR. CROSNE
(PICKLED CROSNE MARTINI)

I love a good dry martini, and my father preferred a Gibson. Because I was an obedient daughter, I came to love a Gibson, too, and switched, always ordering a Gibson just like he did, with an extra cocktail pick skewered with pickled cocktail onions. When I tasted the pickled crosnes, I knew I had to make a pickled crosne martini. I prefer mine stirred, icy cold, and dry. Plan ahead and put the gin and a martini glass in the freezer.

SERVES 1

Ice cubes

2 fl oz/60 ml gin, well chilled

¼ fl oz/7 ml dry vermouth

3 Pickled Crosnes (page 109)

Half fill a mixing glass with ice. Add the gin and vermouth and stir for about 15 seconds so it is icy cold but not diluted. Strain into a chilled cocktail glass. Thread the crosnes onto a cocktail pick and garnish the martini. Serve immediately.

GALANGAL

Alpinia galanga

GREATER GALANGAL / GALINGALE / THAI GINGER / LAOS *(INDONESIAN)* / LENGKAUS *(MALAYSIAN)* / KHA *(THAI)*

HISTORY AND LORE A member of the ginger family (Zingiberaceae), galangal is a leafy perennial herb with stems that grow to nearly 6 feet/2 meters tall, long dark green sword-shaped leaves, and robust underground rhizomes. The word *galangal* comes from the Cantonese *ko-liang-kiang,* which means "a mild ginger from Ko," the ancient name for a prefecture in Guangdong Province. Interestingly, according to Frederich Flückiger and Daniel Hansbury, who published a history of drugs of vegetable origin in 1879, galangal was being used by the Arabs as early as the ninth century, suggesting they knew about galangal and its origin before the Europeans. Marco Polo noted its cultivation in southern China and Java in the thirteenth century. Flückiger and Hansbury also write of its popularity in medieval Europe, especially England, where it was used fresh and dried.

Although galangal is common to Thai, Malaysian, and Indonesian cooking, in the West it has been used primarily to make liqueurs and bitters. Medicinally, it has a long history as an aphrodisiac and digestive stimulant. In the past, it was also reportedly used to "spike" race horses in the Middle East.

VARIETIES Within the ginger family, there are two plant species that are referred to by the common name galangal: greater galangal and lesser galangal.

Greater galangal (*Alpinia galanga*), which grows in the tropics and is native to South Asia and Indonesia, is cultivated primarily in Malaysia, Laos, and Thailand. Grown for its fibrous, woody, aromatic pink shoots, it is similar in flavor to ginger but more peppery and pungent, with a lemony, almost medicinal taste. It is the best known and most widely available of the two species and is the rhizome called for in the recipes in this book, where I refer to it simply as galangal. It is a common ingredient in Thai soups, curry pastes, and curries and is used almost as much as ginger in much of the cooking of Southeast Asia.

Lesser galangal (*Alpinia officinarum*) is grown in warm but not tropical climates. Although India is the second largest exporter of lesser galangal, the plant is native to China, where it grows mainly along the southeast coast. The rhizomes, which are smaller than those of greater galangal, have reddish brown skin and flesh. They also have a stronger, more intense flavor and a sweeter taste, with notes of cinnamon. In Russia, the rhizomes are used for flavoring vinegar, tea, and a popular liqueur.

NUTRITION A handful of galangal carries a significant amount of vitamin C, but because it is never used in that quantity in cooking, its nutritional worth is unimportant. Its value lies primarily in its medicinal or personal hygiene use. For example, in India, it is used as a breath purifier and as a deodorant, and a paste made from the rhizomes is used to treat skin infections. A tonic made from galangal and lime juice is considered an energy booster in parts of Southeast Asia.

AVAILABILITY AND SELECTION Galangal is available year-round in Asian markets and in some supermarkets serving a large Asian population. The rhizomes have pale, yellow-flushed skin, with distinct brown, ridged bands spaced equidistant along the thick stems. Pink-colored shoots often extend upward from the stem. Typically, the rhizomes are kept in a moist spot, often in a shallow pan of water. Look for firm rhizomes without soft spots, mold, or shriveling skin. If the clusters are large and you need only a small amount, ask to have a smaller piece cut for you, as galangal is considerably more expensive than ginger and doesn't keep as long.

STORAGE Wrap galangal in dry paper towels, slip it into a loosely sealed plastic bag, and refrigerate for up to 1 week. Galangal can also be frozen for up to 3 months: cut it into thick slices and freeze it in a freezer-strength lock-top plastic bag.

BASIC USE AND PREPARATION Galangal is used grated, chopped, sliced, or ground into a paste to flavor dishes or marinades. Unlike fresh ginger, which is often eaten raw, sliced or chunked galangal is quite fibrous and should be removed from dishes before serving. Before using, wash the rhizome well under cool running water and blot dry with paper towels. Using a sharp paring knife, scrape or peel off and discard the skin. Cut the galangal into thin slices and then grind the slices to a paste in a mortar. Otherwise, grate on a grater or use a sharp knife to slice, chop, mince, or cut into chunks, as directed in individual recipes.

YIELDS

1-in/2.5-cm piece galangal = 1 oz/30 g

2-in/5-cm piece galangal = 2 oz/55 g

1 tbsp finely grated galangal = about 1 oz/30 g

RED CURRY PASTE

Although curry paste is a condiment that is easy enough to buy ready-made, why not venture into a great DIY project and make your own? This homemade version uses fewer red chiles than some recipes I've seen, so feel free to add more if you want a really fiery sauce. The paste is traditionally made with a mortar and pestle; however, our busy lives might suggest the whirl of a food processor, mini-chop, or blender to speed the task. If you opt for a machine, add a tad bit of water, just a teaspoon at a time, to create a coarse paste.

MAKES ⅓ CUP/75 ML

6 dried small red chiles such as *prik haeng* or *chile de árbol*

¼ tsp kosher or fine sea salt

3 tbsp minced garlic

2 tbsp minced lemongrass

2 tbsp minced shallot

1 tbsp minced galangal

1 tsp finely chopped fresh cilantro roots or stems

1 tsp freshly grated kaffir lime zest or regular lime zest

1 tsp Thai shrimp paste (see Cook's Note)

1 Remove the stems and seeds from the chiles. In a small bowl, combine the chiles with hot water to cover and let soak until softened, about 20 minutes. Drain well and chop coarsely.

2 Using a mortar and pestle, pound the chiles with the salt until they are reduced to a coarse paste. Add the garlic and continue to pound and stir to a fine paste.

3 Repeat with the lemongrass, shallot, galangal, cilantro, and lime zest, working each ingredient into a fine paste before adding the next. Add the shrimp paste and mix to combine. The curry paste will keep in a tightly capped container in the refrigerator for up to 2 weeks.

COOK'S NOTE

An essential component of Thai curry pastes, Thai shrimp paste is fermented sun-dried shrimp ground to a pungent pulp. Similar pastes are used in other Southeast Asian and southern Chinese cuisines. Look for Thai shrimp paste, sometimes labeled *kapi* or *gapi*, in Asian supermarkets.

GALANGAL-TARRAGON SAUCE FOR SEAFOOD

You can substitute fresh ginger for the galangal in this recipe, but the latter gives the sauce an added depth, and it finishes with a delicate accent of spice rather than the bite of heat that ginger delivers. The sauce is made in the same way as mayonnaise is made, but the proportion of liquid turns it into a thin emulsion, perfect for pooling on a plate with a cooked fish fillet set on top. Serve it with grilled, broiled, or pan-seared salmon or halibut. It's also terrific with shrimp. For a dinner party, I sometimes grill salmon on a cedar plank, grill some shiitake mushrooms, and then I spoon a small ladleful of sauce on each dinner plate, put a grilled fillet on top, arrange a trio of grilled mushrooms alongside the fish, and scatter snipped chives over the salmon. The sauce can be prepared in advance, making this menu an easy and elegant way to entertain.

MAKES ABOUT 1¾ CUPS/420 ML

2-in/5-cm piece galangal, peeled and coarsely chopped

¼ cup/60 ml fresh lime juice

¼ cup/60 ml unseasoned rice vinegar

2 egg yolks

2 tsp kosher or fine sea salt

1 cup/240 ml canola or other neutral oil

¼ cup/15 g lightly packed fresh tarragon leaves

1 In a blender or food processor, combine the galangal, lime juice, and vinegar and process until the galangal is pulverized. Add the egg yolks and salt and process until well combined. With the machine running, drizzle in the oil in a slow, steady stream until the mixture is emulsified and has the consistency of a very thin mayonnaise. Add the tarragon and blend until the sauce turns a lovely soft green and the leaves are fully puréed.

2 Strain the sauce through a fine-mesh sieve into a container with a tight-fitting lid. Cover and refrigerate until ready to serve. It will keep for up to 2 days.

TOM KHA GAI
(THAI GALANGAL CHICKEN SOUP)

Perhaps the most ubiquitous use of this aromatic rhizome is in the popular Thai soup *tom kha gai* (*kha* is "galangal" in Thai). This version is quick and easy, with a big return in flavor. Although the ingredients may seem exotic, it's a simple fix for a weeknight dinner served with a scoop of steamed jasmine rice alongside.

SERVES 4

1 lemongrass stalk

2½ cups/360 ml homemade chicken stock or canned low-sodium chicken broth

1-in/2.5-cm piece galangal, peeled and cut into matchsticks

4 small shallots, quartered

5 fresh kaffir lime leaves (see Cook's Note), or 1 tsp freshly grated lime zest

5 Thai bird chiles, stemmed and smashed (see Cook's Note, page 40)

2 skinless, boneless chicken breasts, about 6 oz/170 g each, cut crosswise into slices ¼ in/6 mm thick

1½ lb/680 g oyster mushrooms, stems trimmed and cut in half

One 13½-oz/405-ml can unsweetened coconut milk

3 tbsp fresh lime juice

2 tbsp Asian fish sauce

Kosher or fine sea salt

⅓ cup/20 g firmly packed fresh cilantro leaves

1   Trim off the root end from the lemongrass stalk, then cut off and discard the tough green tops. You should have a bulb about 4 in/10 cm long. Peel away the tough outer leaves, cut the bulb crosswise into 2-in/5-cm pieces, and then smash the pieces. Place the pieces in a large pot and add the stock, galangal, shallots, lime leaves, and chiles. Place over medium-high heat, bring to a simmer, and cook for 5 minutes to infuse the flavors. Add the chicken and mushrooms and simmer until the chicken pieces are opaque and fully cooked, about 3 minutes. Reduce the heat to low. Stir in the coconut milk, lime juice, and fish sauce and heat through. Season with salt.

2   Ladle the soup into warmed soup bowls and garnish with the cilantro. Serve immediately.

COOK'S NOTE

Kaffir lime leaves are used extensively in Thai and other Southeast Asian cuisines to infuse soups and stews with a floral lime flavor. In Asian markets, look for fresh leaves in the produce section or fresh-frozen leaves in the freezer case. Alternatively, you may find kaffir leaves in dried form. I prefer the fresh leaves as they are more intensely aromatic. If you use dried leaves, increase the number of leaves by one-third or one-half.

SNAKE BEAN COCONUT CURRY

Also known as yard-long beans, Chinese long beans, or asparagus beans, snake beans are the pods of a vigorous climbing annual plant widely grown in Southeast Asia and southern China. The pods grow from 14 to 30 inches/ 35.5 to 76 centimeters in length and are dark green, crisp, tender, and nutty tasting. Typically the beans are cut into shorter lengths for vegetable dishes and salads. Look for them in Asian markets or check vendors selling Asian vegetables at farmers' markets. Buy plump-looking beans without any wrinkling or shriveling at the ends.

SERVES 4

2 tbsp canola or other neutral oil

4 shallots, thinly sliced

1-in/2.5-cm piece galangal, peeled and thinly sliced

2 garlic cloves, thinly sliced

2 fresh small kaffir lime leaves (see Cook's Note, page 121), or ½ tsp freshly grated lime zest

2 Thai bird chiles, stemmed and smashed (see Cook's Note, page 40)

1 lb/455 g snake beans, ends trimmed and cut into 3-in/ 7.5-cm lengths

¾ cup/180 ml unsweetened coconut milk

½ cup/120 ml water

2 tsp Red Curry Paste (page 119 or store-bought)

2 tsp firmly packed dark brown sugar

2 tsp kosher or fine sea salt

1 In a large sauté pan, warm the oil over medium-low heat and swirl to coat the pan. Add the shallots, galangal, garlic, lime leaves, and chiles and sauté, stirring frequently, until the shallots are softened and just beginning to turn golden, 5 to 6 minutes. Raise the heat to medium, add the beans, and sauté, stirring to coat them with the oil, for 2 minutes longer.

2 Stir in the coconut milk, water, curry paste, brown sugar, and salt and bring the liquid to a simmer. Cover and cook gently, stirring occasionally, until the beans are tender but not mushy, about 20 minutes. If necessary, reduce the heat to medium-low to keep the liquid at a gentle simmer. Remove the lid, raise the heat to medium-high, and cook to reduce the liquid slightly, about 3 minutes longer. Taste and adjust the seasoning, adding more salt if needed.

3 Transfer the beans and sauce to a warmed serving bowl, discarding the galangal, lime leaves, and chiles. (They are seasonings and not meant to be eaten.) Serve immediately.

RED CURRY AND GALANGAL GRILLED CHICKEN DRUMETTES

Who doesn't love to nibble on finger food? These grilled chicken drumettes are marinated in turmeric-tinted coconut milk infused with a heady amount of garlic, shallots, galangal, and red curry paste. Grilled and basted over direct heat, the skin gets divinely crisp, slightly burnished at the edges, and bronzed. Complete the meal with steamed jasmine rice and Asian Pear and Daikon Salad with Yuzu Vinaigrette (page 260). The drumetttes are also good party fare, served along with a bowl of crudités for dipping into Carrot Top Pesto (page 79).

MAKES 30 TO 36 DRUMETTES

6 large garlic cloves, peeled but left whole

2 large shallots, quartered

1-in/2.5-cm piece galangal, peeled and cut into small pieces

1 tbsp kosher or fine sea salt

2 tsp ground turmeric

1 tbsp Red Curry Paste (page 119 or store-bought)

One 13½-oz/405-ml can unsweetened coconut milk

3¾ lb/1.7 kg chicken drumettes (30 to 36 pieces)

Vegetable oil for brushing the grill grate

1 In a food processor, combine the garlic, shallots, galangal, salt, and turmeric and process until minced, stopping to scrap down the sides of the work bowl once or twice. Add the curry paste and coconut milk and process until completely combined. Measure 1 cup/240 ml of the marinade, transfer it to a covered container, and refrigerate until ready to grill. (This will be used to baste the chicken.)

2 Place the drumettes in a large bowl and pour the remaining marinade over the top. Using tongs or a rubber spatula, toss the chicken until evenly coated. Cover and refrigerate for at least 8 hours or up to 2 days. Alternatively, put the drumettes in a large, freezer-strength lock-top plastic bag, pour the marinade over the top, squeeze out all of the air, and seal the bag. Massage the bag to coat all of the chicken pieces evenly with the marinade. Place on a rimmed baking sheet and refrigerate.

3 Remove the drumettes and basting sauce from the refrigerator 1 hour before you plan to begin grilling. Drain the drumettes, discarding the marinade. Prepare a medium fire in a charcoal grill or preheat a gas grill to medium.

4 Brush the grill grate with oil. Place the chicken, without crowding, directly over the fire and cover the grill. Cook until seared on one side, about 2 minutes. Uncover the grill and brush the top sides of the drumettes with half of the basting sauce. Re-cover the grill and cook the chicken for 5 minutes longer. Using tongs, turn the drumettes over and brush the top sides with the remaining basting sauce. Re-cover the grill and cook until the chicken is cooked through and bronzed with nice grill marks on the second side, about 5 minutes longer.

5 Pile the drumettes on a warmed serving plate. Serve immediately or keep warm until ready to serve.

BANANA LEAF–WRAPPED GRILLED SALMON WITH A GALANGAL-LEMONGRASS MARINADE

In Latin American, Chinese, and Southeast Asian cuisines, banana leaves are used to wrap foods for steaming and grilling. It's an artful and natural way to enclose foods, protecting them from direct heat and sealing in moisture. In addition, the leaves impart a subtle grassy flavor. It is important to wipe the leaves clean before wrapping, to remove the whitish dusty coating. The directions for this recipe are long, but they are straightforward. I wanted to give detailed directions on how to wrap the fish. Refreeze the extra banana leaves in the package; they're handy to have on hand for grilling other fish, such as halibut and cod, which tend to stick to the grill grate.

SERVES 4

1 lemongrass stalk

2 green onions, white part coarsely chopped and green tops thinly sliced

2 large garlic cloves, smashed with the side of a chef's knife

1 tbsp finely chopped fresh cilantro stems, plus sprigs for garnish

1 tbsp peeled and grated galangal

1 Thai bird chile, stemmed and halved lengthwise (see Cook's Note, page 40)

1 tbsp fresh lime juice

1 tbsp kosher or fine sea salt

2 tsp granulated sugar

½ tsp freshly ground pepper

Four 6-oz/170-g salmon fillets, skin and pin bones removed

9 pieces frozen banana leaf, 6 by 10 in/15 by 25 cm each, thawed (see Cook's Note, page 126)

Vegetable oil for brushing the grill grate

4 lime wedges for garnish

1 Trim off the root end from the lemongrass stalk, then cut off and discard the tough green tops. You should have a bulb about 4 in/10 cm long. Peel away the tough outer leaves, cut the bulb crosswise into ½-in/12-mm pieces, and then smash the pieces. Drop the pieces into a food processor. Add the white part of the green onions, the garlic, cilantro stems, galangal, chile, lime juice, salt, sugar, and pepper and pulse until finely minced, stopping to scrape down the sides of the work bowl once or twice.

2 Using a sharp knife, lightly score the flesh on the nonskin side of each fillet, cutting no more than ⅛ in/3 mm deep and making diagonal cuts about 1 in/2.5 cm apart. The cuts will allow the marinade to penetrate the fish. Place the fillets in a glass baking dish. Using a rubber spatula, coat the fish fillets on the scored side with the marinade, dividing it equally. Cover and refrigerate for 1 hour.

3 Prepare a medium-hot fire in a charcoal grill or preheat a gas grill to medium-high.

4 While the grill is heating, assemble the banana-leaf packages. First wipe each piece of leaf clean with a damp paper towel. Using two leaves for each piece of fish, arrange one leaf horizontally and the other one vertically, in the shape of a cross. Place a fillet, marinated-side up, in the center, where the pieces cross. Working carefully (the leaves tear easily), bring the top of the vertical piece over to cover the fillet, tucking it under the bottom of the fish. Bring the bottom piece up and fold it over the top. Holding the folded bottom piece in place with one hand if needed, bring the left side of the horizontal leaf up and over the fillet, tucking it underneath. Repeat on the right side to enclose the fish in a rectangular parcel. It is fine, actually desirable, to have the fish overwrapped with several layers. This will seal in the juices. Set the packet aside while you wrap the remaining three fish fillets the same way.

...CONTINUED

5 Use the extra banana leaf to cut eight long, ribbonlike strips. Use these strips as ties to secure each parcel, tying each one in two places, as if securing a gift.

6 When ready to grill, to create a cool zone, bank the coals to one side of the charcoal grill or turn off one of the burners of the gas grill. Brush the grill grate with vegetable oil. Place the banana-leaf parcels directly over the medium-hot fire. Cover the grill and cook on one side for 5 minutes. Using a wide spatula, carefully turn the parcels over and re-cover the grill. Cook on the second side for 2 minutes. Move the parcels to the cool side of the grate and continue to cook until an instant-read thermometer inserted, through the wrapper, into the center of a fillet registers between 122°F/50°C and 125°F/52°C, about 2 minutes longer.

7 Transfer the parcels to a large baking sheet. The outer leaf on each parcel will be brittle, charred, and cracked. Carefully remove and discard it. Then, using a spatula, transfer each parcel to a warmed dinner plate. Open the leaves to reveal the fish and artfully tuck the edges of the leaves underneath the fish. Garnish each serving with a couple of cilantro sprigs, and place a lime wedge next to each fillet. Serve immediately.

COOK'S NOTE

Banana leaves are available in the frozen foods section of Chinese, Southeast Asian, and Latin American markets. Occasionally, I see them fresh in the produce aisle. The leaves are usually imported from Thailand or the Philippines and come in 1-pound/455-gram packages. Each cellophane bag contains about twenty whole leaves. Partially thaw the package (this only takes a few minutes) and remove the number of leaves you need for the recipe. Reseal the package, pressing out all of the air, and freeze the leaves for later use. They will keep for several months.

LACY GALANGAL BRANDY CRISPS

Delicate and elegant like a fine piece of lace, these crisp spiced cookies are pliable when hot, allowing you to form them into rolled cylinders or even little cups. While the dough is a cinch to make—nothing more than stirring ingredients together on top of the stove—the molding takes quick work and nimble fingers. The simplest thing is to let them harden as flat cookies. For cannoli-shaped cookies, you can roll them around a thick dowel (I use the handle of a wooden spoon). Or, mold each hot cookie inside a rounded custard cup, turning it into a dessert bowl for ice cream, sorbet, or an airy mousse.

MAKES ABOUT 70 COOKIES

½ cup/115 g unsalted butter, plus more for the pans

¼ cup/60 ml unsulfured dark molasses (not blackstrap)

¼ cup/60 ml brown rice syrup

1¼ cups/120 g sifted cake flour

⅔ cup/130 g granulated sugar

¼ tsp kosher or fine sea salt

2 tbsp peeled and finely grated galangal

2 tbsp brandy

1 tbsp dark rum

1 Position a rack in the center of the oven and preheat to 300°F/150°C/gas 2. Butter two baking sheets, preferably nonstick.

2 In a small saucepan, combine the molasses and brown rice syrup over medium heat and bring to a boil. Add the butter and stir until melted. Remove from the heat and stir in the flour, sugar, salt, and galangal. Set aside to cool for 10 minutes and then stir in the brandy and rum.

3 Using a ½-tsp measuring spoon, drop rounded spoonfuls onto the prepared baking sheets, spacing the cookies 2 in/5 cm apart. (The cookies really spread as they bake.) Place one baking sheet in the oven and bake the cookies until they have spread, are bubbly with lacy holes, and are fragrant, 6 minutes. Transfer the pan to a wire rack and immediately put the second baking sheet in the oven. (It is important to set a timer each time, because even though the cookies look done at 4 or even 5 minutes, they are still too soft to work with.) Let the baked cookies sit for 1 minute. Using the tip of a paring knife, lift the edge of a cookie to get under it and then use a small spatula to carefully lift off the cookie.

4 You have a few options for shaping these cookies. You can simply transfer them to a wire rack to cool and harden into flat cookies, but if you decide to shape them, you must work quickly before the warm cookies harden. (If they do harden on the pan, return the pan to the oven to warm the cookies for about 1 minute to make them pliable again. This is why I only bake one sheet at a time.) Once you have shaped them, transfer them to wire racks to cool.

5 Let the pans cool slightly and lightly butter them before baking another batch. The cookies can be made up to 1 day in advance. Layer the cookies between sheets of waxed paper in an airtight container and store at room temperature. These cookies freeze beautifully and keep best if they are frozen the moment they have fully cooled. They can be frozen for up to 1 month. Remove them from the freezer 1 hour before you plan to serve them.

CHOCOLATE-GALANGAL CRINKLE COOKIES

While I am never one to double dip into the cookie jar, let alone triple dip, I can't resist these chocolaty, deeply spiced cookies. Of course, classic crinkle cookies don't have chunks of chocolate in them, let alone galangal, but I always want to up the chocolate quotient, so I added hand-chopped chocolate pieces to the dough. Use a good-quality bittersweet chocolate. My preferred brand is Valrhona for its creamy texture that melts richly and evenly on the tongue. You can use fresh ginger if you can't find galangal, but the galangal imparts a uniquely nuanced sweet spiciness as the flavors finish on the palate.

MAKES 40 TO 45 COOKIES

½ cup/115 g unsalted butter, at room temperature

7½ oz/215 g bittersweet chocolate (not less than 64 percent cacao), chopped

1½ tbsp peeled and grated galangal

¾ cup/90 g all-purpose flour

¼ cup/20 g unsweetened Dutch-process cocoa

1 tsp baking powder

1 tsp ground cinnamon

½ tsp kosher or fine sea salt

¾ cup/150 g granulated sugar

¼ cup/50 g firmly packed dark brown sugar

2 large eggs

1 tsp pure vanilla extract

Confectioners' sugar for rolling the cookies

1 Select a large heatproof bowl that will rest on the rim of a medium saucepan. Fill the saucepan one-third full with water and bring to a simmer. Place the butter, 3 oz/85 g of the chocolate, and the galangal in the bowl, and set the bowl over (not touching) the simmering water. Turn the heat to low. Heat, stirring frequently, until the chocolate and butter are fully melted and completely smooth. Remove from the heat and let cool for about 10 minutes.

2 In a medium bowl, whisk together the flour, cocoa powder, baking powder, cinnamon, and salt. Set aside.

3 Stir the granulated sugar and brown sugar into the melted chocolate, mixing well. Add the eggs, one at a time, and whisk well after each addition. Whisk in the vanilla. Stir in the flour mixture just until the flour is absorbed. Fold in the remaining chopped chocolate. Cover and refrigerate the dough until well chilled and firm, at least 2 hours or up to overnight.

4 Position one rack in the upper third and a second rack in the lower third of the oven and preheat to 350°F/180°C/gas 4. Line two baking sheets with parchment paper.

5 Put some confectioners' sugar in a small, shallow bowl. Scoop up a nugget of the dough and roll it between your palms into a ball 1 in/2.5 cm in diameter. When all of the balls are formed, roll them in the confectioners' sugar, coating them generously and evenly without shaking off the excess. Arrange the coated balls on the prepared baking sheets, spacing them 2 in/ 5 cm apart.

6 Place the baking sheets in the oven and bake the cookies until the tops are cracked and the centers are still soft and chewy, 10 to 12 minutes. For even baking, at the midpoint, switch the pans between the racks and rotate them front to back. Remove from the oven and transfer the cookies to wire racks to cool. The cookies can be made ahead and stored between sheets of waxed paper in an airtight container at room temperature for up to 3 days or frozen for up to 2 weeks.

POACHED ASIAN PEARS WITH GALANGAL AND HONEY

Poached pears, especially crisp Asian pears, are one of my favorite fall and winter desserts. They're simple to make, perfect for a family meal, and ideal for entertaining because they can be made in advance. Immersed in syrup made from honey and brown sugar and laced with galangal, star anise, and cinnamon, the pears turn out sweet, tart, and sprightly. Pair them with coconut ice cream for dessert, or slice them and serve them in a spinach salad with candied walnuts or pecans.

SERVES 4 TO 8

4 Asian pears, about 3 lb/1.4 kg

1 cup/240 ml water mixed with 2 tbsp fresh lemon juice

½ cup/120 ml dry white wine

½ cup/120 ml honey

¼ cup/50 g firmly packed light brown sugar

3-in/7.5-cm piece galangal, peeled and thinly sliced

2 star anise pods

1½-in/4-cm piece cinnamon stick

1 Peel the pears, halve them lengthwise, and remove the cores. Place the pear halves, cut-side down, in a single layer in a large baking dish and cover with the lemon water to prevent them from browning.

2 In a wide, shallow pan just large enough to hold the pears in a single layer, combine the wine, honey, brown sugar, galangal, star anise, and cinnamon stick. Bring to a boil over medium-high heat, stirring to dissolve the honey and sugar. Reduce the heat to a low simmer. Add the pear halves, cut-side down, and just enough of the soaking water to immerse them. Cover the pan partially and simmer until the pears are tender when pierced with a fork, 40 to 45 minutes.

3 Using a slotted spoon, transfer the pears to a heatproof bowl. Increase the heat to high and boil the poaching liquid, stirring occasionally, until it thickens to a syruplike consistency, about 10 minutes. Strain the syrup through a fine-mesh sieve into the bowl holding the pears, and toss the pears gently in the syrup.

4 Serve the pears warm with the syrup drizzled over the top. The pears can be made up to 2 days in advance and kept in a covered container in the refrigerator. Rewarm before serving, or serve chilled.

GINGER

Zingiber officinale

STEM GINGER / GINGERROOT / CANTON GINGER/ JAMAICA GINGER / JIANG *(MANDARIN CHINESE)* / SHOGA *(JAPANESE)*

HISTORY AND LORE Ginger, the best-known member of the ginger family (Zingiberaceae), is a tropical herbaceous perennial with large leaves rising from underground creeping, branching rhizomes. It is believed to have originated in northeastern India or southern China and has been cultivated in tropical Asia since ancient times. It was one of the first spices—and the most prized—carried along the Silk Road from China to Europe. Although it was known to the ancient Greeks and Romans and was available throughout Europe by the tenth century, it did not become popular in Europe until the Middle Ages, when it was the second most coveted spice, after pepper. The Portuguese took ginger to the western coast of Africa in the fifteenth century, and the Spanish introduced it to the New World a century later, carrying it to Jamaica and Mexico. By the end of the sixteenth century, Jamaica was exporting big shiploads of ginger to Spain.

Today, India and China are numbers one and two in global production of the tropical rhizome, which is used in all kinds of cookies, biscuits, cakes, and other sweets around the world, including the famous gingerbread of Great Britain and its French equivalent, *pain d'epice.* Ginger is also widely used in the making of extracts, oils, teas, carbonated drinks, liqueurs, beer, and brandy and

has been shown to lessen the symptoms of the common cold and to ease the nausea that accompanies morning sickness, sea sickness, and chemotherapy treatment.

VARIETIES Fresh ginger can vary slightly, depending on where it is grown, but what distinguishes most of the ginger you find in the market is the age at which it was harvested. Mature ginger, which is ideally harvested when the plant is 7 to 10 months old, is what you most commonly find. Young ginger, harvested at 3 to 4 months, before the skin has fully formed, is available seasonally. The latter, which has ivory flesh and rosy pink tips where the stems are beginning to develop, is milder and less pungent than mature ginger. Japanese ginger *(Zingiber mioga),* known as *myoga* in Japan, is native to East Asia and is now being farmed in Hawaii. This species is cultivated not for its rhizome, which is inedible, but instead for its flower clusters and buds, which are considered a delicacy in Japan.

NUTRITION Ginger is particularly high in potassium, but because it is used in only a small quantity in any recipe, its nutritional value is limited.

AVAILABILITY AND SELECTION Fresh mature ginger is available year-round in Asian markets and almost all supermarkets. The best-quality ginger comes from Hawaii and is at its peak from December to April. Hawaiian ginger is less fibrous and more fragrant and juicy than the ginger grown in Asia (China and the Philippines, in particular), perhaps because it is harvested earlier than mature ginger is elsewhere. Look for young ginger in Asian markets beginning in late December and throughout the spring.

Large pieces of ginger come in handlike formations with several knobby branches. The bulbous branches can be 1 to 2 inches/2.5 to 5 centimeters in diameter and anywhere from 4 to 8 inches/10 to 20 centimeters long. They should be firm with no wrinkles or spongy spots. The skin of ginger is thin, shiny, and taupe, with pale to bright yellow flesh that appears juicy. When ginger is sold loose, it is perfectly acceptable to break off a small portion from the hand. Fresh young ginger should have smooth, moist skin, and feel firm, with a bright, spicy fragrance.

STORAGE Wrap ginger in a dry paper towel, place in an unsealed plastic bag, and refrigerate. It will keep for 3 to 4 weeks. If you see any spots of mold, just cut them off, replace the paper towel, and use the remainder. For longer storage, you can slice ginger, wrap the slices, and freeze them for up to 2 months. The ginger will lose its firm texture, however. Use frozen ginger when a recipe calls for grated, juiced, or smashed ginger. Another option is to peel any extra knobs of young or mature ginger, put them in a jar, fill the jar with inexpensive pale dry sherry, and store in the refrigerator for several months. You can use the ginger-infused sherry in marinades and savory sauces.

BASIC USE AND PREPARATION Ginger can be consumed raw, pickled, preserved in syrup, or crystallized, or cooked by a variety of methods. It is also dried and ground to a powder. Ginger is typically grated or minced for marinades, dressings, and beverages, and can be very finely grated to a paste on a Japanese ceramic or metal grater or a Microplane or other fine-rasp grater. It can also be sliced, cut into matchsticks, or chopped for simmering, stir-frying, braising, or steeping.

To prepare mature ginger, cut or break off only the amount you will need for a recipe. Trim any nodules of their rough ends. Compared to galangal, the skin of ginger is very thin, and if the ginger is quite fresh, with taut smooth skin that shines, I scrape away only the thicker skin between the nodules and leave the remainder. If the ginger is firm but the skin looks a bit rough, then I use a swivel-bladed peeler, paring knife, or the edge of a spoon to scrape or peel the skin. For slices, cut the ginger thinly across the grain. For matchsticks, stack the slices and cut into long strips. To mince, stack the slices, cut long strips, and then cut crosswise into tiny pieces.

To prepare young ginger, cut or break off only the amount you will need for a recipe. Trim any nodules of their rough ends. Young ginger does not need to be peeled except to remove blemishes. For sliced, matchstick-cut, or minced young ginger, handle as you would mature ginger.

YIELDS

½ oz/15 g peeled, trimmed, and minced fresh ginger = 2 tbsp

1 oz/30 g peeled, trimmed, and minced fresh ginger = ¼ cup

2 oz/55 g peeled, trimmed, and grated fresh ginger = ½ cup

6 oz/170 g lightly packed peeled, trimmed, and sliced fresh ginger = 1 cup

SUSHI-STYLE PICKLED GINGER

For sushi and sashimi lovers, making your own pickled ginger is a treat and easy to do. I like to have it on hand as a condiment for grilled seafood. If you see fresh young ginger in the market, nab some and pickle it. Young ginger is less fibrous than mature ginger and has a wonderful texture when pickled. Whether you use young or mature ginger, the easiest way to slice it is on a Japanese-style mandoline. You'll end up with paper-thin uniform slices.

MAKES ONE 1-PT/480-ML JAR

2 cups/340 g lightly packed peeled and thinly sliced fresh ginger

2¼ tsp kosher or fine sea salt

½ cup plus 1 tbsp/135 ml unseasoned rice vinegar

3 tbsp water

⅓ cup plus 1 tbsp/80g granulated sugar

1 Wash a 1-pt/480-ml heatproof glass jar with a tight-fitting lid in hot, soapy water and dry thoroughly. Alternatively, run the jar through the regular cycle of your dishwasher and wash the lid by hand.

2 Fill a medium saucepan two-thirds full of water and bring to a boil over high heat. Add the ginger slices and cook for 1 minute. Drain the ginger slices in a large colander, spreading them out in a single layer, and leave them to dry for 2 to 3 minutes. Sprinkle the ginger with ¼ tsp of the salt and toss to coat evenly. Firmly pack the ginger while it is still warm into the prepared jar.

3 Meanwhile, in a small saucepan, combine the vinegar, water, sugar, and the remaining 2 tsp salt and bring to a boil over high heat, stirring constantly until the sugar dissolves. Boil the pickling liquid for 1 minute and remove from the heat.

4 Using a widemouthed funnel, ladle or pour the hot pickling liquid into the jar, covering the ginger completely and leaving ½-in/12-mm headspace. The ginger will turn a faint pink. Use a spoon to press down on the ginger to submerge it completely in the liquid. Wipe the rim clean and attach the lid. Let stand at room temperature until cool.

5 Place the jar in the refrigerator for at least 2 days before using to allow the flavors to permeate the ginger. The pickled ginger will keep in the refrigerator for up to 3 months.

GINGER VINAIGRETTE
WITH CILANTRO AND GREEN ONION

This boldly flavored vinaigrette is heady with fresh ginger and classic Asian accents. Serve it with grilled shrimp or eggplant, or as a dip for chicken satay, lettuce wraps, or Salmon Salad Rolls with Cellophane Noodles, Jicama, and Green Onions (page 178).

MAKES ⅔ CUP/165 ML

¼ cup/60 ml canola or other neutral oil

3 tbsp peeled and minced fresh ginger

2½ tbsp fresh lime juice

1 tbsp unseasoned rice vinegar

1 tsp granulated sugar

1 tsp Asian sesame oil

½ tsp *sambal oelek* (see Cook's Note)

½ tsp minced garlic

½ tsp kosher salt

¼ tsp freshly ground pepper

3 tbsp finely chopped fresh cilantro

2 tbsp thinly sliced green onion, including green tops

1 In a small sauté pan, heat the oil over medium heat. Add the ginger and sauté until aromatic and golden, 2 to 3 minutes. Transfer the ginger and oil to a small heatproof bowl and let cool slightly, about 5 minutes.

2 While the oil is still warm, add the lime juice, vinegar, sugar, sesame oil, *sambal oelek*, garlic, salt, and pepper and whisk to combine. Stir in the cilantro and green onion. Use immediately, or transfer to a jar with a tight-fitting lid and refrigerate for up to 3 days.

COOK'S NOTE

Sambal oelek (or *sambal ulek*) is an Indonesian hot chile paste made from chiles, salt, vinegar, and sometimes garlic and tamarind. It is a fiery paste with bright flavors, and a little goes a long way. Other Asian chile pastes flavored with garlic can be substituted, but this one is a favorite of mine. It is sold in jars in Asian markets and some supermarkets. Once the jar is opened, store it in the refrigerator; it will keep indefinitely.

DUNGENESS CRAB CAKES WITH GINGER

Packed with chunks of fresh crabmeat, these crab cakes are made with homemade fresh bread crumbs to keep them light and tasting like crab. A healthy dose of minced ginger infuses these patties with a bright, clean flavor. Because they are made without a lot of binders and fillers, you'll need to use a delicate touch when frying and turning the cakes to keep them intact.

MAKES SIXTEEN 2½-IN/6-CM CRAB CAKES; SERVES 8 AS A FIRST COURSE

1 large egg, beaten

6 tbsp/90 ml mayonnaise

2 tbsp Dijon mustard

2 tsp fresh lemon juice

2 tsp Worcestershire sauce

1½ tsp Tabasco sauce

1 tsp minced fresh thyme

½ tsp paprika

¼ tsp freshly ground pepper

½ cup/80 g diced red bell pepper

½ cup/30 g finely chopped fresh flat-leaf parsley

¼ cup/35 g minced shallot

3 tbsp peeled and minced fresh ginger

1 lb/455 g fresh crabmeat, well drained and picked clean of shell

2½ cups/135 g lightly packed fresh bread crumbs (see Cook's Note, page 136)

SRIRACHA CREAM SAUCE

½ cup/120 ml mayonnaise

¼ cup/60 ml sour cream

4 tsp fresh lemon juice

1½ tsp Sriracha sauce (see Cook's Note, page 136)

½ tsp Asian sesame oil

4 tbsp/55 g unsalted butter, plus more if needed

4 tbsp/60 ml canola or other neutral oil, plus more if needed

1 In a medium bowl, whisk together the egg, mayonnaise, mustard, lemon juice, Worcestershire sauce, Tabasco, thyme, paprika, and ground pepper until thoroughly combined.

2 In a large bowl, mix together the bell pepper, parsley, shallot, and ginger. Using a rubber spatula, fold in the crabmeat. Add the mayonnaise mixture and gently fold everything together. Add the bread crumbs and use a light touch to fold them into the crabmeat mixture (overmixing will result in gummy crab cakes). Gently form 16 crab cakes. An easy way to form uniform cakes is to use a ¼-cup/60-ml scoop with a release lever. Release the scoops directly onto a large rimmed baking sheet, and use your fingertips to form them into patties 2½ in/6 cm in diameter and about 1 in/2.5 cm thick. Cover the pan with plastic wrap and refrigerate for at least 30 minutes. (The patties can be prepared up to 8 hours ahead.)

3 To make the cream sauce, in a small bowl, whisk together the mayonnaise, sour cream, lemon juice, Sriracha sauce, and sesame oil until thoroughly combined. Cover and refrigerate until ready to serve.

4 When ready to fry the crab cakes, line two rimmed baking sheets with paper towels. Place two large frying pans, preferably cast iron, over medium-high heat. Add 2 tbsp each of the butter and oil to each pan. When the butter melts, swirl to coat the pan bottoms and add half of the crab cakes, not touching, to each pan. If necessary to avoid crowding, fry the crab cakes in batches, adding more butter and oil to each pan as needed. Cook, turning once with a spatula, until golden brown on both sides and hot throughout, 3 to 4 minutes on each side. If the crab cakes are browning too quickly, reduce the heat to medium. As the crab cakes are ready, transfer them to the towel-lined baking sheets to drain briefly. If cooking a second batch, keep the crab cakes warm in a preheated 200°F/95°C oven while frying the second batch.

5 Arrange the crab cakes on a warmed platter or individual plates. Pass the sauce at the table when serving.

...CONTINUED

COOK'S NOTE

To make fresh bread crumbs, remove the crusts from three or four slices of firm white sandwich bread, then gently tear the bread into small pieces. Place the pieces in a food processor and pulse until reduced to fine crumbs.

Sriracha sauce, a hot chile sauce made from sun-dried chiles, vinegar, garlic, sugar, and salt, is named after the southern Thai city of the same name. In the United States, it has been popularized by Huy Fong Foods, which packages it in a tall, clear plastic bottle with a bright green squirt top and a rooster on the label. It is widely available in Asian markets and in supermarkets with an Asian foods section. Once it is opened, store it in the refrigerator; it will keep indefinitely.

KOREAN-STYLE GRILLED SHORT RIBS

For those who like to have finger-lickin' grilled foods to nibble, these beef short ribs, marinated in a Korean-style soy marinade seasoned with garlic, green onions, and lots of fresh ginger, are a savory, smoky budget-friendly treat. Serve accompanied with Biwa Daikon Kimchi (page 252), or buy prepared kimchi, the fiery Korean pickled cabbage stocked in Asian markets or in the Asian foods section of large supermarkets. Many Asian markets sell beef short ribs cut flanken style, but you may need to order these from your butcher. Ask for beef chuck with ribs, sawed crosswise through the bones into strips about ½ inch/12 millimeters thick.

SERVES 4 OR 5 AS A MAIN COURSE

MARINADE

⅔ cup/165 ml soy sauce

⅓ cup/75 ml mirin (Japanese sweet cooking wine)

⅓ cup/75 ml unseasoned rice vinegar

⅓ cup/65 g firmly packed dark brown sugar

3 tbsp Asian sesame oil

¼ cup/30 g peeled and minced fresh ginger

2 tbsp finely minced garlic (about 7 cloves)

4 green onions, including green tops, minced

½ tsp freshly ground pepper

3 to 3½ lb/1.4 to 1.6 kg beef short ribs, cut flanken style (½ in/12 mm thick across the bones)

Vegetable oil for brushing

1 To make the marinade, in a medium bowl, whisk together the soy sauce, mirin, vinegar, brown sugar, sesame oil, ginger, garlic, green onions, and pepper.

2 Arrange the beef ribs in a large baking dish, pour the marinade over the top, and turn the meat several times until well coated. Cover and refrigerate for at least 3 hours or up to 8 hours. Alternatively, put the beef ribs in a jumbo-size, freezer-strength lock-top plastic bag, pour the marinade over the top, squeeze out all of the air, and seal the bag. Massage the bag to coat all of the beef evenly with the marinade. Place on a rimmed baking sheet and refrigerate.

3 Remove the beef from the refrigerator 1 hour before you plan to begin grilling. Remove the beef ribs from the marinade, drain or blot lightly, and place on a rimmed baking sheet. Discard the marinade. Prepare a medium-hot fire in a charcoal grill or preheat a gas grill to medium-high.

4 Brush the grill grate with vegetable oil. Place the beef ribs, without crowding, directly over the fire and cover the grill. Cook until nicely seared on one side, about 3 minutes. Using tongs, turn the ribs, re-cover, and cook until seared on the second side, 3 to 4 minutes longer. The meat should be lightly charred at the bones and cooked through with no pink.

5 Remove from the grill, pile on a warmed platter, and serve immediately.

GINGERBREAD CAKE WITH CRÈME ANGLAISE

David Lebovitz, a friend and colleague, is the author of several dessert cookbooks, including *Room for Dessert*, which has this recipe for his famous ginger cake. In the introduction to the recipe, he writes, "This is the most-often requested recipe in my repertoire, and I've passed it on to many, many people." He mentions that it frequently appears on Bay Area menus, sometimes called Dave's ginger cake. I asked David via e-mail (lucky guy, he lives in Paris) if I could adapt his recipe, and he agreed. It is simply the most delectable, moist, and ginger-packed cake I have ever eaten.

SERVES 10 TO 12

1 tbsp unsalted butter, at room temperature

3¾ cups/485 g all-purpose flour, plus more for dusting the pan

1½ tsp ground cinnamon

¾ tsp ground cloves

¾ tsp freshly ground pepper

1½ cups/360 ml unsulfured dark molasses (not blackstrap)

1½ cups/300 g granulated sugar

1½ cups/360 ml canola oil or peanut oil

1½ cups/360 ml water

1 tbsp baking soda

⅔ cup/90 g packed, peeled and minced fresh ginger (see Cook's Note)

3 large eggs, beaten

CRÈME ANGLAISE

1 cup/240 ml heavy whipping cream

1 cup/240 ml milk

4 egg yolks

¼ cup/50 g granulated sugar

¼ tsp kosher or fine sea salt

1½ tsp pure vanilla extract

Confectioners' sugar for dusting

1   Position a rack in the lower third of the oven and preheat to 350°F/180°C/gas 4. Grease a 10-in/25-cm (12-cup/2.8-L) Bundt pan, preferably nonstick, with the butter. Sprinkle the pan with a big spoonful of flour, and then tilt and tap the pan to distribute the flour evenly. Turn the pan upside down over the sink and gently shake out the excess flour. Set aside.

2   In a large bowl, sift together the flour, cinnamon, cloves, and pepper. In another large bowl, whisk together the molasses, granulated sugar, and oil.

3   In a 2½-qt/1.4-L saucepan, bring the water to a boil over high heat. Remove from the heat and stir in the baking soda. Whisk the water mixture into the molasses mixture and then whisk in the ginger.

4   Add the flour mixture 1 cup/125 g at a time to the molasses mixture, stirring just until the flour is absorbed. Whisk in the beaten eggs. Pour the batter into the prepared pan.

5   Bake the cake until a toothpick inserted near the center comes out clean, about 1 hour. If the cake appears to be browning too quickly, lay a piece of aluminum foil over the top of the pan. Let the cake cool in the pan on a wire rack for 1 hour. Then invert the rack over the top of the pan, and invert the pan and rack together. Lift off the pan and let the cake cool to room temperature on the rack. (The cake can be covered tightly and stored at room temperature for up to 3 days before serving. Or, it can be wrapped tightly and frozen for up to 1 month and then thawed overnight at room temperature.)

6   To make the crème anglaise, in a 2½-qt/1.4-L saucepan, combine the cream and milk over medium-low heat and bring to a simmer. Remove from the heat. (Do not let the milk mixture boil.)

7 Have ready an ice bath. In a medium bowl, whisk together the egg yolks, granulated sugar, and salt until well blended. Slowly add ½ cup/120 ml of the hot milk mixture to the egg yolk mixture while whisking constantly. (This will temper the yolks so they don't curdle when added to the hot liquid.) Then whisk the egg yolk mixture into the milk mixture in the saucepan. Return the pan to low heat and cook, whisking constantly, until the mixture is as thick as whipping cream and coats the back of a spoon, 3 to 5 minutes. (The crème anglaise is ready when it registers 160°F/71°C on an instant-read thermometer.) Remove the sauce from the heat and pour it through a fine-mesh sieve set over a medium bowl, and then nest the bowl in the ice bath. Add the vanilla to the sauce, stir well, and let cool. Stir the sauce every now and again as it cools. Once it has cooled, press plastic wrap directly on the surface to prevent a skin from forming. Cover and refrigerate until ready to use. (The sauce can be made up to 2 days in advance.)

8 Place the cake on a cake plate. Using a small fine-mesh sieve, dust it with confectioners' sugar. Cut the cake into slices. Spoon 2 tbsp or more of the crème anglaise onto the center of each dessert plate. Place a cake slice in the center of each plate and serve immediately.

COOK'S NOTE

You'll need to buy 5 to 6 oz/140 to 170 g of fresh ginger to end up with ⅔ cup/90 g minced ginger. The easiest way to prepare the ginger is to peel it, cut it into small chunks, and mince it in a small or regular-size food processor. You can mince it by hand, but it will take time.

OLD-FASHIONED GINGERSNAPS

Real gingersnaps—a cookie lover's indulgence—are impossible to resist. If you like them crunchy, bake them a little longer than suggested here. If you are in the soft-and-chewy-ginger-cookie camp, bake them a little less. The secret to their addictively delicious crunch? The dough is formed into balls and then rolled in turbinado sugar rather than granulated sugar.

MAKES ABOUT 48 COOKIES

2 cups/255 g all-purpose flour

2 tsp baking soda

2 tsp ground ginger

1 tsp ground cinnamon

½ tsp freshly grated nutmeg

½ tsp ground allspice

½ tsp kosher or fine sea salt

½ cup/115 g unsalted butter, melted and cooled

¼ cup unsulfured dark molasses (not blackstrap)

½ cup/100 g firmly packed light brown sugar

⅓ cup/65 g granulated sugar

3 tbsp peeled and grated fresh ginger

1 large egg, beaten

½ cup/100 g turbinado sugar

1 Position one rack in the upper third and a second rack in the lower third of the oven and preheat to 350°F/180°C/gas 4. Line two baking sheets with parchment paper.

2 In a medium bowl, whisk together the flour, baking soda, ground ginger, cinnamon, nutmeg, allspice, and salt. Set aside.

3 In a large bowl, whisk together the melted butter, molasses, brown sugar, granulated sugar, grated ginger, and egg. Add the flour mixture and stir to combine thoroughly.

4 Put the turbinado sugar in a small, shallow bowl. Scoop up a nugget of the dough and roll it between your palms into a ball 1 in/2.5 cm in diameter. When all of the balls are formed, roll them in the turbinado sugar, coating them evenly. Arrange the coated balls on the prepared baking sheets, spacing them 2 in/5 cm apart.

5 Place the baking sheets in the oven and bake the cookies until the edges are crisp and the centers are still chewy, 10 to 12 minutes. For even baking, at the midpoint, switch the pans between the racks and rotate them front to back. Remove from the oven and transfer the cookies to wire racks to cool. The cookies can be made ahead, stored between sheets of waxed paper in an airtight container at room temperature for up to 5 days or frozen for up to 2 weeks.

GINGER PANNA COTTA

Light and punctuated with bright ginger flavor, this creamy *panna cotta* is dessert heaven in my book. You can make it year-round, changing the fruit to match the season. In summer, add a shower of fresh blueberries or raspberries; in fall, add a garnish of sliced fresh or poached peaches; in winter, include some chopped candied ginger and satsuma mandarin segments; and in spring, fresh strawberries are perfect.

SERVES 8 OR 9

3 cups/720 ml heavy whipping cream

½ cup/120 ml milk

2½ oz/70 g fresh ginger, peeled and minced

½ vanilla bean, split lengthwise

One ¼-oz/7-g packet powdered gelatin (scant 1 tbsp)

3 tbsp water

⅔ cup/130 g granulated sugar

Pinch of kosher or fine sea salt

1 In a medium, heavy saucepan, combine the cream, milk, and ginger. Using a small paring knife, scrape the seeds from the vanilla bean halves into the pan and then add the bean halves. Place over medium heat and heat until the liquid begins to foam around the edges of the pan, about 5 minutes. Remove from the heat, cover, and let steep for 15 minutes.

2 Meanwhile, in a small, heat-resistant bowl, stir together the gelatin and water and set aside to allow the gelatin to soften, about 5 minutes. Pour hot water to a depth of 1 to 2 in/2.5 to 5 cm into a slightly larger bowl and rest the base of the gelatin bowl in the water. Stir until the gelatin is dissolved and clear, 2 to 3 minutes.

3 Strain the hot cream mixture through a fine-mesh sieve held over a medium bowl. Stir in the sugar and salt until dissolved and then whisk in the gelatin mixture. Let the mixture cool until it is still warm but not hot, stirring occasionally so the vanilla seeds will be dispersed evenly in the finished dessert.

4 Divide the warm mixture evenly among eight or nine ½-cup/120-ml ramekins. Cover with plastic wrap and refrigerate until set, at least 4 hours. (They will keep for up to 3 days.) Serve chilled.

BROWN SUGAR–GINGER ICE CREAM

Making ice cream is a fun summer weekend activity, whether you're churning it in an old-fashioned hand-cranked maker or going modern with an electric one. Here, the brown sugar delivers a slight molasses note to the extra-rich gingery ice cream. If you like, top each serving with berries, chocolate sauce, sugar-crusted walnuts, or even homemade Candied Young Ginger (facing page).

MAKES ABOUT 1 QT/960 ML

2½ cups/600 ml heavy whipping cream

1¼ cups/300 ml milk

⅔ cup/130 g firmly packed light brown sugar

½ cup/100 g granulated sugar

3 oz/85 g fresh ginger, peeled and minced

¼ tsp kosher or fine sea salt

7 egg yolks, lightly beaten

1 In a medium, heavy saucepan, combine the cream, milk, brown sugar, granulated sugar, ginger, and salt. Place over medium heat and warm the mixture, stirring often to dissolve the sugars, until the liquid begins to foam around the edges of the pan, about 5 minutes. Remove from the heat, cover, and let steep for 15 minutes.

2 Have ready an ice bath. Strain the cream mixture through a fine-mesh sieve placed over a bowl. Return the liquid to the pan, place over medium heat, and cook, stirring occasionally, until the mixture is almost at a simmer. Slowly add ½ cup/120 ml of the hot cream mixture to the beaten egg yolks while whisking constantly. (This will temper the yolks so they don't curdle when added to the hot liquid.) Then whisk the egg yolk mixture into the cream mixture and continue to cook over medium-low heat, whisking constantly, until the custard thickens, 7 to 10 minutes. The custard is ready when it registers 175°F/80°C on an instant-read thermometer. Remove from the heat and pour through a fine-mesh sieve set over a medium heatproof bowl, and then nest the bowl in the ice bath to cool, stirring the custard occasionally.

3 When the custard is well chilled and thick, transfer it to an ice-cream maker and churn according to the manufacturer's directions. Transfer the ice cream to a freezer container with a tight-fitting lid and place it in the freezer until it is solid and scoopable, about 4 hours, before serving.

CANDIED YOUNG GINGER

This is a recipe for anyone who likes to putter in the kitchen doing fun cooking projects. All you will need are a candy thermometer and a fine-mesh cooling rack. Beyond that, it is just a matter of cooking the ginger slices in sugar syrup, letting them dry, and then coating them in sugar. You will want to use young ginger, typically available in the springtime. It is less fibrous than mature ginger and it has a less spicy bite. For delectable food gifts, package the slices in small cellophane bags tied with a ribbon.

MAKES ABOUT 8 OZ/225 G

8 oz/225 g fresh young ginger

2½ cups/500 g granulated sugar

1 Peel the ginger. Then, using a mandoline or a sharp chef's knife, cut it crosswise into rounds ¼ in/6 mm thick. Place the ginger slices in a medium, heavy saucepan, add water to cover, and bring to a boil over high heat. Reduce the heat to a simmer and cook until the ginger is tender, about 20 minutes.

2 Drain the ginger slices and return them to the pan. Add 2 cups/480 ml water and 2 cups/400 g of the sugar and attach a candy thermometer to the side of the pan. Place the pan over high heat, bring to a boil, and cook until the syrup registers 225°F/110°C on the thermometer, 10 to 12 minutes. Remove the pan from the heat and let stand for 1 hour.

3 Pour the ginger and the syrup into a large, flat-bottomed colander placed over a bowl and let drain for 1 hour.

4 Transfer the ginger to a fine-mesh cooling rack, spreading the slices, not touching, in a single layer. Let the ginger dry until it is still tacky but not gooey, about 1 hour.

5 Put the remaining ½ cup/100 g sugar in a deep bowl. Add the ginger slices and toss to coat evenly with the sugar. Shake off the excess sugar and return the ginger slices to the cooling rack, again arranging them so they do not touch one another. Leave the slices at room temperature overnight to finish drying. The candied ginger can be stored in an airtight container at room temperature for up to 1 month.

HOMEMADE GINGER ALE

Who knew it could be so simple to make ginger ale at home? Here's an all-natural version, blissfully free of high-fructose corn syrup and preservatives. When I compared this homemade ginger ale to a national brand, it proved unrivaled in spicy, aromatic ginger flavor. Although the ginger syrup recipe makes enough for just four servings, it is easily doubled. Store the remainder in the refrigerator to use whenever you crave a tall, sparkling glass of refreshing ginger ale.

MAKES 1 CUP/240 ML GINGER SYRUP; ENOUGH FOR 4 DRINKS

GINGER SYRUP

½ cup/55 g grated fresh ginger

1 cup/200 g firmly packed light brown sugar

1 cup/240 ml water

Ice cubes

4 cups/960 ml club soda

¼ cup/60 ml fresh lime juice

1 tbsp plus 1 tsp fresh lemon juice

4 lime wedges

1 To make the ginger syrup, in a small saucepan, combine the ginger, brown sugar, and water and bring to a boil over high heat, stirring constantly until the sugar dissolves. Reduce the heat and simmer for 5 minutes to completely dissolve the sugar and infuse the syrup. Remove from the heat and let the ginger steep in the syrup until cool, about 30 minutes. Strain the syrup through a fine-mesh sieve placed over a container with a tight-fitting lid and then cover and refrigerate until well chilled. (The syrup will keep in the refrigerator for up to 2 weeks.)

2 Fill four 16-oz/480-ml glasses two-thirds full of ice. Pour ¼ cup/60 ml of the syrup, 1 cup/240 ml of the club soda, 1 tbsp of the lime juice, and 1 tsp of the lemon juice into each glass and stir to combine. Garnish each glass with a lime wedge and serve immediately.

HORSERADISH

Armoracia rusticana

HISTORY AND LORE Despite the name, horseradish is not a radish at all, though it does belong to the same big family, Brassicaceae, as the radish does—along with lots of other well-known vegetables, such as cabbage, cauliflower, and broccoli. In 1597, the English herbalist John Gerard, in his highly regarded *Herball, or Generall Historie of Plantes*, described *horse*radish, probably employing the prefix *horse* to denote a coarse and vigorous plant. This hardy perennial, originally cultivated as a medicinal herb, is likely native to southeastern Europe and western Asia. Some claim it was grown in Egypt around 1500 B.C., before the exodus of the Hebrew slaves, but little or no proof exists. However, it has been one of the symbolic "bitter herbs" at the Passover seder since the Middle Ages. The ancient Greeks and Romans reportedly cultivated horseradish, consuming both the root and the leaves, the latter as a potherb.

By the sixteenth century, horseradish had become naturalized in England, though it would not become a popular culinary item for another century. It traveled from England to America with the early colonists and was mentioned as an edible garden plant in Bernard McMahon's *The American Gardener's Catalogue, Adapted to the Seasons of the United States*, published in Philadelphia in 1806. Russians, Scandinavians, Germans, and eastern Europeans, along with the British and French, have a long history of using horseradish as a condiment, and thanks to Scandinavian and eastern European immigrants, the root was widely cultivated in southern Canada and in the U.S. Midwest and Northeast by the nineteenth century.

Today, jars of prepared horseradish are common in almost all supermarkets across America, and we have Henry John Heinz to thank for that. In 1869, in Sharpsburg, Pennsylvania (just outside my hometown of Pittsburgh), H. J. Heinz began packing and peddling processed horseradish grown in his own garden. He distinguished his product by putting it in clear glass bottles and using pure grated horseradish, rather than the turnip filler used by less scrupulous vendors of the time.

VARIETIES Two horseradish cultivars are the most widely grown in the United States. The first, known as Maliner Kren (or common) horseradish, has broad, crinkled leaves with prominent veins. The second, called Bohemian, has big, smooth leaves that taper at the base. Both have large roots, though the roots of Maliner Kren are typically a bit larger. Maliner Kren is also the type usually found in supermarkets.

NUTRITION Although horseradish is an excellent source of vitamin C, has lots of potassium, and is low in calories, it is rarely consumed in quantities sufficient to pass along its nutritional wealth. It has medicinal value as well, as a circulatory stimulant, a diuretic for treating lung and urinary infections, and a pain reliever for stiff muscles and sore joints.

AVAILABILITY AND SELECTION In many supermarkets, fresh horseradish is available year-round. At farmers' markets, however, it is sold only from early spring through late fall. Roots dug in the fall after the first frost are generally regarded as the most flavorful. Fresh horseradish roots should feel firm, look husky yet well formed, and be 6 to 8 inches/15 to 20 centimeters long. The skin should be light brown and blemish free. If the root is freshly dug, especially if purchased at a farmers' market, it will have lots of dirt clinging to it and appear slightly darker. The flesh will be creamy white.

STORAGE Wait to wash the root until just before you use it. Wrap it in a damp paper towel, place it in a sealed plastic bag, and refrigerate it for up to 2 weeks. If stored longer, mold may develop. Trim and discard the moldy spots and wrap the root in fresh paper towels.

BASIC USE AND PREPARATION Horseradish can be eaten raw or cooked. It is typically peeled, grated, and mixed with vinegar, mayonnaise, cream, or other dairy product for vinaigrettes, mustards, hot and cold condiments, relishes, and dips. It is also excellent grated and used in a flavored butter or as a coating for roasted meats, especially beef.

To prepare the root, hold it under cool running water and scrub it clean using a vegetable brush. Trim the ends with a sharp paring knife and then peel the root with the knife or a serrated peeler and discard the peel. Peel only as much as you need at the time, blot the remaining root dry, wrap it in a dry paper towel, place it inside a loosely closed plastic bag, and refrigerate it for up to 3 weeks. If any green patches are visible under the skin, trim them away. Grate the root on a box grater, or cut it into small chunks and process it in a food processor or blender until finely minced. To prevent discoloration, sprinkle the root right after it has been grated with a little lemon juice or white wine vinegar.

A CAUTIONARY NOTE When horseradish is cut and grated, it produces isothiocyanates, a type of mustard oil that is quite pungent. Your sinuses will clear and your eyes will tear, and if you aren't careful, you will shed many tears. If grating horseradish on a box grater, I suggest you wear goggles and keep an arm's distance from the root. (The very cool onion goggles available at gourmet cookware stores really do work!) If using a food processor or blender, stand back and turn away before you remove the cover, to allow the fumes to escape.

YIELDS

2-by-1-in/5-by-2.5-cm piece fresh horseradish root = 2 oz/55 g

5 oz/140 g fresh horseradish root, peeled and grated = ½ cup/115 g

HORSERADISH SOUR CREAM DIP

Every Passover, my maternal grandfather, Irving Miller, made beet horseradish from scratch. He was a gardener with a true green thumb, and he grew his own horseradish. I remember how teary everyone got when he served my grandmother's homemade gefilte fish with his beet horseradish on the side. Through the sniffles, we all expressed delight and assured him that this batch was the hottest and best yet. Horseradish is one of those flavors I have always liked. For all you horseradish aficionados out there, here's a fabulous dip. Use more horseradish if you want to guarantee those sniffles and tears. This dip is terrific served with roasted fingerling potatoes, potato chips, wedges of tart apples, or rolled slices of rare roast beef.

MAKES ABOUT 2 CUPS/480 ML

1 cup/240 ml sour cream

¾ cup/65 g peeled, cored, and minced Granny Smith apple

¼ cup/55 g lightly packed grated horseradish, plus more if desired (see Cook's Note)

2 tbsp minced white onion

2 tbsp fresh lemon juice

½ tsp kosher or fine sea salt

¼ tsp freshly ground pepper

¼ cup/12 g finely snipped fresh chives

In a medium bowl, whisk together the sour cream, apple, horseradish, onion, lemon juice, salt, and pepper. Using a rubber spatula, fold in the chives. Cover and refrigerate for at least 1 hour to allow the flavors to meld and the dip to thicken. It can be prepared up to 1 day in advance. Remove from the refrigerator 10 minutes before serving.

COOK'S NOTE

If you cannot find fresh horseradish, you can substitute ¼ cup/60 ml drained extra-hot prepared horseradish.

LEMON HORSERADISH BUTTER

Every cook who looks for ways to perk up weeknight meals or make spur-of-the-moment entertaining easier ought to have a roll of flavored butter in his or her freezer. Just think: Grill a steak or a piece of fish and finish it with a slice of this horseradish butter. Roast some fingerling potatoes and dab them with the butter. Put it on a humble baked potato to dress up. Soften the butter, spread it on crostini, and top it with a slice of smoked salmon for an instant appetizer. Having this kind of homemade food on hand takes cooking from good to great.

MAKES ONE 8-IN/20-CM LOG, ABOUT 1½ CUPS/260 G

2-by-1-in/5-by-2.5-cm piece horseradish root, peeled and cut into small chunks

Freshly grated zest of 1 lemon

1 tsp kosher or fine sea salt

1 cup/225 g unsalted butter, at room temperature

2 tbsp minced fresh flat-leaf parsley

1   In a food processor fitted with the metal blade, process the horseradish until finely grated. Scatter the lemon zest and salt over the top and pulse once or twice until evenly distributed. Add the butter and process until smooth, creamy, and well combined. Add the parsley and pulse just until evenly distributed.

2   Lay a long sheet of parchment paper or plastic wrap on a work surface. Using a rubber spatula, spread the butter into a long, rough log about 1½ in/4 cm in diameter. Wrap the parchment snugly around the log and, using your palms, roll the log back and forth to shape it into a smooth, uniform cylinder. Twist both ends like a candy wrapper to seal them closed. Refrigerate for up to 3 days in the refrigerator or in the freezer for up to 3 months.

HORSERADISH VINAIGRETTE

I developed this vinaigrette for the Smoked Whitefish Salad with Horseradish Vinaigrette on page 153, and then I started thinking about how amazing it would be on a grilled steak salad or tossed with Simple Roasted Beets (page 45). Adjust the amount of horseradish to taste. Two tablespoons seems like the right balance to me, enough to give a real kick of heat and open the nasal passages without making you cry.

MAKES ABOUT ⅔ CUP/165 ML

¼ cup/60 ml extra-virgin olive oil

¼ cup/60 ml fresh lemon juice

2 tbsp Prepared Horseradish (page 157 or store-bought, extra-hot)

Freshly grated zest of 1 lemon

½ tsp kosher or fine sea salt

½ tsp freshly ground pepper

1 tbsp finely chopped fresh dill

In a small jar with a tight-fitting lid, combine the oil, lemon juice, horseradish, lemon zest, salt, and pepper. Cover tightly and shake vigorously to blend. Taste and adjust the seasoning. Stir in the dill. Use immediately, or cover and refrigerate until ready to use. The dressing can be made up to 1 day in advance.

HORSERADISH AND BEET GRAVLAX

One of the most delicate and simple salmon preparations is gravlax, a Scandinavian specialty in which the fish is cured in a salt-and-sugar rub. No cooking is involved. I like to think of these paper-thin slices of raw fish as one step beyond Japanese sashimi. Typically, gravlax is seasoned with fresh dill, a brandy such as Cognac, and spruce sprigs. However, in this variation, raw grated beets and fresh horseradish are mixed together and spread on top of the salt cure. The horseradish subtly flavors the salmon and the beets penetrate the top of the flesh, coloring the surface with a ruby glow. It is divine in looks and taste and is simply gorgeous when sliced! Serve the salmon with buttered pumpernickel and thin cucumber slices as appetizers or a first course. The salmon can be garnished with chopped chives, green onions, capers, or with minced shallots.

SERVES 10 AS A FIRST COURSE OR 20 AS AN APPETIZER

½ cup/75 g coarse sea salt or kosher salt

½ cup/100g firmly packed light brown sugar

1 salmon fillet, 2 to 4 lb/ 910 g to 1.2 kg, skin on and pin bones removed

1½ cups/200 g trimmed, peeled, and grated raw beets (from about 8 oz/225 g beets)

1 cup/240 ml Prepared Horse-radish (page 157 or store-bought, extra-hot)

¼ cup/60 ml vodka

1 Select a large rimmed baking sheet and a wire rack that fits inside the baking sheet and is as close as possible to the length of the fish. Cover the rack with a doubled layer of cheesecloth, allowing enough overhang on the sides and length of the rack to fold over and cover the fish completely.

2 In a small bowl, stir together the salt and sugar. Spread half of the mixture on the skin side of the salmon, packing it into place. Lay the salmon, skin-side down, on the cheesecloth. Gently rub the remaining salt mixture over the flesh side of the fillet.

3 In a medium bowl, mix together the beets and horseradish until thoroughly combined. Spread the beet mixture over the top and sides of the salmon fillet. Slowly drizzle the vodka over the fish, being careful not to rinse off the beet and salt cure.

4 Bring up the sides of the cheesecloth and wrap them snugly around the fish. Fold the overhanging ends toward the center. Now seal the entire fillet in a large sheet of plastic wrap. Once secured, arrange the fillet, flesh-side up, on the rack. Select a slightly smaller rimmed baking sheet or baking dish and place it on top of the fish. Put something that weighs about 3 lb/ 1.4 kg in the sheet pan. I use full beer bottles set on their sides. Place the weighted salmon in the refrigerator for at least 2 days or up to 5 days. Turn the packaged salmon once a day, being sure to return the weight(s) after each turn. (Gravlax will keep for up to 1 week in the refrigerator. To freeze the gravlax, wrap in plastic wrap and then in a double layer of aluminum foil and place in the freezer for up to 3 months. Thaw overnight in the refrigerator before serving.)

5 Scrape the cure off the flesh side of the fillet. Skin the fillet, and then cut crosswise into thin slices. Arrange the slices on a platter and serve.

SMOKED WHITEFISH SALAD
WITH HORSERADISH VINAIGRETTE

I grew up eating smoked whitefish, smoked sable, and lox. It was a traditional Sunday brunch for my family, along with toasted bagels, cream cheese, and scrambled eggs. This salad is an extension of all those flavors I crave. Serve it as a smoked fish salad for brunch or mound it on rye bread crostini for an appetizer. It would also pair with crisp Belgian endive leaves: spoon a small mound into the broad end of the canoe-shaped leaves.

SERVES 4 TO 6

1 lb/455 g smoked whitefish, skin and bones removed, then flaked

1 medium cucumber, about 8 oz/225 g, ends trimmed, halved lengthwise, seeded, and cut into ¼-in/6-mm dice

⅓ cup/30 g finely chopped green onions, including green tops

⅔ cup/165 ml Horseradish Vinaigrette (page 150)

In a large bowl, toss together the flaked whitefish, cucumber, and green onion. Give the vinaigrette a last-minute shake, pour over the salad, and toss well. Cover and refrigerate for 1 hour to allow the flavors to meld before serving. (The smoked fish, cucumber, and green onion can be tossed together a day in advance, but do not add the dressing until 2 hours before you plan to serve the salad. If you add the dressing sooner, the water from the cucumber will dilute it.)

SAUTÉED HORSERADISH GNOCCHI

This dish is inspired by The Best Gnocchi, a recipe in Andrew Carmellini's *Urban Italian*. It's hard for me to resist making a celebrated chef's recipe when he or she calls it "the best." Indeed, Carmellini's light and airy pillows of potato goodness are deserving of the description. Riffing off his recipe, I wanted to up the ante with the addition of fresh horseradish. For those horseradish lovers out there, these are for you. The dough can be made, cut, and boiled up to 2 hours in advance, covered, and left at room temperature. Sauté the gnocchi just before serving.

SERVES 4 TO 6

GNOCCHI

2 lb/910 g russet potatoes

1½ cups/190 g all-purpose flour

1½ cups/340 g lightly packed grated horseradish

1 large egg, beaten

2 tbsp freshly grated Parmesan cheese, preferably Parmigiano-Reggiano

1 tbsp extra-virgin olive oil

1 tbsp unsalted butter, melted

1 tbsp plus 1 tsp kosher or fine sea salt

¼ tsp freshly ground pepper

2 tbsp unsalted butter, plus more as needed

1 tbsp extra-virgin olive oil, plus more as needed

Kosher or fine sea salt

2 tbsp finely snipped fresh chives

Freshly grated Parmesan cheese, preferably Parmigiano-Reggiano, for serving

1 To make the gnocchi, position a rack in the center of the oven and preheat to 425°F/220°C/gas 7.

2 Prick each potato several times with a fork and place them on a baking sheet. Place the baking sheet in the oven and bake the potatoes until they are tender enough to be easily pierced with a paring knife, about 1 hour. Remove the potatoes from the oven and set aside until they are just cool enough to handle but still very hot, 5 to 10 minutes.

3 Cut the potatoes in half lengthwise and scoop the flesh from the skins. Discard the skins. Pass the flesh through a food mill or ricer into a large bowl. Add 1 cup/130 g of the flour, the horseradish, egg, Parmesan, oil, melted butter, the 1 tsp of salt, and the pepper. Using your hands, gently fold the ingredients together, working the dough just until it is combined. Shape the dough into a large ball, adding more flour if it seems too moist; the dough should be slightly tacky but not sticky.

4 Transfer the dough to a floured work surface. Lightly flour a rimmed baking sheet. Cut off a baseball-size hunk of dough and roll it between your hands to form a ball. Then, using your palms, roll the ball back and forth on the floured surface into a skinny log, ¾ in/2 cm in diameter and about 15 in/38 cm long. Cut the log crosswise into pieces about 1 in/2.5 cm long and place the pieces on the floured baking sheet. Cover the baking sheet with plastic wrap so the gnocchi do not dry out while you roll and cut the remaining dough the same way.

5 Fill an 8- to 10-qt/7.5- to 9.4-L stockpot two-thirds full of water, add the remaining 1 tbsp salt and bring to a rolling boil over high heat. Add the gnocchi and stir gently once or twice so they don't stick together. After 1 or 2 minutes, the gnocchi will bob to the surface; wait for 1 minute longer and then, using a slotted spoon, transfer the gnocchi to a large platter.

6 In a large sauté pan, melt the butter with the oil over medium heat and swirl to coat the pan bottom. Add about one-third of the gnocchi; they should fit in a single layer without crowding. Sauté, turning as needed, until the gnocchi are golden brown on all sides, 6 to 8 minutes. Transfer the gnocchi to a rimmed baking sheet, cover loosely with foil, and place them in the oven. (The oven should still be warm from baking the potatoes. If you have boiled the gnocchi in advance, preheat the oven to 250°F/120°C/gas ½ before you begin sautéing.) Sauté the remaining gnocchi in the same way, adding more butter and oil to the pan as needed.

7 Sprinkle the gnocchi with salt and with the chives and toss gently to mix. Divide the gnocchi among warmed individual plates and shower with Parmesan. Serve immediately.

PRIME RIB OF BEEF WITH HORSERADISH CREAM

Serving a prime rib, or standing rib roast, for a special occasion or holiday meal makes a spectacular presentation. You may quiver at the price of the roast but you'll be relaxed and confident in the kitchen because a prime rib is easy to cook. All you have to do is season the meat and roast it. I like my prime rib with a crusty, highly seasoned exterior, a uniformly rosy pink interior, and a full-bodied, creamy horseradish sauce on the side. If you have both beef and sauce left over, slather the sauce on whole-grain bread and pile high with thin slices of cold roast beef for a memorable sandwich.

SERVES 10 TO 12

5-bone prime rib roast of beef, about 10 lb/4.5 kg, bones removed and tied back onto the roast

½ cup/75 g kosher salt or flaky sea salt

12 garlic cloves, finely chopped

2 tsp freshly ground coarse pepper

Horseradish Cream or Prepared Horseradish (facing page)

1 Remove the prime rib from the refrigerator 2 hours before you plan to roast so that it will be at room temperature when it goes into the oven. Trim off the fat from the roast, leaving an even layer ½ in/12 cm thick. (A thin layer of fat protects and bastes the beef while it roasts.) In a small bowl, combine the salt, garlic, and pepper. Rub the salt mixture all over the roast, especially in any spaces between the meat and the bones, covering it with a thick layer. Lay the roast, bone-side down, in a shallow roasting pan. The rib bones act as a natural rack, eliminating the need to use a wire rack. Cover the roast loosely with plastic wrap and let it stand at room temperature until you are ready to cook it.

2 About 30 minutes prior to roasting the beef, position a rack in the center of the oven and preheat to 450°F/230°C/gas 8.

3 Roast the beef, uncovered, for 30 minutes. Reduce the heat to 300°F/150°C/gas 2, but do not open the oven door. After roasting the beef for an additional hour begin checking the roast for doneness with an instant-read thermometer, inserting it into the center of the roast away from bone or fat pockets. The roast is ready when the thermometer registers 115° to 120°F/45° to 48°C for rare, 125° to 130°F/51° to 54°C for medium-rare, or 130° to 140°F/54° to 60°C for medium. (Keep in mind that the temperature of the meat will rise another 5° to 10°F/3° to 6°C when the meat is resting, which is why I like to pull my roast when it reaches 115°F/45°C.) The prime rib may be done in 2 to 2¼ hours (which was the case for a 10-lb/4.5-kg prime rib roast cooked to 115°F/45°C), or it may take a little longer, depending on your oven, the exact weight of the meat, and the desired level of doneness.

4 Transfer the meat to a carving board, tent with aluminum foil, and let rest for at least 20 minutes to allow the juices to set.

5 Remove the twine that held the rib bones to the meat. Use a carving fork to hold the roast in place. Slice the meat across the grain into the thickness you prefer. Cut between the rib bones to separate them and then offer the bones to any bone-loving guests. Accompany the roast with the horseradish cream.

HORSERADISH CREAM

Count me in as a horseradish lover and connoisseur. No bottled stuff for me. I make my own horseradish cream, and here I am offering up my all-time favorite recipe. You can vary the pungency by increasing or reducing the amount of horseradish. I serve this with roast beef, poached salmon, and even spoon it over a baked potato.

MAKES ABOUT 1 CUP/240 ML

1 cup/240 ml sour cream

¼ cup/55 g lightly packed grated horseradish, plus more if desired

1 tsp fresh lemon juice

1 tsp Dijon mustard

½ tsp kosher or fine sea salt

In a small bowl, combine the sour cream, horseradish, lemon juice, mustard, and salt and mix well. Taste and adjust the seasoning, and add more horseradish if desired. Cover and refrigerate for at least 1 hour to allow the flavors to meld. It will keep for up to 3 days in the refrigerator.

PREPARED HORSERADISH

I have tears of joy every time I make this recipe, because it reminds me of holiday dinners at my grandparents' home. To keep from shedding buckets of tears, please read the Cautionary Note on page 148 before you begin.

MAKES ABOUT 1 CUP/120 ML

8 oz/225 g horseradish root, peeled and cut into chunks

½ cup/120 ml white wine vinegar

2 tbsp water

2 tbsp granulated sugar

½ tsp kosher or fine sea salt

In a food processor fitted with the metal blade, process the horseradish until finely grated. Add the vinegar, water, sugar, and salt and process until a thick paste forms. Transfer to a covered container and refrigerate overnight to allow the flavors to meld. It will keep in the refrigerator for up to 1 month.

JERUSALEM ARTICHOKE

Helianthus tuberosus

SUNCHOKE / SUNFLOWER CHOKE / TOPINAMBUR *(ITALIAN)* / TOPINAMBOUR *(FRENCH)*

HISTORY AND LORE Indigenous to North America, the Jerusalem artichoke, a member of the aster (or sunflower) family (Asteraceae), was cultivated by Native Americans before the arrival of the Europeans. It became popular with the early settlers and was taken by seafarers to France at the beginning of the seventeenth century. These nutrient-rich tubers were favorably received and spread throughout Europe as an important food, until the potato gained popularity in the mid-eighteenth century.

The name of this root is confusing, and there is much speculation as to its origin, since it does not come from Jerusalem and is not a type of artichoke, though both are members of the aster family. One suggested source was an early-seventeenth-century description of the tuber by the explorer Samuel de Champlain, who described its flavor as tasting like an artichoke. The suggested explanation for the word *Jerusalem* is that it is an English corruption of the Italian word *girasole* and the Spanish *gerasol*, both of which mean "sunflower." However, it is also suggested that *Jerusalem* is a corruption of Terneuzen, a city in the Netherlands from which the tubers were introduced to England. The overwhelming popularity of the potato reduced these oddly named vegetables to a minor crop in most parts of the world. Today, however, with the proliferation of farmers' markets and specialty growers and the interest of chefs, these crisp, sweet, nutty-tasting tubers are making their way back into the U.S. culinary repertoire.

VARIETIES Jerusalem artichokes are the edible, fleshy underground stem tubers of a frost-hardy deciduous perennial herb that grows up to 6 feet/2 meters in height and has yellow sunflowerlike flowers.

You are likely to find two kinds of Jerusalem artichoke in the market: the roundish western sunchoke, which is pale beige and plump; and the midwestern or northeastern type, which is long and knobby with reddish skin. More than a dozen popular cultivars exist, however. Here are just five of them.

Fuseau A traditional favorite of French growers, the white-fleshed tubers are long and smooth with no knobs, making them easy to clean or peel.

Jacks Copperclad Dark coppery purple tubers with great taste.

Mulles Rose Large white tubers with rose-purple eyes.

Stampede A common early-season cultivar that produces particularly large tubers.

Sun Choke An easy-to-grow cultivar with white flesh and a very nutty taste.

NUTRITION These tubers are carbohydrate rich and low in calories (32 calories per 3½-ounce/100-gram serving), with high levels of potassium and phosphorus. They are a significant source of iron, thiamine, and vitamin C and are high in dietary fiber, which helps reduce blood cholesterol and lessens the incidence of colon cancer. They are also a good potato substitute for diabetics and those on a low-carb diet.

AVAILABILITY AND SELECTION Although available year-round, Jerusalem artichokes are at their best from late fall to midwinter. Some varieties are left in the ground over the winter and harvested in the spring. The tubers should be very firm and free of blemishes, soft spots, or signs of sprouting. Choose tubers of the same size so they will finish cooking at the same time.

STORAGE Wait to wash Jerusalem artichokes until just prior to use. To store them, wrap in a paper towel, place in a loosely sealed plastic bag, and refrigerate for up to 2 weeks.

BASIC USE AND PREPARATION Jerusalem artichokes can be eaten raw or cooked. Used raw, they can be grated, sliced, or julienned and added to salads. If you opt to cook them, they can be steamed, boiled, roasted like potatoes, or baked in a gratin. When sliced, cubed, or diced, they can be sautéed slowly until crisp-tender, or they can be stir-fried like water chestnuts for a crisp crunch. For puréed soups or mashes, cut them into chunks and simmer until soft enough to purée.

To prepare Jerusalem artichokes, wash the tubers thoroughly to remove any dirt stuck in the knobs and then scrub them clean using a vegetable brush. To peel them, blanch them in boiling water for 2 to 3 minutes, drain, rinse under cool running water, and then peel with a paring knife. They can be eaten with their skins on, as well, though the skins are less appealing when the tubers are mashed for purées or soups. If using raw, sprinkle the tubers with a little lemon juice or white wine vinegar as you cut them to prevent discoloration.

A CAUTIONARY NOTE Although Jerusalem artichokes are indeed a nutritious food and good alternative to potatoes, one caveat must not be overlooked. The storage carbohydrate in Jerusalem artichokes is not starch but inulin (not to be confused with insulin), which is not digested or absorbed in the stomach. It is known to cause bloating, stomachaches, and flatulence in some people. In June 2010, a study published in the *Journal of the American Dietetic Association* reported that most subjects experienced little discomfort—most often minor bloating, gas, and stomach cramps—but some subjects could tolerate only the smallest amount of inulin. This is not new news! In 1621, English botanist John Goodyer, in an edition of Gerard's *Herbal*, wrote: "which way soever they be dressed and eaten, they stir and cause a filthy loathsome stinking wind within the body, thereby causing the belly to be pained and tormented, and are a meat more fit for swine than men."

YIELDS

14 to 16 small Jerusalem artichokes = 1 lb/455 g

10 medium Jerusalem artichokes = 1 lb/455 g

8 large Jerusalem artichokes = 1 lb/455 g

1 lb/455 g Jerusalem artichokes, peeled and thinly sliced = 3 cups/400 g

PICKLED JERUSALEM ARTICHOKES

Looking for a wintertime pickling project? Think about Jerusalem artichokes. They deliver the desired crunch and bite of other pickles, but you put them up long after canning season is over. It's a lazy-day weekend cooking project, requiring not much time and delivering delicious results.

MAKES TWO 1-PT/480-ML JARS

1 lb/455 g Jerusalem artichokes, peeled and cut into rounds ¼ in/ 6 mm thick

4 fresh thyme sprigs

1½ cups/360 ml white wine vinegar

½ cup/120 ml water

2 tbsp honey

1 tsp peppercorns

1 tsp fennel seeds

½ tsp yellow mustard seeds

1 Wash two 1-pt/480-ml heatproof glass jars with tight-fitting lids in hot, soapy water and dry thoroughly. Alternatively, run the jars through the regular cycle of your dishwasher and wash the lids by hand.

2 Pack the prepared jars half full with the Jerusalem artichokes. Nestle two thyme sprigs in each jar, spacing them evenly down the sides of the jars. Fill the jars with the rest of the Jerusalem artichokes.

3 In a medium saucepan, combine the vinegar, water, honey, peppercorns, fennel seeds, and mustard seeds and bring to a boil over high heat, stirring constantly until the honey dissolves. Boil the pickling liquid for 1 minute and remove from the heat.

4 Using a wide-mouthed funnel, ladle or pour the hot pickling liquid into the jars, covering the Jerusalem artichokes completely and leaving ½-in/12-mm headspace. Wipe the rims clean and attach the lids. Let stand at room temperature until cool.

5 Place the jars in the refrigerator for at least 5 days before using to allow the flavors to permeate the Jerusalem artichokes. The Jerusalem artichokes will keep in the refrigerator for up to 1 month.

JERUSALEM ARTICHOKE SOUP

It's the smooth, deeply earthy taste of Jerusalem artichokes that makes this soup taste so creamy and rich. Only a small amount of cream is added to finish the soup, which owes its full-flavored nuttiness to the reddish-skinned, knobby tuber. Of course, it doesn't hurt that the vegetables are sautéed in a little bacon fat! The soup is filling, so serving it in small portions is advised.

MAKES ABOUT 6 CUPS/1.4 L; SERVES 8

10 peppercorns

1 bay leaf

4 fresh sage sprigs

4 fresh thyme sprigs

1 tbsp extra-virgin olive oil

2 oz/55 g thick-cut bacon, cut crosswise into strips ¼ in/6 mm wide

2 large garlic cloves, smashed with the side of a chef's knife and roughly chopped

1 large leek, 8 oz/225 g, white and light green part only, halved lengthwise and thinly sliced crosswise into half-moons

1 large celery rib, 4 oz/115 g, thinly sliced

1 lb/455 g Jerusalem artichokes, unpeeled, cut into ½-in/12-mm chunks

1 small russet potato, about 5 oz/140 g, peeled and cut into 1-in/2.5-cm chunks

1 tbsp kosher or fine sea salt

4 cups/960 ml homemade chicken stock or canned low-sodium chicken broth

¼ cup/60 ml heavy whipping cream

Freshly ground white pepper

1   Cut an 8-in/20-cm square of cheesecloth and place the peppercorns, bay leaf, sage, and thyme in the center. Bring up the edges to form a bag and tie securely with kitchen twine to make a bouquet garni. Set aside.

2   Line a plate with paper towels. In a 4- to 6-qt/3.8- to 5.7-L saucepan, heat the oil over medium heat and swirl to coat the pan bottom. Add the bacon and fry, stirring often, until the bacon is browned and crisp, about 5 minutes. Using a slotted spoon, transfer to the paper-lined plate and reserve for garnish.

3   Add the garlic, leek, and celery to the bacon fat in the pan and sauté over medium heat, stirring frequently, until softened but not browned, about 5 minutes. Add the Jerusalem artichokes, potato, salt, stock, and the bouquet garni and bring to a boil. Reduce the heat to a simmer and cook uncovered, using a large spoon to skim off the foam that occasionally rises to the top, until the Jerusalem artichokes and potato are tender when pierced with a fork, about 35 minutes. Remove from the heat, discard the bouquet garni, and let cool slightly.

4   Working in batches, purée the soup in a blender or food processor. Return the puréed soup to the saucepan, place over low heat, add the cream, and season with white pepper. Warm the soup until steaming hot. Do not allow to boil. Taste and adjust the seasoning. (The soup can be prepared up to 3 days in advance. Let cool, transfer to a covered container, and refrigerate. Rewarm over low heat just before serving.)

5   Ladle the soup into a warmed tureen or individual soup bowls. Garnish with the bacon and serve immediately.

WINTER GREENS, SUNCHOKES, CARROTS, FENNEL, AND RADISHES WITH GRAINY-MUSTARD VINAIGRETTE

Inspired by a salad I ate at Grüner, an Alsatian restaurant in Portland, Oregon, owned by Chris Israel, I use raw Jerusalem artichokes and other winter roots to give this salad color and crunch. I simplified the garnish by buying roasted and salted pumpkin seeds for scattering on top, but Chris turns homemade soft pretzels into croutons and tosses them with the salad. That's easy enough to do if you make your own, happen to live in a big city with soft pretzels sold on street corners, or want to buy frozen soft pretzels and bake them. All you'll need to do is cut them into small chunks and dry them in the oven until crisp. It's a novel alternative with an extra kick from the coarse, crunchy pretzel salt.

SERVES 6 TO 8

DRESSING

½ cup/120 ml extra-virgin olive oil

2 tbsp balsamic vinegar

2 tsp whole-grain mustard

1 tsp granulated sugar

1 tsp kosher or fine sea salt

Freshly ground pepper

10 oz/280 g tender inner leaves curly endive, torn into bite-size pieces

5 oz/140 g baby arugula

1 fennel bulb, about 10 oz/280 g, trimmed, quartered lengthwise, cored, and thinly sliced lengthwise

8 oz/225 g Jerusalem artichokes, peeled and thinly sliced

1 bunch radishes, about 8 oz/225 g, root ends and tops trimmed and cut crosswise into paper-thin rounds

2 small carrots, about 4 oz/115 g, trimmed, peeled, and cut crosswise into paper-thin rounds

½ cup/70 g salted roasted pumpkin seeds

1 To make the dressing, in a small bowl or measuring cup, combine the oil, vinegar, mustard, sugar, and salt. Season with pepper and whisk to combine. Taste and adjust the seasoning. Set aside until ready to toss the salad.

2 In a very large bowl, toss together the endive, arugula, fennel, Jerusalem artichokes, radishes, and carrots. (The salad components can be assembled up to 2 hours in advance, covered with damp paper towels, and then covered with plastic wrap and refrigerated until ready to serve.)

3 Whisk the dressing briefly, then pour over the salad. Toss gently and divide among individual salad plates. Garnish with the pumpkin seeds and serve immediately.

SAUTÉED JERUSALEM ARTICHOKES

A simple sauté of thinly sliced Jerusalem artichokes is an ideal side dish—nourishing, hearty, easy to prepare—for fall and winter meals. The big hit of garlic here will be a delight for garlic lovers, though others may want to use less.

SERVES 4 AS A SIDE DISH

1 lb/455 g Jerusalem artichokes

Kosher or fine sea salt

2 tbsp extra-virgin olive oil

6 large garlic cloves, thinly sliced

1 tbsp chopped fresh
flat-leaf parsley

1 tsp fresh lemon juice

¼ tsp freshly ground pepper

1 Fill a 6-qt/5.7-L saucepan two-thirds full of water. Add the Jerusalem artichokes and 1 tsp salt, cover partially, and bring to a boil over high heat. Reduce the heat to a simmer and cook, uncovered, until the Jerusalem artichokes are just tender when pierced with a knife, about 15 minutes.

2 Meanwhile, have ready a large bowl of ice water. As the Jerusalem artichokes become tender (they may not all be ready at the same time), using tongs or a slotted spoon, transfer them to the ice water to cool. When completely cool, drain and pat dry. Slice into rounds ¼ in/6 mm thick.

3 In a large sauté pan, heat the oil over medium-high heat and swirl to coat the pan bottom. Add the Jerusalem artichokes, sprinkle with a little salt, and sauté until golden brown, about 5 minutes. Add the garlic and continue sautéing until it just begins to turn golden brown around the edges, about 2 minutes. Add the parsley, lemon juice, and pepper and toss to coat. Taste and adjust the seasoning. Serve immediately.

ROASTED JERUSALEM ARTICHOKES WITH LEMON, ROSEMARY, AND GARLIC

You don't need to peel Jerusalem artichokes. In fact, especially when roasted, the peels add delicious flavor, color, and texture. Once you have sliced Jerusalem artichokes, work quickly to toss with oil and lemon so they don't discolor.

SERVES 4 AS A SIDE DISH

1 lb/455 g Jerusalem artichokes, unpeeled, cut into slices ¼ in/
6 mm thick

1 medium lemon, cut crosswise into thin slices

12 garlic cloves, peeled but left whole

2 tbsp extra-virgin olive oil

2 tsp minced fresh rosemary

1 tsp kosher or fine sea salt

1 Position a rack in the center of the oven and preheat to 375°F/190°C/gas 5.

2 In a large roasting pan, toss together the Jerusalem artichokes, lemon slices, garlic, oil, rosemary, and salt. Spread them evenly in the pan. Roast, stirring once or twice, until the Jerusalem artichokes are golden brown and tender when pierced with a knife, about 35 minutes. Serve immediately.

PAN-ROASTED JERUSALEM ARTICHOKES AND BUTTERNUT SQUASH

The sweetness of butternut squash not only balances the earthiness of Jerusalem artichokes, but also brightens the appearance of this side dish, lending an autumn hue to these pan-roasted vegetables. It is a good accompaniment to roast pork loin, beef brisket, or pot roast. But it is also hardy enough to stand on its own as a vegetarian main course with a quick sauté of leafy, dark greens, such as Tuscan kale or Swiss chard.

SERVES 4 TO 6

3 tbsp canola or other neutral oil

1 lb/455 g Jerusalem artichokes, unpeeled, cut into slices ½ in/ 12 mm thick

1 butternut squash, about 1¾ lb/800 g, halved lengthwise, seeded, peeled, and cut into 2-in/5-cm chunks

½ tsp kosher or fine sea salt

1 leek, white and light green part only, thinly sliced (about 1½ cups/130 g)

¼ cup/60 ml maple syrup

3 tbsp water

2 tbsp soy sauce

⅛ tsp Asian sesame oil

1 tsp sesame seeds, toasted (see Cook's Note, page 64)

1 Position a rack in the center of the oven and preheat to 375°F/190°C/gas 5.

2 In a large ovenproof sauté pan, heat the canola oil over medium-high heat. Add the Jerusalem artichokes and squash and sauté, stirring frequently, until the edges are golden brown, 8 to 10 minutes. Stir in the salt, transfer the pan to the oven, and roast the vegetables, uncovered, until fork-tender and caramelized, about 10 minutes.

3 Return the pan to the stove top over medium heat, remembering that the handle of the pan is very hot. Add the leek, maple syrup, water, soy sauce, and sesame oil and cook, stirring frequently, until the sauce thickens to a glaze, about 8 minutes. Transfer to a warmed serving bowl. Garnish with the sesame seeds and serve immediately.

JERUSALEM ARTICHOKE AND ARTICHOKE HEART LINGUINE

Despite their names and their common family, the Jerusalem artichoke and the globe artichoke aren't at all alike—one is a tuber, the other a thistle. Yet, flavorwise, they relate perfectly in this pasta dish. Add some slivers of red onion, lots of garlic, a kick of red pepper flakes, a squeeze of lemon juice, and a shower of thinly sliced fresh mint and you have a boldly seasoned pasta dish worthy of serving to company yet easy enough for a family meal.

SERVES 4 TO 6

1 tbsp kosher or fine sea salt, plus 1 tsp

1 lb/455 g dried linguine

3 tbsp extra-virgin olive oil

1 lb/455 g Jerusalem artichokes, cut on the diagonal into slices ¼ in/6 mm thick

¼ tsp freshly ground pepper

⅛ tsp red pepper flakes

1 small red onion, thinly sliced

One 14-oz/400-g can quartered artichoke hearts in water, drained and patted dry

6 large garlic cloves, thinly sliced

1 tsp fresh lemon juice

¼ cup/15 g thinly sliced fresh mint

Freshly grated Pecorino Romano cheese for garnish

1 Fill a large pot two-thirds full of water, add the 1 tbsp salt, and bring to a boil over high heat. Add the pasta and stir. Cook the pasta until al dente (cooked through but still slightly chewy), 7 to 8 minutes.

2 While the pasta water is heating and pasta is cooking, in a large sauté pan, heat the oil over medium-high heat and swirl to coat the pan bottom. Add the Jerusalem artichokes, the remaining 1 tsp salt, the pepper, and red pepper flakes and sauté until the Jerusalem artichokes begin to brown on the edges, about 5 minutes. Add the onion and sauté until translucent, about 5 minutes more. Add the artichoke hearts and garlic and continue sautéing until the artichoke hearts are heated through and the garlic is soft but not brown, about 3 minutes. Add the lemon juice and toss to coat.

3 When the pasta is ready, drain it in a colander, reserving 1 cup/240 ml of the cooking water. Add the pasta and the mint to the sauté pan and toss to combine with the Jerusalem artichoke mixture. Add just enough of the reserved pasta water, a little at a time, as needed to moisten. Taste and adjust the seasoning. Divide the pasta among warmed individual bowls and shower with the cheese. Serve immediately.

JICAMA

Pachyrhizus erosus

YAM BEAN / MEXICAN POTATO OR **POTATO BEAN / SHAGE** *(MANDARIN CHINESE)* **/**
SHA KOT *(CANTONESE)* **/ JICAMA DE AGUA** OR **JICAMA DE LECHE** *(SPANISH)*

HISTORY AND LORE A member of the legume family (Fabaceae or Leguminosae), jicama is an herbaceous, climbing annual with a single thick, smooth or lobed edible tuber. The erect flower clusters develop edible pods, though only the young ones can be cooked and eaten, because once mature, the pods are poisonous. Researching this root by its botanical name clarifies the confusion caused by the same plant being labeled jicama in English-language texts on food plants and yam bean in books that focus on Asian food plants. Jicama grew wild in Mexico and Central America and was cultivated in ancient times by the Aztec and Maya. In the seventeenth century, the Spaniards introduced it to the Philippines, from which it spread farther into Asia and the Pacific and then to western Africa.

VARIETIES Three species of the genus *Pachyrhizus* have been domesticated, but you will only see the best known and most widely cultivated Mexican species, *P. erosus*, sold in supermarkets and in Latin American and Asian markets. For clarity and completeness, it is interesting to note the two other species: *P. ahipa*, or Andean yam bean, and *P. tuberosus*, or Amazonian yam bean.

NUTRITION Enjoy the crunch and sweet juiciness of jicama, because it is a dieter's choice, with only 41 calories for each 4-ounce/115-gram serving. It is high in dietary fiber and is a good source of vitamin C and potassium. These tubers store the carbohydrate inulin instead of starch, which contributes to its sweet flavor. (See pages 160 and 280 for more information on inulin.)

AVAILABILITY AND SELECTION Jicama is available year-round at supermarkets, specialty produce stores, and Latin American and Asian markets. Select firm, medium-size roots that feel heavy and dense for their size. The skin should be uniformly light tan and dry, with no blemishes or soft or dark spots. A large jicama can be fibrous and dry, and small ones are harder to peel. Avoid roots with shriveled skin or cracks. (On occasion, I see jicama sold with a waxed coating, which preserves its moisture and freshness. The wax comes off as you peel the jicama.)

STORAGE An uncut jicama will keep in a cool, dry, dark spot for several days or in the refrigerator for 2 to 3 weeks. Do not store it in a plastic bag, as it needs to have air circulating around it to prevent spoilage. Once a jicama is cut, wrap the unused portion tightly in plastic wrap and refrigerate for up to 1 week.

BASIC USE AND PREPARATION Jicama, with a texture similar to an Asian pear, can be served both raw and cooked. Serve raw as crudités, tossed into salads, diced for salsa, or matchstick cut for slaw. It can be blanched briefly to remove some of its floury taste and then tossed into stir-fries much as you would water chestnuts or bamboo shoots. You can also treat it as you would potatoes or sweet potatoes: it can be boiled, steamed, creamed, braised, or diced or chunked for soup.

To prepare jicama, use a paring knife to trim the top and then remove the thin skin. It comes off easily, almost in long strips, exposing the creamy white flesh. The flesh will not discolor, so it can be prepped ahead of time. To brighten the taste of jicama, give it yet more crunch, and remove some of its water, toss cut jicama with a teaspoon or two of salt and place it in a colander in the sink to drain for 30 minutes. Blot dry with paper towels. It is now ready to use for either raw or cooked preparations.

YIELDS

1 small jicama = 12 oz/340 g

1 medium jicama = 1 to 1½ lb/455 to 680 g

1 large jicama = 2 lb or more/910 g or more

8 oz/225 g jicama, peeled and diced = 1½ cups/190 g

8 oz/225 g jicama, peeled and cut into matchsticks (2-in/5-cm strips) = about 1½ cups/190 g

12 oz/340 g jicama, peeled and diced = about 2 cups/300 g

12 oz/340 g jicama, peeled and cut into matchsticks (2-in/5-cm strips) = about 2 cups/300 g

JICAMA, ROASTED CORN, AND BLACK BEAN SALSA

This recipe calls for grilling the corn, which brings out its natural sugars and adds a wonderful caramelized flavor to the salsa. If that step seems too time-consuming, or you aren't planning to fire up a grill for the rest of your meal, here is a simpler alternative: Cut the corn kernels from the cob with a sharp knife and cook them in 2 teaspoons olive oil in a heavy-bottomed frying pan, preferably cast iron, over medium heat until they are caramel brown, about 3 minutes. Be sure to stir frequently so the corn doesn't blacken. Another option is to use a stove-top grill pan and grill the corn as directed for outdoor grilling.

MAKES ABOUT 3 CUPS/720 ML

1 large ear yellow corn, husk on

2 tsp extra-virgin olive oil

1¼ tsp kosher or fine sea salt

Freshly ground pepper

Juice of 2 limes

1 tsp ground cumin

1 tsp ground coriander

2 tsp firmly packed light brown sugar

One 15-oz/430-g can black beans, drained and rinsed

¾ cup/110 g peeled and diced jicama

¼ cup/35 g diced red onion

1 serrano chile, stemmed and finely minced (see Cook's Note, page 40)

2 green onions, including green tops, thinly sliced on the diagonal

⅓ cup/20 g chopped fresh cilantro

1 Prepare a medium-hot fire in a charcoal grill, preheat a gas grill to medium-high, or place a stove-top ridged grill pan over medium-high heat.

2 Pull back the husk from the corn but do not remove it. Remove the silk and brush the kernels with 1 tsp of the oil. Sprinkle the corn lightly with ¼ tsp of the salt and a little pepper. Pull up the husk to re-cover the ear and twist closed at the top.

3 When the grill is ready, put the corn on the grill grate directly over the fire and cover the grill. Cook the corn on the first side for about 5 minutes. Turn the corn over, re-cover the grill, and cook for about 3 minutes. Give the corn one more turn and continue grilling just until the corn begins picking up color without blackening, about 2 minutes longer. Remove the corn from the grill and let cool. Remove the husk from the corn once it is cool enough to handle.

4 Meanwhile, in a medium bowl, whisk together the lime juice, cumin, coriander, brown sugar, and the remaining 1 tsp salt until dissolved. Whisk in the remaining 1 tsp oil.

5 Trim the base of the corn ear so it is even. Stand the ear upright, stem-side down, in a very shallow bowl. (This helps catch the kernels, which otherwise go flying everywhere if cut on a cutting board.) Using a sharp knife, cut downward along the cob, removing the kernels and rotating the ear a quarter turn after each cut. Discard the cob and scoop the kernels into the bowl with the dressing. Add the beans, jicama, red onion, and serrano chile and mix gently to coat with the dressing. Fold in the green onions and cilantro. Taste and adjust the seasoning.

6 Transfer to a serving bowl, cover, and set aside for at least 1 hour before serving to allow the flavors to meld. (This salsa can be prepared up to 2 days in advance. Cover and refrigerate. Remove from the refrigerator 45 minutes before serving.)

BLOOD ORANGE SALAD WITH JICAMA, ARUGULA, AND OIL-CURED OLIVES

This minty citrus salad is a refreshing accompaniment to a wintertime dinner or buffet. Every component of the salad can be prepared and ready to serve well in advance. You can also make the dressing several hours or even a day ahead. Buy washed and ready-to-use arugula or mâche in 5-ounce/140-gram bags. It takes time to cut the jicama and to peel and slice the blood oranges, so get those tasks done ahead. Arrange the oranges on a plate, cover with plastic wrap, and set aside at room temperature until ready to assemble the salad.

SERVES 8

DRESSING

⅓ cup/45 g thinly sliced shallot

¼ cup/60 ml extra-virgin olive oil

¼ cup/60 ml fresh lemon juice

2 tbsp finely minced fresh mint

2 tsp Dijon mustard

1 tsp granulated sugar

1¼ tsp kosher salt

⅛ tsp freshly ground pepper

8 oz/225 g jicama, trimmed, peeled, and cut into matchsticks 2 in/5 cm long and ¼ in/6 mm thick

½ tsp kosher or fine sea salt

8 blood oranges

5 oz/140 g arugula or mâche (about 8 cups lightly packed)

24 oil-cured black olives

Freshly ground pepper

1 To make the dressing, in a small jar with a tight-fitting lid, combine the shallot, oil, lemon juice, mint, mustard, sugar, salt, and pepper. Cover tightly and shake vigorously to blend. Taste and adjust seasoning. Set aside. (The dressing can be made 1 day in advance and refrigerated. Remove from the refrigerator 2 hours before serving.)

2 Meanwhile, toss the jicama with the salt and place in a colander in the sink to drain for 30 minutes. Blot dry with paper towels.

3 Working with one orange at a time, cut a slice from the top and bottom to reveal the flesh. Stand the orange upright and slice away the peel from the sides in wide strips, cutting downward, following the contour of the fruit, and removing all of the white pith. Cut the orange crosswise into slices ¼ in/ 6 mm thick. Repeat with the remaining oranges.

4 Divide the orange slices evenly among individual salad plates, arranging them in a ring and leaving the center open. In a bowl, toss together the arugula and jicama to mix well. Drizzle the dressing over the top and toss to coat evenly. Divide the salad evenly among the plates, mounding a cluster of it in the center of each plate so that it overlaps the oranges slightly. Arrange 3 olives on each plate. Grind a little pepper over each salad. Serve immediately.

COMPOSED JICAMA, AVOCADO, AND GRAPEFRUIT SALAD WITH CILANTRO DRIZZLE

Here is a festive salad in which the tart yet bright taste of grapefruit is combined with creamy slices of avocado and crunchy strips of jicama and then dressed with an herbal, flavor-intensive cilantro vinaigrette. Pair it with chile-rubbed grilled pork, seared scallops, grilled rare tuna, or skewered shrimp.

SERVES 6

1 small jicama, about 12 oz/340 g, trimmed, peeled, and cut into matchsticks 2 in/5 cm long and ¼ in/6 mm thick

1 tsp kosher or fine sea salt

2 medium grapefruit, about 1 lb/455 g each

6 tbsp/90 ml extra-virgin olive oil

1½ tsp granulated sugar

¼ tsp freshly ground pepper

2 cups/115 g loosely packed fresh cilantro leaves

2 large Hass avocadoes, about 8 oz/225 g each, halved, pitted, peeled, and each half cut lengthwise into 6 wedges

Fleur de sel for sprinkling

Chile powder for sprinkling

1 Toss the jicama with ½ tsp of the salt and place it in a colander in the sink to drain for 30 minutes. Blot dry with paper towels.

2 Working with one grapefruit at a time, cut a slice from the top and bottom to reveal the flesh. Stand the grapefruit upright and slice away the peel from the sides in wide strips, cutting downward, following the contour of the fruit, and removing all of the white pith. Holding the grapefruit over a bowl, use a sharp paring knife to cut along both sides of each segment, releasing the segments and allowing the juice and segments to drop into the bowl. Discard any seeds from the segments or that dropped into the bowl. Squeeze any remaining juice from the pith into the bowl. Repeat with the other grapefruit. (This technique is called supreming.) Strain the juice from the grapefruit segments, reserving ¼ cup/60 ml.

3 In a blender, combine the oil, reserved grapefruit juice, sugar, the remaining ½ tsp salt, and the pepper and process until emulsified. Pour ¼ cup/60 ml of the vinaigrette into a medium bowl. Add the prepared jicama to the bowl and toss to coat evenly with the dressing. Set aside.

4 Add the cilantro to the remaining vinaigrette in the blender and process on high speed until the cilantro is completely puréed and the dressing is liquefied, about 30 seconds. Strain the cilantro vinaigrette through a fine-mesh sieve placed over a small bowl. Taste and adjust seasoning.

5 Divide the grapefruit segments and avocado slices evenly among individual salad plates, alternating them in an overlapping ring. Sprinkle each salad with a pinch of fleur de sel. Divide the jicama evenly among the plates, mounding it in the center of each ring. Drizzle the cilantro vinaigrette in a circle over the grapefruit and avocado. Sprinkle a pinch of chile powder over each mound of jicama. Serve immediately.

JICAMA AND WATERMELON SALAD WITH THAI BASIL AND PINK PEPPERCORN VINAIGRETTE

Perfect for a summer picnic, buffet, or potluck, this pretty pink salad has floral overtones from the crushed pink peppercorns. You can crush the peppercorns in a mortar with a pestle, or you can put them in a lock-top plastic bag and pound them with a heavy spoon or the side of a rolling pin. Because the watermelon begins to release water once it is mixed with the vinaigrette, this salad is best made no more than 6 to 8 hours before serving.

SERVES 6

1 small jicama, about 12 oz/340 g, trimmed, peeled, and cut into ½-in/12-mm cubes

1½ tsp kosher or fine sea salt

¼ cup/60 ml extra-virgin olive oil

2 tbsp red wine vinegar

1½ tsp pink peppercorns, coarsely crushed

1 small seedless watermelon, about 3½ lb/1.6 kg, rind removed and cut into ¾-in/2-cm cubes

3 tbsp thinly sliced fresh Thai basil

1 Toss the jicama with ½ tsp of the salt and place in a colander in the sink to drain for 30 minutes. Blot dry with paper towels.

2 In a large bowl, whisk together the oil, vinegar, pink peppercorns, and the remaining 1 tsp salt. Add the watermelon, jicama, and basil and toss to combine. Taste and adjust the seasoning. Transfer to a serving bowl, cover, and refrigerate until ready to serve. Serve chilled.

WINTERTIME JICAMA SLAW

Most folks associate a vegetable slaw with summertime picnics and barbecues. I happen to think of it as a refreshing salad or accompaniment in the winter, especially with all of the seasonal varieties of citrus in the market. This slaw would be a delightful accent to crab cakes or salmon cakes. It would also be good alongside a fish or shrimp dish or grilled or roast pork tenderloin.

SERVES 4

3 tbsp extra-virgin olive oil

Juice of 1 lime

1 tsp Dijon mustard

¾ tsp ground cumin

½ tsp sugar

¾ tsp kosher or fine sea salt

Freshly ground pepper

1 small jicama, 12 oz/340 g, trimmed, peeled, and cut into matchsticks 2 in/5 cm long and ¼ in/6 mm thick

½ small red onion, halved lengthwise and cut into thin wedges

3 satsuma mandarins, peeled, white pith removed, and segmented

⅓ cup/20 g chopped fresh cilantro

1   In a small bowl, whisk together the oil, lime juice, mustard, cumin, sugar, ¾ tsp salt, and a few grinds of pepper. Taste and adjust the seasoning.

2   In a large bowl, combine the jicama, onion, satsumas, and cilantro and toss to mix well. Whisk the dressing briefly, then pour it over the jicama mixture and toss to coat evenly. Taste and adjust with more salt and pepper if needed. Cover and refrigerate for at least 1 hour to allow the flavors to meld. (The slaw can be made up to 1 day in advance.) Remove from the refrigerator 30 minutes before serving. Toss again just before serving.

SHRIMP AND JICAMA CEVICHE

Buy only the freshest shrimp to make ceviche. I like to use the sweet wild pink shrimp from the Gulf Coast, or, when available, the wild shrimp from the Florida Keys. For casual entertaining, mound the ceviche in a festive bowl and accompany with tortilla chips. To serve as a dressed-up first course, spoon into martini or margarita glasses and garnish with a wedge of lime.

SERVES 4 TO 6 AS AN APPETIZER OR FIRST COURSE

12 oz/340 g large (26 to 30 count per 1 lb/455 g) shrimp, peeled, deveined, and cut into ½-in/ 12-mm pieces

¾ cup/180 ml fresh lime juice (about 6 limes)

¾ cup/180 ml fresh lemon juice (about 3 lemons)

1 small jicama, about 12 oz/340 g, trimmed, peeled, and cut into ¼-in/6-mm dice

½ tsp kosher or fine sea salt

1 small jalapeño chile, stemmed, halved lengthwise, seeded, deribbed, and minced (see Cook's Note, page 40)

¾ cup/40 g loosely packed fresh cilantro leaves

4 green onions, including green tops, sliced paper-thin

2 tbsp extra-virgin olive oil

1 In a medium bowl, combine the shrimp, lime juice, and lemon juice. Gently press down on the shrimp to submerge them in the citrus juice. Cover and refrigerate for 45 minutes to 1 hour to "cook" the shrimp in the citrus. Give the shrimp a stir; if they appear opaque throughout, they are ready.

2 Meanwhile, toss the jicama with the salt and place in a colander in the sink to drain for 30 minutes. Blot dry with paper towels.

3 Drain off and discard all but 2 tbsp of the citrus juice from the shrimp. In a medium bowl, toss together the shrimp, reserved citrus juice, jicama, chile, cilantro, green onions, and oil. Transfer to a serving bowl. Serve immediately, or cover and refrigerate for up to 4 hours before serving. Remove from the refrigerator 20 minutes before serving so the ceviche is cold but not refrigerator cold.

SALMON SALAD ROLLS WITH CELLOPHANE NOODLES, JICAMA, AND GREEN ONIONS

Flavorful, healthful, and beautiful to look at, these salad rolls make perfect appetizers, a first course to kick off an Asian meal, or picnic fare for a summer outing. Even though the ingredient list is long, these are quick to put together and easy to assemble. I like to make them when I have leftover grilled salmon in the refrigerator. Green onions and cilantro are perfect with the jicama strips, but I often just use whatever interesting greens or herbs I have on hand, such as watercress, mesclun, and a little mint. Make this dipping sauce—it's terrific—but if you are short on time, bottled peanut sauce will work, too.

MAKES 8 SALAD ROLLS; SERVES 8 AS AN APPETIZER OR FIRST COURSE

HOISIN-PEANUT DIPPING SAUCE

2 tbsp chunky natural peanut butter, warmed slightly to soften

¼ cup/60 ml hoisin sauce

¼ cup/60 ml water

1 tbsp Asian fish sauce

¾ tsp peeled and minced fresh ginger

¼ tsp red pepper flakes

2 tbsp soy sauce

1 tbsp fresh lemon juice

2 tsp peeled and minced fresh ginger

1 tsp honey

One 12-oz/340-g salmon fillet, skin and pin bones removed

8 oz/225 g jicama, trimmed, peeled, and cut into matchsticks 3 in/7.5 cm long and ⅛ in/3 mm thick

½ tsp kosher or fine sea salt

One 2-oz/55-g package bean thread noodles (see Cook's Note)

8 round rice paper wrappers, 8 to 9 in/20 to 23 cm in diameter (see Cook's Note)

4 green onions, including green tops, halved lengthwise and cut into 4-in/10-cm lengths

32 fresh cilantro sprigs

1 To make the dipping sauce, in a small bowl, stir together the peanut butter, hoisin sauce, water, fish sauce, ginger, and red pepper flakes until well blended. Cover and set aside until ready to serve.

2 In a small bowl, stir together the soy sauce, lemon juice, ginger, and honey. Place the salmon in a shallow baking dish just large enough to accommodate it and pour the marinade over the top. Turn the salmon several times until it is well coated with the marinade and then set aside for 20 minutes.

3 Meanwhile, toss the jicama with the salt and place in a colander in the sink to drain for 30 minutes. Blot dry with paper towels.

4 Place the bean thread noodles in a medium bowl, add warm water to cover, and let stand until softened, about 20 minutes. Drain in a colander and then blot dry with paper towels. Set aside.

5 Position an oven rack about 4 in/10 cm from the heat source and preheat the broiler. Remove the salmon from the marinade and discard the marinade. Place the salmon, skinned-side up, on a small, rimmed baking sheet and broil until bronzed, about 3 minutes. Turn the salmon over and broil until it is bronzed on the second side and flakes slightly when nudged with a fork, about 3 minutes. Remove and set aside to cool. When cool enough to handle, cut the salmon into eight long, thin strips.

6 Have ready a large bowl of warm water, a clean, dry linen towel, and a platter. Working with one rice paper wrapper at a time, dip the wrapper in the water for 5 seconds, turning to dampen both sides, and then transfer to the towel. You will use one-eighth of each ingredient for each roll. To assemble the first roll, lay a small portion of jicama, horizontally, on the bottom third of the wrapper. Top with a small mound of noodles, spreading them horizontally. Place a piece of salmon, two pieces of green onion, and two cilantro sprigs horizontally on top. Roll the edge of the wrapper nearest you over the filling, creating a tight cylinder. Roll it half-way over again and then fold in the sides of the cylinder, envelope style. Continue rolling the wrapper into a finished cylinder and place the roll on the platter. Repeat to make seven more rolls. (It is important that all of the ingredients are rolled into a snug cylinder. If it is not snug, the filling will fall apart when you cut or bite into the roll.) Cover the rolls with a damp paper towel and then with plastic wrap and set aside at room temperature until ready to serve. (The salad rolls can be made up to 2 hours ahead.) Cut each salad roll in half on the diagonal. Arrange on a platter or on individual small plates and serve with little bowls of the dipping sauce.

COOK'S NOTE

Bean thread noodles, also called cellophane noodles or glass noodles, are translucent threads made from the starch of mung beans. They have a wonderful texture once softened. Typically, the noodles come in 2-oz/55-g cellophane packets, usually six to eight packets bundled together in a neon pink or clear plastic-mesh bag. Look for them in well-stocked supermarkets or in Asian grocery stores.

Rice paper wrappers (*banh trang*) are sometimes labeled "spring roll wrappers." These are thin, translucent, dried sheets made from ground white rice, water, salt, and usually a little tapioca flour. They come in various sizes and shapes (round, square, or triangular) and are softened in warm water before using. They are typically rolled around fillings and then served fresh or deep-fried. Rice paper wrappers are sold primarily in Asian grocery stores, but many well-stocked supermarkets also carry them.

LOTUS ROOT

Nelumbo nucifera

ASIAN LOTUS / SACRED LOTUS / RENKON *(JAPANESE)* / LIAN OU *(MANDARIN CHINESE)* / LEEN NGAU *(CANTONESE)*

HISTORY AND LORE Lotus root was originally classified in the water lily family (Nymphaeaceae), but it is now recognized as its own family, Nelumbonaceae. This is an important yet nuanced botanical reclassification for a significant plant held sacred by the Buddhists as a symbol of purity. Prized for its rhizomes, blossoms, and seeds, this perennial aquatic plant is native to tropical Asia, the Middle East, and Australia and has been cultivated for more than two thousand years. By around 500 B.C., it was being grown in the Nile Valley for its exceptional beauty, though the poor found greater value in boiling, drying, and grinding the seeds and rhizomes for food. In China, evidence of its cultivation dates to the Han dynasty (207 B.C.–A.D. 220). In India, a golden lotus flower is said to have grown from the navel of the god Vishnu, and in China and Japan, Buddha is often depicted either holding or seated on a lotus blossom.

Both the leaves and the flowers of the lotus plant are prepared as vegetables, and its seeds—more accurately, a one-seeded nut—are eaten as snacks or milled into flour. The rhizomes, which reveal a lacy interior when cut, are sliced for using in many Indian, Chinese, and Southeast Asian specialty dishes. They are also ground and used as a thickener.

VARIETIES The genus *Nelumbo* includes two similar species, both commonly known as lotus. The recipes in this book call for the commercially cultivated Asian species, *N. nucifera*. Its edible parts include the young root (technically rhizome), the flower, the stem, and the leaf. The second species, *N. lutea*, commonly known as water-chinquapin, water-nut, duck acorn, American marsh lotus, and nelumbo, is native to the eastern and southern parts of the United States, from Florida to Texas. Native American women traditionally gathered the roots, roasting them like potatoes and using the seeds in a variety of ways, including grinding them for flour.

NUTRITION Lotus root is low in calories and rich in dietary fiber and potassium. It is also a good source of vitamins C and B_6, phosphorus, magnesium, calcium, and iron.

AVAILABILITY AND SELECTION Rarely will you find fresh whole lotus roots in a supermarket. Instead, head to an Asian market, preferably one that caters to a large Chinese or Japanese population. (On occasion, large Indian markets will sell fresh lotus root; however, I have most often seen it either canned or presliced in vacuum-sealed bags.) It is usually imported from China or Japan and is available year-round. A lotus root forms three or four sections that resemble stiff, plump sausage links separated from one another by narrow joints, often referred to as necks. Examine the lotus root carefully, especially if a joint is broken and you can see the beautiful, distinctive lacy perforations, which should be white with no signs of brownish mold. The roots should be firm, without cracks or soft spots, and have pale brown, smooth, unblemished skin. Buy an entire section or "link" (or more), rather than a cut portion or the precut slices packed in water in vacuum-sealed bags.

STORAGE If you have purchased two or more links, do not separate them. Wrap in damp paper towels, place inside a loosely sealed plastic bag, and refrigerate. Lotus root will keep for up to 2 weeks, though it is best to use it as fresh as possible.

BASIC USE AND PREPARATION Lotus root is used for both sweet and savory dishes. It can be deep-fried to make delicate lacy-looking chips or battered and then deep-fried for tempura. Lotus root can be blanched and pickled, used in salads, stir-fried, braised, simmered with other vegetables, or added to soups. On the sweet side, it can be grated and added to cakes, muffins, or cookies for crunch. It can also be candied and served as a snack or as a garnish for cakes or other desserts.

To prepare lotus root, cut or break into sections at the narrow joints. Trim off and discard the joints that connected them. Wash the links, using a vegetable brush to remove any clinging dirt and then rinse under cool running water. Use a vegetable peeler to remove the thin skin. The flesh will discolor once it is cut, so have a bowl of acidulated water handy (water with a few drops of vinegar or lemon juice added). Slice crosswise with a knife or mandoline. Depending on the recipe, lotus root may need to be blanched or parboiled before it is pickled, stir-fried, braised, or used in a salad.

YIELDS

1 untrimmed, unpeeled medium lotus root section, about 4 in/10 cm long = 6¼ oz/175 g

1 trimmed, peeled medium lotus root section, about 4 in/10 cm long = 5¼ oz/150 g

1 cup trimmed, peeled, and thinly sliced lotus root = 6 oz/170 g

1 cup trimmed, peeled, and grated lotus root = 5 ¼ oz/150 g

BARBARA TROPP'S LEMON-PICKLED LOTUS ROOT

In the late 1980s, I had the good fortune to take cooking classes from Barbara Tropp, a true scholar and master cooking teacher. She wrote two tomes on Chinese cooking and this recipe is adapted from her second cookbook, *China Moon Cookbook*. She loved to create seasoned nuts, pickles, and nibbles and served these snacks at her acclaimed San Francisco Chinese bistro, China Moon. She describes lotus root as "crunchy, sweet, and possessing the beautiful look of a wheel spoked with dewdrops." I think these pickles are especially delicious with grilled skewers of pork or seafood.

MAKES ABOUT ONE 1-QT/960-ML JAR

1 tbsp unseasoned rice vinegar, plus 2 cups/480 ml

1 lb/455 g lotus root

½ cup/100 g granulated sugar

½ tsp red pepper flakes

½ tsp kosher or fine sea salt

⅛ tsp freshly ground pepper

1 tbsp finely julienned lemon zest

1 tbsp peeled and finely julienned fresh ginger

1 Fill a medium bowl two-thirds full with cold water and add the 1 tbsp of vinegar. Trim and peel the lotus root, then cut into slices 1/16 in/2 mm thick. As you cut the lotus root, add the slices to the vinegar water to keep them from discoloring.

2 Fill a medium saucepan two-thirds full with water and bring to a boil over medium-high heat. Drain the lotus root slices, add them to the boiling water, and blanch, stirring occasionally, just until pleasantly crunchy, about 3 minutes. Drain immediately into a colander and rinse under cool running water until completely cooled. Drain thoroughly and blot dry with paper towels.

3 Rinse the saucepan and add to it the remaining 2 cups/480 ml rice vinegar, the sugar, red pepper flakes, salt, pepper, lemon zest, and ginger. Place over medium-high heat and bring to a boil, stirring to dissolve the sugar. Simmer for 1 minute and then remove from the heat. Cover and let stand 5 minutes.

4 Transfer the lotus root slices to a widemouthed 1-qt/960-ml glass jar with a tight-fitting lid or a similar-size glass, ceramic, or plastic container with a lid. Pour in the hot pickling mixture, stir well, and let stand, uncovered, until cool. Cover and refrigerate for 2 days before serving. Serve cool or at room temperature. The pickles will keep for up to 2 weeks in the refrigerator.

LOTUS ROOT SALAD WITH SPICY THAI VINAIGRETTE

Lotus root and water chestnuts are both white and have a similar crisp texture. But lotus root delivers something that water chestnuts cannot: tremendous beauty. Its flowerlike slices turn this salad into "art in a bowl." Bright green cilantro leaves and chile slices and deep red specks of *sambal oelek* provide a nice contrast to the snow white lotus root rounds.

SERVES 6

DRESSING

6 tbsp/90 ml fresh lime juice

4 tbsp/60 ml canola or other neutral oil

1 tbsp *sambal oelek* (see Cook's Note, page 134)

1 tbsp Dijon mustard

2 tsp Asian fish sauce

1 tsp Asian sesame oil

1 small garlic clove, minced

¼ tsp kosher or fine sea salt

¼ tsp granulated sugar

⅛ tsp freshly ground pepper

10 oz/280 g lotus root, ends trimmed, peeled, and cut into slices ⅛ in/3 mm thick

1 medium Granny Smith apple, peeled, quartered, cored, and cut lengthwise into slices ¼ in/6 mm thick

1 cup/85 g coarsely shredded napa cabbage

¼ small sweet onion such as Vidalia or Walla Walla, cut into wedges ¼ in/6 mm thick

1 small jalapeño chile, stemmed, halved lengthwise, seeded, deribbed, and thinly sliced (see Cook's Note, page 40)

½ cup/30 g lightly packed fresh cilantro leaves

1 To make the dressing, in a small bowl, whisk together the lime juice, oil, *sambal oelek*, mustard, fish sauce, sesame oil, garlic, salt, sugar, and pepper. Taste and adjust the seasoning. Set aside.

2 Fill a medium saucepan two-thirds full with salted water and bring to a boil over medium-high heat. Add the lotus root slices and blanch for only 1 minute so they remain very crisp. Drain immediately into a colander and rinse under cool running water until completely cooled. Drain thoroughly and blot dry with paper towels.

3 In a large bowl, toss together the lotus root slices, apple slices, cabbage, onion, jalapeño, and cilantro. Re-stir the dressing briefly, then pour over the salad and toss gently to mix well. Serve immediately, or cover and set aside for up to 2 hours before serving. (The salad can be made up to 2 days in advance, covered, and refrigerated. Remove from the refrigerator 30 minutes before serving. Toss again just before serving.)

QUICK LEMON CHICKEN SOUP
WITH LOTUS ROOT, GREEN ONIONS, AND CHILES

Consider this a pan-Asian version of the cure-all chicken soup known as Jewish penicillin. It was a cold, rainy day when I developed this recipe, and having a second bowlful right away and then another one later in the day wasn't a hardship. In fact, it was so delicious that I welcomed the chance to eat three big bowlfuls. Plus, it is pretty to look at, with lacy lotus root slices and deep green cilantro leaves floating in the broth. If you keep your pantry stocked with some basic Asian ingredients, this becomes a quick soup to make for a weeknight supper.

SERVES 6

1 tsp freshly grated lemon zest

⅓ cup/20 g firmly packed fresh cilantro leaves

2 green onions, including green tops, thinly sliced

8 cups/2 L homemade chicken stock or canned low-sodium chicken broth

3 tbsp fresh lemon juice

1 or 2 Thai bird chiles, stemmed and cut into paper-thin rounds (see Cook's Note, page 40)

1-in/2.5-cm piece fresh ginger, peeled and cut into matchsticks

2 tbsp Asian fish sauce

1 boneless, skinless chicken breast, 5 oz/140 g, cut crosswise into slices ¼ in/6 mm thick

1½ cups/130 g bean sprouts

6 oz/170 g lotus root, ends trimmed, peeled, and cut into slices ⅛ in/3 mm thick

1 In a small bowl, stir together the lemon zest, cilantro, and green onions. Set aside.

2 In a large pot, combine the stock, lemon juice, chiles, ginger, and fish sauce, bring to a simmer over medium-high heat, and cook for 3 minutes to infuse the flavors. Add the chicken and simmer until it is opaque and cooked through, about 5 minutes. Add the bean sprouts and lotus root, reduce the heat to medium-low, and cook at a very slow simmer until the vegetables are heated through but still crisp, about 3 minutes.

3 Ladle the soup into warmed soup bowls and garnish with the lemon zest mixture. Serve immediately.

LOTUS ROOT, SHRIMP, AND VEGETABLE TEMPURA

While it might seem challenging to make tempura at home, it is simply a matter of organization, planning, and timing. Making tempura is both fun to do and gratifying to master and eating the crispy golden foods that emerge hot from the pan is wonderful. If frying always seems like a messy affair, try it in a wok. I find the pan's broad shape gives me more room to maneuver the foods and results in much less splattering. The secret to lacy, golden-crisp tempura is to make a lumpy batter. I never understood how tempura batter should look until I read Shizuo Tsuji's *Japanese Cooking: A Simple Art:* "The marks of good tempura batter are the powdery ring of flour at the sides of the mixing bowl and a mixture marked with lumps of dry flour."

SERVES 4 TO 6

DIPPING SAUCE

½ tsp instant dashi granules (see Cook's Note, page 71)

⅔ cup/165 ml warm water

¼ cup/60 ml soy sauce

2 tbsp mirin (Japanese sweet cooking wine)

1 tbsp fresh lime juice

1 tbsp peeled and finely grated fresh ginger

1 tsp Asian sesame oil

About 6 cups/1.4 L peanut oil for deep-frying

¼ cup/60 ml Asian sesame oil

12 to 16 large (26 to 30 count per 1 lb/455 g) shrimp, peeled and deveined

2 medium sweet potatoes, peeled and cut on the diagonal into slices ⅛ in/3 mm thick

1 large lotus root section, ends trimmed, peeled, and cut into rounds ¼ in/6 mm thick

1 fennel bulb, trimmed, halved lengthwise, and cut into wedges ½ in/12 mm thick, leaving the core intact

1 To make the dipping sauce, in a 2-cup/480-ml measuring cup, combine the dashi granules and warm water and stir to dissolve the granules. Add the soy sauce, mirin, lime juice, ginger, and sesame oil and stir until thoroughly combined. Set aside until ready to serve. (The dipping sauce can be made up to 1 day in advance. Remove from the refrigerator 2 hours before serving.)

2 Have ready a large, deep frying pan or wok and a deep-frying thermometer. Line a baking sheet with a double thickness of paper towels and set it near the stove. Set a slotted spoon or a wire-mesh skimmer alongside the baking sheet, along with a pair of cooking chopsticks. The oil for deep-frying is a blend of peanut and sesame oil. Add the oils to the pan or wok. The oils should be at least 3 in/7.5 cm deep. Have the shrimp, sweet potatoes, lotus root, fennel, green beans, and *shiso* leaves prepared and in bowls or on plates ready to coat and deep-fry. (Be sure all of the foods are patted dry so they don't splatter during the deep-frying.) Put the flour for dredging in a shallow bowl.

3 Heat the oil to 340°F/170°C on the thermometer.

4 To make the batter, select two medium bowls and put an egg yolk in each bowl. Set aside one bowl. Lightly beat the egg yolk in the second bowl and then pour in 1 cup/240 ml of the ice water, stroking it a few times with chopsticks or a fork to combine. Add 1 cup/100 g of the flour all at once. Using the chopsticks or fork, make long strokes back and forth just until all of the ingredients are loosely combined but the batter is still very lumpy. Overmixing results in a sticky batter that won't yield a lacy, light coating. When the first batch of batter is nearly used up and is looking limp, make the second batch of batter the same way with the remaining ingredients.

8 to 12 green beans, stem
end trimmed

4 to 6 fresh *shiso* (perilla) leaves
or curly parsley sprigs

½ cup/65 g all-purpose flour
for dredging

Kosher or fine sea salt

BATTER

2 egg yolks

2 cups/480 ml ice water

2 cups/200 g sifted
all-purpose flour

5 Working in small batches so as not to crowd the pan, use your fingers to dip each food item first into the flour, shaking off the excess, and then into the batter. Slide the coated foods into the hot oil and fry, turning once or twice for even cooking, until golden. The shrimp needs to cook for about 2 minutes, and the vegetables will take 1½ to 2 minutes. Cook the *shiso* leaves last and dip them only in the batter and fry them only on one side. They will cook in 10 to 15 seconds. Make sure the oil is at 340°F/170°C before you add a new batch.

6 Using the slotted spoon or skimmer, transfer the deep-fried foods to the towel-lined baking sheet to drain briefly. (To hold the shrimp and vegetables for up to 10 minutes, keep them warm in a 250°F/120°C/gas ½ oven until ready to serve.) Arrange the tempura on a warmed platter or individual plates and serve immediately with the dipping sauce on the side.

STIR-FRIED LOTUS ROOT AND SNOW PEAS

Characteristic of the crisp vegetable dishes common to Cantonese cooking, this quick stir-fry is as beautiful as it is crunchy, with brilliant green snow peas set against a backdrop of delicate, snowy white lotus root half-moons. The sauce glazes the vegetables with the subtle flavor of soy and sesame oil. For a bolder finish, increase the amount of soy sauce.

SERVES 4 TO 6

SAUCE

1½ tsp soy sauce

1½ tsp Chinese rice wine or pale dry sherry

1½ tsp Asian sesame oil

1 tsp cornstarch dissolved in 1 tbsp water

¼ tsp granulated sugar

Pinch of freshly ground white pepper

1 tbsp canola or other neutral oil

2 tsp peeled and minced fresh ginger

1 large garlic clove, minced

8 oz/225 g lotus root, ends trimmed, peeled, halved lengthwise, and cut crosswise into slices ⅛ in/ 3 mm thick

12 oz/340 g snow peas, stem end trimmed and strings removed

¼ cup/60 ml homemade chicken stock or canned low-sodium chicken broth

1 To make the sauce, in a small bowl, stir together the soy sauce, rice wine, sesame oil, cornstarch mixture, sugar, and pepper until the sugar is dissolved and the sauce is smooth. Set aside.

2 In a wok or a large, deep frying pan, heat the oil over high heat and swirl to coat the pan bottom and sides. Add the ginger and garlic and stir-fry just until fragrant but not brown, about 15 seconds. Scatter in the lotus root slices and stir-fry for 1 minute. Add the snow peas and stir-fry for 1 minute longer. Pour the stock over the top, give the vegetables a quick toss, cover, and simmer for 45 seconds. Uncover, toss the vegetables once and then add the sauce. Continue to stir-fry until the sauce thickens and glazes the vegetables, about 30 seconds. Transfer to a warmed serving dish and serve immediately.

LOTUS ROOT CHIPS

As a fun, just-playing-in-the-kitchen activity, there is nothing like cooking up some hot, crispy-fresh root-vegetable chips. Deep-frying thin lotus root slices yields a batch of lacy, crisp beauties that are an unusual, hard-to-resist nibble for a cocktail party. Use a mandoline, Japanese vegetable slicer, adjustable ceramic mandoline, or a very sharp knife to cut the root into paper-thin slices.

SERVES 6 AS A NIBBLE

14 oz/400 g lotus root

About 5 cups/1.2 L peanut, grape seed, or vegetable oil for deep-frying

Kosher or fine sea salt

1 Just before you are ready to begin frying, trim the ends, peel, and cut the lotus root into slices 1/16 in/2 mm thick.

2 Line two rimmed baking sheets with a double thickness of paper towels and set it near the stove. Set a slotted spoon or a wire-mesh skimmer alongside the baking sheet. Pour the oil to a depth of about 3 in/7.5 cm into a deep, heavy pot, a wok, or an electric deep fryer and heat to 370°F/185°C on a deep-frying thermometer. (If using an electric deep fryer, follow the manufacturer's instructions for heating the oil.)

3 Fry the lotus root slices in small batches. Add a handful of slices to the hot oil and fry, stirring once or twice, until golden brown, about 2 minutes. (The timing will vary slightly, so look for color first and then sample a slice, testing for crispiness.) Using the slotted spoon or skimmer, transfer the chips to a towel-lined baking sheet to drain. Sprinkle lightly with salt. Continue frying in small batches until all of the slices have been fried. Make sure the oil is at 370°F/185°C before you add a new batch.

4 Transfer the chips to a basket or serving bowl and serve immediately. The chips are best when fried just before serving, but they can be cooked up to 4 hours in advance and stored uncovered at room temperature.

CANDIED LOTUS ROOT

Crisp, lacelike lotus root cries out for a sweet preparation. I began by candying slices, simmering them in a simple syrup flavored with fresh ginger, star anise, and lemon. They turned out sweetly coated and delicately crisp, with a nuanced spiciness. You can use them as a gorgeous garnish for a dessert plate, a bowl of green tea ice cream, or the Brown Sugar–Ginger Ice Cream on page 142. Best of all, make the Lotus Root Upside-Down Cake on page 192—it's an unexpected showstopper.

MAKES ABOUT 3 CUPS/850 G, INCLUDING THE SYRUP

14 oz/400 g lotus root

SYRUP

1½ cups/300 g granulated sugar

1½ cups/360 ml water

3 quarter-size slices fresh ginger

1 star anise pod

1 lemon peel strip, about ½ in/ 12 mm wide and 2 in/5 cm long

1½ tbsp fresh lemon juice

1 Fill a medium saucepan two-thirds full with water. Trim the ends, peel, and cut the lotus root into slices $1/16$ in/2 mm thick. As you cut the slices, slip them into the pan of water to prevent them from browning. When all of the slices are in the pan, place the pan over medium-high heat and bring just to a boil. Immediately remove from the heat and drain the slices into a colander in the sink. Return the slices to the pan, fill the pan two-thirds full with water, and again bring just to a boil over medium-high heat. Drain immediately, and then repeat the boiling and draining one more time.

2 To make the syrup, in a large saucepan, combine the sugar, water, ginger, star anise, and lemon peel and juice and stir to dissolve the sugar.

3 Add the drained lotus root, place over medium-high heat and bring to a simmer. Adjust the heat to maintain a slow simmer, cover partially, and simmer until the syrup is thick and the lotus root is crisp-tender, about 40 minutes.

4 Remove from the heat, uncover, and let the lotus root and syrup cool to room temperature. Transfer the syrup and slices to an airtight container and refrigerate until ready to use. The candied root will keep for several months.

LOTUS ROOT UPSIDE-DOWN CAKE

It took four tries, but I was determined to create this cake! After I candied the lotus root, I got a "bee in my bonnet" to turn the pineapple upside-down cake, a homespun classic, into a candied lotus root beauty. I couldn't resist the idea of a caramelized, lacy-topped upside-down cake. It's as scrumptious as it is beautiful, and here is proof: I took the cake to a dinner party at a friend's home and cut enough slices to serve eight guests, leaving a quarter of the cake on the serving plate. When it was time to go home and gather my cake plate, there was nothing but crumbs. The hosts and another friend devoured the remaining slices while they were clearing the dishes. Serve the cake with whipped cream or vanilla ice cream.

SERVES 10 TO 12

BROWN SUGAR SMEAR

4 tbsp/55 g unsalted butter, at room temperature

½ cup/100 g firmly packed light brown sugar

1 tbsp honey

½ tsp dark rum

¼ tsp pure vanilla extract

Pinch of kosher or fine sea salt

1½ tsp unsalted butter for the pan

Well-drained Candied Lotus Root slices (page 191)

CAKE

1⅓ cups/150 g cake flour

½ tsp baking powder

½ tsp baking soda

½ tsp kosher or fine sea salt

2 large eggs

½ cup/120 ml heavy whipping cream

1 tbsp fresh lemon juice

1¼ tsp pure vanilla extract

½ cup plus 1 tbsp/130 g unsalted butter, at room temperature

¾ cup/150 g turbinado sugar

1 Position a rack in the lower third of the oven and preheat to 375°F/190°C/gas 5.

2 To make the smear, in a small bowl, using a fork or small rubber spatula, combine the butter and brown sugar until completely blended. Mix in the honey, rum, vanilla, and salt. Stir until completely combined. Set aside.

3 Butter only the sides of a well-seasoned 10-in/25-cm cast-iron frying pan. Using a small rubber spatula or offset spatula, spread the smear evenly over the bottom of the pan. Beginning at the perimeter of the pan and working your way toward the center, arrange the lotus root slices in concentric circles, overlapping the slices by almost half. Use the prettiest slices along the outside edge and at the center, filling in any spaces with partial slices. (Use about three-quarters of the lotus root slices to cover the smear generously, making a beautiful, thick lacy layer.) Set aside.

4 To make the cake, sift together the flour, baking powder, baking soda, and salt. Set aside. In a medium bowl, beat the eggs until blended and then discard 2 tbsp of the beaten egg. (You will end up with ⅓ cup/75 ml beaten egg.) Whisk in the cream, lemon juice, and vanilla. Set aside. (The mixture will look like it has curdled and that is okay.)

5 In a stand mixer fitted with the paddle attachment, beat together the butter and turbinado sugar on low speed until well blended, about 1 minute. On low speed, add the dry ingredients all at once and mix on low speed just until they are moistened. Scrape down the sides of the bowl. Add the egg mixture and beat on medium speed just until incorporated, about 1 minute. Scrape down the sides of the bowl.

6 Using a rubber spatula, lift globs of the batter and gently plop them on the lotus root in the frying pan, covering the surface with mounds. Now take the rubber spatula and gently spread the batter to cover the surface carefully and evenly. Bake the cake until deeply browned on top and a cake tester or wooden toothpick inserted in the center comes out clean, 30 to 35 minutes. Let cool in the pan on a wire rack for at least 5 minutes but for no more than 10 minutes.

7 Run a table knife around the inside edge of the pan to loosen the cake sides. Invert a cake plate on top of the pan, centering the cake under the plate, and invert the plate and pan together. Carefully lift off the pan. Serve warm or at room temperature. The cake is best when eaten the same day it is baked.

MALANGA

Xanthosoma sagittifolium

YAUTÍA *(PUERTO RICAN)* **/ TANNIA** *(ENGLISH-SPEAKING WEST INDIES)* **/**
MACAL *(COSTA RICA AND NICARAGUA)* **/ TAYER** *(SURINAME AND THE NETHERLANDS)* **/**
NEW COCOYAM / AMERICAN TARO / ARROWLEAF ELEPHANT'S EAR /
MALANGA AMARILLA *(YELLOW MALANGA)* **/**
MALANGA BLANCA or **TANIA** *(WHITE MALANGA)*

HISTORY AND LORE A genus of the tropical and subtropical flowering plant family Araceae, *Xanthosoma* has more than forty species, all native to tropical America. Several species, including malanga (*X. sagittifolium*), are grown for their starch-bearing roots (corms), making them a valuable food crop of tropical regions. There is a great deal of confusion and mislabeling when it comes to tropical tubers. Taro is the common name for four different root crops grown in tropical areas around the world. They are *X. sagittifolium*, or American taro, the focus of this chapter; *Colocasia esculenta,* or true taro; *Cyrtosperma chamissonis*, or giant swamp taro; and *Alocasia macrorrhiza*, known as both false taro and giant taro. The first two, the most widely cultivated taro types, are featured in this book (see page 309 for true taro). The latter two are only rarely cultivated commercially.

As you can see from the long string of common names listed above, what this species of taro is called depends on what country you are in. In the United States, most markets label it malanga, though I have seen it labeled *yautía* in markets that serve a Puerto Rican population.

I have never seen it labeled American taro, however, hence my decision to refer to *Xanthosoma sagittifolium* as malanga in the book. Spanish and Portuguese seafarers are believed to have been responsible for its dispersal into Europe and probably into Africa, though conflicting information exists on who actually introduced it to Africa. Some sources say the root was transported to Sierra Leone in 1792 by former North American slaves. But the more accepted date is 1843, when missionaries carried it from the West Indies to Ghana.

VARIETIES The many species of the genus *Xanthosoma* are rarely differentiated in markets. All of them that I have seen have shaggy brown skin. However, some are shaped like a plump sweet potato and others are longer and more tapered. The color of the flesh will vary, too. I most often see ivory-fleshed tubers in the market but on occasion have seen yellow or pinkish purple. Despite these differences, they all seem to cook and taste the same. The malanga, or America taro, also has a more pronounced, earthier flavor, reminiscent of walnuts or hazelnuts, than the blander *Colocasia esculenta*, or true taro.

NUTRITION Malanga is high in starch (a form of carbo-hydrate), which means it is also high in calories, with about 340 calories in a 3½-ounce/100-gram serving. It is a good source of potassium, vitamin B$_6$, riboflavin, and thiamine. The starch granules are easily digested through the blood stream, making malanga an ideal food for any-one who is gluten intolerant or has digestive problems.

AVAILABILITY AND SELECTION Malanga is available year-round in Latin American markets or in large super-markets catering to a Hispanic population. The shaggy-haired corms should be very hard, with no soft spots, shriveled skin, cracks, or signs of mold. For ease of peeling, look for evenly shaped specimens.

STORAGE Use immediately, or store in a closed brown-paper bag in a cool, dark spot for up to 5 days. A malanga will soften quickly if left in a plastic bag or refrigerated.

BASIC USE AND PREPARATION Malanga, which must never be eaten raw, can be used in both sweet and savory preparations. It can be coarsely grated and turned into crisp, delicious fritters, or it can be finely grated and mixed with plantains to make the classic meat-filled fried croquettes called *alcapurrias* (see page 200). The finely grated flesh is also used to make a sweet custard filling for pie, or can be mixed with coconut and then shaped into balls and deep-fried. Malanga can be boiled and mashed or sliced and served as a side dish, added to a soup or stew, or sliced paper-thin and deep-fried for chips.

To prepare malanga, wear disposable gloves and use a vegetable brush to scrub it well under cool running water. Slice off the ends and, using a paring knife or vegetable peeler, pare away the hairy skin, continuing to peel until you reach the firm white or other-colored flesh. Cut away any blemished flesh or dark brown spots. Rinse again and pat dry. If not using immediately, submerge in a bowl of cold water to keep it from discoloring.

A CAUTIONARY NOTE There are two precautions related to malanga. First, although selection over the years has reduced the oxalic-acid crystals in the outer layer of the corm, it is important to wear disposable surgical gloves when peeling the vegetable to prevent skin irritation, especially if you have sensitive skin. Second, never eat malanga raw, as these oxalic-acid compounds may irritate the throat. Malanga must always be thoroughly cooked.

YIELDS

1 small malanga = 7 oz/200 g

1 medium malanga = 12 oz/340 g

1 large malanga = 1 to 2 lb/455 to 910 g

1 cup trimmed, peeled, and diced malanga = 8 oz/225 g

2¼ cups trimmed, peeled, and diced or chunked malanga = 1 lb/455 g

---

CREAM OF MALANGA SOUP WITH MALANGA CRISPS

Malanga has a nutlike flavor and a smooth, soft texture when boiled, making it a good candidate for a cream-based puréed soup. Its natural starchiness makes the soup thick and rich on its own, so using half-and-half rather than heavy cream is sufficient to give it that desirable silky finish. It is quite enough to use a little chopped cilantro for garnish, giving the soup a flourish of color and a delicate herbal note, but I couldn't resist cutting a small malanga into matchsticks and frying them for an additional topping. They are irresistibly crisp and tasty, especially with a sprinkle of salt. Perfect for entertaining, the soup can be made up to 2 days in advance.

SERVES 6 TO 8

2 lb/910 g malanga

2 tbsp unsalted butter

2 medium yellow onions, about 12 oz/340 g, coarsely chopped

2 large garlic cloves, finely chopped

1½ tsp kosher or fine sea salt

¼ tsp ground allspice

⅛ tsp cayenne pepper

4 cups/960 ml homemade chicken stock or canned low-sodium chicken broth

GARNISH

1 small malanga, about 7 oz/200 g

About 1 cup/240 ml canola oil or other neutral oil for deep-frying

Kosher or fine sea salt

1 cup/240 ml half-and-half

⅛ tsp freshly grated nutmeg

⅓ cup/20 g coarsely chopped fresh cilantro

1 Fill a large bowl two-thirds full of cold water. Trim, peel, and rinse the malanga, then cut into 1-in/2.5-cm chunks. Drop the chunks into the water as you work to keep them from discoloring.

2 In a stockpot or heavy soup pot, melt the butter over medium-low heat and swirl to coat the pot bottom. Add the onions and garlic and sauté, stirring constantly, until the onions and garlic are well coated with the butter, about 2 minutes. Reduce the heat to low, cover the pot, and cook until the onions are softened but not brown, about 5 minutes. Add the salt, allspice, and cayenne and sauté, stirring constantly, for 1 minute longer.

3 Drain the malanga and add it to the pot along with the stock. Raise the heat to medium-high and bring to a boil. Reduce the heat and simmer, partially covered, until the malanga is soft enough to purée, about 30 minutes. Remove from the heat and let cool for about 10 minutes.

4 Meanwhile, make the garnish. Trim, peel, and rinse the malanga, then cut into matchsticks and place in a small bowl. Line a plate with a double thickness of paper towels and place near the stove. Set a slotted spoon alongside the plate. Pour the oil to a depth of 1 in/2.5 cm into a small, deep frying pan and place over medium-high heat until the oil shimmers but is not smoking. (The oil should register about 340°F/170°C on a deep-frying thermometer.) Working in small batches, add the malanga sticks to the hot oil and fry until golden and crisp like potato sticks, about 1½ minutes. Using a slotted spoon, transfer to the towel-lined plate to drain. Sprinkle lightly with salt. Continue deep-frying in small batches until all of the malanga has been fried. Set aside.

5 Working in small batches, process the soup to a smooth purée in a blender or food processor. Return the puréed soup to the pot and add the half-and-half and nutmeg. Cook over low heat, stirring occasionally, until the soup is steaming hot. Do not allow the soup to boil. Ladle the soup into warmed bowls and garnish with the crisp malanga sticks and the cilantro. Serve immediately.

MALANGA FRITTERS WITH SERRANO CHILES AND GARLIC

Bravo to Jack Bishop, author of *Vegetables Every Day*, for writing such a compelling headnote for his malanga fritters: On reading it, I immediately shredded the malanga I had on hand and made these fritters. These "crisp, wispy fritters," as he calls them, are simple to make, splatter-free when fried, and addictively delicious. There are lots of possible variations beyond the chiles and garlic, such as adding bits of ham and cheese, diced bacon and chives, grated Mexican Cotija cheese, or diced bell peppers and onions. I also like to serve the fritters as canapés, like a little potato latke, topped with a thin slice of smoked salmon, a tiny dollop of sour cream or crème fraîche, and a sprinkle of finely minced chives.

MAKES ABOUT TWENTY-FOUR 2-IN/5-CM FRITTERS

1½ lb/680 g malanga

½ cup/25 g lightly packed fresh flat-leaf parsley leaves

¼ cup/30 g all-purpose flour

3 garlic cloves, minced

1 to 2 serrano chiles, stemmed, seeded, and minced (see Cook's Note, page 40)

1½ tsp kosher or fine sea salt

About ½ cup/120 ml canola oil or other neutral oil for frying

1 or 2 limes, cut into wedges

1 Fill a large bowl two-thirds full of cold water. Trim, peel, and rinse the malanga. Cut it into large chunks if you are shredding it in a food processor. Otherwise, cut it in half crosswise. Submerge the malanga pieces in the water as you work to keep them from discoloring. Drain and blot dry before shredding.

2 Using the coarse holes on a box grater or a food processor fitted with the coarse shredding disk, shred the malanga. Transfer to a large bowl. Add the parsley, flour, garlic, chiles, and salt. Toss well until evenly combined.

3 Scoop up a rounded tablespoonful of the malanga mixture and shape into a flat disk 2 in/5 cm in diameter. (The edges should look ragged, with stringy bits of malanga.) Place on a baking sheet.

4 Preheat the oven to 250°F/120°C/gas ½. Line a baking sheet with a double thickness of paper towels and set near the stove. Set a slotted spatula alongside the baking sheet. Pour the oil to a depth of ¼ in/6 mm into a large frying pan, preferably cast iron, and heat over medium-high heat until the oil shimmers but is not smoking.

5 Working in batches so as not to crowd the pan, add the fritters to the hot oil and fry, turning once, until crisp and golden brown on both sides, 5 to 6 minutes total. Using the slotted spatula, transfer the fritters to the towel-lined baking sheet. Keep warm in the oven while you fry additional batches. Serve hot, accompanied with the lime wedges for squeezing over the top.

> **COOK'S NOTE**
> The fritters are at their best when freshly fried, but they can be made up to 2 hours in advance and set aside at room temperature. Warm them in a 250°F/120°C/gas ½ oven before serving. The fritters also freeze well. Let the fried fritters cool completely, layer between sheets of waxed paper in a covered container, and freeze for up to 1 month. Do not thaw before reheating. Arrange the frozen fritters on a rimmed baking sheet and reheat in a preheated 400°F/200°C/gas 6 oven just until hot, about 7 minutes.

ALCAPURRIAS

Sold as street food throughout Puerto Rico and elsewhere in the Caribbean, these hard-to-resist, shallow-fried fritters are filled with a boldly flavored ground beef mixture that is seasoned with homemade or bottled *sofrito*, diced pimiento, chopped Spanish olives, and a coriander and annatto seasoning mix. The dough that surrounds the meat filling is made from finely grated plantains and malanga mashed together with a little salt. I found it helpful to wear disposable surgical gloves when forming the fritters because they kept the dough from sticking to my hands. You can moisten your hands with a little water to keep the dough from sticking, but it may cause splatters when you put the fritters in the hot oil.

MAKES EIGHT 4-BY-2½-IN/10-BY-6-CM FRITTERS

FILLING

1 tbsp canola or other neutral oil

12 oz/340 g lean ground beef

1 tbsp dried oregano

1½ tsp Sazón Goya coriander and annatto seasoning (see Cook's Note)

¾ cup/180 ml *sofrito*, Goya brand (see Cook's Note) or homemade (see page 396)

1½ tbsp diced pimiento

⅓ cup/55 g finely chopped pimiento-stuffed Spanish olives

2 tbsp tomato paste

DOUGH

1 lb/455 g malanga

4 plantains, about 9 oz/255 g each, ends cut off, halved lengthwise, peeled, and cut into 1-in/2.5-cm chunks

2 tsp kosher or fine sea salt

Canola or other neutral oil for frying

1 To make the filling, in a large frying pan, heat the oil over medium heat and swirl to coat the pan bottom. Add the beef and cook, breaking it up with the side of a spatula, until brown and almost cooked through, about 4 minutes. Stir in the oregano and the coriander and annatto seasoning and sauté, stirring constantly, for 1 minute. Add the *sofrito,* pimiento, olives, and tomato paste and sauté, stirring frequently, until the mixture thickens and the flavors meld, about 4 minutes longer. Remove from the heat and set aside to cool while you make the dough.

2 To make the dough, fill a large bowl two-thirds full of cold water. Trim, peel, and rinse the malanga and then cut into 1-in/2.5-cm chunks. Drop the chunks into the water as you work to keep them from discoloring. Drain and blot dry before mashing.

3 In a food processor, process the malanga and plantains in small batches until minced to a fine pasty mash. As each batch is ready, transfer it to the same large bowl. (Because the malanga discolors quickly when exposed to air, I process the plantains first and then process the malanga, immediately adding it to the mashed plantains to keep it from discoloring.) Add the salt to the malanga-plantain mash and knead it briefly in the bowl to form a heavy dough.

4 Have the filling handy on the work surface, along with a ¼-cup/60-ml measure and a baking sheet. To form the fritters, you need to make sixteen balls of dough total. Using the ¼-cup/60-ml measure, scoop up a portion of dough and roll it into a ball. Make seven more balls the same way. Then, using 3 tbsp of dough for each ball, make eight more balls. Flatten each of these smaller balls into an oval pancake about ¼ in/6 mm thick. Set them aside on a clean work surface or on a baking sheet. (If you have leftover dough, see the Cook's Note for how to use it up.)

5 Wearing disposable gloves to keep the dough from sticking to your hands, or moistening your hands with a little water, place one of the larger balls in the palm of your hand and pat it down to form a pancake ¼ in/6 mm thick and the length and width of your palm (about 4 in/10 cm long and 2½ in/ 6 cm wide). Cup your hand slightly to form the dough into a shallow bowl. Scoop a scant ¼ cup/60 ml of the meat filling into the center of the dough. Lay one of the small preformed pancakes on top (it should cover the meat filling). Pinch together the edges of the two pancakes to enclose the meat and form a stuffed, oval-shaped packet about 4 in/10 cm long, 2½ in/6 cm wide, and 1 in/2.5 cm high. Set aside on the baking sheet. Repeat to make seven more fritters.

6 Preheat the oven to 250°F/120°C/gas ½. Line a baking sheet with a double thickness of paper towels and set near the stove. Set a slotted spatula alongside the baking sheet. Pour the oil to a depth of ½ in/12 mm into a deep 12-in/30.5-cm frying pan, preferably cast iron, and heat to 325°F/165°C on a deep-frying thermometer.

7 Using the slotted spatula, gently lower three or four *alcapurrias* into the hot oil, being careful not to crowd the pan. Fry them until they are deeply golden brown on the underside, about 8 minutes. Using the slotted spatula, carefully turn them over and fry until they are the color of a ballpark corn dog, about 8 minutes longer. It is important not to underfry them or the dough will be raw in the center. Using the spatula, transfer to the prepared baking sheet to drain and keep warm in the oven while you fry additional batches. Make sure the oil is at 325°F/165°C before you add a new batch, and add more oil to the pan if needed. Serve hot.

COOK'S NOTE

Look for Sazón Goya brand coriander and annatto seasoning and Goya *sofrito* (tomato sauce base) at markets selling Latin American or West Indian foods. The *sofrito* is available either bottled or frozen.

If you have leftover dough, form small pancakes from it and fry them in the same oil until they are deeply golden on both sides, about 2 minutes. Each pancake will puff up to form a hollow center, like a pita bread.

ROASTED GARLIC MASHED MALANGA

Like many root vegetables, malanga can be turned into a flavorful mash by peeling it, cutting it into chunks, and boiling it in water or broth. This mash has a subtle nutty quality all on its own, but I prefer it with a big kick of flavor, so I roast a head of garlic and add it to the mash. Serve the mashed malanga with a Caribbean-style vegetarian or meaty stew or as an accompaniment to grilled meats, especially jerk chicken or pork.

SERVES 4 TO 6 AS A SIDE DISH

1 medium head garlic

⅓ cup/75 ml extra-virgin olive oil

2 lb/910 g malanga

Kosher or fine sea salt

¾ to 1 cup/180 to 240 ml homemade chicken stock or canned low-sodium chicken broth or vegetable broth

Freshly ground pepper

1 Position a rack in the center of the oven and preheat to 375°F/190°C/gas 5. Peel the loose, papery outer layers of skin off the head of garlic and trim any roots from the bottom. Cut off enough of the top of the head to expose the cloves. Place the garlic in a small ovenproof dish or pan and pour the oil over the top. Cover the dish with aluminum foil, sealing it well, and roast the garlic until it feels soft when pierced with a knife, 35 to 40 minutes.

2 Remove from the oven, uncover, and let the garlic cool to room temperature. Squeeze the roasted cloves from the skins into a small bowl. Reserve the oil in the baking dish in a separate small dish. Mash the pulp with a fork; you should have at least 2 tbsp. Set aside.

3 Meanwhile, fill a large saucepan half full of cold water. Trim, peel, and rinse the malanga, then cut crosswise into slices about 1 in/2.5 cm thick. Drop the slices into the water as you work to keep them from discoloring.

4 Add 1 tsp salt to the water. Check to make sure there is enough water in the pan to cover the malanga by 2 in/5 cm and add more water if needed. Place the pan over high heat and bring the water to a boil. Reduce the heat so the water just simmers and cook the malanga until it is fork-tender, about 35 minutes.

5 Drain the malanga and transfer it to a stand mixer fitted with the paddle attachment. Add ½ cup/120 ml of the stock, the roasted garlic pulp, and the roasted garlic oil. Begin with the mixer on low speed and then gradually increase the speed to medium and beat until the malanga is fluffy and almost smooth. Add more stock until the mash is as soft and moist as you like. Season with salt and pepper.

6 Serve immediately, keep warm in the top of a double boiler, or cover and rewarm in a microwave oven.

GOLDEN MALANGA COCONUT BALLS

If you love tender-in-the-center coconut macaroons as much as I do, you will love these. They are pure decadence and wonderfully simple: grated malanga and shredded coconut are mixed with sugar and bound with egg white, shaped into balls, and deep-fried. After developing the recipe for the savory Malanga Fritters with Serrano Chiles and Garlic on page 198, I was inspired by their crispy texture to create a coconut confection with the malanga. Just try to eat only one!

MAKES ABOUT 18 BALLS; SERVES 8 TO 10

1 egg white

½ cup/100 g granulated sugar

1⅓ cups/115 g unsweetened medium-shred dried coconut

8 oz/225 g malanga

Canola or other neutral oil for deep-frying

1 In a medium bowl, whisk the egg white just until frothy, about 30 seconds. Add the sugar and whisk to combine. Using a rubber spatula, fold in the coconut.

2 Fill a large bowl two-thirds full of cold water. Trim, peel, and rinse the malanga. Cut it into large chunks if you are shredding it in a food processor. Otherwise, cut it in half crosswise. Submerge the malanga pieces in the water as you work to keep them from discoloring. Drain and blot dry before shredding.

3 Using the coarse holes on a box grater or a food processor fitted with the fine shredding disk, shred the malanga. Stir it into the coconut mixture, mixing until evenly combined.

4 Scoop up a slightly rounded spoonful of the malanga mixture and shape into a firmly formed ball about 1½ in/4 cm in diameter (about the size of a walnut). Place on a baking sheet. Repeat with the remaining mixture. You should have about 18 balls. Set aside.

5 Preheat the oven to 250°F/120°C/gas ½. Line a baking sheet with a double thickness of paper towels and set it near the stove. Set a slotted spoon or a wire-mesh skimmer alongside the baking sheet. Pour the oil to a depth of about 3 in/7.5 cm into a deep, heavy pot, a wok, or an electric deep fryer and heat to 340°F/170°C on a deep-frying thermometer. (If using an electric deep fryer, follow the manufacturer's instructions for heating the oil.)

6 Working in small batches, add the malanga balls to the hot oil and fry, turning them in the oil for even cooking, until deeply golden, 2½ to 3 minutes. Test one to make sure it is cooked all the way through. Using the slotted spoon or skimmer, transfer the deep-fried balls to the towel-lined tray and keep warm in the oven. Continue frying in small batches until all of the balls have been fried. Make sure the oil is at 340°F/170°C before you add a new batch.

7 Serve the balls immediately or keep them warm in the oven for up to 20 minutes. They are best when served warm, but they will stay crisp at room temperature for up to 2 hours.

CUBAN MALANGA PIE

Malanga has intriguing qualities when grated raw. Its natural starchiness is still apparent, but the grated raw pieces don't dissolve, which adds a lovely texture to sweets. This is the pie for anyone who loves custard pies. The shredded malanga rises to the top of the cinnamony rich custard as it bakes, sculpturing the surface with thin, lacy threads. It looks beautiful and has become a new favorite.

If this pie is appealing but you aren't a pie baker, simplify things and buy prepared pie dough or a frozen pastry shell. Just know that this pie dough is really easy and satisfying to work with, and will bring success to even a beginning pie maker.

SERVES 8 TO 10

DOUGH

1¼ cups/160 g all-purpose flour, plus more for dusting

1½ tbsp granulated sugar

1 tsp kosher or fine sea salt

½ cup/115 g ice-cold unsalted butter, cut into small pieces

3 tbsp ice water

1½ tsp fresh lemon juice

FILLING

One 14-oz/300 ml can sweetened condensed milk

½ cup/100 g firmly packed dark brown sugar

3 large eggs, lightly beaten

1 tsp pure vanilla extract

1 tsp ground cinnamon

1 tsp ground ginger

1 tsp kosher or fine sea salt

¼ tsp freshly grated nutmeg

1¼ lb/570 g malanga

Confectioners' sugar for dusting

Sweetened whipped cream, vanilla ice cream, or coffee ice cream for serving (optional)

1 To make the dough, in a food processor, combine the flour, sugar, and salt and pulse a few times to mix. Scatter the butter over the top and pulse until the mixture resembles coarse meal. Add the ice water and lemon juice and process for a few seconds, just until a ball of dough begins to form. Do not overprocess. (To make the dough by hand, whisk together the dry ingredients in a large bowl and then use a pastry blender to cut the butter into the flour mixture. Add the ice water and lemon juice and mix just until the dough comes together in a rough mass.)

2 Transfer the dough to a floured work surface, gathering all of the loose bits, and form into a disk about 1 in/2.5 cm thick. Wrap in plastic wrap and refrigerate for at least 30 minutes. (If wrapped well, the dough will keep for up to 2 days in the refrigerator or up to 2 months in the freezer. Thaw the frozen disk in the refrigerator overnight.)

3 Transfer the dough to a lightly floured work surface. Dust the top of the dough with flour. Using a lightly floured rolling pin, roll the dough out into a round 11 in/28 cm in diameter and about ⅛ in/3 mm thick. Roll the dough around the rolling pin, lift it over a 9-in/23-cm pie pan, and unroll the dough over the pan. Adjust the dough as needed to center it on the pan and then press it gently onto the bottom and sides. Trim the excess dough, leaving a ½-in/12-mm overhang, and then tuck the overhang under itself to form a double thickness around the rim of the pan. Crimp the edges with a fork or your fingers. Chill the crust for 20 minutes.

4 Position a rack in the center of the oven and preheat to 350°F/180°C/gas 4.

5 Line the pie shell with aluminum foil or parchment paper and fill with pie weights. Bake the crust until pale gold and set, about 20 minutes. Carefully remove the pie weights and foil, return the pie shell to the oven, and bake for 5 minutes longer. Let cool for about 10 minutes before filling.

6 Make the filling while the pie shell is prebaking and cooling. In a large bowl, whisk together the condensed milk, brown sugar, eggs, vanilla, cinnamon, ginger, salt, and nutmeg until completely combined. Set aside.

7 Fill a large bowl two-thirds full of cold water. Trim, peel, and rinse the malanga. Cut it into large chunks if you are shredding it in a food processor. Otherwise, cut it in half crosswise. Submerge the malanga pieces in the water as you work to keep them from discoloring. Drain and blot dry before shredding.

8 Using the coarse holes on a box grater or a food processor fitted with the coarse shredding disk, shred the malanga. Measure 1¾ cups/455 g of the grated malanga and add it to the filling mixture. Stir until evenly combined.

9 Pour the filling into the prebaked pie shell and use a rubber spatula to distribute it evenly. Bake until the filling is set, 50 to 60 minutes. (To keep the pie crust from overbrowning at the edges, check the pie at about 40 minutes to see if the crust is darkening too much. Use a pie-crust shield if you have one, or fashion one out of aluminum foil and carefully place it over the crust to shield it from further darkening.) Let the pie cool completely on a wire rack.

10 Cut the pie into wedges. Dust the wedges with confectioners' sugar and serve with whipped cream if desired.

PARSLEY ROOT

Petroselinum crispum var. tuberosum

HAMBURG PARSLEY / TURNIP-ROOTED PARSLEY / ROOTED PARSLEY

HISTORY AND LORE Prized for its fleshy taproot, parsley root is a member of the family Apiaceae, home to such well-known root vegetables as carrots and parsnips. The plant's flat, dark green leaves, which are coarser than flat-leaf parsley, are edible, too. An Old World vegetable popular in central Europe and the Netherlands, parsley root is just beginning to catch on in the United States, where it is most commonly found at farmers' markets. It was grown and used in Germany in the sixteenth century and was introduced to England from the Netherlands in the eighteenth century, though it never really caught on with cooks there.

In central Europe, parsley root was one of several vegetables and herbs known as *Suppengruen*, or "soup greens," which were traditionally added to the water in which poultry or beef was boiled for use in a soup or stew. If you ask a grandmother of Jewish or central European descent for a list of the essential ingredients in chicken soup, she is likely to include parsley root—my maternal grandmother did!

VARIETIES A number of varieties of parsley are grown for their tops, but only Hamburg parsley is grown for its good-size, fleshy, edible root. American seed catalogs seem to list only one variety, referring to it as either parsley root or Hamburg parsley, and they picture it as a long, whitish tapered root. Apparently, varieties with a round turnip-shaped taproot are known, but I have not found them in U.S. seed catalogs.

NUTRITION The leaves and roots are a good source of vitamin A, vitamin C, and iron.

AVAILABILITY AND SELECTION Typically harvested in late fall and in winter, parsley root is hard to find in many locales. But if you see it—check your farmers' market— buy it. It is delicious and guaranteed to be a root you will grow to like. Look for pale, creamy beige roots that are firm and uniformly sized. The roots resemble small parsnips, but you will know them when you see their leaves, which look like curly-leaf parsley leaves.

STORAGE If parsley roots are purchased with their feathery tops attached, remove the tops as soon as you get home, leaving 1 inch/2.5 centimeters of the stem attached. If the tops are left attached, they draw moisture, flavor, and nutrients out of the roots. Store the roots and tops separately. Put the roots unwashed in a loosely closed plastic bag lined with a paper towel, which wicks away any trapped moisture and keeps them fresh longer. Refrigerate the roots for up to 2 weeks. To store the tops, remove the bottom stems, wrap the leafy tops in a paper towel, put inside a sealed plastic bag, and refrigerate. For peak freshness, use the young green tops within a day or two of purchase.

BASIC USE AND PREPARATION These aromatic roots are usually, but not always, eaten cooked. Prepared and eaten like celery or parsnips, parsley roots can be boiled, steamed, simmered, roasted, or added to soups and braises. The feathery tops can be plucked from their fine stems and used raw in salads or added to soups or braises.

To prepare a parsley root, scrub with a vegetable brush under cool running water, then trim off the ends and peel with a swivel or serrated peeler. Shred, grate, or cut as directed in individual recipes.

YIELDS

1 small parsley root = 2 oz/55 g

1 medium parsley root = 3 to 5 oz/85 to 140 g

1 large parsley root = 6 to 7 oz/170 to 200 g

4 to 6 medium parsley roots = 1 lb/455 g

1 lb/455 g parsley roots, trimmed, peeled, and sliced or diced = 3 cups/415 g

PARSLEY ROOT, APPLE, AND WATERCRESS SALAD

Raw parsley root gives this colorful salad the perfect crunch. To make quick work of cutting the apple and parsley root into matchsticks, I first use a small ceramic mandoline to cut thin slices. I then stack several slices and cut them into matchsticks with a sharp knife. Serve this salad immediately after you toss it, as the delicate, soft leaves of watercress will begin to wilt right away.

SERVES 4

DRESSING
5 tbsp/75 ml extra-virgin olive oil

1½ tbsp fresh lemon juice

1 tsp Dijon mustard

1 tsp freshly ground pepper

½ tsp kosher or fine sea salt

½ tsp granulated sugar

6 oz/170 g parsley root, trimmed, peeled, and cut into matchsticks

1 medium crisp red apple such as Gala or Honeycrisp, about 6 oz/170 g, halved, cored, and cut into matchsticks

2 bunches watercress, about 7 oz/200g, leaves and very tender top stems only

1 To make the dressing, in a small bowl, whisk together the oil, lemon juice, mustard, pepper, salt, and sugar.

2 In a large bowl, toss together the parsley root and apple. Add the dressing and mix gently to coat evenly. Set aside to marinate for 10 minutes. Add the watercress and toss gently to combine. Serve immediately.

PARSLEY ROOT TORTILLA ESPAÑOLA

Here, I have added parsley root to Spain's national dish, giving it an unusual herbaceous accent. Serve it for breakfast, cut into squares for a tapas party, or as a lunch or light dinner main course. If you have some *romesco* sauce on hand, pass it at the table.

SERVES 6 TO 8

¼ cup/60 ml extra-virgin olive oil

12 oz/340 g parsley root, trimmed, peeled, and thinly sliced using a mandoline or sharp chef's knife

8 oz/225 g Yukon Gold potatoes or other waxy variety, peeled and thinly sliced into rounds using a mandoline or sharp chef's knife

1 medium yellow onion, thinly sliced

Kosher or fine sea salt

Freshly ground pepper

8 large eggs

1 In a 10-in/25-cm cast-iron frying pan or ovenproof nonstick sauté pan, heat the oil over medium-high heat. Add the parsley root, potatoes and onion. Season with salt and pepper, reduce the heat to medium, and cook, stirring occasionally, until the vegetables are tender when pierced with a fork, 15 to 20 minutes. Adjust the heat as needed so that the vegetables do not brown.

2 Position an oven rack about 4 in/10 cm from the heat source and preheat the broiler.

3 In a medium bowl, whisk the eggs until blended and then season with salt and pepper. Using a wooden spoon, spread the vegetables evenly in the pan and pour in the eggs. The eggs should just barely cover the vegetables. Reduce the heat to medium-low and cook until the eggs are set around the edges and just about set in the center but still moist, 10 to 15 minutes.

4 Transfer the pan to the broiler and broil until the top is set and golden brown, about 3 minutes. Allow the tortilla to rest for at least 5 minutes before serving. Run a table knife around the inside edge of the pan to loosen tortilla sides. Invert a platter on top of the pan, invert the pan and platter together, and lift off the pan. Slice into wedges. Alternatively, cut and serve the tortilla directly from the pan. Serve hot or at room temperature.

PARSLEY ROOT AND BUTTERNUT SQUASH GRATIN

On dreary rainy weekends during the fall and winter, I stay indoors and putter in the kitchen. I want the oven on for additional warmth, and I often get hungry for a crusty Parmesan-topped vegetable gratin. This humble dish, with multiple layers of potato, butternut squash, and parsley root, is scented with garden herbs—whatever mixture pleases you—and baked with just enough cream and Parmesan to add richness. The parsley root adds a subtle, rustic earthiness to the gratin. I prefer to buy a small butternut squash, but it's sometimes hard to find one. You'll most likely end up with a bigger squash than you need for this gratin. Use the top portion that does not contain the seeds for this dish, and cube the remainder for a quick sauté on another night.

SERVES 6 TO 8

4 tbsp/60 ml extra-virgin olive oil

1 large yellow onion, 10 oz/280 g, thinly sliced

Kosher or fine sea salt

Freshly ground pepper

2 tbsp minced mixed fresh herbs such as rosemary, thyme, sage, and parsley

12 oz/340 g Yukon Gold potatoes, peeled and cut into slices ¹⁄₁₆ in/ 2 mm thick

One 12-oz/340-g butternut squash, trimmed, halved lengthwise, seeded, peeled, and cut into slices ¹⁄₁₆ in/2 mm thick

3 tbsp heavy whipping cream

½ cup/55 g freshly grated Parmesan cheese, preferably Parmigiano-Reggiano

12 oz/340 g parsley root, trimmed, peeled, and cut into slices ¹⁄₁₆ in/ 2 mm thick

¾ cup/45 g lightly packed fresh bread crumbs (see Cook's Note, page 136)

1 large garlic clove, minced

1   Position a rack in the center of the oven and preheat to 350°F/180°C/gas 4. Grease a 2-qt/2-L shallow, broiler-safe baking or gratin dish with ½ tbsp of the oil.

2   In a large sauté pan, heat 1½ tbsp of the oil over medium-high heat. Add the onion, season with salt and pepper, and sauté until translucent, about 4 minutes. Add the herbs and toss to combine. Remove the pan from the heat.

3   Arrange half of the potato slices in a tight, overlapping layer on the bottom of the prepared baking dish. Sprinkle lightly with salt and pepper. Spread half of the sautéed onions evenly over the top. Arrange half of the squash slices on top of the onions in a tight, overlapping layer. Sprinkle lightly with salt and pepper. Drizzle 1½ tbsp of the cream over the squash and scatter 1 tbsp of the Parmesan over the top. Next, arrange half of the parsley root in an even layer on top and season with salt and pepper. Repeat the layers exactly as you have just done, using all of the remaining vegetables and cream and 1 tbsp of the cheese.

4   Cover the dish tightly with aluminum foil. Bake until the squash and potatoes are tender when poked with a fork, 35 to 45 minutes.

5   Meanwhile, heat the remaining 2 tbsp oil in a small sauté pan over medium heat. Add the bread crumbs and garlic and stir to toast lightly, about 3 minutes. Remove from the heat and transfer to a shallow bowl to cool for 10 minutes. Add the remaining 6 tbsp/40 g Parmesan cheese to the bread crumbs and toss to combine.

6   Remove the gratin from the oven, uncover, and sprinkle the bread crumb mixture evenly over the top. Position an oven rack about 4 in/10 cm from the broiler and turn the oven setting to broil. Place the gratin under the broiler to crisp and brown the top, 3 to 5 minutes. Set aside to rest for 10 minutes before serving. Cut into wedges or squares and serve directly from the baking dish.

SMASHED PARSLEY ROOTS AND POTATOES WITH CRÈME FRAÎCHE

There is nothing "skinny" about this deliciously decadent combination of parsley root and potato made with butter and crème fraîche. However, the recipe can easily be lightened up by using a tad less butter and substituting low-fat milk for the crème fraîche. Either way, the earthy, herbal flavor of the parsley root adds depth and aroma, making this side dish decidedly more interesting than classic mashed potatoes.

SERVES 4

8 oz/225 g parsley root, trimmed, peeled, and cut into 2-in/5-cm chunks

1 lb/455 g russet potatoes, peeled and cut into 2-in/5-cm chunks

2 tsp kosher or fine sea salt

4 tbsp/55 g unsalted butter, melted

½ cup/120 ml crème fraîche

1 Place the parsley root and potatoes in a large saucepan and add cold water to cover. Place over high heat, cover partially, and bring to a boil. Add 1 tsp of the salt and reduce the heat so the water boils gently. Cook until the parsley root and potatoes are very tender when pierced with a knife, 12 to 15 minutes.

2 Drain the vegetables in a colander or sieve. Return them to the pan and set over medium heat for just a few seconds to remove any moisture from the pan. Remove the pan from the heat. Using a potato masher, mash the parsley root and potatoes. Add the melted butter and continue to mash and stir until the butter is absorbed. Stir in the crème fraîche and the remaining 1 tsp salt. Serve immediately, or cover and keep warm until ready to serve.

GRANDMA ROSE'S PULLED CHICKEN SOUP WITH PARSLEY ROOTS, CARROTS, AND HERBS

Both of my grandmothers were amazingly skilled in the kitchen, but I always thought of my paternal grandmother (Grandma Becky) as the artful baker and my maternal grandmother (Grandma Rose) as the inspired cook. Every time I make Grandma Rose's pulled chicken soup I feel like I am honoring her Jewish traditions and the old-world recipes she prepared while I was growing up. Since I no longer live in an area with a kosher butcher selling freshly killed chickens, I buy a plump, fresh natural or organic free-range chicken. I like to cut it up myself so I can use the entire carcass for the broth. It's easy to do, and I have provided detailed directions at the start of the recipe. Of course, you can instead ask your butcher to do it for you. Just make sure he wraps up all the parts, including the neck and gizzards.

SERVES 8

1 whole chicken, preferably natural or organic free-range, 3½ to 4 lb/ 1.6 to 1.8 kg

Kosher or fine sea salt

Freshly ground pepper

4 medium carrots, 8 oz/225 g, trimmed and peeled

14 oz/400 g parsley root, trimmed and peeled

2 celery ribs, including leafy tops, cut into 1-in/2.5-cm chunks

4 fresh thyme sprigs

4 fresh flat-leaf parsley sprigs

10 peppercorns

4 oz/115 g dried fine egg noodles

3 tbsp finely minced fresh flat-leaf parsley

1 Set a large soup pot and a dinner plate near your workspace. Place the chicken on a large cutting board. Reach inside the body cavity and remove the neck and packet of giblets. Add the neck and giblets to the soup pot, reserving the liver for another use (say, sautéing it for a four-legged furry friend). Using a sharp knife, preferably a flexible boning knife, cut off the wings and add them to the pot. Cut down between the thigh and body until you feel bone. Pull back on the thigh until you see the thigh joint and angle your knife to separate the thigh from the body. Then angle the knife to separate the leg from the thigh. Repeat on the other side. Add the legs to the pot and place the thighs on the plate. Now remove each breast from the bone. Start at the keel bone that runs along the top of the breast and use the tip of the knife to cleanly cut the skin along the top of one breast half. Angle the knife and cut between the bone and breast meat until you can separate the meat from the bone. Repeat on the other side. Place the boneless breasts on the plate. At this point you should have the carcass left. I like to cut it into a few pieces so it fits more easily into the pot. Generously season the thighs and breasts on both sides with salt and pepper and set them aside.

2 Cut two of the carrots and one medium parsley root into chunks. Add them to the soup pot along with the celery, thyme, parsley sprigs, and peppercorns. Now add the seasoned thighs and breasts to the pot. Add cold water to cover the solids by 1 in/2.5 cm. Place the pot over medium-high heat, bring to a boil, and then reduce the heat so the liquid simmers steadily. Using a large spoon or soup skimmer, skim off the brown foam that rises to the top. After 5 minutes or so, the foam will become white and no more skimming will be necessary.

...CONTINUED

3 Partially cover the pot and adjust the heat so the broth barely simmers. Cook for 30 minutes. Using a slotted spoon or tongs, remove the thighs and breasts to the plate and set aside until cool enough to handle, about 15 minutes. Re-cover the pot partially and continue to simmer the broth for 1 hour longer.

4 When the cooked meat is cool enough to handle, use your fingers or a fork to pull the meat from the bones into large bite-size shards. (You will lose the rustic, homespun look of the soup if you cut the meat with a knife.). Set aside the pulled chicken and throw the thighbones back into the simmering broth. Continue simmering the broth, partially covered, until it has a rich color and tastes like chicken. The total cooking time for the broth is 1½ to 2 hours. While the broth is simmering, cut the remaining two carrots and the parsley root into thin rounds. Set aside.

5 When the broth is done, set a large, fine-mesh sieve over a large, clean soup pot. Using a slotted spoon or a fine-mesh skimmer, transfer the bones, meat, and vegetables to the sieve, capturing all of the juices in the pot. Discard the solids. Pour the broth through the sieve into the pot.

6 Place the pot over medium-high heat and bring to a simmer. Add the sliced carrots and parsley root and 1½ tsp salt and cook for 5 minutes. Add the egg noodles and cook until tender, about 8 minutes longer. At this point the vegetables should be fork-tender. Add the shredded chicken to the soup along with 1 tbsp of the minced parsley. Taste the soup and adjust the seasoning with more salt and pepper if needed.

7 Ladle the soup into warmed bowls and garnish with the remaining 2 tbsp minced parsley. Serve immediately.

COOK'S NOTE

The broth can be made a day or two in advance. Let the strained broth cool before transferring it to a covered container. Refrigerate the pulled chicken and broth separately. To serve, bring the broth to a simmer over medium-high heat and add the sliced vegetables, noodles, and shredded chicken as directed.

CHICKEN FRICASSEE WITH PARSLEY ROOTS AND CHANTERELLE MUSHROOMS

This is a lovely French dish of tender bone-in chicken pieces braised in white wine, with the sauce reduced and finished with a classic liaison of egg yolks and crème fraîche. I like to cut up the chicken in the traditional French manner, separating it into eight pieces: two thighs, two legs, and each breast half cut in half crosswise and with the wing attached to the upper portion. The wing tips are always removed, leaving just the two wing joints attached. You can begin by buying a cut up chicken, but it is more economical to buy the whole bird. An added bonus is to use the neck, wing tips, giblets, and back to make a small batch of homemade chicken stock.

SERVES 6 TO 8

1 whole chicken, preferably natural or organic free-range, 3½ to 4 lb/ 1.6 to 1.8 kg, cut into 8 serving pieces without the back and wing tips (see headnote)

Kosher or fine sea salt

Freshly ground pepper

½ cup/115 g unsalted butter, plus 2 tbsp

3 medium leeks, 1 lb/455 g, white and light green part only, halved lengthwise and thinly sliced cross- wise into half-moons

¼ cup/30 g all-purpose flour

4 fresh flat-leaf parsley sprigs, folded into a bundle and tied with kitchen twine

1 large garlic clove, smashed with the side of a chef's knife

One 750-ml bottle crisp dry white wine

½ cup/120 ml homemade chicken stock or canned low-sodium chicken broth

1 tbsp granulated sugar

2 lb/910 g parsley root, trimmed, peeled, and cut into pieces about 1½ in/4 cm long by ½ in/12 cm wide and thick

1   Arrange the chicken pieces in a single layer on a large plate or baking sheet and season generously on both sides with salt and pepper. Set aside.

2   In a 12-in/30.5-cm shallow braising pan with a tight-fitting lid, melt the ½ cup/115 g butter over medium-low heat. Add the leeks and sauté, stirring constantly, for 1 minute. Cover the pan and cook the leeks until meltingly soft, about 5 minutes. Uncover and, using tongs, add the chicken, skin-side down, in a single layer. Increase the heat to medium and cook the chicken on all sides until the skin turns opaque and the flesh is no longer pink, about 10 minutes total. (You don't want to brown the chicken; instead, you want to remove the rawness from the flesh and skin.) When the chicken is cooked on all sides, stir the flour into the fat in the pan and cook for 2 minutes longer. Tuck the parsley bundle and the garlic clove in the pan. Add the wine, stock, and sugar and bring to a simmer. Cover the pan tightly and cook, adjusting the heat so the liquid barely simmers, until the chicken is partially cooked, about 30 minutes.

3   Using a large spoon or tongs, add the parsley root to the pan, nudging the pieces into the liquid and between the chicken pieces. Make sure they are covered with liquid and can braise evenly. Cover the pan and continue to cook until the parsley root is fork-tender and the chicken is cooked through, 15 to 20 minutes longer.

...CONTINUED

12 oz/340 g chanterelle mushrooms, ends trimmed and cut into large pieces (see Cook's Note)

¼ cup/15 g coarsely chopped fresh flat-leaf parsley

3 egg yolks

½ cup/120 ml crème fraîche or heavy whipping cream

4 Meanwhile, in a medium frying pan, melt the remaining 2 tbsp butter over medium heat and swirl to coat the pan bottom. Add the mushrooms and sauté until tender but not mushy, about 5 minutes. Add half of the chopped parsley, toss to combine, and sauté for 1 minute longer. Remove from the heat and keep warm.

5 In a small bowl, whisk together the egg yolks and crème fraîche. Set aside until ready to use.

6 When the chicken is done, use a large slotted spoon to transfer the chicken and the parsley root to a warmed serving platter that is deep enough to contain the sauce. Cover with aluminum foil and keep warm. Discard the garlic and parsley bundle. Turn the heat to high and boil the liquid in the pan until reduced to about 2 cups/480 ml, about 7 to 10 minutes. Reduce the heat to low. Spoon some of the hot braising liquid into the egg yolk mixture, stir well, and then quickly stir the whole mixture into the sauce in the pan. Heat the sauce through, stirring constantly, until thickened, about 2 minutes. Do not allow to boil.

7 Spoon the sauce over the chicken and then spoon the sautéed mushrooms over the top. Garnish with the remaining parsley and serve immediately.

COOK'S NOTE

I love the color contrast of the golden chanterelle mushrooms against the creamy blonde sauce cloaking the chicken, but it isn't always possible to find chanterelles. This dish will work equally well with other wild mushrooms, such as lobster or hen-of-the-woods, or even with shiitakes.

PARSNIP

Pastinaca sativa

HISTORY AND LORE Parsnips, which grow wild in temperate Europe and western Asia, have been cultivated since Roman times. In the first century A.D., Pliny the Elder used the Latin word *pastinaca* for both carrots and parsnips. During the Middle Ages, before the introduction of the potato and when sugar and honey were scarce and expensive, this sweet, starchy member of the family Apiaceae did double duty in Europe: it was a staple vegetable and a sweetener, the latter made by evaporating its juices and using the brown residue that remained like honey. Parsnips were regular fare for the lower classes of central and northern Europe, especially for observant Catholics on fasting days. In the nineteenth century, both the English and the Irish made parsnip wine, which some consumers considered reminiscent of a sweet Madeira, and parsnip beer was popular in the northern part of Ireland. Today, Italian farmers who breed pigs for the manufacturers of Parma prosciutto often include parsnips in the pigs' diet.

Parsnips were introduced to the West Indies in the sixteenth century and carried to North America by the colonists. They were being grown in Virginia by 1609, and Native Americans quickly adopted the plant, using it as a primary root vegetable until the potato replaced it in the nineteenth century. Nowadays, the consumption of parsnips is confined mainly to northern Europe. But with the proliferation of farmers' markets and CSAs in the United States, this old-fashioned vegetable, valued as a winter crop for soups and stews, is slowly gaining favor.

VARIETIES Even in farmers' markets, parsnips are rarely sold by variety. However, gardeners can seek out several popular types, distinguished by their root shape: bulbous (stocky roots with rounded shoulders), wedge (broad and long), and bayonet (narrow and long).

All American These hefty wedge-type roots have a sweet, nutty flavor and grow to 12 inches/30.5 centimeters long and 3 inches/7.5 centimeters wide.

Harris Model This plant yields hardy, flavorful, snow white roots about 15 inches/38 centimeters long that can be overwintered for a spring harvest.

Hollow Crown One of the oldest cultivated varieties, it produces wide, smooth roots with a mellow, sweet, nutlike flavor. The roots, which grow to 15 inches/38 centimeters long and 3 inches/7.5 centimeters wide, can be harvested in the fall or left in the ground until spring for improved flavor.

White Gem This variety has wedge-shaped to bulbous, smooth roots with nutty, sweet flesh.

NUTRITION Parsnips are a good source of vitamin C and a significant source of folate and manganese. They also carry plenty of potassium, with 365 milligrams in a ½-cup/55-gram serving.

AVAILABILITY AND SELECTION Although available year-round, the most flavorful parsnips are harvested right after the first frost, when their starches turn to sugar, sweetening the root and adding an herbaceous, nutty flavor. Choose roots that are smooth, with pale creamy skin free of cracks and blemishes. They should feel heavy for their size, with knobby heads and fleshy forms that taper to a long root end. Parsnips are always sold with their green tops already removed. Pass up roots that have started to sprout, an indication of a fibrous, woody core.

STORAGE Store unwashed and untrimmed parsnips in a plastic bag lined with a paper towel, which wicks away any trapped moisture and keeps the roots fresh longer. They will keep in the refrigerator for up to 2 weeks.

BASIC USE AND PREPARATION Parsnips are woefully underused, but once most people try them, they are surprised by how sweet and pleasantly complex they taste. They are typically cooked, though are deliciously sweet when grated raw and added to the batters for baked goods. The creamy white roots can be prepared exactly like carrots: boiled, steamed, sautéed, roasted, or braised. They can also be shallow- or deep-fried as a garnish or snack.

To prepare parsnips, scrub them clean with a vegetable brush under cool running water, trim the ends, and peel them using a swivel or serrated peeler. Shred, grate, or cut them as directed in individual recipes.

YIELDS

1 small parsnip = 2 to 3 oz/55 to 85 g

1 medium parsnip = 4 to 5 oz/115 to 140 g

1 large parsnip = 8 to 10 oz/225 to 280 g

1 cup trimmed, peeled, and sliced parsnips = 4 oz/115 g

1½ cups trimmed, peeled, and grated parsnips = 12 oz/340 g

PARSNIP AND POTATO SOUP WITH CRISP DICED BACON

I like to make this soup in the fall and early winter when parsnips are at their peak. They must remain in the ground until after the first frost, which converts their starches to sugar. In fact, parsnips were once (incorrectly) considered poisonous if they were pulled before the ground had frozen. Deeply flavored and aromatic, this soup is perfect cool-weather comfort food.

SERVES 8

3 fresh thyme sprigs

3 fresh flat-leaf parsley sprigs

2 bay leaves

4 tbsp/55 g unsalted butter

1 large yellow onion, chopped

1½ lb/680 g parsnips, peeled and cut into 1-in/2.5-cm chunks

1 lb/455 g russet potatoes, peeled and cut into 1-in/2.5-cm chunks

¼ cup/60 ml dry sherry (fino)

6 cups/1.4 L homemade chicken stock or canned low-sodium chicken broth

1 cup/240 ml heavy whipping cream

Kosher or fine sea salt

Freshly ground white pepper

5 slices bacon, cut into ½-in/ 12-mm dice

1 Cut an 8-in/20-cm square of cheesecloth and place the thyme, parsley, and bay leaves in the center to make a bouquet garni. Bring up the edges to form a bag and tie securely with kitchen twine. Set aside.

2 In a stockpot or heavy soup pot, melt the butter over medium-low heat and swirl to coat the pot bottom. Add the onion, cover, and cook, stirring occasionally, until the onion is soft but not browned, about 8 minutes. Add the parsnips and potatoes and cook, stirring constantly, until well coated with the butter, about 2 minutes. Add the sherry, raise the heat to medium-high, and sauté the vegetables, stirring constantly, until most of the liquid has evaporated, about 1 minute. Add the stock and the bouquet garni to the pot and bring to a boil. Reduce the heat to maintain a simmer, cover partially, and cook, stirring occasionally, until the vegetables are tender when pierced with a fork and soft enough to purée, about 30 minutes. Remove from the heat and let cool for about 10 minutes.

3 Discard the bouquet garni. Working in batches, process the soup to a smooth purée in a blender or food processor. Return the puréed soup to the pot, place over low heat, and add the cream. Warm the soup until steaming hot. Do not allow to boil. Season with salt and pepper. Set aside and keep warm.

4 Line a plate with paper towels. In a frying pan, cook the bacon over medium heat until crisp, about 5 minutes. Using a slotted spoon, transfer to the towel-lined plate to drain.

5 Ladle the soup into a warmed tureen or individual bowls, garnish with the bacon, and serve immediately.

> **COOK'S NOTE**
> The soup can be made up to 3 days in advance. Let cool completely and refrigerate in a covered container. Rewarm gently just before serving. The bacon can be cooked up to 1 day in advance and stored, covered, in the refrigerator. Just before serving, recrisp it in a frying pan over medium heat or on a microwave-safe plate lined with paper towels on medium power in a microwave oven.

SILKY PARSNIP PURÉE

Here is a lovely alternative to a potato purée. Cooking the parsnips in milk and infusing the mixture with garlic deepens the flavor. Serve alongside roasted meats or poultry.

MAKES 3 CUPS/720 ML; SERVES 4 TO 6 AS A SIDE DISH

2 lb/910 g parsnips, trimmed, peeled, and diced

1½ cups/360 ml milk

1 garlic clove, minced

2½ tsp kosher or fine sea salt

2 tbsp unsalted butter, at room temperature

In a medium saucepan, combine the parsnips, milk, garlic, and salt. Bring to a simmer over medium heat, cover partially and cook until the parsnips are very tender when pierced with a fork, 15 to 20 minutes. (Keep the milk at a slow simmer so it doesn't curdle.) Remove from the heat and let cool slightly. Transfer the contents of the pan to a food processor and process until a silky, smooth purée forms. Add the butter and process until incorporated. Taste and adjust the seasoning. Serve immediately or keep warm until ready to serve. (The parsnip purée can be made up to 3 days in advance, cooled, covered, and refrigerated. Reheat in a double boiler or microwave oven.)

ORANGE-BRAISED PARSNIPS WITH CUMIN AND MINT

Layers of flavor make this easy braised side dish a favorite for entertaining. It might seem odd to begin the cooking by melting and caramelizing sugar. But trust me, it accents and deepens the natural, earthy sweetness of the parsnips. The parsnips are delicately glazed with a mixture of butter, orange juice, stock, and a splash of vinegar and then finished with a hint of cumin and fresh mint for a pop of color.

SERVES 4 TO 6 AS A SIDE DISH

1½ lb/680 g parsnips

1 tbsp granulated sugar

2 tbsp unsalted butter, cubed

½ cup/120 ml fresh orange juice

¼ cup/60 ml homemade chicken stock or canned low-sodium chicken broth

2 tsp white wine vinegar

¾ tsp kosher or fine sea salt

½ tsp ground cumin

¼ tsp freshly ground pepper

1½ tbsp finely minced fresh mint

1 Trim and peel the parsnips. Cut them into sticks about 2 in/5 cm long by ½ in/12 mm wide and ½ in/12 mm thick.

2 In a 10-in/25-cm heavy frying pan, heat the sugar over medium heat until it starts to melt. Cook the sugar, lifting and tilting the pan as needed so the sugar melts evenly and turns a golden brown. Immediately add the butter and stir constantly until the sugar and butter are evenly combined. Add the parsnips and cook, stirring constantly, until evenly coated, about 2 minutes.

3 Add the orange juice, stock, vinegar, salt, cumin, and pepper. Reduce the heat to low, cover, and simmer until the parsnips are fork-tender, 10 to 12 minutes. Remove the lid and stir occasionally until the liquid is reduced and the parsnips are glazed and caramelized, about 3 minutes longer. Stir in the mint and serve immediately.

PARSNIPS WITH GOAT'S MILK BUTTER AND THYME

Goat's milk butter is commonly sold at natural foods stores and specialty food shops. With a delicious tang and creamy white texture, this distinctive butter delivers a tartness that balances the natural sweetness of the parsnips. Use unsalted cow's milk butter if you can't find goat's milk butter, but it is worth seeking out. I love it spread on a toasted baguette with a spoonful of orange marmalade. To keep the butter fresh tasting, store the unused portion in the freezer.

SERVES 4

1 lb/455 g parsnips

4 tbsp/55 g goat's milk butter

½ cup/120 ml homemade chicken stock or canned low-sodium chicken broth

½ tsp kosher or fine sea salt

1 tsp minced fresh thyme

⅛ tsp freshly ground pepper

1 Trim and peel the parsnips. Cut them into sticks about 2 in/5 cm long by ½ in/12 mm wide and ½ in/12 mm thick.

2 In a 10-in/25-cm heavy frying pan, melt the butter over medium heat and swirl to coat the pan bottom. Add the parsnips and sauté, stirring constantly, until evenly coated with the butter, 2 minutes. Add the stock and salt, stir briefly, cover, and reduce the heat to medium-low. Cook the parsnips until they are fork-tender, about 4 minutes.

3 Remove the lid, add the thyme and pepper, and stir occasionally until the liquid is reduced and the parsnips are glazed and caramelized, 1 minute longer. Serve immediately.

ROASTED PARSNIPS AND CARROTS WITH FRESH DILL

This vegetable dish needs no last-minute attention, making it an ideal choice for busy cooks. The ivory and orange root vegetables, flecked with fresh dill, complement roasted poultry and are a colorful addition to a wintertime meal or a good addition to a Thanksgiving buffet, especially because they can be made in advance and reheat well.

SERVES 8 TO 10

8 medium parsnips, about 2½ lb/ 1.2 kg

1½ lb/680 g tender carrots

⅓ cup/75 ml extra-virgin olive oil

2 tbsp chopped fresh dill

1 tsp freshly ground pepper

2 tsp kosher or fine sea salt

1 Position a rack in the center of the oven and preheat to 400°F/200°C/gas 6.

2 Trim and peel the parsnips and carrots. Cut them into sticks about 3 in/ 7.5 cm long by ½ in/12 mm wide and ½ in/12 mm thick.

3 In a large roasting pan or oven-to-table baking dish, toss the parsnips and carrots with the oil, dill, pepper, and salt. Roast, stirring once or twice, until the vegetables are tender when pierced with a knife and lightly caramelized in spots, about 45 minutes. Serve immediately, or cover and keep warm for up to 1 hour before serving. (The roasted vegetables can be made up to 1 day in advance, covered, and refrigerated.)

SEARED DUCK BREAST OVER PARSNIP PURÉE WITH PORT REDUCTION

Parsnip purée and seared duck breasts—now this is an elegant pairing. Many home cooks shy away from searing duck breasts (or roasting a whole duck), thinking it is challenging, when, in fact, it isn't. The trick is to be organized, have a good-quality sauté pan, and cook the duck breasts slowly over medium heat to achieve a bronzed, crisp skin. With the breasts cooked skin-side down, the fat is rendered, spooned off, and saved. Don't discard that fat! It is a treat to have some on hand for decadently delicious sautéed potatoes (see page 240).

SERVES 4

Three 12-oz/340-g boneless Muscovy or Pekin (Long Island) duck breasts

Kosher or fine sea salt

Freshly ground pepper

Freshly grated nutmeg

2 tbsp canola or other neutral oil

1½ tbsp finely minced shallot

1 large garlic clove, minced

⅔ cup/165 ml good-quality tawny port

1 cup/240 ml homemade chicken stock or canned low-sodium chicken broth

1 tsp minced fresh thyme

2 tsp fresh lemon juice

3 tbsp unsalted butter, cut into 3 equal pieces

3 cups/720 ml Silky Parsnip Purée (page 222)

1 Position a rack in the center of the oven and preheat to 400°F/200°C/gas 6. Place a wire rack large enough to hold the duck breasts in a rimmed baking sheet.

2 Using a sharp knife, score a ½-in/12-mm crosshatch pattern in the skin of each breast. Pat dry with paper towels. Season both sides generously with salt, pepper, and nutmeg.

3 Heat a 12-in/30.5-cm heavy-bottomed sauté pan over medium-low heat. Add the oil and swirl to coat the pan bottom. Carefully arrange the duck breasts, skin-side down, in the pan and sear them, moving them every few minutes with a flexible spatula for even browning and to ensure they aren't sticking to the pan. As the fat is rendered from the breasts, use a large spoon to transfer the excess to a small heatproof bowl and reserve for another use. Cook the duck until the skin is beautifully bronzed and crisp, 20 to 25 minutes. Turn the breasts flesh-side down and cook for 1 minute, just enough to barely sear the flesh. Transfer the breasts to the wire rack, skin-side up. Using an instant-read thermometer, check the temperature of the duck. It should be about 120°F/48°C.

4 Put the duck breasts in the oven and roast until they register 125°F/52°C for a rosy medium-rare. This should take about 7 to 10 minutes. Remove from the oven and let rest for 5 to 10 minutes.

5 While the duck breasts are roasting and then resting, prepare the pan sauce. Pour off all but 1 tbsp of the duck fat from the sauté pan, leaving behind the crusty brown bits. Place the pan over medium heat, add the shallot and garlic, and sauté, stirring constantly, until the shallot and garlic are just coated with the oil, about 30 seconds. Add the port, increase the heat to medium-high, and scrape the pan bottom with a wooden spoon to release the brown bits. Boil until the port is reduced by half, about 2 minutes. Add the stock and boil until the liquid is reduced to ½ cup/120 ml. Reduce the heat to low and stir in the thyme and lemon juice. Add the butter, 1 tbsp at a time, and swirl with the spoon until emulsified. Season with salt and pepper. Cover and keep warm while you slice the duck breasts.

6 Transfer the duck breasts to a carving board and cut on the diagonal across the grain into thin slices. Divide the parsnip purée among warmed dinner plates, placing it in the center of each plate. Fan the duck slices over the top, dividing them evenly. Drizzle with the sauce and serve immediately.

SPAGHETTI CARBONARA
WITH PARSNIPS, PANCETTA, AND PEAS

Here's a traditional dish with a twist! Earthy, sweet parsnips and a burst of color from the peas turn classic *spaghetti alla carbonara* into a new, interesting dish. It's the magical blending of the eggs and Parmesan that turns these components into a creamy sauce. This pasta is easy enough for a weeknight meal but special enough to serve to guests.

SERVES 6

1 tbsp kosher or fine sea salt

4 tbsp/60 ml extra-virgin olive oil

6 oz/170 g thinly sliced pancetta, cut into ½-in/12-mm pieces

3 medium parsnips, about 12 oz/ 340 g, trimmed, peeled, and cut into ¼-in/6-mm dice

2 tsp coarsely ground pepper

1 lb/455 g spaghetti

1¾ cups/200 g freshly grated Parmesan cheese, preferably Parmigiano-Reggiano

1 large egg plus 3 egg yolks, lightly beaten

1 cup/140 g frozen green peas, thawed

1 Warm a large bowl suitable for tossing the pasta. Set aside.

2 Fill a large pot two-thirds full of water, add the salt, and bring to a boil over high heat.

3 Meanwhile, in a 10-in/25-cm sauté pan, heat the oil over medium heat. Add the pancetta and cook slowly, stirring occasionally, until beautifully browned but not crisp, 6 to 8 minutes. Using a slotted spoon, transfer the pancetta to the warmed bowl.

4 Add the parsnips to the sauté pan and cook, stirring occasionally, until crisp-tender and caramelized at the edges, about 4 minutes. Stir in the pepper and cook until fragrant, about 1 minute. Transfer the contents of the pan to the bowl with the pancetta and let cool for 5 minutes.

5 While the parsnips are cooling, add the pasta to the boiling water, stir, and cook until al dente (cooked through but still slightly chewy), 8 to 10 minutes.

6 Add 1½ cups/170 g of the Parmesan, the egg, and the egg yolks to the parsnips and pancetta in the bowl and stir to combine. Sprinkle the peas over the top and fold in gently. Set aside.

7 When the pasta is ready, drain it in a colander, reserving ¾ cup/180 ml of the cooking water. Immediately transfer the pasta to the bowl holding the pancetta mixture and toss to coat the pasta evenly, adding just enough of the reserved pasta water, a little at a time, to make the sauce creamy.

8 Divide the pasta among warmed individual bowls, spooning any peas, pancetta, or parsnips that have fallen to the bottom of the large bowl over the top. Sprinkle 1 tbsp of the remaining Parmesan cheese over each portion and serve immediately.

THREE-LAYER PARSNIP CAKE
WITH CREAM CHEESE FROSTING

Think carrot cake, but with parsnips—a natural switcheroo! You get the same delightfully moist texture and sweet flavor from ivory white parsnips that you get from carrots. I am a confirmed chocoholic when it comes to cakes, but I am completely won over by this one. It's big and tall, with a generous amount of cream cheese frosting to satisfy everyone (like my husband) who loves a creamy dab with each bite of cake. I like the rustic look, with just the layers and top frosted, leaving the sides of the cake exposed. If you prefer the sides generously swirled with frosting, too, you'll need to make one and a half times the amount of frosting.

SERVES 12

CAKE

Unsalted butter for the cake pans, at room temperature

2 cups/255 g all-purpose flour, plus more for dusting the pans

2 tsp baking powder

2 tsp baking soda

2 tsp ground cinnamon

1 tsp kosher or fine sea salt

½ tsp freshly ground nutmeg

3 cups/680 g grated parsnips, about 8 trimmed and peeled parsnips (see Cook's Note, page 229)

1 cup/85 g sweetened flaked dried coconut

1 cup/115 g chopped walnuts

½ cup/85 g golden raisins

2 cups/400 g granulated sugar

1 cup/240 ml canola or other neutral oil

4 large eggs

1 To make the cake, position one rack in the center and a second rack in the lower third of the oven and preheat to 350°F/180°C/gas 4. Butter three 9-in/23-cm cake pans with 1½-in/4-cm sides. Line the bottom of each pan with a circle of parchment paper. Butter the parchment paper. Sprinkle one pan with a spoonful of flour, and then tilt and tap the pan to distribute the flour evenly. Turn the pan upside down over the sink and gently shake out the excess flour. Repeat with the second and third pans.

2 In a large bowl, sift together the flour, baking powder, baking soda, cinnamon, salt, and nutmeg. In another bowl, stir together the parsnips, coconut, walnuts, and raisins.

3 In a stand mixer fitted with the paddle attachment, or in a large bowl using a handheld mixer, beat together the sugar and oil until smooth, about 2 minutes. Begin the mixer on low speed and then increase to medium speed so the oil doesn't splatter. Add the eggs, one at a time, beating well after each addition until the batter is smooth. On low speed, add the flour mixture and beat just until it disappears. Using a rubber spatula, fold in the parsnip mixture until evenly distributed.

4 Divide the batter among the prepared pans, spreading it evenly in each pan. Bake the cakes until they just start pulling away from the sides of the pan and a toothpick inserted into the center of a cake comes out clean, 40 to 50 minutes. For even baking, at the midpoint, switch the pans between the racks and rotate them front to back. Let the cakes cool in the pans on wire racks for 15 minutes. Run a table knife around the inside edge of each pan to loosen the cake sides. Invert the cakes onto the racks and peel off the parchment paper. Let cool completely before frosting.

...CONTINUED

Two 8-oz/225-g packages cream cheese, at room temperature

1 cup/225 g unsalted butter, at room temperature

2 cups/200 g confectioners' sugar, sifted

1 tbsp fresh lemon juice

½ cup/40 g sweetened flaked coconut for garnish (optional)

5 To make the frosting, in the stand mixer fitted with the paddle attachment, or in a large bowl using the handheld mixer, beat the cream cheese on medium speed until smooth, about 3 minutes. Add the butter and beat until combined, about 2 minutes. Add the confectioners' sugar and lemon juice and beat until fluffy, about 3 minutes.

6 Place one cake layer, top-side down, on a cake plate. Using an offset spatula, spread one-third of the frosting over the top. Spread the frosting right to the edge of the top without frosting the sides. Carefully set the second cake layer on top, placing it top-side down and lining up the edges. Spread half of the remaining frosting on top of the layer the same way. Place the third cake layer on top, right-side up. Spread the remaining frosting over the top of the cake, again without frosting the sides. Swirl the frosting to decorate the top and then garnish the top evenly with the coconut, if desired. Refrigerate the cake for at least 45 minutes to set the frosting. Remove from the refrigerator 30 to 40 minutes before serving.

COOK'S NOTE

If you have a shredding blade for your food processor, you can make quick work of grating the parsnips. Otherwise, use the coarse holes on a box grater.

The cake can be made up to 2 days in advance. Refrigerate until cold and then carefully cover with plastic wrap. The frosted cake also freezes well. Place it in the freezer unwrapped until both the frosting and the cake are firm and set, usually about 3 hours. Wrap the cake airtight in plastic wrap and then aluminum foil. I don't like to freeze baked goods longer than 30 days, as they pick up a stale-freezer taste. Thaw the cake, still wrapped, in the refrigerator overnight.

POTATO

Solanum tuberosum

HISTORY AND LORE Cultivated potatoes all belong to one botanical species (*Solanum tuberosum*), but it includes thousands of varieties that vary by size, shape, color, water content, and starch level. A member of the nightshade family (Solanaceae), the potato is a perennial plant, usually grown like an annual, with fibrous roots and many rhizomes that become swollen at the tip, forming edible tubers. Potatoes are indigenous to the Andean region of South America and remains of wild tubers dating to 11,000 B.C. have been found in southern Chile. They were probably domesticated at least seven thousand years ago in the area around Lake Titicaca, in Bolivia and Peru. Early specimens, which looked nothing like modern potatoes, were most likely dark purple with yellow flesh. In the sixteenth century, Spanish explorers searching for gold observed potato cultivation in Peru, Bolivia, Colombia, and Ecuador, and potatoes were reportedly carried from the port of Cartagena in Colombia to Spain around 1570. From there, the tubers spread throughout Europe, although misinformation regarding the potato's association with the nightshade family kept it from gaining widespread acceptance on the dinner table. Instead, it became a food for the poor and infirmed and for animals. Some ministers preached against eating the "ungodly root," despite the lack of references to it in the Bible.

Interestingly, potatoes did not travel directly from South America to North America. They were late arrivals, introduced to New Hampshire by Irish immigrants in 1719.

In England, potatoes were not universally adopted until the mid-eighteenth century, and in Germany, they were not a field crop until the end of the eighteenth century. The popularity of the potato increased with the regular occurrence of severe winters and prolonged wars, because they could be hoarded and hidden underground, where they remained preserved and less vulnerable to deliberate destruction. From the 1750s through the nineteenth century, the tubers gained widespread prominence across central and eastern Europe and into Russia. They were also introduced to Africa, India, China, and Japan. Today, they are cultivated in about 150 countries around the world, thriving nearly everywhere except for the lowland tropics. Globally, they are considered the fourth most important crop after rice, wheat, and maize.

VARIETIES With close to four thousand varieties, it is best to categorize potatoes in terms of their starch and moisture content to understand how to use them.

MEALY POTATOES (HIGH STARCH, LOW MOISTURE)

Russet, also known as Idaho, Russet Burbank, or baker potatoes.

Potatoes high in starch yield a mealy, granular texture when cooked. They are lower in sugar and moisture than low-starch potatoes, perfect for deep-frying, producing crisp, golden French fries. Ideal for baking: the flesh cooks up fluffy and light; their lack of moisture makes them ideal for mashed potatoes.

MEDIUM-STARCH POTATOES

All-purpose potatoes; most yellow-fleshed potatoes, including Yukon Gold, Yellow Finn, and German Butterball; most purple-skinned, white-fleshed potatoes, including Purple Viking; some fingerling varieties, including Purple Peruvian, Butterfinger, and Ozette; Kennebec, Katahdin, Caribe, Irish Cobbler.

Potatoes with moderate moisture and starch are often referred to as all-purpose potatoes because they are good cooked by nearly any method. They tend to hold their shape when simmered in soups or used for making potato salad. They are also excellent for sautéing, roasting, braising, and stewing. Do as the French do and use yellow varieties to achieve a dense, creamy texture and buttery flavor in puréed or whipped potato recipes.

WAXY POTATOES (LOW STARCH, HIGH MOISTURE)

New potatoes; most fingerling varieties, including Russian Banana, French, and Rose Finn Apple; all red-skinned potatoes, including Red Bliss, Red Pontiac, All Red, Ruby Crescent, and Red Creamer.

Potatoes high in moisture and low in starch are referred to as waxy varieties because of their smooth, velvety texture. Their high moisture content means they cannot absorb much additional moisture, so they hold their shape well when simmered. Waxy potatoes are the best choice for chowders, soups, stews, and salads. They are also well suited for roasting and sautéing because their higher sugar content caramelizes their exteriors to a rich golden brown.

NUTRITION Potatoes have a reputation for being fattening, but they aren't. With 75 calories per 14-ounce/400-gram serving, they are a boon for the weight-conscious eater. Potatoes contain about 80 percent water, 18 percent carbohydrate (most of it starch), and 2 percent protein. They are rich in lysine, have a fair amount of mineral salts (calcium, potassium, and iron), and are a good source of vitamin C. Interestingly, it is the thin layer immediately under the skin that contains most of the potato's flavor and vitamin C.

AVAILABILITY AND SELECTION Harvesting times depend on the cultivar. You will see many potato varieties in the market year-round. Select firm potatoes with taut skin and no cracks, blemishes, sprouts, or any splashes of green. Potatoes with greenish patches have been exposed to excessive amounts of light. Those with sprouts are old and have been stored for too long.

STORAGE Store potatoes in a cool, dark spot away from light and with good air circulation. Avoid refrigerating them or storing them in plastic bags, which promotes softening and sprouting, and protect them from both daylight and artificial light, which can cause them to develop green spots, evidence of increased presence of solanine, a toxin. Protect them from frost. During the cool months, I store potatoes in my basement in a brown-paper sack with the top crumpled over but not tightly sealed. This blocks out light but doesn't trap moisture. During the warmer months, I buy just what I need and use them right away. At 50°F/10°C, potatoes will keep for 2 to 3 months.

BASIC USE AND PREPARATION Potatoes are always cooked and are incredibly versatile. They can be boiled, baked, roasted, steamed, simmered, sautéed, grill-roasted, and deep-fried. Scrub them under cool running water to rid them of dirt. With a paring knife, cut out any eyes that are starting to sprout. If peeling the potatoes before cooking, use a vegetable peeler. Don't peel a potato unless necessary, to preserve the most nutrients. This holds true even when boiling potatoes. If using potatoes cold for salads, plunge the cooked potatoes into a bowl of ice water until cool and then peel and cut them. If using them hot, let the potatoes cool slightly before peeling and then cut as directed.

A CAUTIONARY NOTE When peeling potatoes, any areas of green should be peeled completely away. These patches reveal the presence of solanine, a naturally occurring poisonous alkaloid that intensifies with exposure to light.

Peeled potatoes discolor quickly, so have a bowl of acidulated water handy and drop the potatoes into the water as you peel and cut them.

Use a potato masher, ricer, food mill, or electric mixer to mash potatoes. Never use a food processor, which can result in a gummy, gluey consistency.

YIELDS

1 very small potato = 1½ to 2 oz/40 to 55 g

1 small potato = about 3 oz/85 g

1 medium potato = 7 to 8 oz/200 to 225 g

1 large potato = 9 to 10 oz/255 to 280 g

1 cup cooked and sliced small potatoes = 8 oz/ 225 g

2 cups peeled, cooked, and mashed potatoes = 1 lb/455 g

POTATO AND CORN CLAM CHOWDER WITH FRESH THYME

In this recipe, I skillet-toast the fresh corn for added depth of flavor, and I use fresh herbs, always my preference over dried ones. Head to the deli or meat counter to buy single slices of bacon; otherwise, buy a package and freeze the rest. If you want to trim calories, you can use one slice of bacon and still get that bacon taste, and use milk for the half-and-half.

SERVES 6 AS A LIGHT SUPPER

2 ears yellow corn

½ tsp kosher or fine sea salt

3 slices bacon, finely chopped

1 yellow onion, chopped

2 red-skinned or other waxy potatoes, about 10 oz/280 g each, peeled and cut into ½-in/12-mm cubes

2 cups/480 ml bottled clam juice

1 tbsp fresh thyme leaves

2 cups/480 ml half-and-half

1 lb/455 g small clams such as Littleneck, scrubbed

⅓ cup/20 g minced fresh flat-leaf parsley

Freshly ground pepper

1 Husk the corn and remove all of the silk. Trim the base of each ear so it is even. Stand one ear of corn upright, stem-side down, in a very shallow bowl. (This helps catch the kernels, which otherwise go flying everywhere if cut on a cutting board.) Using a sharp knife, cut downward along the cob, removing the kernels and rotating the ear a quarter turn after each cut. Repeat with the second ear. Discard the cobs.

2 Heat a nonstick frying pan over medium heat. Add the corn and sauté until the kernels are lightly browned and toasted, about 3 minutes. Stir in the salt, remove from the heat, and set aside.

3 In a heavy soup pot, cook the bacon over medium heat until crisp, about 5 minutes. Using a slotted spoon, transfer the bacon to paper towels to drain. Pour off all but 2 tbsp of the fat from the pan and return the pan to medium heat. Add the onion, sauté for 1 minute, and then cover and cook until soft but not brown, about 3 minutes. Add the potatoes, clam juice, and thyme and bring to a boil. Reduce the heat to low, cover, and simmer until the potatoes are tender, 10 to 12 minutes.

4 Add the corn, bacon, half-and-half, and clams; re-cover and cook just below a simmer until the clams open and the soup is piping hot, about 5 minutes. (The half-and-half will curdle if the soup comes to a boil.) Add the parsley and season with pepper.

5 Ladle into warmed soup bowls, dividing the clams evenly and discarding any clams that failed to open. Serve immediately.

GERDA'S AUSTRIAN POTATO SALAD

Born and raised in Austria, Gerda Richards is the mother of my dear friend Roxane Richards Huang. With old-world charm and culinary talent, she whips up an apple strudel in no time, hand stretching her dough over the tabletop to make it leaf thin. It's a work of art, and so is her highly acclaimed potato salad. She made her potato salad in my kitchen, instructing me every step of the way. It was an engaging lesson with a pinch of this, an extra spoonful of that, and the right proportion of vinegar, all the while making sure the potatoes didn't break apart as the ingredients were mixed in.

SERVES 8 TO 10

4 lb/1.8 kg medium red-skinned or other waxy potatoes

Kosher or fine sea salt

9 slices bacon, about 8 oz/225 g, cut into ¾-in/2-cm dice

¾ cup/35 g finely snipped fresh chives

1 cup/140 g diced red onion

1 cup/120 g well-drained and chopped sweet-and-sour pickles (look for German or Polish pickles)

1 tbsp caraway seeds

½ cup/120 ml extra-virgin olive oil

½ cup/120 ml cider vinegar, Champagne vinegar, or unseasoned rice vinegar, plus more as needed

1 Fill a large pot half full with water and bring to a boil over high heat. Add the potatoes and 1 tbsp salt, bring the water back to a boil, and cook until the potatoes are almost tender when pierced with a knife, 15 to 20 minutes. (Gerda says they should be tender but not falling apart; otherwise, they will break apart in the salad.) Drain the potatoes in a colander and let cool for 30 minutes.

2 Meanwhile, cook the bacon. In a 10-in/25-cm nonstick frying pan, cook the bacon over medium heat until crisp and all of the fat is rendered, about 5 minutes. Using a slotted spoon, transfer the bacon to paper towels to drain. Discard the bacon fat or reserve for another use.

3 Use a paring knife to slip off the skins from the potatoes. Cut the potatoes into rounds ¼ in/6 mm thick and place in a large bowl. Add the bacon, chives, red onion, pickles, and caraway seeds. Using a rubber spatula, toss gently to combine. Drizzle on the oil and vinegar and toss to combine. Taste the salad and balance the flavors with additional vinegar; you want a nice acidic edge that is not too sharp. (This is when Gerda carefully tasted, adding a splash of additional vinegar, or even a little water, to balance the flavor and moisture of the salad.)

4 Cover the salad and let the flavors meld for 30 minutes before serving. The salad is best served right away but can be covered and refrigerated for several hours. Bring it to room temperature before serving.

CLASSIC MASHED POTATOES

Several years ago I took a class from Shirley Corriher, expert food scientist and cookbook author. She was discussing potatoes and the absorption of butter into a mashed flaky, fluffy-textured potato such as a russet. She said, "While many cooks mix together the melted butter and warm milk and then add it to the mashed potatoes, you will get a more buttery-tasting potato if you add the melted better first and then stir in the milk. This allows the fat to absorb into the cells of the potato, which have swelled and pulled apart from one another." I'm all for potatoes with a buttery flavor. The milk then loosens and flavors the potatoes, making them softer, creamy, and rich!

SERVES 6 TO 8

4 russet or other floury potatoes, about 2 lb/910 kg

Kosher or sea salt

¾ cup/180 ml milk

6 tbsp/85 g unsalted butter, melted

Freshly ground pepper

1 Peel the potatoes and rinse under cold water. Cut each potato into quarters and place in a large saucepan. Add cold water to cover, place over high heat, cover partially, and bring to a boil. Uncover, add 2 tsp salt, and reduce the heat so the water boils gently. Cook until the potatoes are tender when pierced with a fork, 10 to 12 minutes. Meanwhile, in a small saucepan, heat the milk over medium heat just until steaming hot but not boiling.

2 Drain the potatoes in a colander and return them to the warm pan. Place over low heat and stir for 1 minute to evaporate any excess water. Using a potato masher, ricer, or food mill, mash the potatoes. Add the butter to the potatoes and stir to mix. Mix in the milk, a little at a time, until the potatoes are as soft and moist as you like. Season with salt and pepper. Serve immediately, or keep warm in the top of a double boiler or cover and rewarm in a microwave oven.

BUTTER MASHED YUKON GOLD POTATOES WITH PARMESAN

Deliciously different from russet potatoes, mashed Yukon Golds are creamy rich, with a buttery texture and a lovely golden hue. They have a higher moisture content and are lower in starch than the russet potato, and therefore require a different proportion of milk and butter when puréed. For a busy cook who likes to entertain and avoid last minute chaos in the kitchen, know that it works perfectly well to cook and mash potatoes up to an hour in advance. They can be kept warm in the top of a double boiler set over simmering water, or reheated in a microwave oven just before serving. If you use the do-ahead plan, be sure to add an extra pat or two of butter.

SERVES 6 TO 8

6 large Yukon Gold potatoes, about 2½ lb/1.2 kg

Kosher or fine sea salt

1 cup/240 ml milk

½ cup/120 ml heavy whipping cream

½ cup/115 g unsalted butter, melted

⅓ cup/45 g freshly grated Parmesan cheese, preferably Parmigiano-Reggiano

Freshly ground pepper

1 Peel the potatoes and rinse under cold water. Cut each potato into quarters and place in a large saucepan. Add cold water to cover, place over high heat, cover partially, and bring to a boil. Uncover, add 2 tsp salt, and reduce the heat so the water boils gently. Cook until the potatoes are tender when pierced with a fork, 10 to 12 minutes. Meanwhile, in a small saucepan, heat the milk and cream over medium heat just until steaming hot but not boiling.

2 Drain the potatoes in a colander and return them to the warm pan. Place over low heat and stir for 1 minute to evaporate any excess water. Using a potato masher, ricer, or food mill, mash the potatoes. Add the butter and cheese to the potatoes and stir to mix. Add the milk mixture, a little at a time, until the potatoes are as soft and moist as you like. Season with salt and pepper. Serve immediately, or keep warm in a double boiler or cover and rewarm in a microwave oven.

COLCANNON

In his well-researched and beautifully illustrated *The Country Cooking of Ireland*, Colman Andrews offers a version of this celebrated Irish potato dish from Nenagh, in County Tipperary, toward the southern end of the country. Colcannon is a St. Patrick's Day favorite. Traditionally, the potatoes are mashed with butter and milk and then wilted cabbage and herbs are mixed in. Using curly kale instead of cabbage is another classic variation—and my favorite.

SERVES 6

4 russet or other floury potatoes, about 2 lb/910 kg

Kosher or fine sea salt

6 tbsp/85 g unsalted butter, melted

2 to 3 cups/50 to 75 g lightly packed chopped kale leaves

1¼ cups/300 ml milk

4 green onions, green tops only, minced

Freshly ground pepper

1 Put the potatoes in a large pot and add cold water to cover. Place over high heat, cover partially, and bring to a boil. Uncover, add 2 tsp salt, and reduce the heat so the water boils gently. Cook until the potatoes are tender when pierced with a fork, about 30 minutes.

2 Meanwhile, in a large sauté pan, melt 4 tbsp/55 g of the butter over medium-high heat. Add the kale and cook, stirring frequently, until wilted, about 5 minutes. Remove from the heat.

3 In a medium saucepan, heat the milk just until hot but not boiling. Add the remaining 2 tbsp butter and the green onions and simmer for 2 minutes. Add the kale, using a rubber spatula to scrape any excess butter from the sauté pan into the milk mixture. Stir well to combine, remove from the heat, cover, and keep warm.

4 When the potatoes are ready, drain them in a colander and let cool for 10 minutes or until just cool enough to handle. Use a paring knife to slip off the skins from the potatoes and then return them to the pan. Mash with a potato masher. Stir the milk mixture into the potatoes and mash to distribute the kale evenly. Season with salt and pepper. Serve immediately, or keep warm in the top of a double boiler or cover and rewarm in a microwave oven.

> **COOK'S NOTE**
> Traditionally, each serving is spooned onto a plate, the back of the serving spoon is used to create a hollow in the center, and a pat of softened butter is placed in the hollow.

GRANDMA ROSE'S LATKES

This is my maternal grandmother's recipe for latkes, or potato pancakes, which I enjoyed every Hanukkah when I was growing up. Fried in a very hot frying pan, they are crisp and thin, with wavy shreds of delicately browned potato at the edges. It is hard to resist breaking off the crunchy edge pieces as you move the pancakes from the oil to the wire rack. I consider those fabulous shards a treat for the cook (me!), though I also remember my grandmother sharing generously with me.

MAKES ABOUT TWENTY 2-IN/5-CM LATKES

3 lb/1.4 kg russet or other floury potatoes

1 medium yellow onion, halved

1 large egg, lightly beaten

2 tbsp all-purpose flour

½ tsp baking powder

1 tsp kosher or fine sea salt

Freshly ground pepper

Canola or other neutral oil for frying

1 cup/240 ml sour cream

1 cup/240 ml applesauce

1 Have a colander and a large bowl of cold water ready. Peel the potatoes and rinse under cold water. Using the coarse holes on a box grater or a food processor fitted with the coarse shredding grating disk, coarsely grate the potatoes. Place the grated potatoes in the cold water for 1 minute and then drain in the colander. Rinse the potatoes under cold water once or twice until the water runs clear. This removes the starch and keeps the potatoes from turning reddish. Use your hands or the back of a broad spoon to press out as much liquid as possible. Dry the bowl and transfer the potatoes to the bowl.

2 Using the box grater or the food processor, coarsely grate the onion. Add the onion to the potatoes and mix to combine. Add the egg, flour, baking powder, salt, and a few grinds of pepper and mix to combine. (The potatoes can be set aside at room temperature for up to 1 hour before continuing.)

3 Position a rack in the center of the oven and preheat the oven to 250°F/120°C/gas ½. Have ready a large wire rack set in a rimmed baking sheet.

4 Pour the oil to a depth of ½ in/12 mm into one or two large, heavy frying pans, preferably cast iron, and heat over medium-high heat until the oil shimmers but is not smoking. Scoop up about ¼ cup/60 ml of the potato mixture and gently drop it into the pan. Use a spatula to flatten it slightly, forming a pancake. Form as many additional pancakes as will comfortably fit in the pan without crowding. Fry on one side until golden brown, about 3 minutes. Turn and brown the other side, about 3 minutes longer. Using a slotted spatula, transfer the latkes to the wire rack and keep warm in the oven. Continue frying in batches until all of the potato mixture is used up, adding more oil and adjusting the heat as needed. (The latkes can be made up to this point 1 day ahead if refrigerating or 2 weeks ahead if freezing. Let cool, layer between sheets of waxed paper in a covered container, and refrigerate or freeze. Arrange the latkes, straight from the refrigerator or freezer, in a single layer on a wire rack set in a rimmed baking sheet. Reheat in a preheated 350°F/180°C/gas 4 oven until hot and crisp, 15 to 20 minutes.)

5 Serve immediately or keep warm in the oven for up to 10 minutes. Pass bowls of sour cream and applesauce at the table.

ULTIMATE HAND-CUT FRENCH FRIES

For the adventurous home cook, tackling homemade French fries is one of the ultimate kitchen challenges. I know it was for me, so I collected all of my books on food science and began to study. Thanks to Harold McGee, Shirley Corriher, Russ Parsons, David Joachim, and Andrew Schloss, I now understand the finer points of making perfect fries. It takes potatoes with a high starch content—russets—to make flaky fries with crisp exteriors. Soaking the potatoes is key, because it draws the starch to the surface for a better crust. Selecting the right oil is critical, too. You need an unsaturated fat with a high smoke point, such as peanut, grape seed, or safflower oil. And, most important, the best French fries are fried twice so the interior is cooked through and the surface is crisp.

SERVES 4 AS A SIDE DISH

Kosher or fine sea salt

4 cups/960 ml ice water

2 lb/910 g russet potatoes

Peanut, grape seed, or safflower oil for deep-frying

1 In a large bowl, dissolve 1 tbsp salt in the ice water.

2 Peel the potatoes. (If you prefer a more rustic French fry, leave the peel on.) Using a mandoline or a chef's knife, cut the potatoes into long batons ¼ to ½ in/6 to 12 mm thick. Transfer the potatoes to the ice water and let them soak for 10 minutes. Drain and dry thoroughly with paper towels before frying.

3 Meanwhile, line two baking sheets with a double thickness of paper towels and set near the stove. Set a slotted spoon or a wire-mesh skimmer near the stove. Pour the oil to a depth of about 4 in/10 cm into a deep heavy pot, a wok, or an electric deep fryer and heat to 325°F/165°C on a deep-frying thermometer. (If using an electric deep fryer, follow the manufacturer's instructions for heating the oil.)

4 Fry the potatoes in small batches. Add a handful of potatoes to the hot oil and fry, stirring once or twice, until they are lightly browned at the tips, about 5 minutes. (The timing will vary slightly, so look for color first.) Using the slotted spoon or skimmer, transfer the fries to a towel-lined baking sheet to drain. Continue frying in small batches until all of the potatoes are fried. Make sure the oil is at 325°F/165°C before you add a new batch. At this point, the fries can be set aside at room temperature for up to 2 hours.

5 Just before serving, line the baking sheets with fresh paper towels. Heat the oil to 375°F/190°C. Working in small batches again, fry the potatoes until golden and crisp, about 3 minutes per batch, depending on how deeply golden you like your fries. Using the slotted spoon or skimmer, transfer the fries to the towel-lined baking sheets to drain briefly. Season with salt and serve immediately.

POTATOES SAUTÉED IN DUCK FAT

One rule in my kitchen is never to discard the luscious rendered fat left in the bottom of the pan after roasting a duck, goose, or chicken. I strain the fat and, depending on how soon I think I will be using it, refrigerate or freeze it. All of this fat is a gift from the bird to be used respectfully and deliciously! I can't think of a better way to honor the bird than to cook potatoes in this flavorful fat. Be patient and let the potatoes brown slowly; the less you fuss with them the better they are. It's the crispy sides and crackly edges that make these potatoes so divine. Don't season the potatoes until they have finished cooking. If you season them while they are cooking, they will get soggy.

SERVES 6 AS A SIDE DISH

6 to 8 medium red-skinned or other waxy potatoes, about 3 lb/1.4 kg

Kosher or fine sea salt

4 to 6 tbsp/55 to 85 g rendered duck fat, goose fat, or chicken fat (schmaltz) or clarified butter

1 to 2 tbsp minced fresh parsley, rosemary, thyme, and/or oregano

Freshly ground pepper

1 Fill a large pot half full with water and bring to a boil over high heat. Add the potatoes and 1 tbsp salt, bring the water back to a boil, and cook the potatoes for 8 minutes. They should remain firm but be partially cooked. Drain the potatoes in a colander and let cool for 10 minutes or until just cool enough to handle.

2 Use a paring knife to slip off the skins from the potatoes. (For a more rustic dish, you can leave the skins on.) Cut the potatoes into thick wedges.

3 In a large, heavy sauté pan, preferably cast iron, heat the fat over medium heat until completely melted, then swirl to coat the pan bottom. Add the potatoes and sauté, tossing occasionally, until browned and crisp on all sides, 20 to 30 minutes. (Don't rush the process by turning up the heat. The slow browning delivers a crispier potato.) Toss in the herbs, sauté for 1 minute longer, and immediately remove from the heat.

4 Line a plate with a double thickness of paper towels, then use a slotted spoon to transfer the potatoes to the towel-lined plate. Season generously with salt and pepper. Transfer the potatoes to a warmed serving bowl and serve immediately.

ROASTED NEW POTATOES WITH ROMESCO SAUCE

This classic Catalán sauce keeps for a few months in the refrigerator, so I try to keep a batch on hand at all times for spur-of-the-moment entertaining. It's a perfect sauce to serve with roasted baby potatoes or fingerlings for appetizers. With the sauce made ahead, the only task is to roast the potatoes, and that is simple to do: just cut, roast, and bake.

MAKES 3 CUPS/720 ML SAUCE AND 30 POTATO HALVES; SERVES 8 TO 10 AS AN APPETIZER

ROMESCO SAUCE

2 medium ancho chiles

4 large garlic cloves

1 large red bell pepper, roasted, seeded, deribbed, and coarsely chopped

1 cup/115 g blanched almonds, toasted (see Cook's Note, page 79)

One 14½-oz/415-g can diced tomatoes, drained

2 tbsp red wine vinegar

1¼ tsp kosher or fine sea salt

1 tsp *pimentón* (Spanish smoked paprika)

¼ tsp granulated sugar

⅛ tsp cayenne pepper

3 tbsp extra-virgin olive oil

15 baby new, fingerling, or baby Yukon Gold potatoes, halved lengthwise

2 tbsp extra-virgin olive oil

Kosher or fine sea salt

1 To make the sauce, remove the stems and seeds from the ancho chiles. Place the chiles in a bowl, add hot water to cover, and soak until softened, about 45 minutes. Drain well and tear into small pieces.

2 In a food processor, process the garlic until finely minced. Add the chiles, roasted pepper, almonds, tomatoes, vinegar, salt, *pimentón*, sugar, and cayenne and pulse until uniformly minced, stopping to scrape down the sides of the bowl once or twice. With the machine running, slowly add the oil and process just until combined. Taste and adjust the seasoning. (Feel free to add more cayenne if you desire a spicier sauce.) Transfer to a serving bowl, cover, and set aside for at least 1 hour to allow the flavors to meld. (This sauce keeps, tightly covered, in the refrigerator for up to 3 months. Remove from the refrigerator 45 minutes before serving.)

3 Position a rack in the center of the oven and preheat to 400°F/200°C/gas 6. Have ready a large rimmed baking sheet.

4 In a large bowl, toss the potatoes with the oil. Sprinkle lightly with salt. Arrange the potatoes, cut-side down, in a single layer on the baking sheet. Bake until the potatoes are tender when pierced with a knife and the cut sides are caramelized, 25 to 35 minutes. Let cool in the pan for 10 minutes.

5 Arrange the potatoes on a serving platter and serve warm or at room temperature, with the sauce on the side. (The potatoes can be roasted up to 8 hours in advance. Cover and set aside at room temperature. Warm in a 350°F/180°C/gas 4 oven just before serving if desired.)

GRILLED FINGERLING POTATOES WITH CRUMBLED BLUE CHEESE SAUCE

Grilling lends a smoky flavor to potatoes that cannot be achieved with any other cooking method. The best potatoes to grill-roast are either new red potatoes or small waxy potatoes, such as fingerlings. While traveling and ruminating on potato recipe ideas for this book, I met a friend for a drink and we enjoyed an appetizer of Idaho potato skins with a blue cheese dipping sauce. It made me think about how good a blue cheese sauce can be, especially one packed with fat crumbles of cheese and served with grilled fingerling potatoes. Here's the recipe, which is perfect with a grilled steak.

SERVES 4

1 to 1¼ lb/455 to 680 g fingerling potatoes

2 tbsp extra-virgin olive oil

Kosher or fine sea salt

Freshly ground pepper

Vegetable oil for brushing the grill grate

BLUE CHEESE SAUCE

½ cup/120 ml plain low-fat yogurt or sour cream

½ cup/120 ml mayonnaise

2 tsp Dijon mustard

1 tbsp granulated sugar

½ tsp freshly ground pepper

3 tbsp minced fresh flat-leaf parsley

2 tbsp snipped fresh chives

3 oz/85 g blue cheese, crumbled (see Cook's Note)

1 Prepare a medium-hot fire in a charcoal grill or preheat a gas grill to medium-high.

2 Poke the potatoes in several places with the tines of a fork. Place the potatoes in a bowl and toss with the olive oil. Season with salt and pepper.

3 When ready to grill, to create a cool zone, bank the coals to one side of the charcoal grill or turn off one of the burners of the gas grill. Brush the grill grate with vegetable oil. Arrange the potatoes in a single layer on the cool side of the grill, cover, and grill until the potatoes are tender when pierced with a knife, 18 to 20 minutes.

4 Meanwhile, make the sauce. In a bowl, whisk together the yogurt, mayonnaise, mustard, sugar, and pepper. Using a rubber spatula, gently mix in the parsley, chives, and cheese. (The sauce can be made up to 3 days in advance, covered, and refrigerated. Remove from the refrigerator 30 minutes before serving.)

5 Remove the potatoes from the grill and leave them whole or cut them in half lengthwise. Arrange them in a warmed serving bowl and drizzle the sauce over the top or serve it on the side.

COOK'S NOTE
I am especially fond of tangy, rich blues, such as Point Reyes blue from California, Rogue Creamery blue from Oregon (Rogue also makes a smoked blue and the Gorgonzola-style Oregonzola), and Maytag blue from Iowa.

TWICE-BAKED GRUYÈRE POTATOES WITH LOTS OF GREEN ONIONS

My family called these "put-and-take potatoes" when I was growing up. I have no idea where that name came from. Yiddish? Pittsburghese? It doesn't matter. Although my mother's version of twice-baked potatoes was much simpler than this one, I still remember how special they were when she made them. Baked potato skins with the flesh scooped out, whipped with butter and sour cream, and then mounded back into the potato skins and baked again is homey goodness. My mother added chives, skipped the herbs, and melted shredded Cheddar cheese on top. This dressed-up version is full of flavorful aromatics, a textural crunch of almonds, and has a crusty Parmesan top when finished under the broiler for a minute or two.

SERVES 6 TO 8

4 large russet or other floury potatoes, about 12 oz/340 g each

Canola or other neutral oil for rubbing potatoes

4 tbsp/55 g unsalted butter

⅓ cup/35 g slivered blanched almonds

1 large garlic clove, minced

6 green onions, including green tops, thinly sliced

1½ tbsp finely minced fresh rosemary

4 oz/115 g Gruyère cheese, grated

¾ cup/180 ml sour cream

¾ cup/180 ml plain Greek yogurt

2 to 3 tbsp milk

Kosher or fine sea salt

Freshly ground pepper

2 tbsp fine dried bread crumbs

2 tbsp freshly grated Parmesan cheese, preferably Parmigiano-Reggiano

1 Position a rack in the center of the oven and preheat to 400°F/200°C/gas 6. Using a fork, pierce the potatoes in several spots. (This allows the steam to escape during baking, which keeps the skins from cracking.) Rub the potatoes with oil and place them on a rimmed baking sheet. Bake until the skins are crisp and the potatoes are tender when pierced with a knife, about 1 hour. Set aside until cool enough to handle, about 10 minutes.

2 Meanwhile, in a medium frying pan, melt the butter over medium-high heat. Add the almonds and sauté, stirring constantly, for 1 minute. Add the garlic, green onions, and rosemary. Sauté, stirring frequently, until the onions are soft but not brown, about 2 minutes longer. Transfer to a plate and set aside.

3 Cut the potatoes in half lengthwise. Using a spoon, scoop out the flesh into a bowl, being careful to keep the skins intact and leaving a thin layer of flesh attached to the skins so the shells will be sturdy. Arrange the potato shells, hollow-side up, on a large rimmed baking sheet.

4 Use a potato masher or food mill to mash the potato flesh. Using a rubber spatula, fold in the onion mixture and the Gruyère cheese. Stir in the sour cream and then the yogurt. Add just enough of the milk to create a fluffy mixture that will mound nicely in the shells. Season with salt and pepper.

5 Spoon the potato mixture into the shells, dividing it evenly and mounding it above the rim of each shell. (For a fancier dish, use a pastry bag fitted with a large star tip to swirl the potato mixture into the shells.) In a small bowl, stir together the bread crumbs and Parmesan cheese. Spoon about 1½ tsp of the mixture on the top of each stuffed potato. (The stuffed potatoes can be prepared up to this point and set aside at room temperature for 2 hours.)

6 Bake the potatoes until heated through and nicely browned on top, about 20 minutes. To crisp the top, turn on the broiler and broil until the bread crumb mixture is nicely browned, 2 to 3 minutes. Serve immediately.

SUNEETA'S POTATO CHAAT
WITH CILANTRO-MINT CHUTNEY

A few years ago, Suneeta Vaswani, my wonderful friend and colleague, led me and others on a culinary tour of India. We started in Delhi, headed to Agra and Jaipur, and then south to Kerala and Chennai. Suneeta warned us all that we would be hungry for Indian food after returning home, missing the vibrant spices and intoxicating flavors. She was right. I get hungry for Indian food often and find myself making Indian snacks, the street food of the various regions. I have adapted Suneeta's recipe for potato *chaat—aloo tikki chaat*, as it is known in Delhi—from her amazing cookbook, *Complete Book of Indian Cooking: 350 Recipes from the Regions of India*.

SERVES 6 TO 8

2 lb/910 g baby new potatoes

3½ tsp kosher or fine sea salt

¾ cup/180 ml plain low-fat yogurt

About ¼ cup/60 ml water

⅓ cup/75 ml coriander chutney (see Cook's Note)

⅓ cup/75 ml sweet tamarind chutney (see Cook's Note)

2 tsp *chaat masala* (see Cook's Note)

1 tsp ground cumin

½ to ¾ tsp cayenne pepper

2 to 3 tbsp canola or other neutral oil

½ cup/70 g diced red onion

½ cup Punjabi spice mix (see Cook's Note)

½ cup fine *sev* (see Cook's Note)

3 tbsp finely chopped fresh cilantro

1 Place the potatoes in a large pot, add water to cover by at least 1 in/2.5 cm and 2 tsp of the salt. Place over high heat and bring to a boil. Reduce the heat so the water just simmers and cook the potatoes, uncovered, until they are very tender when pierced with a fork, 8 to 10 minutes.

2 Drain the potatoes in a colander and let cool for 10 minutes or until just cool enough to handle. Working with one potato at a time, place it in the palm of your hand and press gently with the other palm to flatten, forming a patty about ½ inch/12 mm thick. (The edges will split and that is fine.)

3 Place the yogurt in a bowl and stir in enough of the water to make it a thin pouring consistency. Place the coriander chutney and tamarind chutney in separate bowls and stir in a little water. In a small bowl, stir together the *chaat masala*, cumin, the remaining 1½ tsp salt, and cayenne to taste.

4 In a large, heavy frying pan, preferably cast iron, heat 1 tbsp of the oil over medium-high heat until hot but not smoking. Add as many potatoes as will comfortably fit in the pan without crowding. Fry on one side until golden brown, about 3 minutes. Turn and brown the other side, about 3 minutes longer. Transfer the potatoes to a warmed shallow platter, arranging them in a single layer. Fry the remaining potatoes the same way, adding more oil and adjusting the heat as needed.

5 Sprinkle the *chaat masala* mixture over the potatoes. Drizzle the yogurt evenly over the top and then drizzle both chutneys over the top. Scatter the onions over the potatoes, followed by the Punjabi mix, *sev*, and cilantro. Serve immediately.

COOK'S NOTE
Head to a well-stocked Indian grocery to pick up the chutneys, the *chaat masala* (spice mix), the Punjabi spice mix, and the *sev* (vermicelli snack). Alternatively, order them online from www.indianfoodsco.com.

ISTRIAN POTATOES

This is the first of many fabulous recipes I have made from Karen Evenden's informative cookbook, *A Taste of Croatia: Savoring the Food, People, and Traditions of Croatia's Adriatic Coast*. Karen and her husband, Bill, sailed up and down the Adriatic coast, stopping to savor the regional specialties and collect recipes. This recipe comes from Istria, the northern part of Croatia, where Italian influence is strong. The potatoes are tossed with diced prosciutto, tomatoes, garlic, and parsley and baked gratin style, with an irresistible golden-crusted topping of Parmesan cheese.

SERVES 4

2 tsp unsalted butter, at room temperature

1½ lb/680 g German Butterball or Yukon Gold potatoes, peeled and cut into 1-in/2.5-cm cubes

2 oz/55 g prosciutto, diced

1 Roma tomato, halved lengthwise, seeded, and diced

2 tbsp finely minced fresh flat-leaf parsley

2 garlic cloves, minced

1 tbsp extra-virgin olive oil

½ tsp kosher or fine sea salt

¼ tsp freshly ground pepper

¾ cup/180 ml heavy whipping cream

½ cup freshly grated Parmesan cheese, preferably Parmigiano-Reggiano

1 Position a rack in the center of the oven and preheat to 350°F/180°C/gas 4. Generously grease a 1½-qt/1.4-L ovenproof baking dish or gratin dish with the butter.

2 In a large bowl, toss together the potatoes, prosciutto, tomato, parsley, garlic, oil, salt, and pepper. Turn the mixture into the prepared baking dish. Pour the cream over the top.

3 Cover the dish with aluminum foil and bake for 30 minutes. Remove the foil, sprinkle the cheese evenly over the top, and continue to bake until the potatoes are tender when pierced with a fork and the top is golden, 35 to 45 minutes longer. Serve immediately or keep warm until ready to serve.

PARMESAN-CRUSTED POTATO GRATIN WITH FRESH THYME

This creamy, Parmesan-topped potato gratin is perfect for a crowd. The crisp cheese crust, browned and crunchy at the edges, is an ideal foil for multiple layers of paper-thin potato slices scented with thyme, nutmeg, and white pepper. The Parmesan sprinkled on each layer adds just the right amount of saltiness, and the garlic-infused cream brings a rustic earthiness to the gratin.

SERVES 12

3 cups/720 ml heavy whipping cream

1 large garlic clove, finely minced

2 tbsp unsalted butter, at room temperature

6 large red-skinned potatoes, about 4 lb/1.8 kg, peeled and cut into paper-thin slices

1 cup/115 g freshly grated Parmesan cheese, preferably Parmigiano-Reggiano

2 tbsp minced fresh thyme

Freshly grated nutmeg

Freshly ground white pepper

1 In a small saucepan, combine the cream and garlic over medium heat, bring to a simmer, and simmer for 5 minutes. Remove from the heat and let the cream and garlic steep while you prepare the potatoes.

2 Position a rack in the center of the oven and preheat to 325°F/165°C/gas 3. Generously grease a 12- to 14-cup/2.8- to 3.2-L shallow baking dish or gratin dish with the butter.

3 Arrange a layer of potatoes in the bottom of the dish, creating rows and overlapping the slices. Sprinkle the potatoes with 2 tbsp of the Parmesan cheese, a big pinch of thyme, and a smidgen of nutmeg and pepper. Stir the cream and gently pour about ¼ cup/60 ml evenly over the top. Repeat the layering, seasoning each layer with cheese, thyme, nutmeg, and pepper and topping it with about ¼ cup/60 ml of the cream, until all of the potatoes are used. You should have about three layers of potatoes, depending on the shape of the dish. Pour the remaining cream evenly over the top and sprinkle with the remaining Parmesan. Cover the dish with aluminum foil. (The gratin can be made up to this point and set aside for up to 2 hours before baking.)

4 Bake the gratin until the potatoes are almost tender and the liquid is mostly absorbed, about 1½ hours. Uncover the gratin and continue to bake until the liquid is completely absorbed and the potatoes are browned and moist, about 30 minutes longer. If desired, turn on the broiler and broil until the top is browned and crisp, 2 to 3 minutes, making sure the dish is broiler safe.

5 Set aside to rest for 10 minutes before serving. Cut into wedges or squares and serve directly from the dish.

> **COOK'S NOTE**
> You can make this recipe in individual gratin dishes. To serve eight, cut the ingredients by one-third and assemble the gratins in eight 5-in/12-cm round white porcelain gratin dishes. Bake for about 45 minutes and then begin to check for doneness.

RADISH

Raphanus sativus

HISTORY AND LORE *Raphanus sativus* includes a variety of jewel-toned, black-skinned, green-fleshed, and white taproots of diverse shapes and sizes, most with edible leaves. A member of the mustard family (Brassicaceae), the radish is one of the oldest cultivated plant foods. But an absence of archeological records has made it difficult to pinpoint its origin or its original form. Radishes are likely indigenous to Europe and Asia and are believed to have been first cultivated in the eastern Mediterranean before 2000 B.C., probably in Egypt, where they were reportedly included in the daily rations, along with onions and garlic, given to the workers who built the pyramids. They have also been grown in Asia since antiquity, where they were often pickled.

Radishes were among the few vegetables found in the fifteenth-century English kitchen. They traveled to the New World with the colonists, and by 1629, they were being grown in backyards in Massachusetts. Today, Koreans are the top consumers of "Oriental radishes," with the Japanese coming in a distant second.

VARIETIES Radish varieties can be grouped by season—spring, summer, winter, fall—or physical properties. I prefer the latter. Westerners are most familiar with table radishes, also referred to as spring or summer radishes. These are the small, jewel-toned, white-fleshed varieties with bushy green tops. In Asian cuisines, large, long radishes with white or white-and-green skin are prepared in myriad ways. Coarse-skinned black orbs with ivory flesh are common in eastern Europe and Russia.

TABLE RADISHES

Cherry Belle The most common round red table radish found in American supermarkets.

Easter Egg A beautiful bouquet of rose, lavender, white, and red radishes that is a combination of different varieties, rather than a single variety.

French Breakfast Small, cylindrical radishes with crimson tops that fade into white tips. They are crisp-tender and mild and are elegant served with butter and salt.

Icicle Pristine white to red, the tapered shape is reminiscent of icicles, thus the name.

ASIAN TYPES

China Rose Similar in shape but slightly smaller than daikon, with red skin.

Daikon (Japan), mooli (India and the West Indies) White and torpedo shaped, these sweetly pungent radishes are the most common Asian variety available in the United States.

Luo bo (Mandarin Chinese), lo baak (Cantonese), moo (Korean) These names encompass a variety of Asian radishes that are fat and squat, with green tops that fade to white on the bottom. Some are more green than white, others more white than green.

Watermelon (Misato, Red Meat, Rose Heart) These eye-catching beauties have green skin hiding vibrant magenta-veined flesh that makes for a captivating presentation when sliced paper-thin.

BLACK RADISHES

Long Black Spanish Similar to the Round Black Spanish (see following), but shaped like a thick carrot.

Round Black Spanish Round, hardy radish that does well in cold climates. It has tough, black or charcoal skin; dense, dry creamy white flesh; and an extremely spicy flavor.

OTHER RADISHES

Rat-Tailed Grown for its long, crisp, spicy seedpods rather than its root.

NUTRITION Radishes are a low-calorie energy food, with 1 cup/85 grams sliced table radishes carrying only 20 calories. They contain a fair amount of vitamin C and are rich in vitamin B_6, riboflavin, magnesium, copper, and calcium. They are also a good source of ascorbic acid, folic acid, and potassium.

AVAILABILITY AND SELECTION A sure sign of whether a radish is fresh is the vibrancy of its greens. In spring and summer, table radishes abound at farmers' markets, including the colorful Easter Egg ones, but red Cherry Belle radishes can be found year-round at the grocery store. Black radishes are in season from fall through early spring and are usually sold with their greens already clipped. Daikon and other Asian varieties are available year-round at Asian markets and some supermarkets. Some less common varieties, like Watermelon radishes, are available intermittently throughout the year. All radishes should have smooth, unblemished skins and show no sign of dryness or cracking. They should be heavy for their size, an indication of their moisture content.

STORAGE If you purchase radishes with their greens attached, remove them as soon as you get home, leaving a short bit of stem intact. If left attached, the tops draw moisture, flavor, and nutrients from the roots. Store the radishes and tops separately. Store unwashed and untrimmed radishes in a loosely sealed plastic bag lined with paper towels (to wick away any trapped moisture) in the refrigerator. To store the tops, wrap them in a paper towel, then seal them in a plastic bag and refrigerate them for no more than a few days. Table radishes should be eaten within a week or so of being harvested, and Asian types will keep for up to 3 weeks. If kept moisture free, black radishes will keep for several months. Wrap them in newspaper or put them in a perforated plastic bag and store them in the refrigerator.

BASIC USE AND PREPARATION Often referred to as a "salad root," crisp, peppery radishes are, as the nickname implies, an ideal addition to salads. Their pungency comes from oil present mostly in the skin, so you can vary their potency by peeling. Table radishes are sprinkled with salt for a snack or appetizer, thinly sliced and tossed with greens for a salad, or thinly sliced to top an open-faced sandwich. Although Western cooks usually don't cook radishes, they can be roasted, sautéed, steamed, or boiled. Cooking dulls their peppery taste and brings out their sweetness. In Asian cuisines, radish preparations are more diverse: in Japan, they are pickled or grated and used as a condiment; in Korea, they are used for kimchi; and in China, they are made into puddings, braised in clay pots, grated for making steamed savory cakes, pickled, and more.

YIELDS

TABLE RADISHES

1 medium bunch radishes with tops = 8 oz/225 g

1 medium bunch radishes, trimmed and thinly sliced = 2 cups/170 g

Bushy tops from 1 medium bunch radishes = 1⅔ cups/40 g

ASIAN RADISHES

1 large daikon radish = 14 oz/400 g

3 cups trimmed, peeled, and matchstick-cut daikon = 12 oz/340 g

⅔ cup trimmed, peeled, and sliced daikon = 5 oz/ 140 g

SWEET PICKLED DAIKON

Elevated to an art form, the Asian tradition of serving pickles as appetite arousers and palate refreshers has always delighted me. Perhaps that is why my refrigerator shelves are always packed with condiments, chutneys, and assorted pickles—whether Asian or Jewish deli-style ones. As an accompaniment, these simple-to-make sweet and tart daikon pickles cross over a wide range of cuisines. They are equally delicious served as a condiment to an Asian meal as they are served with a French pâté or Norwegian gravlax appetizer.

MAKES THREE ½-PT/240-ML JARS

12 oz/340 g daikon radish

½ cup/120 ml water

½ cup/120 ml unseasoned rice vinegar

½ cup/100 g granulated sugar

1½ tbsp salt

1 Wash three widemouthed ½-pt/240-ml heatproof glass jars with tight-fitting lids in hot, soapy water and dry thoroughly. Alternatively, run the jars through the regular cycle of your dishwasher and wash the lids by hand.

2 Peel the daikon and cut it crosswise into sections 2¼ in/5.5 cm long. Slice the sections into matchsticks ⅛ in/3 mm thick and wide. Pack the matchsticks, standing them upright, in the jars, dividing them evenly.

3 In a medium saucepan, combine the water, vinegar, sugar, and salt over high heat and bring to a boil, stirring to dissolve the sugar and salt. Boil the liquid for 1 minute and then remove from the heat.

4 Using a widemouthed funnel, ladle or pour the hot pickling liquid into the prepared jars, covering the daikon completely and leaving ½-in/12-mm headspace. Wipe the rims clean and attach the lids. Let stand at room temperature until cool and then refrigerate for at least 2 days before serving to allow the flavors to permeate the daikon. The pickled daikon will keep for up to 1 month.

BIWA DAIKON KIMCHI

Gabe Rosen, owner of Biwa, a Japanese *izakaya* (grill-bar) restaurant in Portland, Oregon, shared this recipe with me. It's simply the best kimchi I have ever tasted. With so many variations on this traditional Korean fermented vegetable dish, Gabe's is not too sour and not overly hot. It is balanced and crisp and a wonderful accompaniment to all of the skewered foods and grilled fish (especially the mackerel) on Biwa's menu. My husband always asks for an extra order so he can take some home. To his delight, we now have a homemade batch in the refrigerator, made from the following recipe.

   Gabe had several helpful suggestions in the notes he sent along with the recipe, which he scaled for the home cook. First, he always uses Diamond Crystal brand kosher salt and not iodized table salt. He clarified that the Korean chile powder he uses is the coarse type, not the finely ground type, a tip that was incredibly helpful given the astonishing number of different chile powders at my local Korean market. (See the Cook's Note for further details on the powder.) He also described the container he uses for fermenting the kimchi (a 5-gl/15-L commercial-grade plastic container available at restaurant-supply stores) and what he uses for a weight. I decided to use a 1-gl/3.7-L widemouthed glass jar, a small china bread plate that fit inside the jar, and a tall, narrow glass vase filled with water on top of the plate as the weight. I covered the whole thing with plastic wrap and put it in a cool, dry spot in my basement pantry. Rig whatever container you have on hand, keeping in mind that it must not be more than two-thirds full. Finally, he noted that fermentation works best when the air temperature is cool—below room temperature.

MAKES FOUR 1-QT/960-ML JARS

5 lb/2.3 kg daikon radish, peeled and cut into 1-in/2.5-cm pieces

1 lb/455 g napa cabbage, cut into 1-in/2.5-cm pieces

⅔ cup/85 g kosher salt

1 cup/240 ml water

3 tbsp rice flour

⅔ cup/55 g Korean red chile powder (see Cook's Note)

⅓ cup/65 g granulated sugar

1 bunch green onions, including green tops, cut into 1-in/2.5-cm lengths

1 bunch mustard greens, about 1½ lb/680 g, tough stems discarded and cut into 1-in/2.5-cm pieces

1 medium head garlic, cloves peeled and finely minced

1 tbsp peeled and grated fresh ginger

1 tbsp fresh lemon juice

1 In a very large bowl, combine the daikon and cabbage. Add the salt and toss well to coat the vegetables evenly. Set aside for 3 hours to draw out the excess water from the vegetables.

2 Meanwhile, in a small saucepan, whisk together the water and rice flour. Bring the mixture to a boil over medium-high heat, stirring constantly. Cook for 1 minute, stirring once or twice, and then remove from the heat. (It forms a thick paste and creates "burpy" bubbles. Reduce the heat to low if the paste begins to splatter.) Stir in the chile powder and sugar. (It looks like thick, red chile–colored goo.) Remove from the heat and set aside to cool.

3 Quickly rinse the daikon and cabbage with cold water to remove the excess salt and drain well in a colander. Blot dry with paper towels. Wipe the bowl dry and return the daikon and cabbage to the bowl. Toss the daikon and cabbage with the green onions and mustard greens.

4 Add the cooled chile powder mixture to the bowl and, wearing disposable surgical gloves, use your hands to distribute the goo evenly throughout the vegetables. Add the garlic, ginger, and lemon juice and toss thoroughly to combine.

5 Pack the kimchi into a widemouthed 1-gl/3.8-L glass or ceramic container with straight sides. (A durable, round restaurant-grade storage container also works well.) Place a plate on top of the mixture and press down firmly. Place a weight, such as a closed container filled with water, on top of the plate and press down to force out the moisture in the vegetables. Cover the jar with plastic wrap film and place in a cool, dark place to ferment for 2 to 4 weeks. Every day, press down on the plate to make sure all of the vegetables are submerged. They must be completely submerged for fermentation to occur.

6 After 2 weeks, the kimchi is ready to eat, but it will continue to develop complex flavors if left to ferment for up to 4 weeks. It can be stored in a large, airtight container or packed into four 1-qt/960-ml jars with tight-fitting lids. The kimchi will keep in the refrigerator for up to 6 weeks. (It continues to ferment and the desirable sour flavor continues to develop in the refrigerator.)

COOK'S NOTE

Korean red chile powder (*gochutgaru*) is very spicy with a hint of sweetness. It is made from dried Korean chiles and is available in a fine or coarse grind. You want the coarse grind for making kimchi. It can be found in Korean grocery stores and some Asian markets, or you can order it online from www.koamart.com. It is typically sold in large quantities. The smallest quantity I could buy at G Mart, a Korean grocery store in Portland, Oregon, was a 17½-oz/500-g package. (It wasn't expensive, but that's a lot of chile powder! Make kimchi often; it's a terrific DIY project.) Seal the bag tightly and store the remaining chile powder in a cool, dark place or in the refrigerator.

EASTER EGG RADISH CROSTINI WITH HERBED GOAT CHEESE

When I see bunches of Easter Egg radishes at the farmers' market they make me smile. They're so colorful, almost as if an artist took red and white paints and began tinting the red to create a rainbow of pinkish hues. Do the same thing as you assemble the crostini. Mix up the slices so that each toast includes different shades. The crostini would be a delightful appetizer or first course for an Easter brunch or lunch.

MAKES 16 CROSTINI

16 baguette slices, ¼ in/6 mm thick on the diagonal

Extra-virgin olive oil for brushing

HERBED GOAT CHEESE

8 oz/225 g fresh goat cheese, at room temperature

2 tbsp minced fresh dill

2 tbsp minced fresh tarragon

2 tbsp snipped fresh chives

1 tsp freshly grated lemon zest

½ tsp kosher or fine sea salt

½ tsp freshly ground pepper

1 bunch Easter Egg radishes, about 8 oz/225 g, tops removed and trimmed

Fleur de sel for garnish

Minced fresh dill for garnish

1 Position a rack in the center of the oven and preheat to 350°F/180°C/gas 4. Arrange the baguette slices in a single layer on a rimmed baking sheet. Lightly brush both sides of each slice with olive oil. Bake until lightly browned on one side, about 7 minutes. Turn the slices over and rotate the baking sheet front to back. Continue to bake until lightly browned on the second side, about 5 minutes longer. The crostini should be crunchy but not brittle. Set aside to cool.

2 To make the herbed goat cheese, in a medium bowl, stir together the goat cheese, dill, tarragon, chives, lemon zest, salt, and pepper, mixing well. Taste and adjust the seasoning. Set aside.

3 Using a mandoline set on the narrowest setting, shave the radishes into rounds.

4 Spread a thick layer of the goat cheese on one side of each crostino. Arrange several radish slices on top of each crostino, overlapping the slices to reveal the multicolored skins. Sprinkle with a pinch of fleur de sel and of dill. Serve immediately.

FRENCH BREAKFAST RADISHES WITH HERB BUTTER AND SEL GRIS

The simplicity of this classic appetizer is always welcome. Cool, crisp, good-looking French breakfast radishes are dipped in softened unsalted butter and then in artisanal salt. Bring some fresh herbs with a hint of lemon into the mix and you've created layers of flavor. To serve, use several of the big bushy radish tops on the bottom of the serving plate or bowl and mound the radishes on top. Don't throw out the rest of the tops! Reserve them to make the Radish Top Soup on page 256.

SERVES 6 TO 8 AS AN APPETIZER

HERBED BUTTER

1 cup/225 g unsalted butter, at room temperature

1 tbsp finely chopped fresh tarragon

1 tbsp finely chopped fresh dill

1 tbsp snipped fresh chives

1 tbsp finely chopped fresh flat-leaf parsley

1 tsp minced lemon zest

½ tsp kosher or fine sea salt

2 bunches French breakfast radishes, about 8 oz/225 g each, root ends trimmed and tops trimmed with 1 in/2.5 cm of the green stems attached and leafy tops reserved

Sel gris or other artisanal sea salt for serving

1   To make the herbed butter, in a stand mixer fitted with the paddle attachment, beat the butter on medium speed until it is creamy and light, about 2 minutes. Stop the mixer once or twice to scrape down the sides of the bowl. Scatter the tarragon, dill, chives, parsley, lemon zest, and salt over the top and then beat on medium-low speed until the herbs are evenly distributed. Transfer to a small serving bowl. Serve immediately, or cover and refrigerate and then remove from the refrigerator 45 minutes before serving. (The herbed butter can be refrigerated for up to 2 days or frozen for up to 1 month.)

2   Arrange several of the big, good-looking radish tops on a serving plate or in a shallow bowl, overlapping them slightly. Decoratively mound the trimmed radishes on top. Put the bowl of herbed butter next to the radishes, and set another small bowl filled with the artisanal salt beside it.

RADISH TOP SOUP

Until I began working on this book, I did what most cooks do: I bought beautiful radishes with bushy green tops and lopped off and discarded the tops. Never again. Radish tops are both edible and absolutely delicious, fresh or cooked. This recipe, reminiscent of a classic French potage, takes full advantage of the radish tops, delivering a brilliant green puréed soup with a silky texture and spicy, bright taste. Serve it in the traditional manner as a starter, or offer soup shots for a fun and unexpected appetizer.

MAKES ABOUT 5 CUPS/1.2 L; SERVES 6

2 tbsp unsalted butter

1 leek, white and light green part only, halved lengthwise and thinly sliced crosswise into half-moons

1 small yellow onion, diced

1 carrot, peeled and diced

1½ tsp kosher or fine sea salt

1 medium russet potato, about 6½ oz/185 g, peeled and diced

4 cups/960 ml water

1½ tsp granulated sugar

½ tsp freshly ground pepper

5 cups/120 g lightly packed chopped radish tops (from 3 bushy bunches)

5 or 6 radishes, trimmed and cut into matchsticks

1 In a heavy soup pot, melt the butter over medium-low heat and swirl to coat the pot bottom. Add the leek, onion, carrot, and salt and stir briefly. Cover and cook, stirring once or twice, until the vegetables are very soft but not brown, about 20 minutes. Uncover, add the potato, water, sugar, and pepper, increase the heat to medium-high, and bring to a simmer. Adjust the heat to maintain a simmer, re-cover, and cook, stirring occasionally, until the vegetables are tender when pierced with a fork and soft enough to purée, about 35 minutes. Add the radish tops and stir until the greens are wilted, about 1 minute. Remove from the heat and let the soup cool for about 10 minutes.

2 Working in batches, process the soup to a smooth purée in a blender or food processor. (At this point, the soup can be cooled, covered, and refrigerated for up to 2 days.) Return the puréed soup to the pot and place over medium-low heat. If the soup is too thick, add a little water to achieve a creamy consistency. Heat, stirring occasionally, until steaming hot.

3 Ladle the soup into warmed bowls. Place a little clump of matchstick-cut radishes in the center of each bowl for garnish. Serve immediately.

RED RADISH SALAD AND RADISH GREENS WITH LEMON CRÈME FRAÎCHE

Both the radish tops and roots are used here, giving this salad color and crunch. The creamy lemon-dill dressing is the perfect foil for the sharp, biting flavor of the radishes. Buy red globe radishes with bushy tops so you have enough of the greens to create a mound in the center of each salad plate. Freshly cracked pepper is a terrific accent to the salad.

SERVES 4

DRESSING

¼ cup/60 ml crème fraîche

2 tbsp milk

1 tbsp fresh lemon juice

3 tbsp finely chopped fresh dill

¾ tsp kosher or fine sea salt

2 bunches red globe radishes, about 8 oz/225 g each, root ends and tops trimmed, radishes quartered, and leafy tops reserved

Freshly cracked pepper

1 To make the dressing, in a small bowl, whisk together the crème fraîche, milk, and lemon juice until smooth. Stir in the dill and salt. Cover and refrigerate until ready to serve. (The dressing can be made up to 1 day in advance.)

2 Place the radish greens in a large bowl. Drizzle just enough of the dressing (2 to 3 tbsp) over the top to coat the greens lightly without making them limp and toss to coat evenly. Divide the greens among large individual salad plates, mounding them in the center.

3 In a medium bowl, toss the radishes with the remaining dressing. Divide the radishes evenly among the plates, arranging them in a circle around each mound of greens. Spoon any excess dressing over the top. Garnish each plate with several grinds of pepper. Serve immediately.

SHAVED WATERMELON RADISH AND ASPARAGUS SALAD WITH CASTELVETRANO OLIVES AND GOUDA

My assistant, Andrea Slonecker, developed this recipe for a springtime feature article in *Mix*, the magazine of the *Oregonian*. The salad is a beautiful mosaic of complementary textures and fresh spring flavors. Look for magenta-centered watermelon radishes at farmers' markets. If you can't track them down, substitute another radish variety. Castelvetranos are big, buttery, bright green olives that are found at most specialty markets. White balsamic vinegar adds sweet acidity without the dark color of regular balsamic, allowing the vibrant colors of this dish to shine.

SERVES 8 TO 10

60 medium-large asparagus spears, ends trimmed or snapped away

2 cups/340 g Castelvetrano olives

Good-quality extra-virgin olive oil for dressing

White balsamic vinegar for dressing

Kosher salt

Freshly cracked pepper

4 medium watermelon radishes, trimmed

5 oz/140 g Gouda or other semifirm cheese

1 Have ready a steamer rack and a pan of simmering water. Fill a large bowl with ice water and place near the stove. Line a platter with a double thickness of paper towels and place near the ice water. Working in batches, arrange about one-third of the asparagus on the steamer rack and place the rack over the water, making sure the water is 1 in/2.5 cm or so below the rack. Cover the pan with a tight-fitting lid and steam the asparagus until crisp-tender, about 3 minutes. Using tongs, immediately transfer the asparagus to the bowl of ice water. Let cool for a few minutes and then transfer the asparagus to the towel-lined platter and blot dry. Repeat with the remaining asparagus, steaming and cooling them in two batches.

2 Using a sharp paring knife, slice each asparagus spear in half lengthwise, or in thirds if the spears are particularly thick. Set aside. (The asparagus can be prepared to this point up to 4 hours in advance. Cover and refrigerate.)

3 Pit the olives by crushing them with the side of a chef's knife or other hard, flat object. Work the pits out with your fingers and discard. Place the olives back into the olive juice (to keep their bright green color) and refrigerate until needed. (The olives can be prepared up to 4 hours in advance.)

4 Place the asparagus in a bowl and toss with just enough olive oil to coat without leaving a puddle at the bottom of the bowl. Drizzle with a splash of vinegar, season with salt and pepper, and then gently toss again. Arrange the asparagus on a platter or divide among individual salad plates.

5 Using a mandoline set on the narrowest setting, shave the radishes into rounds and place in a bowl. Toss the radish slices with just enough olive oil to coat, add a splash of vinegar, and then season with salt and pepper and toss again. Spread the radish slices across the center of the plated asparagus. Drain the olives and scatter them around the platter or plates. Using a vegetable peeler, shave thin slices of the cheese over the top. Garnish with pepper and serve immediately.

ASIAN PEAR AND DAIKON SALAD WITH YUZU VINAIGRETTE

Beautiful and contemporary, this salad is white on white with contrasting dark specks from the black sesame seeds. Crisp sticks of Asian pear and daikon are tossed with brightly acidic yuzu vinaigrette. If you can't find yuzu juice, substitute equal parts fresh lemon and lime juice.

SERVES 4

1 tbsp plus 2 tsp yuzu juice (see Cook's Note)

2 tsp grape seed oil

1½ tsp black sesame seeds

½ tsp granulated sugar

½ tsp kosher or fine sea salt

1 medium Asian pear, 15 oz/430 g

8 oz/225 g daikon radish

1 In a medium bowl, whisk together the yuzu juice, oil, sesame seeds, sugar, and salt, dissolving the sugar and salt.

2 Halve and core the pear and cut into sticks about 3 in/7.5 cm long and ¼ in/6 mm thick and wide. As the pear sticks are cut, add them to the dressing and stir to coat to prevent browning. Peel the daikon and cut into sticks the same size. Add them to the bowl and toss to combine. Taste and adjust the seasoning. Cover and refrigerate for at least 1 hour before serving to allow the flavors to meld. (The salad will keep for up to 2 days in the refrigerator.)

COOK'S NOTE

Yuzu is an aromatic citrus fruit native to East Asia. Look for bottled yuzu juice in Asian food stores and some specialty food markets.

DAIKON AND APPLE SLAW

I like to serve this salad in the summertime as a lively and colorful alternative to classic coleslaw. Matchstick-cut crisp daikon and tart green apple are tossed with a sesame seed vinaigrette that carries a fiery-sweet kick of heat from *sambal oelek*.

SERVES 6 TO 8

SESAME SEED VINAIGRETTE

1 tbsp sesame seeds, toasted (see Cook's Note, page 64)

3 tbsp unseasoned rice vinegar

2 tbsp light soy sauce

1 tbsp granulated sugar

1 tbsp canola or other neutral oil

2 tsp Asian sesame oil

2 tsp *sambal oelek* (see Cook's Note, page 134)

1 tsp kosher or fine sea salt

2 green onions, including green tops, thinly sliced

1 large crisp apple such as Granny Smith or underripe Golden Delicious, 8 oz/225 g

1 large daikon radish, 14 oz/ 400 g, peeled

1 To make the vinaigrette, using a mortar and a pestle or a spice grinder, grind the sesame seeds to a powder. In a medium bowl, whisk together the ground sesame, vinegar, soy sauce, sugar, canola oil, sesame oil, *sambal oelek*, and salt. Add the green onions and stir to combine. Set aside.

2 Peel, halve, and core the apple and cut into sticks about 3 in/7.5 cm long and ¼ in/6 mm thick and wide. As the apple sticks are cut, add them to the dressing and stir to coat to prevent browning. Peel the daikon and cut into sticks the same size. Taste and adjust the seasoning. Cover and refrigerate until chilled before serving, about 30 minutes. (The salad will keep for up to 2 days in the refrigerator.)

BLACK RADISH TUNA SALAD SANDWICHES

Here's a terrific spin on traditional tuna salad. Black radishes have a sharp, distinctive taste that livens up the flavor of tuna salad and gives it a nice crunch in place of the usual chopped celery. They have a lower water content than red radishes (or celery, for that matter), so the tuna salad won't "weep" if made a day in advance. Instead of making sandwiches, you can serve a scoop of the tuna salad on a bed of lettuce leaves and tomato slices, or use it as a topping for crostini.

MAKES 1½ CUPS/370 G; ENOUGH FOR 3 OR 4 SANDWICHES

One 6-oz/170-g can good-quality white meat tuna packed in water, drained

1 medium black radish, with peel, grated on the coarse holes on a box grater

½ cup/120 ml mayonnaise

1 tbsp finely minced shallot

1 tbsp chopped fresh dill

1 tbsp chopped fresh flat-leaf parsley

½ tsp freshly grated lemon zest

1 tbsp fresh lemon juice

½ tsp kosher or fine sea salt

¼ tsp freshly ground pepper

1 medium black radish, trimmed and thinly sliced on a mandoline

6 to 8 slices bread such as baguette, whole wheat, rye, or sourdough, lightly toasted

1 In a medium bowl, flake the tuna into small chunks. Add the grated radish, mayonnaise, shallot, dill, parsley, lemon zest and juice, salt, and pepper and stir to combine. Taste and adjust the seasoning.

2 Arrange the radish slices evenly on 3 or 4 bread slices. Spread the tuna salad over the radish slices, dividing it evenly. Top each sandwich with another slice of bread and press gently. Cut the sandwiches in half if desired. Serve immediately.

PANFRIED TROUT WITH ROASTED RADISHES AND RADISH GREEN SALSA VERDE

When bought fresh from the farmers' market, radishes have bushy green tops, which may not be the case at a supermarket. You'll need both the tops and the roots to make this recipe. The roots are roasted to accompany the pan-seared trout, and the tops are combined with capers, garlic, and anchovies to create a variation on *salsa verde*. Spooning the salsa over the crisp-skinned fish delivers a main course worthy of company.

SERVES 4

2 bunches red radishes, including the bushy fresh green tops

1 bunch fresh flat-leaf parsley if needed

2 oil-packed anchovy fillets, rinsed and patted dry

2 large garlic cloves, smashed with the side of a chef's knife

3 tbsp capers, rinsed and drained

Grated zest and juice of 1 lemon

Kosher or fine sea salt

Freshly ground pepper

¾ cup/180 ml plus 1½ tbsp extra-virgin olive oil

4 boned whole trout with head and tail intact, 8 to 10 oz/225 to 280 g each, rinsed and patted dry

6 tbsp/85 g unsalted butter

¾ cup/90 g all-purpose flour

1 Position a rack in the center of the oven and preheat to 450°F/230°C/gas 9.

2 Remove the tops from the radishes and reserve the radishes. Roughly chop the greens; you should have about 4 cups/100 g lightly packed greens. If not, supplement the volume with fresh flat-leaf parsley leaves.

3 In a food processor, process the radish greens, parsley (if using), anchovies, garlic, capers, lemon zest and juice, ¼ tsp salt, and ⅛ tsp pepper until minced. With the machine running, add ½ cup of the oil through the feed tube and process until emulsified. Transfer to a bowl and set aside.

4 Trim the stem and root end from each radish and cut in half lengthwise. Place the radishes on a rimmed baking sheet, drizzle with the 1½ tbsp oil, sprinkle with a little salt and pepper, and toss to coat evenly. Arrange the radishes, cut-side down, in a single layer on the baking sheet. Roast until caramelized and tender, about 15 minutes.

5 Meanwhile, using a sharp knife, score the trout on both sides, making three or four evenly spaced, shallow, diagonal cuts through the skin on each side. Season both sides of the fish generously with salt and pepper. In a small pan, melt 2 tbsp of the butter over low heat and then remove from the heat. Put the flour in a wide, shallow medium bowl. Brush both sides of each fish with the melted butter. Then dredge each fish in the flour, coating both sides evenly and patting to remove any excess flour.

6 Use two large frying pans to cook the fish. In each pan, heat 2 tbsp of the butter and 2 tbsp of the remaining oil over medium-high heat until the butter is completely melted and swirl to coat the pan bottom. Arrange two trout in each pan and fry, turning once, until golden brown on both sides, about 5 minutes on the first side and 3 minutes on the second side.

7 Transfer the trout to warmed dinner plates. Spoon about ¼ cup/60 ml of the salsa across the center of each fish. Scatter the roasted radishes on top and around each fish and serve immediately. Pass the remaining salsa at the table.

RUTABAGA

Brassica napobrassica

HISTORY AND LORE A member of the mustard family (Brassicaceae), the rutabaga is a cross between a turnip and a wild cabbage. It is a relatively young root crop, originating in the late Middle Ages, most likely in either Scandinavia, Bohemia, or Russia. The first written account of the rutabaga dates to 1620, when Swiss botanist Gaspard Bauhin noted that the wild roots were flourishing in Sweden. Rutabagas get their name from a Swedish word, *rotabagge*, or "root bag," though in some English-speaking countries, including England and Australia, they are called swedes. Other common names include Swedish turnip, neep (Scotland), and turnip-rooted cabbage, as it was known in the early 1800s in the United States.

Originally, the rutabaga was grown for animal fodder and only consumed by humans during times of famine; hence, it was regarded as peasant food. It is still an inexpensive staple of northern European and Russian pantries but underrepresented in American kitchens. Because the rutabaga requires cold conditions to sweeten before harvest, consumption is confined mostly to the United States, Canada, northern Europe, and northern Asia.

VARIETIES In the market, you will likely be faced with only one option for rutabagas, but gardeners have the luxury of choosing from a few different types.

American Purple Top This popular variety yields hefty golden roots with deep purple crowns that cook up orange and delightfully tender and sweet.

Laurentian A very sweet flavor and high yield of uniform 6-inch/15-centimeter roots make this a common supermarket variety; often grown in Canada.

Marian These monsters grow as large as 8 inches/ 20 centimeters in diameter and are highly uniform in shape.

NUTRITION The rutabaga is slightly more nutrient rich than its sister, the turnip. It is relatively low in calories, with only 36 calories in a 3½-ounce/100-gram serving, but high in carbohydrates. Deeply colored rutabagas are an excellent source of minerals and nutrients, including vitamin C, potassium, iron, fiber, and folate.

AVAILABILITY AND SELECTION Rutabagas are available in supermarkets year-round but are more bountiful in the fall and winter when they can be found at local farmers' markets. At other times of the year, they are imported from colder regions of northern Canada. Rutabagas are often confused with purple-topped turnips, so note that they have a more golden tan bottom and are usually a deeper plum toward the stem end. They tend to be rather large and are sometimes coated with wax. Although the larger, wax-coated specimens are delicious, if given an option, pick the smallest, wax-free rutabagas for optimum texture and flavor. Choose rutabagas that are heavy for their size, a sure sign that they are moist inside. Avoid those with cracks, bruising, soft spots, or a shriveled appearance. Even though rutabaga greens are edible, the roots are almost never sold with the greens attached.

STORAGE Store unwashed and untrimmed rutabagas in a loosely sealed plastic bag lined with a paper towel to wick away any trapped moisture. They will keep in the refrigerator for a month or more.

BASIC USE AND PREPARATION Rutabagas are one of the hardier root vegetables, with a starchy, low-moisture flesh that takes well to roasting, boiling, mashing, or braising. Scrub them well under cool running water. Trim the stem and root ends and peel the tough outer skin with a sturdy vegetable peeler or a paring knife. Be sure to remove any green-tinted areas to reveal the golden flesh. You'll need to use a hefty chef's knife and a little force to cut this dense root into wedges, chunks, or slices. It can also be shredded or thinly sliced and eaten raw in salads.

YIELDS

1 small rutabaga = 5 to 7 oz/140 to 200 g

1 medium rutabaga = 8 oz/225 g

1 large rutabaga = 9 to 11 oz/255 to 310 g

2 medium rutabagas = 1 lb/455 g

1⅓ cups trimmed, peeled, and cubed rutabagas = 8 oz/225 g

1¾ cups trimmed, peeled, cooked, and puréed rutabagas = 1½ lb/680 g

ROASTED ROOT VEGETABLE STOCK

Making your own vegetable stock is a snap, and there is just no comparison between homemade stock and canned vegetable broth. Roasting the vegetables first yields a stock that is rich tasting and deeply bronzed. I like to make stock on the weekends when I am busy in the kitchen anyway. It is an easy task that doesn't involve precision timing or a lot of thought but does deliver first-rate benefits, especially when I stash some of the stock in my freezer for later use.

MAKES 4 CUPS/960 ML

1 lb/455 g rutabagas, ends trimmed, peeled, and cut into 1-in/2.5-cm chunks

1 lb/455 g purple-topped turnips, ends trimmed, peeled, and cut into 1-in/2.5-cm chunks

1 lb/455 g carrots, trimmed, peeled, and cut into 1-in/2.5-cm chunks

1 lb/455 g yellow onions, cut into 1-in/2.5-cm chunks

2 tbsp extra-virgin olive oil

6 fresh thyme sprigs

8 fresh flat-leaf parsley sprigs

1 large bay leaf

12 peppercorns

1 Position a rack in the center of the oven and preheat to 425°F/220°C/gas 7. Have ready two large rimmed baking sheets.

2 In a large bowl, toss the rutabagas, turnips, carrots, and onions with the oil. Divide the vegetables evenly between the two baking sheets, spreading them in a single layer. Roast, turning the vegetables once or twice with a spatula, until caramelized at the edges, 35 to 45 minutes.

3 Transfer the vegetables to a large soup pot. Add the thyme, parsley, bay leaf, peppercorns, and enough cold water to cover the vegetables by 2 in/5 cm. Place over high heat and bring to a boil. Using a large spoon or soup skimmer, skim off any brown foam that rises to the top. Cover partially, reduce the heat so the stock barely simmers, and cook for 1 hour.

4 Using the slotted spoon or skimmer, transfer the vegetables and herbs to a fine-mesh sieve set over a large bowl to catch all of the juices. Discard the solids. Pour the stock through the sieve into the bowl. Let cool. (To cool the stock quickly, set the bowl in a larger bowl filled with ice water.) Stir the stock occasionally to help cool it down. Use immediately, or cover tightly and refrigerate for up to 5 days or freeze for up to 6 months.

FARRO SALAD WITH ROASTED RUTABAGA, GOAT CHEESE, AND HAZELNUTS

Before I ever had the idea for this cookbook, I read and immediately clipped a recipe for rutabagas that appeared in "A Good Appetite," Melissa Clark's *New York Times* column. The rutabaga was a root vegetable that I had tried once or twice but didn't really know—just like her—until now! This recipe is adapted from her inspired autumnal salad that combines maple-roasted rutabagas with farro, shallots, crumbled *ricotta salata*, and toasted hazelnuts.

SERVES 6 TO 8

1½ lb/680 g rutabagas, ends trimmed, peeled, and cut into ¾-in/2-cm pieces

7 tbsp/105 ml extra-virgin olive oil

1 tbsp maple syrup

Kosher or sea salt

Freshly ground pepper

1½ cups/275 g farro (see headnote on page 86)

2 tsp red wine vinegar, plus more for drizzling

¼ tsp granulated sugar

2 tbsp minced shallot

1 large garlic clove, minced

4 oz/115 g fresh goat cheese, crumbled

½ cup/55 g hazelnuts, toasted and chopped (see Cook's Note, page 79)

4 cups/100 g lightly packed baby arugula

1 Position a rack in the center of the oven and preheat to 400°F/200°C/gas 6. In a medium bowl, toss the rutabagas with 2 tbsp of the oil, the maple syrup, 1 tsp salt, and a generous grind of pepper. Spread in an even layer on a rimmed baking sheet. Roast the rutabagas, stirring occasionally, until fork-tender and browned at the edges, about 30 minutes. Let cool to room temperature.

2 Meanwhile, bring a large pot of salted water to a boil over high heat and add the farro. Reduce the heat so the water just simmers, cover partially, and cook until the farro is tender, 20 to 45 minutes. Add more water if needed. (The cooking time for farro can vary widely depending on the type you buy. Taste along the way and go by texture rather than timing.) Drain the farro in a sieve and shake to remove any excess water. Let cool to room temperature.

3 In a large bowl, whisk together 3 tbsp of the oil, the vinegar, ½ tsp salt, a few grinds of pepper, the sugar, shallot, and garlic. Taste and adjust the seasoning. Add the farro to the bowl and toss to coat the grains with the dressing. Add the rutabagas and toss gently to mix. Add the cheese and hazelnuts and toss until evenly combined.

4 In another bowl, toss the arugula with the remaining 2 tbsp oil, a drizzle of vinegar, and a little salt and pepper.

5 Divide the arugula among individual salad plates or arrange in a large, shallow serving bowl. Mound the farro salad on top and serve immediately. (The farro salad can be made up to 1 day in advance. Cover and refrigerate. Remove from the refrigerator 2 hours before serving.)

BUTTER-ROASTED RUTABAGAS

Use this recipe as a foundation for many variations. For example, you can add fresh herbs to layer the flavors; combine the rutabagas with other root vegetables, such as carrots and parsnips, to create a root vegetable medley; or brush the rutabaga wedges with honey or maple syrup just before they are done roasting to caramelize the edges. Or, you can combine all three suggestions and create a more complex dish. Consider honey-coated roasted root vegetables tossed with finely chopped rosemary, or a combination of balsamic vinegar and honey with just the rutabagas.

SERVES 4 AS A SIDE DISH

2 lb/910 g rutabagas, ends trimmed, peeled, and cut into ½-in/12-mm wedges

2 tbsp unsalted butter, melted

1 tsp kosher or fine sea salt

½ tsp freshly ground pepper

1 Position a rack in the center of the oven and preheat to 425°F/220°C/gas 7.

2 In a large bowl, toss the rutabagas with the butter, salt, and pepper. Turn the rutabagas out onto a large rimmed baking sheet, arranging them in a single layer. Scrape the bowl, drizzling any remaining butter over the top. Roast the rutabagas until they are fork-tender and the edges are caramelized, 25 to 30 minutes. Serve immediately or keep warm until ready to serve.

HONEY-BRAISED RUTABAGAS

Opt for golden rutabagas instead of potatoes as a side dish for roast chicken or lamb. This simple braise delivers terrific flavor with the addition of honey and nutmeg.

SERVES 4 TO 6 AS A SIDE DISH

3 tbsp unsalted butter

2 lb/910 g rutabagas, ends trimmed, peeled, and cut into ¾-in/2-cm cubes

2 cups/480 ml homemade chicken stock or canned low-sodium chicken broth

3 tbsp honey

1 tsp kosher or fine sea salt

¼ tsp freshly grated nutmeg

Freshly ground pepper

1 In a large sauté pan, melt the butter over medium-high heat and swirl to coat the pan bottom. Add the rutabagas, stock, honey, and salt and bring to a boil. Reduce the heat so the liquid just simmers, cover, and cook, stirring occasionally, until the rutabagas are fork-tender but not falling apart, about 20 minutes.

2 Uncover the pan, increase the heat to high, and boil the braising liquid, stirring occasionally, until it reduces to a syrup consistency and coats the rutabagas, about 10 minutes. Stir in the nutmeg and season with pepper. Serve immediately.

MICROBREW-BRAISED RUTABAGAS

Who knew? With a little experimentation, I've discovered rutabagas and beer are made for each other. Add this side dish to a wintertime menu that features roast pork, grilled sausages, braised brisket, or even roast chicken. A porter-style beer works best, delivering a rich malt flavor without a bitter finish.

SERVES 6 AS A SIDE DISH

2 tbsp unsalted butter

1 tbsp extra-virgin olive oil

1 large yellow onion, about 12 oz/ 340 g, thinly sliced

2 tbsp firmly packed dark brown sugar

4 tsp kosher or fine sea salt

½ tsp ground Aleppo chile (see Cook's Note, page 84)

¼ tsp freshly ground black pepper

¼ tsp ground cinnamon

2 lb/910 g rutabagas, ends trimmed, peeled, and cut into ½-in/12-mm wedges

One 12-oz/360-ml bottle porter-style beer

1½ cups/360 ml Roasted Root Vegetable Stock (page 267) or canned low-sodium vegetable broth

2 tsp finely chopped fresh oregano

2 tsp finely chopped fresh thyme

1 In a Dutch oven or other heavy pot, melt the butter with the oil over medium-low heat until the butter is foamy. Add the onion and stir to coat evenly. Cover and cook until the onion begins to soften, about 5 minutes. Uncover and continue to cook, stirring frequently, until the onion is evenly golden brown and caramelized, about 20 minutes.

2 Add the brown sugar, salt, Aleppo pepper, black pepper, and cinnamon and stir constantly until the brown sugar has melted and the spices are aromatic, about 1 minute. Add the rutabagas and stir to coat. Add the beer and stock, pressing down on the vegetables to submerge them. The liquid should just cover the vegetables. If it doesn't, add more stock or water as needed. Increase the heat to medium-high and bring to a boil. Reduce the heat until the liquid is at a simmer, cover, and cook for 20 minutes. Stir in the oregano and thyme, re-cover, and continue to cook until the rutabagas are fork-tender, 5 to 10 minutes more. Using a slotted spoon, transfer the rutabagas and onions to a serving bowl, cover, and keep warm.

3 Increase the heat to high and boil the braising liquid, stirring occasionally, until it reduces to about ¼ cup/60 ml and has thickened to a syrup consistency, 10 to 15 minutes. Reduce the heat to low, return the rutabagas and onion to the pan, and toss to coat in the sauce. Heat until the vegetables are hot and then taste and adjust the seasoning. Serve immediately.

RUTABAGA HASH WITH ONIONS AND CRISP BACON

Make this hash for a weekend brunch or as an easy weeknight supper. I like to serve it with a tossed green salad or a steamed vegetable and a crusty loaf of bread. Pass Tabasco or other hot sauce at the table; the vinegary, smoky flavor of hot sauce complements the rutabagas, bacon, and chiles. Poach eggs to place on top of this hearty hash. The runny soft-cooked eggs are a perfect accompaniment.

SERVES 4 TO 6

6 slices bacon, about 5 oz/140 g, cut into ¾-in/2-cm pieces

2 lb/910 g rutabagas, ends trimmed, peeled, and cut into ½-in/12-mm dice

1 large yellow onion, cut into ½-in/12-mm dice

2 celery ribs, halved lengthwise, then cut crosswise into slices ¼ in/6 mm thick

1 Anaheim chile, stemmed, seeded, and cut into ½-in/12-mm dice (see Cook's Note, page 40)

1 jalapeño chile, stemmed, seeded, and minced

½ tsp kosher or fine sea salt

½ tsp freshly ground pepper

3 tbsp chopped fresh cilantro, plus more for garnish

Tabasco or other hot-pepper sauce for serving

1 In a 12-in/30.5-cm frying pan, preferably cast iron, cook the bacon over medium-high heat until crisp, about 5 minutes. Using a slotted spoon, transfer to paper towels to drain.

2 Pour off all but ¼ cup/60 ml of the fat from the pan. Return the pan to medium-high heat, add the rutabagas and onion, and sauté, stirring constantly, for 2 minutes. Reduce the heat to medium, cover, and cook, stirring once, for 7 minutes to steam the rutabagas. Uncover the pan, increase the heat to medium-high, and cook, stirring, until the vegetables are browned at the edges, about 1 minute longer.

3 Add the celery and both chiles, stir briefly, and then cover and cook for 3 minutes longer. Uncover the pan and add the salt and pepper. Cook, stirring frequently, until the rutabagas are fork-tender and the celery is crisp but not raw tasting. Fold in the cilantro and bacon. Serve immediately, garnished with additional cilantro. Pass the hot-pepper sauce at the table.

SOUR CREAM MASHED RUTABAGAS WITH FRESH DILL

The sweet, delicately flavored pale yellow flesh of rutabagas pairs beautifully with potatoes and transforms a classic mash into a far more intriguing side dish. Add sour cream and flecks of fresh dill and serve with a holiday bird or with a simple roast chicken for a Sunday supper. I turn leftovers into a hearty brunch main course by reheating the mash, mounding it in a warmed wide bowl, and placing two poached eggs on top. Pass the hot sauce or offer some grated cheese for sprinkling.

SERVES 6 AS A SIDE DISH

1½ lb/680 g rutabagas
(about 3 medium)

1½ lb/680 g russet or other
floury potatoes

1 tbsp plus 2 tsp kosher
or fine sea salt

2 tbsp unsalted butter,
at room temperature

½ cup/120 ml sour cream

1 tbsp finely chopped fresh dill

Freshly ground pepper

1 Trim and peel the rutabagas and potatoes and rinse under cold water. Cut the rutabagas into 1-in/2.5-cm chunks. Cut the potatoes into 2-in/5-cm chunks. (The rutabagas take longer to cook, so cutting them into smaller chunks means they will cook in the same amount of time as the potatoes.) Place the rutabagas and potatoes in a large saucepan and add cold water to cover. Add 1 tbsp of the salt, place over high heat, cover partially, and bring to a boil. Reduce the heat so the water boils gently and cook until the potatoes and rutabagas are fork-tender without falling apart, about 15 minutes.

2 Drain the rutabagas and potatoes in a colander, return them to the warm pan, place over low heat, and stir for 1 minute to evaporate any excess water. Use a potato masher to mash the vegetables. Blend in the butter until it melts, and then add the sour cream and the remaining 2 tsp salt, mixing well. Stir in the dill and season with pepper. Serve immediately or keep warm until ready to serve.

> **COOK'S NOTE**
> The rutabaga mash can be made up to 2 hours in advance. Keep warm in the top of a double boiler set over simmering water, or transfer to a covered microwave-safe dish and reheat in a microwave oven just before serving.

DOMENICA MARCHETTI'S POT ROAST WITH HONEY-ROASTED RUTABAGAS

Like me, cookbook author and friend Domenica Marchetti was well into her twenties before she had her first taste of rutabagas. She said, "It's not a vegetable that you see much in Italian cooking. It was at an old family-style restaurant in Detroit called the Blue Pointe, and the rutabagas came mashed, as a side dish. I liked them immediately—earthy and faintly sweet, with dense golden flesh. I had a notion that rutabaga and honey would be a good match, and they are. Here, the vegetable is tossed with honey butter and roasted [together with carrots] and then braised with beef for a delicious twist on classic pot roast."

SERVES 4 TO 6 AS A MAIN COURSE

1½ lb/680 g rutabagas, ends trimmed, peeled, and cut into 2-in/5-cm pieces

1 lb/455 g carrots, peeled, trimmed, and cut into 2-in/5-cm pieces

¼ cup/60 ml honey

4 tbsp/55 g unsalted butter

Kosher or fine sea salt

Freshly ground pepper

2 tbsp extra-virgin olive oil

1 boneless chuck roast, about 3 lb/1.4 kg

1 large yellow onion, finely diced

1½ tsp finely chopped fresh thyme

½ cup/120 ml dry white wine

1 cup/240 ml homemade beef stock or canned low-sodium beef broth

1 Position a rack in the center of the oven and preheat to 400°F/200°C/gas 6.

2 In a large bowl, combine the rutabagas and carrots. In a small saucepan, combine the honey and butter over low heat and heat until the butter is melted, stirring to mix the butter and honey together. Pour the honey butter over the vegetables and toss to coat evenly. Season with ½ tsp salt and a generous grind of pepper. Transfer the vegetables to a rimmed baking sheet and spread them in a single layer. Roast the vegetables, turning them every 15 minutes or so, until they are tender and browned in spots, about 45 minutes. Remove from the oven and set aside. Reduce the oven temperature to 325°F/165°C/gas 3.

3 In a large Dutch oven or other heavy pot, heat the oil over medium-high heat. Season the chuck roast on both sides with a little salt and pepper, add to the pot, and brown until the bottom is nicely seared, 3 to 4 minutes. Turn the roast and brown the other side, another 3 to 4 minutes. Transfer the meat to a deep plate.

4 Reduce the heat to medium-low, add the onion and thyme, and sauté, stirring frequently, until the onion is softened and translucent, 7 to 8 minutes. Raise the heat to medium-high and pour in the wine. Cook at a lively simmer until most of the wine has been absorbed, about 1 minute.

5 Return the meat to the pot along with any juices that have accumulated on the plate. Add the roasted vegetables and the stock, raise the heat to medium-high, and bring to a simmer. Cover the pot and place it in the oven. Let the pot roast braise, turning the meat every 30 to 45 minutes, until fork-tender, 2 to 2½ hours.

6 Transfer the roast to a cutting board and use a knife to slice it or a fork and a knife to pull it into large chunks. Arrange the meat on a warmed serving platter and spoon the vegetables around it. Spoon the sauce over the meat and vegetables and serve immediately.

RUSTIC APPLE AND RUTABAGA TART

A free-form tart, called a *galette* in French, is a boon to novice dessert makers everywhere. The dough is rolled out, a fruit filling is mounded in the center, and the edges are folded over the filling. There's no fitting the dough into a pie plate and no crimping of edges, which can intimidate many cooks. Although it's not traditional to add rutabagas to a fruit dessert, when combined with apples and golden raisins, they take on an earthy, homey flavor that makes the tart completely intriguing, including an herbal accent you can't identify but I promise you'll like.

SERVES 8 TO 10

TART DOUGH

1¾ cups/220 g all-purpose flour, plus more for dusting

1½ tbsp granulated sugar

1 tsp kosher or fine sea salt

¾ cup/170 g ice-cold unsalted butter, cut into small pieces

3 to 4 tbsp ice water

1½ tsp fresh lemon juice

FILLING

1¾ lb/800 g Golden Delicious apples (about 3 large), peeled, halved, cored, and cut into thin wedges

2 tsp fresh lemon juice

1 large rutabaga, 10 oz/280 g, ends trimmed, peeled, and cut into thin wedges

1 cup/140 g golden raisins

1 cup/200 g firmly packed light brown sugar

2 tbsp bourbon whiskey

⅓ cup/65 g granulated sugar

3 tbsp cornstarch

1½ tsp ground cinnamon

½ tsp kosher or fine sea salt

¼ tsp freshly grated nutmeg

1 To make the dough, in a food processor, combine the flour, sugar, and salt and pulse a few times to mix. Scatter the butter over the top and pulse until the mixture resembles coarse meal. Add the ice water and lemon juice and process for a few seconds, just until a ball of dough begins to form. Do not overprocess. (To make the dough by hand, whisk together the dry ingredients in a large bowl and then use a pastry blender to cut the butter into the flour mixture. Add the ice water and lemon juice and mix just until the dough comes together in a rough mass.)

2 Transfer the dough to a floured work surface, gathering all of the loose bits, and form into a disk about 1 in/2.5 cm thick. Wrap in plastic wrap and refrigerate for at least 1 hour. (If wrapped well, the dough will keep for up to 2 days in the refrigerator or up to 2 months in the freezer. Thaw the frozen disk in the refrigerator overnight.)

3 To make the filling, in a large bowl, toss the apples with the lemon juice to prevent them from browning. Set aside.

4 In a heavy saucepan, combine the rutabagas, raisins, brown sugar, and whiskey and stir to combine and moisten the sugar. Place over medium-low heat, bring to a simmer, and cook, stirring constantly, until the sugar is completely dissolved. Cover, reduce the heat to low, and cook until the rutabagas are almost fork-tender but still have a little resistance, about 15 minutes. Using a slotted spoon, transfer the rutabagas and raisins to the bowl with the apples and toss to combine. Return the pan to medium heat and boil the syrup remaining in the pan until it is reduced to 3 tbsp. Pour the syrup over the apple mixture. In a small bowl, stir together the granulated sugar, cornstarch, cinnamon, salt, and nutmeg. Sprinkle over the apple mixture and toss gently until incorporated. Set aside to cool completely.

1 tbsp milk

Turbinado sugar for sprinkling

Sweetened whipped cream or vanilla ice cream for serving (optional)

5 Position a rack in the center of the oven and preheat to 375°F/190°C/gas 5. Line a large rimmed baking sheet with parchment paper.

6 On a lightly floured work surface, roll out the dough into a circle about 14 in/35.5 cm in diameter. (It is fine for the edges to be uneven; it makes the tart look more rustic.) Dust the work surface and dough with a little more flour as needed to keep the dough from sticking. Roll the dough around the rolling pin, lift it over the prepared baking sheet, and unroll the dough over the baking sheet. Adjust the dough as needed to center it on the sheet pan; excess dough will hang over the edges of the pan. Mound the filling in the center of the dough, leaving a 2-in/5-cm border uncovered. Bury the raisins under the apples and rutabagas so they won't burn when the tart bakes. Fold the border of the dough up and over the apples and rutabagas (the center of the tart is open), pleating the edge and pinching to seal any cracks. Brush the crust with the milk and then sprinkle generously with the turbinado sugar.

7 Bake the tart until the crust is well browned and the filling is bubbly, 45 to 55 minutes. Let cool completely on the pan on a wire rack. When ready to serve, using a large, wide metal spatula, slide the tart onto a big plate or platter and cut into wedges. Serve with whipped cream, if desired.

SALSIFY
WHITE SALSIFY / OYSTER PLANT / VEGETABLE OYSTER
Tragopogon porrifolius

AND

SCORZONERA
BLACK SALSIFY / BLACK OYSTER PLANT
Scorzonera hispanica

HISTORY AND LORE I have put salsify and scorzonera together because they are closely related botanically (family Asteraceae) and they can be used interchangeably in the kitchen. Of the two, salsify (*Tragopogon porrifolius*) is better known but still woefully underappreciated as a delicious root vegetable. Native to the eastern Mediterranean, wild salsify was known as a vegetable in ancient times but was not cultivated until the sixteenth century. It was first planted in Italy and France and only later in central and northern Europe. It was brought to North America in the late eighteenth century, and, according to his garden records, Thomas Jefferson planted it at Monticello. Although recipes for the tasty taproot regularly appeared in early American cookbooks, it has nearly disappeared from U.S. gardens and markets in more recent times. Some varieties have a mild oyster flavor, which explains its other most popular common name, oyster plant.

Scorzonera (*Scorzonera hispanica*), with its black skin and narrower profile, is similar to salsify but considered superior in taste. One source suggests that the name comes from the French *scorzon,* or "serpent," due to its early use in Spain as an antidote for snake bites. Another suggests it is drawn from the Italian *scorza,* or "bark," and *nera,* or "black," which describes the root. Scorzonera is native to central and southern Europe and is found as far east as Siberia. It was known to the Greeks and Romans, who used it medicinally, but cultivation as a food plant didn't

begin until the seventeenth century, when it was grown in Spain. Today, Belgium is the most important producer and exporter of scorzonera, followed by France and the Netherlands. Little is cultivated in Britain and the United States, though some home gardeners and some small-scale farmers who sell at farmers' markets have begun growing it. Occasionally, you'll see it at gourmet produce markets, likely imported from Belgium.

VARIETIES Salsify, a biennial, produces a thin, tapering taproot with creamy white flesh that grows up to 15 inches/ 38 centimeters long. It has narrow, leeklike leaves and beautiful, reddish violet edible flowers that are followed by thistlelike seedheads.

Giant Cultivated for its uniformly shaped, consistently long taproot and delicate taste of oysters.

Sandwich Island This salsify is an heirloom variety native to Europe. It has smooth skin and strongly flavored roots mildly reminiscent of oysters.

Scorzonera, a winter-hardy perennial, has darker skin, narrower roots, and a milder flavor than salsify. The plant has slender, tapering leaves and bears yellow flower heads that resemble dandelions. Although only the roots are sold, the leaf stalks, buds, and flowers are edible and often used in salads by home gardeners.

Duplex Appreciated for its long, flavorful roots.

Flandria Long roots (up to 12 inches/30.5 centimeters) with strongly flavored flesh.

Géante Noire de Russie or Russian Giant Black-skinned variety with white flesh, superb flavor, and an extremely long taproot.

Lange Jan (Long John) Long, tapering dark brown roots.

NUTRITION With similar nutritional profiles, salsify and scorzonera are a boon to dieters with only about 70 calories in a 3½-ounce/100-gram serving. The roots are rich in dietary fiber and are a good source of vitamin C, B$_6$, calcium, and potassium. Salsify contains inulin, a complex carbohydrate that yields fructose, rather than glucose, when digested, making the root a good choice for diabetics.

AVAILABILITY AND SELECTION Salsify is in season between October and March. Imported Belgian scorzonera is supplied to markets in the United States almost year-round, lacking only in late summer. Look for salsify or scorzonera that is firm and without any soft spots, bruises, or cracks in the flesh or the skin. The roots are almost always sold individually with their greens trimmed. Avoid roots that are heavily forked, as they are a challenge to peel. Very narrow roots don't leave you much flesh once they are peeled, and roots that are too thick can be tough and fibrous. Medium-size roots are the best choice.

STORAGE If the salsify or scorzonera has its leaves attached, trim them off before storing the roots. Wrap the unwashed roots in a dry paper towel, slip them into a plastic bag, and close loosely. Store them in the refrigerator for up to 2 weeks.

BASIC USE AND PREPARATION Salsify and scorzonera can be prepared and cooked in exactly the same way. The roots can be steamed, simmered, boiled, roasted, sautéed, or fried. In some instances, parboiling the roots before sautéing or roasting is suggested.

To prepare salsify or scorzonera, fill a bowl with acidulated water (water with a few drops of vinegar or lemon juice added). Scrub the roots to remove the dirt, trim the ends, and then peel them with a vegetable peeler. Immediately drop the peeled roots into the acidulated water to prevent discoloring.

YIELDS

1 lb/455 g salsify or scorzonera = about 4 roots, 1 in/ 2.5 cm thick

2 cups trimmed, peeled, and thinly sliced salsify or scorzonera = 1 lb/455 g

---

PARBOILED SALSIFY OR SCORZONERA

Often a recipe calls for salsify or scorzonera to be partially cooked before it is sautéed, simmered in a sauce, or roasted. This is the basic, easy method to follow.

Rice vinegar or distilled white vinegar

Salsify or scorzonera

1 Fill a large saucepan three-fourths full with water and add 1 tbsp unseasoned rice vinegar or distilled white vinegar for every 8 cups/2 L water. Trim and peel the root and cut into thin slices on the diagonal, into 3-in/7.5-cm logs, or into 1-in/2.5-cm chunks, as directed in the recipe you are using. Because the root begins to brown as soon as it is cut, drop the pieces into the vinegar water as you cut them. Let soak for at least 10 minutes or up to 1 hour before cooking.

2 Have ready a large bowl of ice water and a colander. Bring the water in the saucepan to a boil over high heat and cook until crisp-tender, 6 to 7 minutes for thin slices and 8 to 10 minutes for logs or chunks. Drain in the colander and transfer to the ice water to cool completely, about 2 minutes and then drain again. Wrap the pieces in several thicknesses of paper towels to dry.

3 Use immediately, or wrap in dry paper towels, place in a lock-top plastic bag, seal closed, and refrigerate for up to 2 days.

SCORZONERA WRAPPED IN CRISP PROSCIUTTO

Roasted scorzonera is an unexpected and delightful variation on asparagus wrapped in prosciutto. As an elegant do-ahead, it doesn't get much easier. The scorzonera can be roasted ahead, cooled until it can be handled, wrapped with prosciutto, and set aside for an hour or more before crisping the prosciutto in the oven and serving. Another option is to roast the scorzonera a day in advance and then wrap the logs and crisp the prosciutto just before serving.

MAKES 24 APPETIZERS

4 cups/960 ml water

½ lemon

14 oz/400 g scorzonera

1 tbsp extra-virgin olive oil

Kosher salt or fine sea salt

12 paper-thin slices prosciutto, halved crosswise

1 Position a rack in the center of the oven and preheat to 400°F/200°C/gas 6.

2 Pour the water into a bowl and squeeze the juice from the lemon half into the water. Trim and peel the scorzonera, cut into 3-in/7.5-cm-long logs, and immediately drop into the lemon water to prevent discoloration. (If the top of the root is thicker than the tapered bottom, cut the logs in half lengthwise so they will roast evenly.) Drain the scorzonera and blot dry with paper towels before roasting.

3 In a large bowl, toss the scorzonera with the oil and a few pinches of salt. Arrange in a single layer on a rimmed baking sheet and roast until fork-tender, 10 to 15 minutes, depending on the thickness of the logs. Remove from the oven and set aside until cool enough to handle.

4 Wrap a half slice of prosciutto around each scorzonera log. It will wrap about three times. Leave a small portion of one end exposed. This will be the "handle" for picking up the hors d'oeuvre. Arrange the wrapped logs on a rimmed baking sheet, preferably nonstick, spacing them at least ½ in/12 mm apart. Bake until the prosciutto is crisp, 3 to 5 minutes. Serve immediately.

SCORZONERA AND WILD MUSHROOM RAGOUT

This ragout could be served on its own as a silken creamy side dish, but it is divine as a vegetarian main course when served over creamy polenta, buckwheat pasta, or spaetzle. It could even be used as a filling for crêpes. Use a combination of wild mushrooms or pick just one—porcini, chanterelle, or morel—whatever looks fresh and is in season. I like to use a medium-sweet Portuguese Madeira for this dish. In fact, I always keep a bottle of this full-flavored fortified wine on hand for all kinds of sweet and savory cooking.

SERVES 6

3 tbsp extra-virgin olive oil

3 tbsp unsalted butter

4 shallots, about 6 oz/170 g, finely chopped

4 large garlic cloves, finely chopped

1 lb/455 g scorzonera, trimmed, peeled, cut into 1-in/2.5-cm chunks, and parboiled (see page 281)

1 lb/455 g wild mushrooms such as porcini, chanterelle, or morel, stems trimmed and thickly sliced

2 tsp kosher or fine sea salt

½ tsp freshly ground pepper

¼ cup/60 ml medium-sweet Madeira

2 cups/480 ml heavy whipping cream

2 tsp fresh lemon juice

2 tsp finely chopped fresh oregano

1 In a large sauté pan, warm the oil and butter over medium-low heat until the butter melts and then swirl to coat the pan bottom. Add the shallots and garlic and sauté, stirring frequently, until the shallots are translucent, about 3 minutes. Add the scorzonera and mushrooms, sprinkle with the salt and pepper, and sauté, stirring frequently, until the mushrooms soften and have given up most of their liquid, about 5 minutes.

2 Add the Madeira and stir to blend. Use a heat-resistant rubber spatula or a wooden spoon to scrape up any brown bits from the pan bottom. Add the cream and lemon juice and bring to a simmer. Adjust the heat so the ragout slowly simmers and cook, stirring occasionally, until the sauce thickens slightly, about 5 minutes. Stir in the oregano. Taste and adjust the seasoning. Serve immediately.

RED QUINOA WITH SCORZONERA, CARROTS, AND SWISS CHARD

Substantial enough to serve as a vegetarian main course, this colorful dish is vegetable dense and protein rich. Along with the crisp-tender carrots, I like to add scorzonera or salsify whenever I see it in the market, for its added crisp texture and artichoke-like flavor. Not wanting to waste any nutrients or flavor, I use the water in which I parboiled the vegetables to cook the quinoa, which, in turn, imparts a deeper vegetal flavor to the grain. For a lovely color contrast, buy the beautifully hued red quinoa for this dish.

SERVES 6 TO 8

7 cups/1.7 L water

½ lemon

12 oz/340 g scorzonera

1 tsp kosher or fine sea salt

3 medium carrots, about 9 oz/255 g, trimmed, peeled, and thinly sliced on the diagonal

1 bunch Swiss chard with white stalks, about 12 oz/340 g, leaves cut into bite-size pieces and stalks cut into ½-in/12-mm dice

1 cup/180 g red quinoa, well rinsed and drained

SHERRY VINAIGRETTE

½ cup/120 ml extra-virgin olive oil

3 tbsp sherry vinegar

1 tsp kosher or fine sea salt

¾ tsp freshly ground pepper

½ tsp granulated sugar

½ cup/70 g salted roasted pumpkin seeds

2 green onions, including green tops, thinly sliced on the diagonal

1 Pour 4 cups/960 ml of the water into a bowl and squeeze the juice from the lemon half into the water. Trim and peel the scorzonera, cut on the diagonal into thin slices, and immediately drop into the lemon water to prevent discoloration. Drain the scorzonera and blot dry with paper towels before cooking. Have ready a bowl filled with ice water. Line a second bowl with a double thickness of paper towels.

2 In a medium saucepan, bring the remaining 3 cups/720 ml water to a boil. Add the salt, scorzonera, and carrots and parboil for 2 minutes, just until crisp-tender. Transfer the vegetables to the ice water, cool completely, and then scoop them out and place in the towel-lined bowl. Bring the water back to a boil and add the chard leaves and diced stalks. Cook just until tender, about 3 minutes. Transfer the chard and stalks to the ice water until cool and then drain them, blot dry with paper towels, and set aside.

3 Measure 2 cups/480 ml of the vegetable water and discard the rest. Put the vegetable water back into the pan and bring to a boil over medium-high heat. Stir in the quinoa, reduce the heat so the liquid is at a slow simmer, cover the pan, and cook the quinoa until all of the water is absorbed and the quinoa is tender, 15 to 20 minutes. (Raise the heat and stir to evaporate any remaining water.) Transfer the quinoa to a large bowl and let cool.

4 To make the vinaigrette, in a small bowl, whisk together the oil, vinegar, salt, pepper, and sugar. Taste and adjust the seasoning. Set aside.

5 Add the scorzonera, carrots, chard leaves and stalks, pumpkin seeds, and green onions to the quinoa and toss gently to combine. Give the vinaigrette another quick stir and add it to the quinoa mixture. Toss gently to combine. Transfer to a serving bowl and serve immediately, or cover and set aside at room temperature for up to 2 hours until ready to serve. (The quinoa salad can be made 1 day in advance, covered, and refrigerated. Remove from the refrigerator an hour or so before serving so the quinoa is cool but not refrigerator cold.)

SCORZONERA FETTUCCINE IN MUSHROOM CREAM SAUCE

Is it rich? Yes. Is it warming, nourishing, autumnal comfort food? Indeed, a hearty yes. Sometimes a luscious pasta cream sauce is what we want—a decadent reminder that cloaking strands of al dente pasta with Parmesan and cream makes a perfect meal. Look for fresh porcini mushrooms at the farmers' market, though cremini mushrooms will certainly do. Pair with a Chianti, Barbera, or Barbaresco, which complements the woodsy flavor of the mushrooms.

SERVES 6

4 cups/960 ml water

½ lemon

1 lb/455 g scorzonera

Kosher or fine sea salt

1 lb/455 g dried fettuccine

6 tbsp/85 g unsalted butter

12 oz/340 fresh porcini or cremini mushrooms, stems trimmed and sliced

3 cups/720 ml heavy whipping cream

1 cup/115 g freshly grated Parmesan cheese, preferably Parmigiano-Reggiano

¼ cup/15 g minced fresh flat-leaf parsley

1 Pour the water into a bowl and squeeze the juice from the lemon half into the water. Trim and peel the scorzonera, cut on the diagonal into thin slices, and immediately drop into the lemon water to prevent discoloration. Drain the scorzonera and blot dry with paper towels before sautéing.

2 Fill a large pot two-thirds full with water, add 2 tsp salt, and bring to a boil over high heat. Add the pasta and stir. Cook the pasta until al dente (cooked through but still slightly chewy), 8 to 10 minutes.

3 While the water is heating and the pasta is cooking, in a large sauté pan, melt the butter over medium heat. When the butter foams, add the scorzonera and sauté, stirring frequently, for 2 minutes. Add the mushrooms and continue to sauté, stirring frequently, until the mushrooms release their moisture and are cooked through, about 5 minutes. Add the cream, 1 tsp salt, and the Parmesan and bring to a slow simmer. Reduce the heat if needed to maintain a gentle simmer and cook, stirring occasionally, until thickened, about 10 minutes. Taste and adjust the seasoning with salt if needed.

4 When the pasta is ready, drain it in a colander, shaking out the excess water. Add the pasta to the sauté pan and toss to coat with the sauce. Transfer to a warmed serving bowl or divide among warmed individual bowls. Garnish with the parsley and serve immediately.

SALSIFY OYSTER STEW

For oyster lovers like me, this stew is irresistible, especially with the addition of salsify, which gives the stew more texture and a subtle mushroom flavor. Although it can be reheated successfully (gently), oyster stew is best when made right before serving. Have everything measured and ready to cook—the soup is super-easy to put together.

SERVES 6

1 pt/480 ml extra-small shucked oysters (about 30) and their liquor

4 tbsp/55 g unsalted butter

1 tbsp Worcestershire sauce

1½ tsp sweet paprika

½ tsp celery salt

2 cups/480 ml milk

1 cup/240 ml heavy whipping cream

10 oz/280 g salsify, trimmed, peeled, thinly sliced on the diagonal, and parboiled (see page 281)

¼ tsp freshly grated nutmeg

Kosher or fine sea salt

Freshly ground white pepper

2 tbsp minced fresh flat-leaf parsley

1 Drain the oysters through a fine-mesh sieve placed over a small bowl to catch the liquor. Set the oysters aside. Reserve the liquor.

2 In a medium saucepan, melt the butter over medium heat. Stir in the Worcestershire sauce, paprika, and celery salt. Add the oysters and bring to a simmer. Cook just until the edges of the oysters curl, about 3 minutes. Add the oyster liquor to the pan and bring to a simmer. Add the milk, cream, salsify, and nutmeg. Reduce the heat to low and cook, stirring occasionally, just until hot. Do not let the mixture boil. Season with salt and pepper.

3 Ladle the soup into a warmed tureen or individual bowls, garnish with the parsley, and serve immediately.

SALSIFY PROVENÇAL

For a weeknight family meal, pile the salsify into a serving bowl as a jumble of petite logs and scatter the flecks of parsley and garlic over the top. For entertaining, I like to line up the logs on a platter in a neat fashion, making a long, low stack like a wood pile, with the parsley-garlic mixture sprinkled down the center.

SERVES 6 TO 8

3 tbsp minced fresh flat-leaf parsley

2 large garlic cloves, minced

5 tbsp/70 g unsalted butter

2 lb/910 g salsify or scorzonera, trimmed, peeled, cut into 3-in/ 7.5-cm logs, and parboiled (see page 281)

½ tsp kosher or fine sea salt

¼ tsp freshly ground white pepper

1 In a small bowl, mix together the parsley and garlic. Set aside.

2 In a large frying pan, melt 3 tbsp of the butter over medium-low heat. Add the parboiled salsify and toss to coat with the butter. Reduce the heat to low and sauté, stirring frequently, until the salsify is fork-tender, about 10 minutes. Sprinkle with the salt and pepper, give the salsify another stir, and then transfer to a warmed platter.

3 Cut the remaining 2 tbsp butter into small cubes and dot the top of the salsify. Sprinkle the parsley-garlic mixture over the top and serve immediately or keep warm until ready to serve.

ROASTED SALSIFY WITH THYME AND BACON BREAD CRUMBS

If everything tastes better with bacon, then salsify is a natural partner. This dish is as easy as could be. Fry up some bacon, use a bit of the bacon fat to season fresh bread crumbs, and then cut the salsify into logs, toss with some of the bacon fat, and roast until fork-tender. The bacon-bread crumbs get scattered over the top and deliciousness ensues. This would be a terrific accompaniment to roast chicken or pork.

SERVES 4 TO 6

4 cups/960 ml water

½ lemon

1¾ lb/800 g salsify or scorzonera

4 slices bacon (about 3½ oz/100 g)

⅓ cup/30 g lightly packed fresh bread crumbs (see Cook's Note, page 136)

1 tsp minced fresh thyme leaves

½ tsp kosher or fine sea salt

1 Position a rack in the center of the oven and preheat to 400°F/200°C/gas 6.

2 Pour the water into a bowl and squeeze the juice from the lemon half into the water. Trim and peel the salsify, cut into 3-in-/7.5-cm-long logs, and immediately drop into the lemon water to prevent discoloration. (If the top of the root is thicker than the tapered bottom, cut the logs in half lengthwise so they will roast evenly.) Drain the salsify and blot dry with paper towels before roasting.

3 In a medium frying pan, cook the bacon over medium-low heat until very crisp. Transfer to a plate lined with a double thickness of paper towels to drain. Pour off all but 1 tbsp of the fat from the pan, reserving the extra fat.

4 Return the pan to medium heat, add the bread crumbs and thyme, and sauté until the crumbs are well coated and crisp, about 1 minute. Finely crumble the bacon and add it back to the pan, tossing to combine with the crumb mixture. Remove from the heat and set aside.

5 In a large bowl, toss the salsify with 1 tbsp of the reserved bacon fat and the salt. Arrange in a single layer on a rimmed baking sheet and roast until fork-tender, 10 to 15 minutes, depending on the thickness of the logs. Transfer to a warmed serving dish. Sprinkle the bacon-crumb mixture over the top. Serve immediately.

PAN-ROASTED PORK TENDERLOIN WITH SALSIFY, CARROTS, CHICKPEAS, AND CRANBERRIES

While researching salsify and scorzonera for this book, I came across an intriguing recipe in Marcus Samuelsson's excellent *New American Table*. Inspired by his restaurant chef–driven recipe, which pairs poached venison with salsify and carrots and is seasoned with North African flavors, I decided to make a dish more accessible to the home cook. Adapting the recipe, I roasted pork tenderloin in place of the venison and substituted Spanish smoked paprika for the sumac. The delicious results—boldly flavored and colorful on the plate—make this dish perfect for an autumn or wintertime dinner party.

SERVES 6 TO 8

4 cups/960 ml water

½ lemon

1 lb/455 g salsify

1 lb/455 g carrots

Two 1-lb/455-g pork tenderloins, trimmed of fat

Kosher or fine sea salt

Freshly ground pepper

3 tbsp extra-virgin olive oil

½ cup/85 g drained canned chickpeas, rinsed and blotted dry

½ cup/120 ml fresh orange juice

½ cup/120 ml water

2 tbsp unsweetened dried cranberries

1 tbsp firmly packed light brown sugar

1 star anise pod

¼ tsp *pimentón* (Spanish smoked paprika)

1 tbsp unsalted butter

1 tbsp finely chopped fresh flat-leaf parsley

1 tbsp finely chopped fresh oregano

1   Position a rack in the center of the oven and preheat to 400°F/200°C/gas 6.

2   Pour the water into a bowl and squeeze the juice from the lemon half into the water. Trim and peel the salsify, cut into ¾-in/2-cm lengths, and immediately drop into the lemon water to prevent discoloration. (If the top of the root is thicker than the tapered bottom, cut the lengths in half lengthwise so they will cook evenly.) Drain the salsify and blot dry with paper towels before sautéing.

3   Peel and cut the carrots to match the size of the salsify pieces. (If the carrots are thicker at the top, cut the top ends in half lengthwise so they will cook evenly.) Set aside.

4   Season the pork generously on all sides with salt and pepper. Place a 12-in/30.5-cm ovenproof sauté pan over medium-high. Add the oil and heat until it shimmers and then swirl to coat the pan bottom. Add the pork tenderloins and sear on all sides until browned and nicely caramelized, about 6 minutes total. Transfer the pork to a large plate.

5   Add the salsify to the pan and sauté, stirring frequently, for 3 minutes. Add the carrots and continue to sauté, stirring frequently, until the carrots and salsify are browned at the edges, about 5 minutes longer. Add the chickpeas and ½ tsp salt and stir for 1 minute longer. Use a spatula to make two wide channels through the vegetables, and arrange the pork tenderloins, with space between them, in the channels so they rest directly on the pan bottom and the vegetables surround them on all sides.

...CONTINUED

6 Place the pan in the oven and roast the pork until an instant-read thermometer inserted into the center of a tenderloin registers 140° to 145°F/60° to 63°C, about 10 minutes. The center should be rosy when cut into with a knife. Transfer the pork to a carving board and tent loosely with aluminum foil.

7 Place the pan with the vegetables over medium heat. (Remember that the handle is hot!) Add the orange juice, water, cranberries, brown sugar, star anise, *pimentón*, and ¼ tsp pepper and mix well. Bring to simmer and cook, stirring occasionally, until the sauce is reduced by half, about 3 minutes. Stir in the butter, parsley, and oregano. Taste and adjust the seasoning.

8 To serve, cut the pork on a slight diagonal into slices 1 in/2.5 cm thick. Arrange a portion of the vegetables in the center of each warmed dinner plate and fan three or four slices of pork over the top. Serve immediately.

SWEET POTATO

Ipomoea batatas

HISTORY AND LORE Sweet potatoes, which belong to the morning glory family (Convolvulaceae), should not be confused with either ordinary potatoes *(Solanum tuberosum*, page 231*)* or with yams of the genus *Dioscorea* (page 377). They are indigenous to tropical America, in particular to the northwestern areas of South America, but perhaps also to Central America and southern Mexico. According to *The Cambridge World History of Food*, archaeological evidence suggests a date of at least 2000 B.C. for the presence of cultivated sweet potatoes in the New World, and possibly a domesticated form as early as 8000 B.C. They are believed to have originated from the wild Mexican genus *Ipomoea*, whose tubers and leaves were a food source for early inhabitants in North, Central, and South America.

The dispersal of the sweet potato as a food crop is an amazing story of far-flung travel and cultural exchange. Its introduction to Polynesia has been dated to around the time of Christ, though how it got there is a mystery. Some believe the tubers were transported by Polynesian seafarers who had seen them in South America and brought them home. Others theorize they arrived on vines that had clung to vessels long adrift at sea. At the end of the fifteenth century, Christopher Columbus took the sweet potato to Spain, and by the mid-sixteenth century, it had spread deep into Europe. Interestingly, the sweet potato was on European tables nearly a half century before the Irish potato arrived. The Spanish carried sweet potatoes to the Philippines, and Portuguese traders introduced them to the East Indies and India and then to China by the end of the sixteenth century. Although they were in Japan by about 1615, sweet potatoes did not take hold as a food crop until they were reintroduced in the 1670s to stave off a famine.

Early in the sixteenth century, during the days of the slave trade, Portuguese from Brazil and Lisbon introduced the sweet potato to Africa. In 1540, Spanish explorer Hernando de Soto saw Native Americans cultivating sweet potatoes in Louisiana. By the early seventeenth century, they were being grown as far north as Virginia. Today, sweet potatoes are cultivated throughout the world's tropical and subtropical regions, and they rank as one of the world's most important food crops, after rice, wheat, corn, yuca (cassava), and potatoes.

VARIETIES Hundreds of different varieties of sweet potato are grown around the world. They are most often divided into two main types by how they perform when cooked. The "soft" variety has orange flesh that cooks up soft and moist. The "firm" variety has creamy white or yellow flesh that remains mealy and relatively firm. This is where the name confusion comes in. The firm variety was already being grown in the United States when the soft-fleshed type was introduced. To distinguish them, the latter were called yams because they resembled the unrelated African yam of the genus *Dioscorea* (see page 377), and the term stuck. The boniato, or Cuban sweet potato, is a third type of sweet potato, with flesh similar to the firm, mealy type. The following are some of the most widely available sweet potato varieties.

SOFT, MOIST-FLESHED SWEET POTATOES

Garnet, Jewel, Beauregard, Hernandez, Centennial
Moist-type sweet potatoes have a high starch content
that converts to sugar as they cook, which results in a
sweet, rich, almost pumpkinlike flavor. The flesh comes
in shades of salmon-pink, orange, and yellow-orange
and the skin varies from deep tan to red-brown. These
cultivars are ideal for sweet and savory cooking and
baking.

FIRM, MEALY FLESHED SWEET POTATOES

O'Henry, Jersey, White Triumph, Southern Queen,
Kotobuki, Okinawan, Satsuma Firm-type sweet potatoes
have a lower starch content than the soft type, which
makes them less sweet. They are a bit more fibrous, too,
though they are still quite tender when properly cooked.
Their skin is light tan to yellowish brown and their flesh
is pale yellow to white. They are particularly desirable
for baking because their flesh cooks up fluffy and light.
Their lack of moisture allows them to absorb liquid,
which means they are ideal for mashing, too. Kotobuki,
a Japanese cultivar, has light reddish brown flesh and
a chestnutlike flavor. Okinawan, another Japanese
cultivar, has moderately sweet purple flesh and light
brown skin. It keeps its beautiful color when cooked.

Boniato/Cuban Sweet Potato Typically only seen in
markets catering to a Hispanic population, this Cuban
variety is large and heavy for its size. It has brown or red
skin and firm, white flesh that develops a floury, fluffy
texture and chestnutlike taste when cooked.

NUTRITION Sweet potatoes are considered a superfood
and a beta-carotene powerhouse, with 23 milligrams in
1 cup/290 g of the cooked root. Indeed, they have more
beta-carotene than any other vegetable, including carrots. But they shine in other categories, too, scoring at
the top of the class in vitamins A and C, folate, iron,
copper, calcium, and fiber, according to a study of fifty-
eight vegetables by the Center for Science in the Public
Interest.

AVAILABILITY AND SELECTION Most sweet potato varieties are available year-round. Japanese varieties are in the
market from late summer until late spring; the deep
orange– and yellow-fleshed varieties are at their peak from
early fall until late winter; and the Cuban boniatos, if
you can find them, are available year-round. Buy sweet
potatoes that are firm; free of blemishes, cracks, and soft
spots; and feel heavy for their size. The skins should
be firm, wrinkle free, and smooth. If possible, select
medium-size roots that are plump in the middle with
tapered ends. If you will be roasting them, they should
be uniformly sized for consistent baking times.

STORAGE Store unwashed sweet potatoes in a cool, dry
spot with good ventilation. Avoid refrigerating or storing
sweet potatoes in plastic bags, which promote softening
and sprouting. During the cool months of the year, I store
sweet potatoes in my basement enclosed in a loose brown-
paper sack with the top crumpled over but not sealed.
This blocks out light but doesn't trap moisture. During
the warmer months, I buy just what I need for a recipe
and use them right away. At 50°F/10°C, sweet potatoes
will keep for a couple of weeks.

BASIC USE AND PREPARATION Sweet potatoes are versatile and, suitable for sweet and savory dishes. They can
be boiled, baked, roasted, steamed, simmered, sautéed,
grill-roasted, and deep-fried, plus they can be peeled, cut,
and eaten raw as crudités. To rid them of dirt, scrub them
well with a vegetable brush under cool running water. Use
a paring knife to cut off any blemishes, and a vegetable
peeler to pare away the skin. To preserve nutrients, don't
peel a sweet potato before boiling or baking, and boil
them whole, rather than cut up. The flesh of sweet potatoes will darken when exposed to air, so work quickly or
have a bowl of acidulated water handy (water with a few
drops of vinegar or lemon juice added) and drop the potatoes into the water as you cut them.

YIELDS

1 small sweet potato = 7 to 8 oz/200 to 225 g

1 medium sweet potato = 9 to 11 oz/255 to 310 g

1 large sweet potato = 12 to 14 oz/340 to 400 g

8 oz/225 g cooked and mashed sweet potatoes = ¾ cup

1 lb/455 g cooked and mashed sweet potatoes = 1½ cups

1 lb/455 g trimmed, peeled, and diced sweet potatoes =
3 cups

ARACELY'S SWEET POTATO WAFFLES

Knowing how much my nine-year-old friend Aracely Watson loves to help her mother, Paola, cook, I asked her if she had a favorite recipe she would like to contribute to my book. She expressed utter delight at the thought of having her recipe published. These are Aracely's amazingly delicious waffles. Kid friendly and family tested, they are good for breakfast, brunch, or even a Sunday night breakfast-for-dinner supper. Aracely likes her pecans mixed into the batter, and I prefer mine sprinkled on top. Either option works well.

MAKES SIX 6-IN/15-CM ROUND WAFFLES

2 cups/255 g all-purpose flour

2 tsp baking powder

1 tsp baking soda

2 tsp ground ginger

1½ tsp ground cinnamon

1½ tsp kosher or fine sea salt

½ tsp freshly grated nutmeg

2 large eggs, at room temperature

¾ cup/225 g puréed sweet potatoes (see Cook's Note)

1 cup/240 ml milk

½ cup/120 ml sour cream

⅓ cup/65 g firmly packed light brown sugar

4 tbsp/55 g unsalted butter, melted

1 tsp pure vanilla extract

Cooking spray for the waffle iron if needed

½ cup/55 g pecans, toasted and finely chopped (see Cook's Note, page 79)

Maple syrup, warmed, for serving

1 In a large bowl, whisk together the flour, baking powder, and baking soda. Add the ginger, cinnamon, salt, and nutmeg and stir until evenly distributed. Separate the eggs, placing the yolks and whites in separate medium bowls.

2 Add the sweet potatoes to the egg yolks and mix until thoroughly combined. Stir in the milk, sour cream, brown sugar, melted butter, and vanilla. Mix until evenly combined. Using a rubber spatula and a few swift strokes, add the wet ingredients to the dry ingredients and mix just until the dry ingredients are absorbed.

3 Using a whisk or a handheld mixer, whip the egg whites until soft peaks form. Gently fold the egg whites into the waffle batter.

4 Heat a waffle iron according to the manufacturer's directions. If needed, coat the plates of the waffle iron with cooking spray. When hot, ladle in the batter, cover, and cook the waffle until beautifully browned on both sides. Repeat to make a total of six waffles. Transfer to warmed plates, sprinkle with the pecans, and drizzle with maple syrup. Serve immediately.

COOK'S NOTE

You can use either canned puréed sweet potatoes or easily make your own. Cut a medium sweet potato into small cubes and measure 1½ cups/225 g. Steam the cubes until tender enough to mash or purée, or place in a microwave-safe bowl, cover with plastic wrap, and microwave on high power until soft enough to mash or purée, about 3 minutes.

SWEET POTATO BISCUITS

Whether you make these savory yet sweet biscuits for Thanksgiving or Easter, as many families do, or serve them for breakfast, brunch, or dinner, they are an absolute delight. There is nothing like a warm biscuit cut in half, smeared with honey mustard or honey butter, and layered with slices of country ham or turkey. The small pinch of cayenne adds a kick of heat, but it can be omitted if you prefer. If you don't have a biscuit cutter, you can drop the dough by the large spoonful onto the baking sheet—a more rustic look but just as delicious.

MAKES 8 BISCUITS

12 oz/340 g Garnet sweet potatoes, peeled and cut into 1-in/2.5-cm cubes

2 tsp kosher or fine sea salt

2 tbsp firmly packed light brown sugar

1 tbsp unsalted butter, melted, plus 6 tbsp/85 g ice-cold, cut into small pieces

1¾ cups/220 g all-purpose flour, plus more if needed

2½ tsp baking powder

½ tsp baking soda

Pinch of cayenne pepper

⅓ cup/75 ml buttermilk

Honey for serving

1 In a medium saucepan, combine the sweet potatoes, 1 tsp of the salt, and water to cover by 1 in/2.5 cm. Cover partially and bring to a boil over medium-high heat. Reduce the heat to medium and simmer until the potatoes are very tender when pierced with a fork, about 10 minutes. Drain the potatoes, return them to the warm pan, and stir over low heat for 1 minute to evaporate any excess moisture. Use a potato masher, ricer, or food mill to mash the potatoes. Measure out ¾ cup/225 g for the biscuits and reserve the rest for another use. (I eat it on the spot as a healthful snack.) Add the brown sugar to the sweet potatoes while they are still hot, stirring to dissolve the sugar. Then let cool to room temperature, cover, and refrigerate until thoroughly chilled, about 30 minutes.

2 Position a rack in the lower third of the oven and preheat to 425°F/220°C/gas 7. Grease a rimmed baking sheet with ½ tbsp of the melted butter. Set aside.

3 In a large bowl, stir together the flour, baking powder, baking soda, cayenne pepper, and the remaining 1 tsp salt. Scatter the cold butter over the top and, using a pastry blender or your fingertips, work the butter into the flour until the butter pieces are no larger than peas. In a medium bowl, mix together the mashed sweet potatoes and buttermilk. Add the sweet potato mixture to the dry ingredients and stir just until well blended.

4 Turn the dough out onto a lightly floured work surface. If the dough feels too sticky, knead in a little more flour. Using your fingertips, press the dough into a circle about ½ in/12 mm thick. Using a floured 2-in/5-cm round biscuit cutter, cut the dough into rounds, cutting them as close together as possible. Gather together the scraps, reshape the dough, and cut out more biscuits. Arrange the rounds on the prepared baking sheet, spacing them about 1 in/2.5 cm apart. (Alternatively, you can drop the dough by the large spoonful onto the prepared baking sheet for drop-style biscuits.)

5 Brush the biscuits with the remaining ½ tbsp melted butter. Bake the biscuits, rotating the pan front to back midway through the baking time, until golden brown, 20 to 24 minutes. Serve warm with honey.

MOROCCAN SWEET POTATO SALAD

Friend and colleague Laura Russell shared this recipe with me, which was published in the June 2010 issue of the *Oregonian*'s *MIX* magazine. I made it for a summer potluck and it was a huge hit. A perfect do-ahead side dish for entertaining, the sweet potatoes are cubed and roasted until fork-tender and then tossed with Laura's version of *charmoula*, a Moroccan marinade, transformed into a garlicky, tart vinaigrette heady with the flavor of cilantro.

SERVES 6

2½ lb/1.2 kg sweet potatoes, peeled and cut into 1-in/2.5-cm cubes

⅓ cup/75 ml plus 2 tbsp extra-virgin olive oil

¾ tsp kosher or fine sea salt

2 garlic cloves, finely minced

1 tsp ground cumin

1 tsp sweet paprika

⅛ tsp cayenne pepper

3 tbsp fresh lemon juice

⅓ cup/20 g chopped fresh flat-leaf parsley

⅓ cup/20 g chopped fresh cilantro

⅓ cup/35 g sliced almonds, toasted (see Cook's Note, page 79)

1 Position a rack in the center of the oven and preheat to 425°F/220°C/gas 7.

2 In a large bowl, toss the sweet potatoes with the 2 tbsp oil and ¼ tsp of the salt. Transfer the sweet potatoes to a large rimmed baking sheet and spread them out in an even layer. (Set the bowl aside to use for tossing the cooked potatoes.) Roast the potatoes, stirring once at the midpoint of roasting, until they are tender when pierced with a fork but still hold their shape, 15 to 20 minutes.

3 Meanwhile, in a small bowl, mix together the garlic, cumin, paprika, cayenne, lemon juice, and the remaining ½ tsp salt. Whisk in the remaining ⅓ cup/75 ml oil. Add the parsley and cilantro and stir to combine.

4 When the potatoes are ready, return them to the large bowl. Add the vinaigrette and toss gently. Add the almonds if you are planning to serve the salad within a few hours; otherwise, toss them in just before serving so they stay crisp. Serve at room temperature. (The salad can be made up to 2 days in advance, covered, and refrigerated. Remove from the refrigerator 2 hours before serving.)

SUSIE MIDDLETON'S SWEET POTATO "MINI FRIES" WITH LIMY DIPPING SAUCE AND SPICED SALT

I find some foods completely addictive and irresistible, and sweet potato fries are one of them. While I adore the ones that come out of a deep fryer, I am less inclined to make those at home. I bake my fries, and even though they are not as crisp as the deep-fried ones, I am totally satisfied because the flavor, crisp edges, and tender centers are all wonderful.

My favorite recipe for oven-baked sweet potato fries is from Susie Middleton's terrific vegetable lover's cookbook, *Fast, Fresh & Green*. When I e-mailed her to ask if I could include her recipe in my collection, she responded that it was one of the most popular recipes in the book. Once you try them, you will know why.

SERVES 3 OR 4

1 lb/455 g sweet potatoes

¼ cup/60 ml extra-virgin olive oil

Kosher or fine sea salt

LIMY DIPPING SAUCE

⅓ cup/65 g mayonnaise

½ tsp finely grated lime zest

1 tbsp fresh lime juice

½ tsp finely minced garlic

Pinch of kosher or fine sea salt

SPICED SALT (OPTIONAL)

1 tbsp kosher or fine sea salt

½ tsp granulated sugar

¼ tsp ground cinnamon

¼ tsp ground cumin

¼ tsp ground coriander

¼ tsp paprika

1 Position a rack in the center of the oven and preheat to 475°F/245°C/gas 9. Line an 18-by-13-by-1-in/45.5-by-33-by-2.5-cm heavy-duty rimmed baking sheet with parchment paper.

2 Cut the unpeeled sweet potatoes crosswise on a slight diagonal into slices ⅜ in/1 cm thick. (If the sweet potato is very narrow at one end, cut the slices at a sharp angle at that end.) Cut each slice lengthwise into sticks between ¼ and ⅜ in/6 mm and 1 cm wide. (They will be about 2 in/5 cm long.) Put the sticks in a bowl, add the oil and 1 tsp salt, and toss to coat evenly. Spread the sweet potatoes in a single layer on the prepared baking sheet, making sure to scrape all of the oil and salt from the bowl onto them.

3 Roast for 20 minutes. Using a spatula, flip the sticks over and continue cooking, flipping once or twice more, until the fries are nicely browned (some in spots, some all over), about 10 minutes longer.

4 To make the dipping sauce, in a small bowl, whisk together the mayonnaise, lime zest, lime juice, garlic, and salt until well blended. Let stand for 10 to 15 minutes to allow the flavors to marry.

5 If making the spiced salt, in a small bowl, stir together the salt, sugar, cinnamon, cumin, coriander, and paprika until well combined.

6 When the fries are ready, remove them from the oven, sprinkle them with the spiced salt or more kosher or sea salt (be generous and do not skip this step!), and toss well. Serve piping hot with the dipping sauce.

HONEY AND CHIPOTLE ROASTED SWEET POTATO SPEARS

Here, I have given a traditional food an interesting cultural twist. The ingredients—chipotle chile powder, lime juice, honey—reflect the flavors of Southwestern cuisine. This recipe is terrific for the Thanksgiving table or for any fall or wintertime meal.

SERVES 10 AS A SIDE DISH

4 lb/1.8 kg medium sweet potatoes, peeled, halved crosswise, and then cut into ½-in/12-mm wedges

½ cup/115 g plus 1 tbsp unsalted butter, at room temperature

1 tsp chipotle chile powder

½ cup/120 ml honey

⅓ cup/75 ml fresh lime juice

1 tsp kosher or fine sea salt

1 Position a rack in the center of the oven and preheat to 400°F/200°C/gas 6. Put the sweet potatoes in a large bowl. Coat a large rimmed baking sheet with the 1 tbsp of butter.

2 In a small saucepan, melt the remaining ½ cup/115 g butter over medium heat. Whisk in the chile powder and then add the honey, lime juice, and salt. Bring to a simmer, stirring constantly, and simmer for 3 minutes to meld the glaze.

3 Pour the glaze over the sweet potatoes and toss until well coated. Spread the sweet potatoes in a single layer on the prepared baking sheet, making sure to scrape all of the glaze from the bowl onto them. Cover the pan tightly with aluminum foil.

4 Roast the sweet potatoes for 40 minutes. Remove the foil and baste the sweet potatoes with the pan glaze. Continue to bake, basting every 10 minutes, until the sweet potatoes are tender, nicely browned, and caramelized at the edges, about 20 minutes longer. Serve immediately, or keep warm in a low oven for up to 30 minutes and then baste again just before serving.

COOK'S NOTE

The sweet potatoes can be roasted up to 1 day in advance, covered, and refrigerated. Bring to room temperature 2 hours before reheating and then reheat in a 350°F/180°C/gas 4 oven for about 20 minutes. Alternatively, the sweet potatoes can be roasted up to 4 hours in advance and set aside at room temperature. Reheat before serving, basting with the glaze.

GRILLED SWEET POTATOES WITH MAPLE AND ADOBO GLAZE

Whether it is labeled "yam" or "sweet potato" in the market, the Garnet, with its red-rust skin and orange-yellow flesh, is the best sweet potato for grilling. Look for firm, unblemished potatoes that are fairly uniform in size so that all of the slices are about the same diameter. Pair the Garnets with grilled pork tenderloin or pork chops. They are equally delicious alongside grilled chicken.

SERVES 4

6 tbsp/85 g unsalted butter

3 tbsp maple syrup

1 tbsp adobo sauce from canned chipotle chiles

2 lb/910 g sweet potatoes, preferably Garnet, peeled and cut on the diagonal into slices ½ in/12 mm thick

Kosher or fine sea salt

Vegetable oil for brushing the grill grate

1 Prepare a medium fire in a charcoal grill or preheat a gas grill to medium.

2 In a small saucepan, melt the butter over medium heat. Pour or ladle 3 tbsp of the butter into a small heatproof bowl or measuring cup. Set aside. Add the maple syrup and adobo sauce to the butter in the pan and whisk until smooth. Keep warm.

3 Arrange the potato slices in a single layer on a large rimmed baking sheet. Brush them on both sides with the reserved melted butter and sprinkle with salt.

4 When ready to grill, to create a cool zone, bank the coals to one side of the charcoal grill or turn off one of the burners of the gas grill. Brush the grill grate with vegetable oil. Arrange the potatoes directly over the medium fire, cover the grill, and grill until dark brown grill marks appear on the underside, about 3 minutes. Turn, re-cover, and grill until dark grill marks appear on the second side, about 3 minutes longer. Move the potatoes to the cooler part of the grill, brush generously on both sides with the maple-butter mixture, re-cover, and grill until the potatoes are tender when pierced with a knife, 3 to 5 minutes longer.

5 Transfer the potatoes to a warmed platter and brush with any remaining maple-butter mixture. Serve immediately or keep warm until ready to serve.

GARNET SWEET POTATO CASSEROLE WITH PECAN STREUSEL

This recipe is from my first holiday cookbook, *The Thanksgiving Table*. It has been an all-time favorite since it was published, so forget about leftovers because there never are any. The children sneak back for seconds, and some adults sneak back for thirds. It's that good. My husband, the dishwasher in the family, can be found scraping leftover caramelized, crusty bits of streusel from the pan before he puts it in the sink to soak.

SERVES 8 TO 10

6 large Garnet or other dark orange–fleshed sweet potatoes, about 5 ½ lb/2.5 kg

¾ cup/180 ml milk

½ cup/115 g unsalted butter

3 large eggs, lightly beaten

¾ cup/150 g firmly packed dark brown sugar

PRALINE STREUSEL

4 tbsp/55 g unsalted butter

¾ cup/150 g firmly packed dark brown sugar

½ tsp kosher or fine sea salt

½ tsp ground cinnamon

½ tsp freshly grated nutmeg

¾ cup/180 ml heavy whipping cream

1½ cups/170 g coarsely chopped pecans

2 tsp pure vanilla extract

1 Position a rack in the center of the oven and preheat to 350°F/180°C/gas 4. Pierce each sweet potato several times with a fork and place in a baking pan. Bake until the potatoes are tender when pierced with a fork, 1¼ to 1½ hours. Set aside until cool enough to handle.

2 In a small saucepan, heat the milk and butter until the butter has melted and the mixture is hot but not boiling. Remove from the heat and keep hot.

3 Cut the potatoes in half lengthwise and scoop the flesh into a large bowl, discarding the skins. Use a potato masher, ricer, or food mill to mash the potatoes. Stir the milk mixture into the potatoes until well mixed. Whisk in the eggs and continue whisking until well combined with the potato mixture. Add the brown sugar and stir until thoroughly blended.

4 Butter a 9-by-13-in/23-by-33-cm baking pan or an 11-in/28-cm round oven-to-table casserole. Spread the sweet potato mixture evenly in the casserole. Set aside. Increase the oven temperature to 375°F/190°C/gas 5.

5 To make the streusel, in a 2-qt/2-L saucepan, melt the butter over low heat. Stir in the brown sugar, salt, cinnamon, nutmeg, cream, and pecans and bring to a simmer. Cook, stirring constantly, until the sugar has dissolved and the mixture is thick, about 5 minutes. If the mixture begins to boil and splatter, turn down the heat to maintain a simmer. Remove from the heat and stir in the vanilla.

6 Pour the streusel evenly over the sweet potatoes, spreading it with a rubber spatula. (Alternatively, make the sweet potato filling and the streusel 1 day in advance and store separately, tightly covered, in the refrigerator. Warm the streusel and spread it over the potato mixture just before baking.)

7 Bake the casserole until the streusel is slightly crusty and set, about 30 minutes. Serve immediately.

JEWEL SWEET POTATO RAVIOLI WITH SAGE BROWN BUTTER SAUCE

If you like to make fresh pasta dough, make a batch and roll it out for these ravioli. Alternatively, buy fresh pasta sheets, then roll them slightly thinner and cut them into strips to form individual ravioli. Store-bought wonton wrappers make this recipe even easier for anyone who doesn't have a lot of time to spend in the kitchen.

MAKES 32 RAVIOLI; SERVES 8 AS A FIRST COURSE OR 4 OR 5 AS A MAIN COURSE

1¾ lb/800 g Jewel or other dark orange–fleshed sweet potatoes, halved lengthwise

1 tbsp extra-virgin olive oil

1 tbsp unsalted butter

2 garlic cloves, minced

1½ tsp finely minced fresh sage

1 tsp kosher or fine sea salt

¼ tsp freshly ground pepper

64 wonton wrappers (from a 1 lb/455 g package), kept refrigerated until ready to use

BUTTER SAUCE

¾ cup/170 g unsalted butter

12 large fresh sage leaves, stacked and cut crosswise into thin shreds

Pinch of kosher or fine sea salt

Grated pecorino cheese for sprinkling

1 Position a rack in the center of the oven and preheat to 425°F/220°C/gas 7.

2 Rub the cut sides of the sweet potatoes with the oil. Place the potato halves, cut-side down, on a rimmed baking sheet and roast until very tender when pierced with a fork, 30 to 45 minutes. Set aside until cool enough to handle. Scoop the flesh into a bowl, discarding the skins. Use a potato masher, ricer, or food mill to mash the potatoes until completely smooth.

3 In a small frying pan, melt the butter over medium heat. Add the garlic and sauté until soft but not brown, about 1 minute. Add the sage and crisp in the butter for 30 seconds. Remove from the heat and stir in the salt and pepper. Add to the sweet potatoes in the bowl and mix to combine.

4 Line a baking sheet with parchment paper. On a clean work surface, arrange eight wonton wrappers in a row. Keep the remaining wrappers covered with a damp paper towel to prevent them from drying out. For each raviolo, measure a level 1 tbsp of the filling and mound it in the center of a wrapper. Lightly brush the edges of wrapper with water to moisten them. Place another wonton wrapper on top and gently press around the filling to release any air pockets. Using a 2¾-in/7-cm round biscuit cutter or fluted cookie cutter, cut out the raviolo and press gently to seal the edges. Or, use a ravioli cutter to shape the raviolo and crimp the edges. As the ravioli are formed, transfer them to the prepared baking sheet. Repeat to make the remaining ravioli.

5 To make the butter sauce, in a small frying pan, melt the butter over medium heat and heat until it just begins to brown, 2 to 3 minutes. Add the sage and crisp in the butter for 30 seconds. Remove from the heat and season with the salt. Set aside and keep warm until ready to serve.

6 Bring a large pot of salted water to a boil and gently add the ravioli. Reduce the heat so the water boils gently (otherwise the ravioli could split apart) and cook until tender, 4 to 5 minutes. Using a large slotted spoon or a wire skimmer, transfer the cooked ravioli to individual warmed plates or shallow bowls. Spoon the sauce over the ravioli and finish with a generous sprinkling of pecorino. Serve immediately.

SWEET POTATO-TOPPED TURKEY POTPIE

Old-fashioned potpies typically call for lining a deep baking dish with pastry dough, adding a filling of blanched chopped vegetables and chopped meat in a cream-based sauce, and then topping the pie with flaky pastry, biscuit dough, or dumplings. This recipe is a colorful twist on that classic, using mashed sweet potatoes as the topper and eliminating the bottom crust (which usually ends up soggy, mushy anyway).

MAKES 5 SINGLE-SERVING POTPIES

TOPPING

1½ lb/680 g dark orange–fleshed sweet potatoes such as Garnet or Jewel, peeled and cut into 1-in/2.5-cm cubes

2 tsp kosher or fine sea salt

3 tbsp unsalted butter, melted

1 tbsp firmly packed light brown sugar

¼ tsp freshly grated nutmeg

Freshly ground pepper

FILLING

2 tbsp unsalted butter

2 tbsp canola or other neutral oil

1 large yellow onion, about 12 oz/340 g, diced

¾ cup/100 g diced celery

¾ cup/105 g peeled and diced carrot

Kosher or fine sea salt

3 tbsp all-purpose flour

1½ cups/360 ml homemade chicken or turkey stock or canned low-sodium chicken broth

½ cup/120 ml heavy whipping cream

2½ cups/375 g shredded roast turkey or chicken

2 tbsp finely chopped fresh flat-leaf parsley

1 tbsp finely chopped fresh sage

1 tbsp minced fresh thyme

Freshly ground pepper

1 To make the topping, in a saucepan, combine the sweet potatoes, 1 tsp of the salt, and water to cover by 1 in/2.5 cm. Cover partially and bring to a boil over medium-high heat. Reduce the heat to medium and simmer until the potatoes are very tender when pierced with a fork, about 10 minutes.

2 Drain the potatoes, return them to the warm pan, and stir over low heat for 1 minute to evaporate any excess moisture. Use a potato masher, ricer, or food mill to mash the potatoes. Stir in the melted butter, brown sugar, nutmeg, and the remaining 1 tsp salt and season with a few grinds of pepper. Set aside. (The sweet potatoes can be made up to 2 days in advance, covered, and refrigerated. Bring to room temperature before using.)

3 To make the filling, position a rack in the center of the oven and preheat to 400°F/200°C/gas 6. Have ready five 1-cup/240-ml ramekins or wide ovenproof mugs or cups.

4 In a large saucepan or deep 10-in/25-cm frying pan, melt the butter with the oil over medium heat until the butter foams. Add the onion, celery, and carrot and sauté until they begin to soften, about 2 minutes. Stir in 1 tsp salt, cover partially, reduce the heat to medium-low, and simmer gently until the vegetables are very tender, about 12 minutes.

5 Sprinkle the flour over the cooked vegetables and stir until well blended. Slowly stir in the stock, bring to a simmer, and cook, stirring, until smooth and thickened, about 2 minutes. Add the cream, stir to blend, and bring to a simmer. Add the turkey, parsley, sage, and thyme; stir to combine; and return the mixture to a simmer. Season with salt and pepper and then remove from the heat. Spoon the filling into the ramekins, dividing it evenly and filling to within ¾ in/2 cm of the rim.

6 Using a rubber spatula, carefully spread and mound spoonfuls of the mashed sweet potatoes over the filling, leaving little random peaks here and there. (I like to spread the filling almost to the edge, but not fully covering the filling, so that a bit of the bubbly filling is visible when the potpies are served.)

7 Arrange the potpies on a rimmed baking sheet. Bake until bubbly and piping hot, about 20 minutes. Serve immediately.

ROAST TURKEY AND SWEET POTATO CHOWDER

When Thanksgiving leftovers beckon and another turkey sandwich seems boring, reach for the soup pot and whip up this hearty, soulful chowder chock-full of vegetables. Wander the produce aisles to see what looks fresh. Sweet potatoes are always plentiful in winter and add an underlying sweetness to the soup. Choose Swiss chard, with either red or white ribs, or another dark leafy green. Red potatoes and onions are always stacked high in the fall. Although zucchini is overly abundant in summer, it's in the market year-round. Add it to the pot just before the soup is ready so it remains bright green. Accompany the chowder with crusty French bread.

SERVES 6

3 slices bacon, diced

1 medium yellow onion, cut into ½-in/12-mm dice

2 large celery ribs, cut into ½-in/12-mm dice

2 large red potatoes, about 8 oz/225 g each, peeled and cut into ½-in/12-mm dice

1 lb/455 g sweet potatoes, peeled and cut into ½-in/12-mm dice

7 cups/1.7 L homemade chicken stock or canned low-sodium chicken broth

1 medium zucchini, trimmed and cut into ½-in/12-mm dice

2 cups/60 g firmly packed chopped Swiss chard, green leaves only

10 oz/280 g roast turkey, cut into ½-in/12-mm dice

1 tbsp minced fresh thyme

2 tbsp minced fresh flat-leaf parsley

Kosher or fine sea salt

Freshly ground pepper

1 In a heavy soup pot, cook the bacon over medium heat, stirring frequently, until browned. Remove with a slotted spoon to a plate. Set aside. Pour off all but 2 tbsp of the bacon fat, and return the pot to medium heat. Add the onion and celery and sauté until the vegetables are soft but not brown, 3 to 5 minutes.

2 Add the potatoes, sweet potatoes, and stock; raise the heat to high; and bring to a boil. Reduce the heat to a simmer, cover partially, and cook until the potatoes are tender, about 15 minutes. Add the zucchini, Swiss chard, turkey, thyme, parsley, and reserved bacon and cook for 5 minutes longer.

3 Season with salt and pepper and ladle the soup into warmed individual bowls or mugs. Serve immediately.

SWEET POTATO PIE WITH A GINGERBREAD CRUST AND BOURBON WHIPPED CREAM

This pie is so divinely smooth and creamy that even a little sliver is satisfying. The rich-tasting roasted sweet potato filling, spiced with cinnamon and nutmeg, pairs perfectly with the gingersnap crust. A leftover slice of this pie and a cup of coffee is one of my favorite breakfasts.

SERVES 10 TO 12

GINGERBREAD CRUST

½ cup/115 g unsalted butter, melted

2 cups/225 g gingersnap crumbs (see Cook's Note)

FILLING

1¾ lb/800 g dark orange–fleshed sweet potatoes (2 large or 3 medium)

2 tbsp unsalted butter, at room temperature, cut into small cubes

¾ cup/150 g firmly packed light brown sugar

2 large eggs, lightly beaten

½ cup/120 ml unsweetened coconut milk

½ cup/120 ml heavy whipping cream

2 tbsp bourbon whiskey

1 tsp pure vanilla extract

1 tsp ground cinnamon

½ tsp freshly grated nutmeg

½ tsp kosher or fine sea salt

BOURBON WHIPPED CREAM

1 cup/240 ml heavy whipping cream

2 tbsp confectioners' sugar

1 tbsp bourbon whiskey

1 Position one rack in the center and a second rack in the lower third of the oven and preheat to 350°F/180°C/gas 4. Line a large rimmed baking sheet with parchment.

2 To make the crust, butter a 9-in/23-cm deep-dish glass pie plate with 1 tbsp of the melted butter. In a medium bowl, combine the gingersnap crumbs and the remaining butter and toss and stir until the crumbs are evenly moistened. Press the crumb mixture evenly in the bottom and up the sides of the pie plate, stopping within about ½ in/12 mm of the rim. Bake the crust in the lower third of the oven until crisp and lightly colored, 10 to 12 minutes. Let cool completely on a rack.

3 To make the filling, pierce each sweet potato several times with a fork and place on the prepared baking sheet. Bake until the potatoes are very tender when pierced with a fork, 1 to 1½ hours, depending on the size of the potatoes. Remove from the oven, cut each potato in half lengthwise, and let cool for 10 minutes.

4 Scoop the flesh from the sweet potato halves into a large bowl, discarding the skins. Use a potato masher to mash the potatoes with the butter. Add the brown sugar and continue to mash. (The potatoes should be warm enough to melt the butter and dissolve most of the brown sugar.) Using a wooden spoon, stir in the eggs. Add the coconut milk, cream, bourbon, vanilla, cinnamon, nutmeg, and salt and stir until the mixture is smooth and light. (Alternatively, beat the ingredients with a handheld mixer or a stand mixer.)

5 Gently pour the filling into the cooled crust. Place the pie in the center of the oven and bake until the sides are slightly puffed, about 45 minutes. The very center of the filling will still be a bit soft and will even jiggle a little when you shake the pie plate gently. Turn off the oven, set the oven door ajar, and leave the pie in the oven, undisturbed, for another 10 minutes. Transfer the pie to a wire rack and let cool completely.

6 To make the whipped cream, in a medium bowl, combine the cream, confectioners' sugar, and bourbon. Using a whisk or a handheld mixer, whip the cream until soft peaks form. Use immediately or cover and refrigerate for up to 4 hours.

7 Cut the pie into wedges with a warm, wet knife, wiping the knife clean after each cut. Top with the whipped cream and serve.

COOK'S NOTE

Use store-bought gingersnap cookies labeled old-fashioned and packaged in a 1-pound/455-gram box. The ones I buy are crisp, thin, and about 2 inches/5 centimeters in diameter. You will need only half of the box. To make finely ground crumbs, use a food processor or blender and grind in two batches. Alternatively, place the gingersnaps in a large, freezer-strength, lock-top plastic bag, squeeze out all of the air, seal the bag, and crush the cookies into even, fine crumbs with a rolling pin.

TARO

Colocasia esculenta

TRUE TARO / OLD COCOYAM *(WEST AFRICA)* / EDDOE, EDDO, OR DASHEEN *(WEST INDIES)* / TARO *(PACIFIC ISLANDS)* / ELEPHANT'S EAR / YU TOU *(MANDARIN CHINESE)* / SATOIMO *(JAPANESE)*

HISTORY AND LORE Often called the "potato of the tropics," taro is a member of the tropical and subtropical flowering plant family Araceae. There is a great deal of confusion and mislabeling when it comes to all kinds of tropical tubers, and taro is no exception. It is the common name for four different tropical root crops around the world, as explained in the chapter on malanga, also known as American taro *(Xanthosoma sagittifolium)*, on page 195. And like malanga, this taro *(Colocasia esculenta)*, sometimes called true taro, can appear under various names in the marketplace because it is cultivated across such a broad swath of the globe.

Thought to be indigenous to India or Burma, true taro is among the world's oldest cultivated food plants. References suggest that it has been domesticated for over five thousand years in tropical Southeast Asia, cultivated even before rice or millet. It was transported both east and west, making its way throughout the Orient, the islands of the Pacific, westward along the Mediterranean, and to Africa south of the Sahara. It flourished in Egypt at the time of Alexander's expedition, and was considered an important culinary staple in both Athens and Rome. Spanish explorers and slave traders carried taro across the Atlantic to the New World, where it became an important crop in tropical Central and South America and in the West Indies.

VARIETIES Although there are more than one hundred varieties of taro in the species *Colocasia esculenta*, only two are important to most cooks: dasheen (*C. esculenta* var. *esculenta*) and eddoe (*C. esculenta* var. *antiquorum*). They are rarely differentiated by name in markets, however. Eddoe forms a relatively small main tuber, the size of a duck egg, with numerous little oval tubers on the stem. These smaller corms, favored by the Chinese and Japanese, are blander, similar to a potato, but with a slightly sweet, nutty flavor. They are often boiled in their jackets and then peeled and eaten. Dasheen has a large main tuber, usually 4 inches/10 centimeters in diameter and 6 to 8 inches/15 to 20 centimeters long, and just a few subsidiary tubers. Both are covered with shaggy brown skin and have distinct rings at regular intervals along their length. Although they are very different in size, they are similar in taste and can be used interchangeably.

NUTRITION Taro is high in starch, which means it is also high in calories, with 107 calories in a 3½-ounce/100-gram serving. It is also a significant source of potassium and vitamin B_6 and carries a good dose of vitamin C, phosphorus, and iron. The starch granules in taro are easily digested, which makes it an ideal food for anyone who is gluten intolerant or has digestive problems.

AVAILABILITY AND SELECTION Taro is available year-round in most supermarkets and in Asian, Indian, and Latin American markets. Both the eddoe and dasheen varieties are roughly spherical, but the eddoe is small, varying between the size of a golf ball and a tennis ball, and the dasheen can be quite large, up to 9 inches/23 centimeters in diameter. The flesh can be creamy white, pale pink, white with speckles of purple, or even mauve. Select taro that is very firm with no soft spots, wrinkled skin, cracks, or signs of mold. The more evenly shaped the roots are, the easier they are to peel. Large taro roots, which tend to be more cylindrical, are often cut and sold in smaller sections. Look at the cut ends to make sure they are fresh and free of mold.

STORAGE Use immediately or store in a closed brown-paper bag in a cool, dark spot for up to 5 days. Taro softens quickly if left in a plastic bag or refrigerated.

BASIC USE AND PREPARATION Taro, which must always be cooked, is used in both sweet and savory foods. It can be coarsely grated and fashioned into crisp fritters, finely grated and mixed with vegetables or fish to make croquettes, cooked and puréed or riced for a sweet dessert filling, cooked and mashed like potatoes, cooked and sliced and served as a side dish, or sliced and added to soups or stews. Taro can also be sliced paper-thin on a mandoline and the slices deep-fried for chips. Poi, a Polynesian staple, is cooked taro mashed to a paste and allowed to ferment.

To prepare taro, wear gloves and use a vegetable brush to scrub the root under cool running water. Slice the ends off the root and then, using a paring knife or vegetable peeler, pare away and discard the hairy skin. Continue to trim until you get to the firm flesh. Rinse the root again and pat dry. If not using immediately, submerge the root in a bowl of cold water to keep it from discoloring. In general, large taro roots should be peeled and cut up before cooking; small roots are usually scrubbed and then boiled or baked in their jackets.

A CAUTIONARY NOTE There are two precautions related to taro. First, although selection over the years has reduced the amount of oxalic acid crystals in the outer layer of the corm, it is important to wear disposable surgical gloves or to coat your hands with cooking oil when peeling taro to prevent skin irritation, especially for anyone with sensitive skin. Second, never eat taro raw, as the oxalic acid compounds can irritate the throat. Taro must always be cooked thoroughly.

YIELDS

1 small taro = 4 oz/115 g

4 small taro = 1 lb/455 g

1 cup trimmed, peeled, cooked, and mashed taro = 8 oz/225 g

2¼ cups trimmed, peeled, and diced or chunked taro = 1 lb/455 g

TARO CHIPS

Like yuca chips, taro chips fry with virtually no splatter. Buy small roots, about the size of a turnip, which make the perfect-size chips. If possible, buy both purple- and white-fleshed roots and fry up a colorful combination of chips. Use a mandoline, Japanese vegetable slicer, or a very sharp knife to cut the roots crosswise into paper-thin slices. Season the chips with salt as soon as they come out of the fryer. They are irresistible.

MAKES ABOUT 120 CHIPS

About 5 cups/1.2 L peanut, grape seed, or vegetable oil for deep-frying

1 lb/455 g small taro roots

Kosher or fine sea salt

1 Have ready two baking sheets lined with a double thickness of paper towels. Set a slotted spoon or a wire-mesh skimmer alongside the baking sheets. Pour the oil to a depth of about 3 in/7.5 cm into a deep, heavy pot, a wok, or an electric deep fryer and heat to 320°F/160°C on a deep-frying thermometer. Taro chips fry best at a slightly lower temperature than what is used for most deep-fried foods. (If using an electric deep fryer, follow the manufacturer's instructions for heating the oil.)

2 While the oil is heating, trim, peel, and rinse the taro. Cut crosswise into paper-thin rounds.

3 When the oil is ready, fry the taro in small batches. Add a handful of slices to the hot oil and deep-fry, stirring once or twice, until golden brown, about 4 minutes. (The timing will vary slightly, so look for color first and then sample a chip, testing for crispiness.) Using a slotted spoon or a wire-mesh skimmer, transfer the chips to a towel-lined baking sheet to drain. Sprinkle lightly with salt. Continue frying in small batches until all of the slices are fried. Make sure the oil is at 320°F/160°C before you add a new batch.

4 Transfer the chips to a basket or serving bowl and serve immediately. While it is delightful to have warm chips right out of the fryer, taro chips keep well and will stay deliciously crisp for several days. Store in an airtight container at room temperature.

PANKO-CRUSTED TARO

Here, slices of boiled taro root are coated first with flour, then with beaten egg, and finally with coarse Japanese bread crumbs (*panko*) and deep-fried until golden and crisp. Serve them with a generous sprinkling of salt and a squeeze of lime juice. This is an easy appetizer because the taro can be boiled well in advance, the coated slices will keep on a baking sheet for a while until you are ready to fry them, and the frying is splatter-free because of the low-moisture content of taro root.

SERVES 6

6 small taro roots, about
1½ lb/680 g

Kosher or fine sea salt

½ cup/65 g instant flour, such as
Wondra brand, or all-purpose flour

2 large eggs, beaten

2 cups/110 g *panko* (Japanese
bread crumbs)

About 1 cup/240 ml canola or
other neutral oil for frying

2 limes, cut into wedges

1 In a large saucepan, combine the unpeeled taro roots with water to cover by 2 in/5 cm and bring to a boil over high heat. Reduce the heat so the water simmers and cook until the taro is fork-tender, 13 to 15 minutes. Drain the taro in a colander. When cool enough to handle, use a paring knife to remove the skins. Rinse the taro and blot dry with paper towels. Cut crosswise into rounds ⅓ in/8 mm thick.

2 Season each slice on both sides with salt. Put the flour, eggs, and bread crumbs into three separate shallow bowls. Working with one slice at a time, dredge it in the flour, coating lightly; dip it in the eggs; and then coat it with the bread crumbs, gently pressing the crumbs to coat thoroughly and evenly on both sides. Set aside on a baking sheet.

3 Have ready a dinner plate lined with a double thickness of paper towels. Pour the oil to a depth of about ¾ in/2 cm into a large frying pan and heat until the oil shimmers but is not smoking. Carefully place the taro slices into the oil and fry until golden brown on both sides, about 2 minutes. Using a slotted spoon, transfer the fried slices to the towel-lined plate to drain. Sprinkle with salt. Serve immediately with the lime wedges.

SAUTÉED TARO WITH A SESAME, GARLIC, AND HONEY GLAZE

In this recipe—a tropical alternative to potatoes as a side dish—cooked cubes of taro are sautéed, slicked with a honey glaze and a heady dose of garlic, and then garnished with toasted sesame seeds and cilantro.

SERVES 4

1 lb/455 g large taro roots, trimmed, peeled, rinsed, and cut into 1-in/ 2.5-cm cubes

2 tsp kosher or fine sea salt

2 tbsp canola or other neutral oil

1 tbsp Asian sesame oil

2 tbsp honey

2 tbsp unseasoned rice vinegar

2 garlic cloves, minced

2 tbsp finely chopped fresh cilantro

1 tsp sesame seeds, toasted (see Cook's Note, page 64)

1 In a medium saucepan, combine the taro, 1 tsp of the salt, and water to cover by 2 in/5 cm and bring to a boil over high heat. Reduce the heat so the water simmers and cook until the taro is almost tender, about 5 minutes. (The taro needs to be tender but still hold its shape.) Carefully drain the taro in a colander so the cubes don't break, shaking to remove any excess water.

2 In a large sauté pan, preferably nonstick, heat the canola and sesame oil over medium-high heat and swirl to coat the pan bottom. Add the taro and sauté, stirring frequently, until golden brown on all sides, about 5 minutes. Add the honey, vinegar, garlic, and the remaining 1 tsp salt. Toss gently to coat and cook just long enough to glaze the taro, about 1 minute. Transfer to a warmed serving bowl. Garnish with the cilantro and sesame seeds. Serve immediately.

SOBA NOODLES IN MUSHROOM BROTH
WITH TARO AND KABOCHA SQUASH

I couldn't wait to dive into this big bowl of nourishment. Japanese *soba* noodles swim in a savory mushroom broth dense with taro root, daikon, carrot, and kabocha squash. A Japanese market is where you will find: *Naga negi*, which looks like an oversize green onion (you can substitute a leek); *bunashimeji* mushrooms are petite, brown button-topped mushrooms sold in clusters (enoki mushrooms can be used in their place); look for precooked *soba* noodles, in either the frozen foods section or the refrigerator case; you'll find *shichimi togarashi*, a Japanese spice blend, in the spice aisle.

SERVES 4

10 dried shiitake mushrooms

5 cups/1.2 L boiling water

½ cup/120 ml light soy sauce

⅓ cup/75 ml mirin (Japanese sweet cooking wine)

1 lb/455 g refrigerated or frozen precooked *soba* noodles (do not thaw the frozen noodles)

1 tsp Asian sesame oil

½ tsp granulated sugar

2 tbsp sake or mirin

12 oz/340 g small taro roots, trimmed, peeled, rinsed, halved lengthwise, and cut crosswise into slices ¼ in/6 mm thick

4 oz/115 g daikon radish, peeled, halved lengthwise, and cut crosswise into slices ¼ in/6 mm thick

1 medium carrot, 4 oz/115 g, peeled and cut on the diagonal into ovals ¼ in/6 mm thick

1 *naga negi*, white and light green part only, trimmed and cut on the diagonal into ovals ¼ in/6 mm thick

3½ oz/100 g *bunashimeji* mushrooms, trimmed and pulled apart

1 lb/455 g kabocha squash, seeded, unpeeled, and cut into bite-size cubes

Shichimi togarashi for serving

1 Place the mushrooms in a heatproof bowl and pour the boiling water over the top. Place a plate on top of the mushrooms to keep them submerged and let soak for 1 hour. Remove the mushrooms from the water, rinse them to remove any grit, blot dry, and cut off and discard the stems. Cut the mushrooms into halves or quarters, depending on their size. Set aside. Strain the soaking liquid through a fine-mesh sieve into a bowl. Add the soy sauce and mirin and set aside.

2 While the mushrooms are soaking, cook the *soba* noodles. Have ready a large bowl of ice water. Bring a large pot of water to a rapid boil over high heat. Add the *soba* but do not stir until the water has returned to a boil. Use a long wooden spoon or long chopsticks to separate the noodles, and then immediately lift out the noodles with a sieve. Transfer the noodles to the ice water, give them a stir to remove any additional starch, and as soon as they are cool, drain them thoroughly. Set aside.

3 In a large saucepan or soup pot, heat the sesame oil over medium heat. Add the mushrooms and sauté, stirring constantly, for 1 minute. Add the sugar and stir just until the sugar is dissolved, about 30 seconds. Add the sake and stir to deglaze the pan, scraping up any brown bits on the pan bottom. Add the mushroom liquid, taro, daikon, carrot, *naga negi*, and *bunashimeji* mushrooms; increase the heat to high; and bring to a boil. Reduce the heat to a simmer and cook for 5 minutes. Add the squash and continue to cook until the squash is fork-tender, 5 to 7 minutes longer.

4 Divide the noodles evenly among the warmed soup bowls. Make sure the soup is piping hot and then ladle it over the noodles in each bowl and serve immediately. Pass the *shichimi togarashi* at the table.

VIETNAMESE PORK AND TARO STEW WITH GREEN GARLIC

I love to make this deeply satisfying country stew in the early spring when green garlic is in season and available at the farmers' market. Green garlic is harvested before the bulb forms and looks like green onions or very small leeks. It has a mild garlic flavor, much more herblike and delicate than mature heads. If you can't find green garlic, you can substitute 2 large garlic cloves.

SERVES 4

3 tbsp canola or other neutral oil, plus more if needed

1½ lb/680 g boneless pork shoulder, trimmed of fat and cut into ½-in/ 12-mm cubes

Kosher or fine sea salt

Freshly ground pepper

2 large shallots, thinly sliced

6 stalks green garlic, white and light green part only, cut crosswise into thin rounds

2 tbsp soy sauce

2 tbsp Asian fish sauce, preferably Vietnamese *nuoc mam*

4 cups/960 ml water

1 lb/455 g small taro roots, trimmed, peeled, rinsed, and cut crosswise into rounds ¼ in/6 mm thick

2 star anise pods

One 3-in-/7.5-cm-long cinnamon stick

GARNISHES

1 cup/60 g bean sprouts

8 fresh cilantro sprigs

4 lime wedges

2 serrano chiles, stemmed and thinly sliced (see Cook's Note, page 40)

Sambal oelek (see Cook's Note, page 134)

1 In a Dutch oven or other heavy pot, heat the oil over medium heat and swirl to coat the pan bottom. Add half of the pork to the pan, season lightly with salt and pepper, and sauté, stirring frequently, until nicely browned on all sides, about 5 minutes. Using a slotted spoon, transfer the pork to a plate. Repeat with the remaining pork.

2 Tilt the pan to check the amount of oil remaining. If there is not at least 1 tbsp oil, add a little more. (The brown bits sticking to the pan bottom will be absorbed into the sauce once the pan is deglazed.) Add the shallots and green garlic, and sauté over medium heat, stirring frequently, until soft but not brown, about 4 minutes. Add the soy sauce and fish sauce, increase the heat to high, and cook, stirring constantly, to release the brown bits sticking to the pan bottom, about 1 minute.

3 Add the water, taro, reserved pork and any accumulated juices, star anise, and cinnamon stick. Bring the liquid to a boil, reduce the heat to maintain a slow simmer, cover, and cook, stirring once or twice, until the pork and taro are tender, 15 to 20 minutes.

4 While the stew is simmering, arrange the garnishes on a large plate or in individual bowls. Ladle the stew into warmed deep soup bowls to serve. Pass the garnishes at the table. (The stew can be made up to 2 days in advance, covered, and refrigerated. Reheat gently before serving.)

THAI-STYLE SWEET PANCAKES WITH TARO ROOT LEMON CREAM FILLING

When working in the kitchen with my fabulous assistant, Andrea Slonecker, we are disciplined eaters, knowing how much we have to taste and sample in a full day of recipe development. But restraint went out the window when we made these pancakes—we couldn't stop eating them. We just looked at each other and laughed. We were stuffed and every bite was worth it. Make these for breakfast, brunch, or dessert, serving them with a tropical fruit purée such as mango or passion fruit, plus a dusting of confectioners' sugar.

MAKES 12 PANCAKES

FILLING

1 lb/455 g small taro roots, trimmed, peeled, rinsed, and cut into 1-in/2.5-cm chunks

⅔ cup/130 g granulated sugar

1 tbsp freshly grated lemon zest (from 2 lemons)

3 tbsp fresh lemon juice

¼ tsp kosher or fine sea salt

1 cup/240 ml heavy whipping cream

PANCAKES

1 cup/130 g all-purpose flour

1 tbsp baking soda

1 tsp kosher or fine sea salt

1 large egg

¼ cup/50 g granulated sugar

1½ cups/360 ml evaporated milk

2 tbsp unsalted butter, melted, plus more for buttering the pan

1 tsp pure vanilla extract

Confectioners' sugar for dusting

1 To make the filling, in a medium saucepan, combine the taro and water to cover by 2 in/5 cm and bring to a boil over high heat. Reduce the heat so the water simmers and cook until the taro is fork-tender and just beginning to fall apart, about 10 minutes. Drain the taro in a colander, shaking to remove any excess water. Pass the taro through a food mill or ricer into a large bowl. Add the sugar, lemon zest, lemon juice, and salt and mix well to dissolve the sugar. Let cool completely.

2 In a medium bowl, using a whisk or a handheld mixer, beat the cream until soft peaks form. Gently fold the whipped cream into the cooled taro mixture. Set aside while you make the pancakes.

3 To make the pancakes, sift together the flour, baking soda, and salt into a medium bowl. In a large bowl, whisk the egg until fluffy and light, about 1 minute. Add the sugar and whisk until well blended. Add the milk, melted butter, and vanilla and stir to mix. Stir in the flour mixture just until all of the flour is absorbed but a few lumps are still visible. (The batter is thinner than traditional pancake batter.) Set the batter aside to rest for 20 minutes.

4 Heat a large griddle or frying pan, preferably nonstick, over medium-low heat. When the surface is hot, brush it with butter. For each pancake, ladle ¼ cup/60 ml of the batter onto the hot surface and, using the back of the ladle, lightly spread the batter into a 6-in/15-cm pancake. Repeat to add as many more pancakes as will fit without crowding. Cook until golden brown, puffed, and little holes have formed on top, about 1 minute. Flip and cook until nicely browned on the second side, about 30 seconds longer. Fill each pancake with 2 tbsp of the filling. Spoon the filling onto the center of the pancake and spread it to form a thick line across the center. Roll the pancake around the filling to enclose it and place it seam-side down on a warmed serving plate. Repeat until you have used all of the batter and the filling, buttering the pan for each batch. Dust with confectioners' sugar and serve warm.

TURMERIC

Curcuma longa

HISTORY AND LORE A member of the ginger family (Zingiberaceae), turmeric is a robust, herbaceous perennial plant believed to be indigenous to India, though it has never been found in the wild. It looks like the ginger plant, with yellowish leaves rising from edible yellow rhizomes. The latter have been used for centuries as a dye, spice, and medicine. Turmeric is believed to have reached China by the eighth century, East Africa by the ninth century, West Africa four centuries later, and Jamaica by the eighteenth century. In many languages, the name for turmeric means "yellow root." In others, the name is often linked to its botanical kin, ginger, such as the Chinese *jiang huang*, or "yellow ginger."

Turmeric is mentioned in ancient Sanskrit texts, and its usage dates back nearly four thousand years to the Vedic culture of northern India, where it was used as a culinary spice and in religious rituals. For Hindus in the south, the yellow color symbolizes the sun, and during the harvest festival of Pongal, a whole turmeric plant, including the fresh rhizomes, is offered as a gift of thanks to Suryan, the Sun God. Today, Erode, a large city in the southern Indian state of Tamil Nadu, is the world's largest producer of turmeric. Not surprisingly, its nickname is Yellow City. While turmeric's vibrant color suggests a relationship between turmeric and saffron, and it has been known as a poor man's saffron, it is nothing like it in flavor or aroma.

VARIETIES Turmeric is widely cultivated throughout the tropics. Botanists have so far recognized some thirty species of turmeric in the genus *Curcuma*. Among these, *C. longa* is economically the most crucial, accounting for more than 90 percent of the commercial crop, and is what you will see in your local market.

NUTRITION One cup/220 g of turmeric is a significant source of iron, potassium, and vitamin C, but, of course, it is never used in that quantity in a single dish, so its nutritional value is unimportant. It does have medicinal value in smaller amounts, however. In India, turmeric has been used in traditional Ayurvedic medicine as a remedy for poor digestion, to treat heart disease, and to heal wounds. The yellow compound found in the rhizome is curcumin, which has been the focus of several recent scientific studies into its anti-inflammatory and anticancer potential, based on its antioxidant strength.

AVAILABILITY AND SELECTION Fresh turmeric is available year-round in Indian and Asian markets, some natural foods stores, and in some specialty produce markets. Select fresh, plump turmeric "fingers" that are firm and free of soft spots or shriveled skin.

STORAGE Wrap turmeric in a dry paper towel and place inside an unsealed plastic bag in the refrigerator. It will keep for 1 to 2 weeks. If you see any spots of mold, just cut them off, replace the paper towel, and use the remainder. For longer storage, you can slice, wrap, and freeze turmeric for up to 2 months; however, it will lose its firm texture. Use frozen turmeric when a recipe calls for minced or mashed turmeric.

BASIC USE AND PREPARATION Fresh turmeric is used extensively in Indian, Thai, Cambodian, and other Southeast Asian cuisines as a coloring and flavoring spice. The fresh roots are pounded and ground into a paste for classic Thai herbal pastes. It is minced, grated, or thinly sliced for chutneys and pickles, and it is simmered with coconut milk for vegetable, meat, and fish curries. It is also used in rice dishes and eaten on ceremonial and festive occasions. It is a natural dye for drinks, confectionery, and sauces, including mustards and Worcestershire sauce.

Prepare only the amount you will need for a recipe. Trim the rough ends and use a vegetable peeler or paring knife to remove the skin. Finely slice, mince, or grate the turmeric as directed in the recipe. Cut thin slices across the grain. To mince, stack the slices, cut into long strips, and then cut crosswise into fine pieces.

A CAUTIONARY NOTE Fresh turmeric is a natural dye. I always wear disposable gloves when working with it to keep my fingers from being stained yellow. Look for the gloves at a pharmacy or in a supermarket in the aisle with bandages and first-aid supplies. Turmeric will also stain countertops and cutting boards. But if you clean up quickly and use a diluted bleach solution, the golden yellow dye will fade almost completely away. If not, leave your cutting board in a sunny spot. The dye is not light-proof and will fade away when left in the sun for an hour or so.

YIELDS

2-in/5-cm finger fresh turmeric = ½ oz/15 g

Two 2-in/5-cm fingers fresh turmeric = 1 oz/30 g

1 tbsp peeled and minced fresh turmeric = ½ oz/15 g

2 tbsp peeled and minced fresh turmeric = 1 oz/30 g

¼ cup/60 ml peeled and minced fresh turmeric = 2 oz/55 g

THAI KAO SOI PASTE

The first step to making this deliriously fragrant paste is to grill the chiles, ginger, shallots, garlic, and fresh turmeric. Heightening the flavor of these aromatics with the smoke from the grill deepens the taste of the paste, making it heady and vibrant. Cooking the shallots and garlic until their skins char and their flesh softens removes their rawness, develops their flavor, and contributes necessary moisture to the paste. Use the paste for making Chiang Mai Curry Noodles (page 328) or Crisp-Fried Tofu and Vegetables in Kao Soi Coconut Broth (page 330), or smear it on firm-fleshed fish, such as cod or halibut, for braising in coconut milk.

MAKES ½ CUP/120 ML

4 dried small red chiles such as *prik haeng* or *chile de árbol*

5 thick slices peeled fresh ginger (¼ in/6 mm thick)

4 shallots, unpeeled

4 large garlic cloves, unpeeled

½-oz/15-g piece fresh turmeric, peeled and cut on the diagonal into slices ½ in/12 mm thick

1 tsp coriander seeds, toasted and ground (see Cook's Note, page 324)

½ tsp kosher or fine sea salt

30 fresh cilantro stems, cut into ½-in/12-mm pieces

Canola or other neutral oil for storage

1 Immerse five 10-in/25-cm bamboo skewers in water for at least 30 minutes.

2 Stem the chiles, slit lengthwise, and remove the seeds. In a small bowl, combine the chiles with warm water to cover and let soak until softened, about 20 minutes. Drain and blot dry.

3 Prepare a medium-hot fire in a charcoal or gas grill. Use a stove-top grill pan if you have a good hood fan for ventilation.

4 While the grill is heating, thread the chiles onto one skewer, weaving them in and out so they are securely attached. Thread the ginger onto another skewer and do the same with the shallots, garlic, and turmeric, leaving space between the pieces so all surfaces can color and char.

5 Place the skewers directly over the fire and grill, turning as needed, to char on all sides. The chiles, ginger, and turmeric need only a light char, about 5 minutes. The garlic takes about 10 minutes to char the skins completely and soften the clove. The shallots need about 20 minutes to char the skins completely and soften the flesh. As the skewers finish grilling, remove them to a plate.

6 Using a large mortar and pestle or a mini food processor, grind together the chiles, coriander seeds, and salt until reduced to the texture of a coarse spice blend. Peel the shallots and garlic cloves. Using a sharp knife, roughly chop the shallots, garlic, and ginger, keeping them separate. Add the shallots to the chiles and grind until finely mashed. Next, add the garlic and grind until finely mashed. Proceed to add the ginger, the turmeric, and finally the cilantro, grinding to a coarse paste after each addition. If using a food processor, stop the machine several times and use a rubber spatula to scrape down the sides of the work bowl to incorporate all of the ingredients. If the paste is too stiff to grind, add 1 to 2 tbsp water.

7 Transfer the paste to a jar with a tight-fitting lid. It will keep in the refrigerator for up to 5 days. After 3 days, add a thin layer of oil to the top of the paste to preserve its freshness.

CAMBODIAN KROEUNG PASTE

This fresh herbal paste is the essence of Cambodian cooking. It is used in many Khmer recipes, just as curry pastes are used in Thai dishes, to season soups, stir-fried dishes, and satay. In this book, it is used as a flavoring rub for Chicken Skewers with Cambodian Kroeung Paste on page 327.

MAKES ¾ CUP/180 ML

2 lemongrass stalks

6 garlic cloves, smashed with the side of a chef's knife

1 large shallot, coarsely chopped

1-oz/30-g piece fresh turmeric, peeled and coarsely chopped

1-oz/30-g piece galangal, peeled and coarsely chopped

4 fresh kaffir lime leaves (see Cook's Note, page 121), ribs removed and torn into small pieces

1 tsp kosher or fine fine sea salt

2 tbsp canola or other neutral oil, plus more for storage if needed

1 Trim off the root end from each lemongrass stalk, then cut off and discard the tough green tops. You should have a bulb about 4 in/10 cm long. Peel away the tough outer leaves and then finely chop the bulb.

2 Using a large mortar and pestle or a mini food processor, grind together the lemongrass, garlic, shallot, turmeric, galangal, lime leaves, and salt to form a fine paste. If using a food processor, stop the machine several times and use a rubber spatula to scrape down the sides of the work bowl to incorporate all of the ingredients. Add the oil and continue to grind to incorporate the oil fully. The oil will help to break down the hard-to-blend ingredients.

3 Transfer the paste to a jar with a tight-fitting lid. It will keep in the refrigerator for up to 5 days. After 3 days, add a thin layer of oil to the top of the paste to preserve its freshness.

YELLOW RICE

This vivid rice is a lovely accompaniment to braised or roast chicken, such as the Roasted Lemongrass Chicken with Arrowhead on page 39. Many variations and embellishments to the dish are possible. For example, you can stir in chopped roasted peanuts or cashews, cooked peas or asparagus tips, thin rings of green onion, or small pieces of crisp-tender green beans. To make the recipe vegetarian, use vegetable stock or broth in place of the chicken stock or broth. Or, make it richer by cooking the rice in a combination of stock and coconut milk, using 1 cup/240 ml unsweetened coconut milk and 1¼ cups/300 ml stock.

SERVES 4 TO 6

1½ cups/300 g jasmine or basmati rice

1 tbsp canola or other neutral oil

2 tbsp finely chopped shallot

1 large garlic clove, minced

1 tbsp peeled and minced fresh turmeric

3 fresh kaffir lime leaves (see Cook's Note, page 121), crumpled in your hand

2¼ cups/540 ml homemade chicken stock or canned low-sodium chicken broth

1 tsp kosher or fine sea salt

1 Place the rice in a medium bowl, cover with cold water, swish the rice around with your hand, and drain the cloudy water. Repeat two or three times until the water runs clear. On the final washing, drain the rice very well and set aside.

2 In a wide, heavy saucepan, heat the oil over medium heat and swirl to coat the pan bottom. Add the shallot, garlic, and turmeric and sauté, stirring constantly, until the garlic just begins to brown, about 2 minutes. Add the rice and lime leaves and sauté, stirring constantly, until the grains are well coated with the oil. Add the stock and salt and bring to a boil. Reduce the heat to low, cover, and cook at a slow simmer until the liquid is absorbed and the rice is tender, 18 to 20 minutes.

3 Fluff the rice with a fork and serve immediately or keep warm until ready to serve.

OKRA CURRY

I'm an okra lover and I can't resist buying it when I see it fresh in the market—not too big, firm, and a lovely pale green without any blemishes or darkened tips. Typically, in the Indian style, I dry-fry it over high heat with spices to make a quick, crisp sauté. While researching fresh turmeric, I came across a recipe for okra simmered in coconut milk that inspired this easy-to-make braised side dish. It pairs beautifully with the Yellow Rice on page 323.

SERVES 6

1 tbsp canola or other neutral oil

1 medium yellow onion, about 8 oz/225 g, halved lengthwise and cut into very thin wedges

2 serrano chiles, stemmed, halved lengthwise, and seeded (see Cook's Note, page 40)

2 large garlic cloves, minced

1½ tsp peeled and minced fresh ginger

2 tbsp peeled and minced fresh turmeric

12 oz/340 g okra, cut crosswise into ¾-in/2-cm pieces

1 tsp cumin seeds, toasted and ground (see Cook's Note)

1 tsp coriander seeds, toasted and ground (see Cook's Note)

1½ cups/360 ml unsweetened coconut milk

½ cup/120 ml water

2 tsp kosher or fine sea salt

In a 12-in/30.5-cm straight-sided sauté pan, heat the oil over medium-low heat. Add the onion and sauté until soft and golden brown, about 10 minutes. Add the chiles, garlic, ginger, and turmeric and sauté, stirring constantly, for 1 minute. Add the okra and sauté, stirring frequently, until they lose some of their rawness but are still very crisp, 3 to 4 minutes. Stir in the cumin, coriander, coconut milk, water, and salt and bring to a simmer. Cover partially and cook, stirring occasionally, until the okra is tender, 12 to 15 minutes. Taste and adjust the seasoning. Serve immediately.

COOK'S NOTE

Dry-roasting whole spices in a frying pan and then grinding them maximizes their flavor and scent. Place a small, heavy frying pan, preferably cast iron, over high heat. Add the spices to the pan and toast, stirring constantly, until fragrant and lightly browned, about 2 minutes. Transfer to a plate to cool. The spices can then be ground in a mortar and pestle, spice grinder, or blender to a powder. Or, lacking these tools, place the toasted spices in a heavy lock-top plastic bag and pound with a rolling pin or the bottom of a small, heavy saucepan.

INDIAN-SPICED CAULIFLOWER, POTATOES, AND PEAS

Serve this classic Punjabi recipe as a vegetarian main course or as a hearty side dish. Ground turmeric can be substituted for the fresh, but the nuanced sour-sweet, savory flavor of fresh turmeric really blossoms when sautéed in the oil, adding more depth and complexity to the vegetables.

SERVES 4 TO 6

3 tbsp canola or other neutral oil

5 quarter-size slices fresh ginger, peeled and minced

4 garlic cloves, minced

1 tbsp peeled and minced fresh turmeric

3 dried small red chiles such as *prik haeng* or *chile de árbol*, stemmed and seeded

1 bay leaf

1½ tsp kosher or fine sea salt

1 tsp ground coriander

1 tsp ground cumin

½ tsp freshly ground pepper

1½ cups/360 ml canned crushed tomatoes in thick purée

1 cup/240 ml water

1½ lb/680 g white boiling potatoes, peeled and cut into 1-in/2.5-cm cubes

2 lb/910 g head cauliflower, trimmed, cored, and cut into 2-in/5-cm florets

1 cup/140 g frozen green peas, thawed

½ cup/30 g chopped fresh cilantro

1 In a large, deep sauté pan with a tight-fitting lid, warm the oil over medium heat and swirl to coat the pan bottom. Add the ginger, garlic, and turmeric and sauté, stirring constantly, until the garlic turns light brown, about 1 minute. Add the dried chiles, bay leaf, salt, coriander, cumin, and pepper and sauté until the spices are fragrant, 2 minutes longer.

2 Add the tomatoes and water, stir in the potatoes and cauliflower, and bring the liquid to a simmer. Reduce the heat to low, cover, and simmer, stirring occasionally, until the vegetables are fork-tender, 15 to 20 minutes. Stir in the peas and cook, uncovered, until the peas are tender, about 3 minutes longer. Stir in the cilantro, saving 2 tbsp to sprinkle over the top. Transfer to a warmed serving dish, sprinkle with the reserved cilantro, and serve immediately.

SPICY TURMERIC-SCENTED KOHLRABI

Kohlrabi, a relative of cabbage, has the crunch of water chestnuts or lotus root and the subtle taste of broccoli stalks. In this braised dish, it turns a gorgeous translucent gold after the turmeric sauce is reduced to a fiery glaze.

SERVES 4

1 tbsp canola or other neutral oil

2 large garlic cloves, minced

2 tbsp peeled and minced fresh turmeric

¼ tsp red pepper flakes

1 lb/455 g kohlrabi, trimmed and peeled, cut in half crosswise, and sliced into half-moons ⅛ in/3 mm thick

1 tsp granulated sugar

½ tsp kosher or fine sea salt

¾ cup/180 ml water

1   In a large sauté pan, heat the oil over medium heat and swirl to coat the pan bottom. Add the garlic, turmeric, and red pepper flakes and sauté until the garlic is soft but not brown, about 30 seconds. Add the kohlrabi, sugar, and salt and cook, stirring constantly, for 2 minutes. Add the water and bring to a boil. Reduce the heat to maintain a slow simmer, cover, and cook until the kohlrabi is tender, about 15 minutes.

2   Uncover the pan, raise the heat to medium-high, and cook, stirring frequently, until the sauce thickens to a glaze, about 5 minutes. Taste and adjust the seasoning. Serve immediately.

CHICKEN SKEWERS WITH CAMBODIAN KROEUNG PASTE

If you make the flavoring paste in advance—say, on a relaxed weekend day—it takes only a minute to cut up the chicken, toss it with the paste, and marinate the meat. Although skewers are always fun for a family meal—a good excuse for eating with your fingers—keep this recipe in mind as an appetizer for summer entertaining, too.

MAKES 16 TO 18 SKEWERS

1¼ lb/570 g boneless, skinless chicken thighs, trimmed of excess fat

¾ cup/180 ml Cambodian Kroeung Paste (page 322)

Vegetable oil for brushing the grill grate

Lime wedges for serving

1 Cut the chicken thighs lengthwise into strips ¾ in/2 cm wide and about ¼ in/6 mm thick. (At the thickest part of the thigh, you may need to cut the chicken crosswise in half in order to get uniformly thick pieces.) Place the chicken in a bowl and rub it with the paste until evenly coated. Cover and marinate in the refrigerator for at least 2 hours or up to 8 hours.

2 Remove the chicken from the refrigerator 1 hour before you plan to grill. Immerse sixteen to eighteen 10-in/25-cm bamboo skewers in water to soak for at least 30 minutes.

3 Prepare a medium-hot fire in a charcoal grill or preheat a gas grill to medium-high.

4 While the grill is heating, thread the chicken onto the skewers, dividing it evenly and weaving each slice to pierce it two or three times. Bunch the meat a bit, so it covers about 8 in/20 cm of each skewer.

5 Oil the grill grate. Fold a piece of aluminum foil 12 in/30.5 cm long in half lengthwise and lay it on the grill grate. Arrange the skewers so the exposed bamboo is protected from the flame by the foil and the meat is directly over the fire. Use two pieces of foil if necessary. Grill the skewers, turning them once, until the chicken is cooked through and the edges are slightly caramelized and charred, about 3 minutes per side. Cover the grill when cooking the skewers on the second side. Arrange the skewers on a warmed serving platter along with the lime wedges. Serve immediately.

CHIANG MAI CURRY NOODLES

A sunny, hearty one-bowl meal, this dish is named after Chiang Mai, Thailand's northern capital. Soft egg noodles are cloaked in a deeply rich curry sauce and then topped with crunchy deep-fried egg noodles. You can skip the step of frying some of the egg noodles for garnish, but it is quick to do and not messy at all. Plus, the crunchy noodles are addictively good. Look for dried noodles imported from Thailand labeled "Chinese-style egg noodles" and/or *bamee*. Traditionally, many different condiments are served with this dish, such as chopped shallots and Thai-style pickled cabbage. I have kept it simple with green onions, cilantro, and lime wedges.

SERVES 4

One 13½-oz/405-ml can unsweetened coconut milk

2 cups/480 ml plus 1 tbsp canola or other neutral oil

½ cup/120 ml Thai Kao Soi Paste (page 321)

12-oz/340-g boneless sirloin tip or steak, trimmed of fat and cut into ¾-in/2-cm chunks

1 tbsp granulated sugar

2 cups/480 ml water

2 tbsp Asian fish sauce

1 tbsp dark soy sauce

1 tsp kosher or fine sea salt

1 tbsp fresh lime juice

1 lb/455 g dried Chinese-style egg noodles (bamee)

3 green onions, including green tops, thinly sliced

⅔ cup/10 g lightly packed fresh cilantro leaves

1 lime, cut into wedges

1 Open the can of coconut milk without shaking it. Spoon out the thick cream that has separated out at the top of the can. Set aside. (There should be about 1 cup/240 ml.) Pour off the thin coconut milk and set it aside. (There should be about ¾ cup/180 ml.)

2 In a large, heavy pan or wok, heat 1 tbsp of the oil over medium-high heat and swirl to coat the pan bottom. Add the paste and stir-fry to soften it in the oil, about 30 seconds. Add the thick coconut cream and cook, stirring constantly, until it comes to a simmer. Add the beef and sugar and cook, stirring occasionally, until the beef changes color and is partially cooked through, about 5 minutes. Add the thin coconut milk, the water, fish sauce, soy sauce, and salt. Bring to a simmer, stirring once or twice, and simmer until the meat is cooked through, about 10 minutes. Remove from the heat and stir in the lime juice. Cover and keep warm while you cook the noodles. (Set the soup aside for up to 1 hour. Reheat before serving.)

3 Frying some of the noodles to use as a garnish is optional but easy to do. Remove 2 oz/55 g of the noodles from the package. Line a plate with a double thickness of paper towels. Set a wire skimmer or tongs alongside the plate. Pour the remaining 2 cups/480 ml oil into a small, deep frying pan and heat to 375°F/190°C on a deep-frying thermometer. Carefully add about one-fourth of the noodles to the hot oil. They will sizzle and puff up and then turn golden brown within about 30 seconds. Using the wire skimmer or tongs, transfer them to the towel-lined plate. Repeat to fry the remaining noodles. Set aside at room temperature for up to 3 hours.

4 Bring a large pot two-thirds full of water to a rapid boil over high heat. Add the remaining noodles and cook until tender but not mushy, about 5 minutes. Drain well in a colander, shaking out any excess water. Divide the noodles evenly among warmed large soup bowls. Ladle the hot curry over the top. Top each serving with a portion of the crispy noodles, if desired. Sprinkle each serving with an equal amount of the green onions and cilantro. Serve immediately. Pass the lime wedges for squeezing on top.

CRISP-FRIED TOFU AND VEGETABLES IN KAO SOI COCONUT BROTH

Here, I have tweaked a classic Malaysian vegetarian one-dish meal, using my homemade Thai Kao Soi Paste as the flavoring base. The green beans, carrots, and cabbage, combined with deep-fried tofu triangles to soak up the golden coconut broth, makes this humble soup comforting and nourishing all at once. The recipe goes together quickly if you make the paste ahead of time and have it on hand in the refrigerator. Although you can skip the step of deep-frying the tofu and just add drained tofu to the soup, I find the contrast in textures worth the effort.

SERVES 4 TO 6

3 galangal slices, ½ in/12 mm thick

7 unsalted macadamia nuts

3 tbsp canola or other neutral oil, plus more for deep-frying

½ cup/120 ml Thai Kao Soi Paste (page 321)

½-oz/15-g piece fresh turmeric, peeled and minced

1 cup/240 ml unsweetened coconut milk

2 cups/480 ml water

6 oz/170 g green beans, stem end trimmed and cut on the diagonal into 1½-in/4-cm lengths

1 tbsp granulated sugar

1½ tsp kosher or fine sea salt

2 medium carrots, about 7 oz/200 g, trimmed, peeled, and cut into sticks about 1½ in/4 cm long and ⅓ in/8 mm wide

5 oz/140 g green cabbage, cored and cut into 1-in/2.5-cm squares

1 block firm tofu, about 15 oz/430 g, drained, pressed to release more moisture, and blotted dry

1 cup/130 g rice flour

2 green onions, including green tops, sliced paper-thin on the diagonal

¼ cup/15 g chopped fresh cilantro

1 Place the slices of galangal on a cutting board and bruise until juicy with the bottom of a small, heavy frying pan. Set aside. Place the macadamia nuts in a small lock-top plastic bag and pulverize with the side of a rolling pin until finely ground. Set aside.

2 In a large saucepan, heat the 3 tbsp oil over medium heat until a drop of the paste sizzles on contact. Add the paste, turmeric, and crushed nuts and sauté, stirring constantly, until fragrant and softened, about 1 minute. Add the galangal and stir to coat with the paste, about 1 minute longer. Add the coconut milk and water and bring to a gentle simmer, stirring occasionally. Add the green beans, sugar, and salt; reduce the heat to medium-low; and simmer, uncovered, for 5 minutes. Add the carrots and cabbage and cook until fork-tender, about 10 minutes longer. Remove and discard the galangal. Keep warm.

3 While the soup is simmering, fry the tofu. Cut the tofu lengthwise into slabs ½ in/12 mm thick. Cut each slab on the diagonal to form two triangles. Blot each piece with paper towels. Place the rice flour in a deep plate or shallow, wide bowl. Lightly coat each piece of tofu with the rice flour, tapping to remove the excess. Place on a baking sheet.

4 Line a second baking sheet with a double thickness of paper towels. Set a slotted spoon or spatula alongside the baking sheet. Pour the oil to a depth of 2 in/5 cm into a wok or deep frying pan and heat to 340°F/170°C on a deep-frying thermometer. Working in small batches, add the tofu triangles to the hot oil and fry, turning them once, until lightly colored and crisp on all sides, about 3 minutes total. Using the slotted spoon or spatula, transfer the fried tofu to the towel-lined baking sheet. Continue deep-frying until all of the tofu has been fried. Make sure the oil is at 340°F/170°C before you add a new batch. Set aside at room temperature until ready to serve.

5 Divide the tofu triangles evenly among warmed shallow individual bowls. Ladle the hot soup over the top and garnish with a sprinkling of green onions and cilantro. Serve immediately.

TURMERIC-BRAISED HALIBUT STEAKS WITH GARLIC

If you cannot find halibut, you can substitute cod, tilapia, or even salmon or arctic char. You can also opt for fillets rather than steaks, but be sure to ask your fishmonger to skin them for you. The aromatic flavor of this dish comes from first searing the fish on both sides and then braising it in the coconut milk infused with a bountiful amount of garlic and turmeric. Serve the halibut with steamed jasmine or basmati rice and a simple sautéed or steamed vegetable, such as asparagus, snow peas, or baby bok choy.

SERVES 4

Four 8-oz/225-g halibut steaks

2½ tsp kosher or sea salt

2 tbsp canola or other neutral oil

¼ cup/55 g peeled and minced fresh turmeric

12 garlic cloves, minced

1½ cup/360 ml unsweetened coconut milk

4 serrano chiles, stemmed and halved lengthwise (see Cook's Note, page 40)

1 tsp freshly ground pepper

1 Blot the fish steaks dry with paper towels and place on a large plate. Season the fish on both sides with 1 tsp of the salt.

2 In a large frying pan, heat the oil over medium-high heat and swirl to coat the pan bottom. Carefully add the fish and sear, turning once, until golden brown on both sides, about 3 minutes on each side. Transfer the fish to a plate.

3 Return the pan to medium heat, add the turmeric and garlic, and sauté, stirring constantly, until the aromatics are soft but not brown, about 1 minute. Add the coconut milk, chiles, pepper, and the remaining 1½ tsp salt and bring to a simmer. Reduce the heat to low and return the fish to the pan. Spoon the sauce over the fish, cover, and continue to cook, spooning the sauce over the fish once or twice more, until the fish flakes easily when pierced with a knife, about 8 minutes. Arrange the fish on warmed dinner plates, spoon some of the sauce over each fillet, and serve immediately.

TURNIP

Brassica rapa var. rapa

HISTORY AND LORE A swollen taproot with edible greens, the turnip belongs to the mustard family (Brassicaceae), which also counts among its members such popular roots as horseradish, rutabaga, and radish. One of the world's oldest domesticated root crops, the turnip is believed to be indigenous to the region between the Baltic Sea and the Caucasus, from which it spread throughout Europe. Most research concludes that cultivation dates back at least four thousand years. Its longevity as a crop is primarily due to two factors: it thrives in poor soil and it stores well, which made it a dependable food source for both people and their livestock. Greek and Roman writers wrote of the turnip's virtues and importance for feeding "the poorer classes and country folk." First-century Roman author and naturalist Pliny the Elder considered turnips one of the most important agricultural products north of the Po River and recommended eating the green tops.

Turnips spread to eastern Asia, specifically China, before the Middle Ages and later to Japan. European colonists brought the roots to North America in the late sixteenth and early seventeenth centuries, where they became a summer crop in the north and a winter crop in the south. They were a common part of the diet of African American slaves, who ate both the tops and roots. Today, turnip greens cooked with a ham hock is an iconic soul food dish.

VARIETIES In most markets in the United States, you will find only large purple-topped turnips year-round. In springtime and early fall, farmers' markets and specialty grocers have beautiful, tender baby turnips. Perfectly spherical, these quick-growing varieties are sold with their bushy green tops still attached. The flesh can range from bright white to orange. The skin is usually white toward the root end and purple near the stem, although heirloom varieties can be all white, orange, red, or green. Smaller turnips tend to be sweeter; larger specimens carry more of the root's characteristic peppery bite that mellows after cooking.

Golden Ball A deep amber color characterizes this relatively small, round variety with succulent flesh.

Purple Top White Globe These are the quintessential large, round roots that sometimes appear slightly flattened, with bright purple shoulders and a white bottom. The smaller the root, the sweeter the flavor and the better the texture.

Shoigun (or Shogun) This variety is grown specifically for its edible foliage.

Tokyo Types (Tokyo Cross, Tokyo Market, Tokyo White) These small, tender, white sphere-shaped turnips are picked when they are 1 to 3 inches/2.5 to 7.5 centimeters in diameter. They are sold in bunches of 8 to 12 with their tender greens still attached and are sometimes labeled baby turnips.

White Egg (Snowball) As the name implies, this is a white, egg-shaped variety with a delicate, sweet flavor. They are typically sold in bunches with their greens attached.

NUTRITION Turnips are low in calories, with just 25 calories in a 3½-ounce/100-gram serving. The roots are relatively devoid of most vitamins and nutrients, with the exception of a healthy dose of vitamin C. Turnip leaves, on the other hand, are an excellent source of vitamins A, C, and K as well as calcium, folate, and potassium.

AVAILABILITY AND SELECTION Turnips are available in supermarkets year-round and in farmers' markets in the spring and fall. Buy baby turnips with their fresh, bushy, crisp greens still attached, a sure sign of freshness. Mature turnips should be free of cracks, bruising, and soft spots. Avoid roots with an old, shriveled appearance. Smaller turnips tend to be more tender and moist; larger turnips can be tough and sometimes woody.

STORAGE If turnips are purchased with their greens attached, remove the greens as soon as you get the turnips home, leaving 1 inch/2.5 centimeters of the stem attached to the roots. If the tops are left attached, they will draw moisture, flavor, and nutrients from the roots. Store the turnips and tops separately. Store unwashed and untrimmed turnip roots in a plastic bag lined with a paper towel in the refrigerator. The paper towel wicks away any trapped moisture and keeps the roots fresh longer, up to a few weeks for the larger storage turnips but only a few days for baby turnips. To store the tops, remove the bottom stems, wrap the leafy greens in a paper towel, slip them into a plastic bag, seal the top, and refrigerate. For peak freshness, the young green tops should be used within a day or two of purchase.

BASIC USE AND PREPARATION Turnip roots are most commonly roasted, sautéed, pickled, or stewed in soups. To prepare the roots, scrub them well under running cool water. Trim the stem and root ends and peel the tough, bitter skin and any fibrous matter found underneath. Small roots with tender skins do not need to be peeled. Cut the turnips into wedges, chunks, or slices as directed in individual recipes. You can also shred or finely slice turnips and eat them raw in salads. Rinse the leafy tops in several changes of cold water to rid them of sand and dirt. Discard the fibrous part of the stalks and cook the greens by blanching, sautéing, or stewing.

YIELDS

ROOTS

1 small turnip = 3 to 5 oz/85 to 140 g

1 medium turnip = 6 to 7 oz/170 to 200 g

1 large turnip = 8 to 10 oz/225 to 280 g

1 bunch baby turnips, including green tops = about 12 oz/340 g

1½ cups trimmed, peeled, and diced turnips = 10 oz/280 g

3 cups trimmed, peeled, and diced turnips = 1 ¼ lb/570 g

GREENS

Bushy green tops from 1 bunch turnips, stemmed = 4 cups/100 g lightly packed leaves

ROASTED TURNIP GHANOUSH

In 2000, Michael Bauer authored *The Secrets of Success Cookbook*, a collection of recipes from San Francisco's top chefs. I've cooked a number of recipes from his book and have always been delighted with the results. One recipe I particularly like is chef Yahya Salih's Hudhud Ghanoush, a twist on baba ghanoush, the traditional Middle Eastern dip made with eggplant. It uses turnips in a unique way—first roasting them and then puréeing them—and sweetens the spread with date purée, easily made by boiling dates in water and then puréeing them until smooth. Use the extra purée at breakfast time, spread on toasted wheat bread along with creamy goat cheese.

MAKES 4 CUPS/960 ML

2 lb/910 g turnips (about 6 medium)

1 cup/170 g pitted dates

1 cup/240 ml water

½ cup/120 ml low-fat plain Greek yogurt

⅓ cup/75 ml roasted tahini

3 tbsp fresh lemon juice

1 tbsp minced garlic

2 tsp kosher or fine sea salt

¼ tsp freshly ground pepper

1 tbsp finely minced fresh flat-leaf parsley

Pita bread, baked pita chips, or crudités for serving

1 Position a rack in the center of the oven and preheat to 375°F/190°C/gas 5.

2 Place the unpeeled turnips on a rimmed baking sheet and roast until very soft, 30 to 45 minutes. Transfer them to a heatproof bowl, cover with plastic wrap, and let cool. The steam will make them easier to peel.

3 While the turnips are roasting, in a small saucepan, combine the dates and water and bring to a boil over medium-high heat. Cook until the dates have softened, about 5 minutes. Transfer to a food processor and process until puréed. Set aside to cool. Measure ⅓ cup/75 ml purée to use for the recipe. (Cover and refrigerate the remaining purée for another use. It will keep for up to 1 month.)

4 When the turnips are cool enough to handle, peel them and transfer to a food processor. Add the yogurt, date purée, tahini, lemon juice, garlic, salt, and pepper and process until smooth and creamy. Taste and adjust the seasoning. Transfer to a serving bowl and garnish with the parsley. Serve immediately with pita bread, or cover and refrigerate until ready to serve. (The dip can be prepared up to 1 day in advance, covered, and refrigerated.)

TURNIP AND CARROT KRAUT WITH CARAWAY

The minute I tasted this kraut I became hungry for a Reuben sandwich and wished I had corned beef in the refrigerator and rye bread in the cupboard. It also made me hungry for a grilled kosher hot dog tucked inside a soft bun, smeared with grainy mustard and topped with this turnip and carrot kraut. For those who have never fermented any foods, this is a great way to start—a small batch recipe with big-flavored results.

MAKES 2½ CUPS/600 ML

1 lb/455 g turnips, peeled and cut into large chunks

4 oz/115 g carrots, peeled and cut into large chunks

2½ tsp kosher salt

½ tsp caraway seeds, toasted (see Cook's Note, page 324)

1 Using the coarse holes on a box grater or a food processor fitted with the coarse shredding disk, grate the turnips and carrots. Transfer the grated vegetables to a large glass container with straight sides, such as a 1-qt/960-ml glass measuring cup. Add the salt and toasted caraway seeds and toss to combine thoroughly. Place a glass or china plate on top of the mixture and press down firmly. Place a weight, such as a closed container filled with water, on top of the plate and press down to squeeze out the moisture that is released by the vegetables. Cover the container with a clean kitchen towel and place in a cool, dark place to ferment for 1 week.

2 Every day, press down on the plate to make sure the vegetables are submerged. The salt will continue to draw out moisture from the vegetables during fermentation, and pressing on the plate helps to extract the brine. The vegetables must be completely submerged for fermentation to occur and to avoid mold from developing on the surface. If mold does form, skim it off and discard it. (Don't worry, the kraut is still safe to eat!)

3 After 1 week, the kraut will be tangy and ready to eat. If left to ferment for 2 weeks or more, it will continue to develop complex flavors. When you think the kraut has fermented long enough, you can store it in a covered container in the refrigerator and enjoy it for several weeks.

CREAMY TURNIP SOUP WITH GREENS

In French cooking, a thick soup made from puréed vegetables is called a *potage*. This soup is a potage, but because some cooks may not be familiar with the term, I chose to use the word *creamy* in the recipe title. The soup tastes rich and creamy, yet there isn't even a teaspoon of cream in the ingredients list. And because of that, the soup is quite low in calories and packed with nutrients. To make the lovely swirled garnish of puréed turnip greens, you'll need to buy a bunch of small, snowy white turnips with their bushy tops still attached.

MAKES 7 CUPS/1.7 L; SERVES 6 TO 8

10 peppercorns

4 fresh parsley sprigs

4 fresh thyme sprigs

2 bay leaves

1½ tbsp extra-virgin olive oil

1 medium yellow onion, diced

2 leeks, white and light green part only, halved lengthwise and thinly sliced crosswise

Kosher or fine sea salt

Freshly ground pepper

1½ lb/680 g turnips, peeled, trimmed, and diced

1 medium russet potato, about 8 oz/225 g, peeled and diced

4 cups/960 ml homemade chicken stock or canned low-sodium chicken broth

Pinch of freshly grated nutmeg

1 cup/35 g lightly packed chopped turnip greens

1 Cut an 8-in/20-cm square of cheesecloth and place the peppercorns, parsley, thyme, and bay leaves in the center. Bring up the edges to form a bag and tie securely with kitchen twine to make a bouquet garni. Set aside.

2 In a heavy soup pot, heat the oil over medium-low heat and swirl to coat the pan bottom. Add the onion, leeks, 1 tsp salt, and ¼ tsp pepper, stir briefly, and then cover and cook, stirring once or twice, until the vegetables are very soft but not brown, about 10 minutes. Add the bouquet garni to the pot along with the turnips, potato, and stock. Increase the heat to medium-high and bring to a boil. Reduce the heat to maintain a simmer, cover, and cook, stirring occasionally, until the vegetables are tender when pierced with a fork and soft enough to purée, about 20 minutes. Remove from the heat, discard the bouquet garni, and let the soup cool for about 10 minutes.

3 Working in batches, process the soup to a smooth purée in a blender or food processor. Return the puréed soup to the pot. If the soup seems too thick, add about ½ cup/120 ml water to achieve a creamy consistency. Add the nutmeg and season with salt and pepper. Set aside and keep warm.

4 Transfer ½ cup/120 ml of the puréed soup to the blender or food processor. Add the turnip greens and process to a smooth purée. Season with a pinch each of salt and pepper.

5 Bring the soup to a simmer and ladle into warmed soup bowls. Using a large spoon, swirl some of the puréed turnip greens on the top of each serving and serve immediately.

COOK'S NOTE

The soup and garnish can be made up to 3 days in advance. Let the soup cool, transfer to a covered container, and refrigerate. The garnish of puréed greens must be chilled quickly to preserve its bright green color. Transfer to a small bowl, place the bowl in an ice-water bath to cool, and then cover and refrigerate. Rewarm the soup and garnish just before serving.

WHITE BALSAMIC–GLAZED TURNIPS

For anyone not familiar with white balsamic vinegar, it is made with white wine vinegar rather than the red wine vinegar used to make traditional dark balsamic. It is milder and less sweet than the dark vinegar, and it doesn't color the food to which it is added, making it perfect to use with white baby turnips.

SERVES 4 TO 6

4 tbsp/55 g unsalted butter

1½ lb/680 g baby turnips, green tops removed and saved for another use, roots trimmed and quartered

¼ cup/60 ml water

¼ cup/60 ml white balsamic vinegar

1 tbsp granulated sugar

1 tsp kosher or fine sea salt

¼ tsp freshly ground white pepper

2 tbsp chopped fresh flat-leaf parsley

1 In a large sauté pan, melt the butter over medium heat and swirl to coat the pan bottom. Add the turnips and stir to coat. Add the water and bring to a simmer. Reduce the heat to maintain a slow simmer, cover, and cook until the turnips are tender, about 8 minutes.

2 Uncover the pan and add the vinegar, sugar, salt, and white pepper. Increase the heat to medium-high and cook, stirring frequently, until the sauce thickens to a glaze, 3 to 5 minutes. Taste and adjust the seasoning. Remove the pan from the heat and toss in the parsley. Serve immediately.

ROASTED TURNIPS WITH THYME

Basic and delicious—that's the beauty of these lovely roasted turnips. Serve them as an alternative to potatoes to accompany a braised beef or pork dish. They would also complement a roast chicken and can be scattered around the bottom of the roasting pan. To ensure the chicken is fully roasted yet the turnips don't overcook, add the turnips to the roasting pan about 15 minutes after you begin roasting the chicken.

SERVES 4 TO 6

2 lb/910 g medium purple-topped turnips, trimmed, peeled, and cut into 1½-in/4-cm wedges

2 tbsp extra-virgin olive oil

2 tbsp minced fresh thyme

2 tsp kosher or fine sea salt

¼ tsp freshly ground pepper

1 Position a rack in the center of the oven and preheat to 375°F/190°C/gas 5.

2 On a rimmed baking sheet, toss together the turnips, oil, thyme, salt, and pepper. Place in the oven and roast, stirring twice at regular intervals during roasting, until the turnips are golden brown and tender when pierced with a knife, 35 to 45 minutes. Serve immediately.

TURNIPS AND LEEKS IN MISO BUTTER

After a full day's work, I can't imagine a more satisfying dinner in such a short time. The pungent bite of the turnips is an inspired and balanced counterpoint to savory white miso paste and soft, sweet leeks. Aromatic jasmine rice is a natural partner for this vegetarian dish. It steams in about the same time that it takes to cook the turnips, and that makes for a quick, weeknight meal.

SERVES 2 AS A MAIN COURSE, OR 4 AS A SIDE DISH

1 tbsp unsalted butter

1 lb/455 g medium purple-topped turnips, peeled, halved lengthwise, and sliced crosswise into half-moons ¼ in/6 mm thick

1 large leek, white and light green part only, thinly sliced

2½ tbsp white miso paste

¼ cup/60 ml hot water

¼ cup/60 ml mirin (Japanese sweet cooking wine)

Kosher or fine sea salt

2 tbsp chopped fresh cilantro

2 tsp sesame seeds, toasted (see Cook's Note, page 64)

1   In a large sauté pan, melt the butter over medium heat and swirl to coat the pan bottom. Add the turnips and leek and sauté, stirring occasionally, until the leek is softened and the turnips are crisp-tender, about 10 minutes.

2   Dissolve the miso in the hot water and add it to the turnip mixture. Add the mirin and bring to a simmer. Reduce the heat to maintain a slow simmer, cover, and cook until the turnips are tender when pierced with a fork, 5 to 7 minutes.

3   Remove the pan from the heat, season with salt, and toss in the cilantro. Garnish with the sesame seeds and serve immediately.

KASHMIRI-STYLE TURNIPS WITH GREENS

This is an adaptation of a recipe from Raghavan Iyer's splendid *660 Curries*, using baby turnips with their bushy greens instead of the kohlrabi Iyer suggests. Like kohlrabi, turnips "come alive in the presence of sweet fennel, pungent ginger, hot chiles, and smoky cardamom." I used two leafy bunches of baby turnips in this recipe, cutting the turnips into halves or quarters, depending on their size. I used more than half of the greens from the tops. Since the greens cook down so much, you could chop and add all of them if you wanted to, adding a tad more cream at the end of the cooking time to make enough sauce.

SERVES 4

2 tbsp canola or other neutral oil

1 serrano chile, stemmed, halved lengthwise, seeded, deribbed, and finely minced (see Cook's Note, page 40)

1 tbsp peeled and minced fresh ginger

2 black cardamom pods (see Cook's Note, page 87)

1 tsp fennel seeds, ground in a mortar or spice grinder

14 oz/400 g baby turnips, trimmed and halved or quartered, depending on their size

⅔ cup/165 ml water

1 tsp kosher or fine sea salt

About 4 cups/120 g lightly packed chopped turnip greens (from just over 2 bunches baby turnips)

2 tbsp heavy whipping cream

1 In a medium saucepan, heat the oil over medium heat. Add the chile and ginger and sauté until fragrant and soft but not brown, about 2 minutes. Add the cardamom pods and fennel and sauté just until aromatic, about 20 seconds. Add the turnips, water, and salt and bring to a boil. Reduce the heat to low, cover, and simmer, stirring occasionally, until the turnips are almost tender when pierced with a fork, about 5 minutes. Pack the greens on top, cover, and let the greens wilt, about 3 minutes longer.

2 Give the greens and turnips a gentle stir and then add the cream. Simmer, uncovered, over low heat until slightly thickened, about 2 minutes. Taste and adjust the seasoning. Serve immediately.

TURNIP GREENS GUMBO Z'HERBES

This recipe is a delicious way to use up the tasty turnip tops you end up with after making Pancetta-Wrapped Baby Turnips (facing page) or White Balsamic–Glazed Turnips (page 338). If you don't have enough greens to yield 12 cups/300 g, it is fine to substitute another root vegetable top, such as radish tops or beet greens, or any other hardy green, such as kale, mustard greens, or Swiss chard. Traditionally, this vegetarian Creole dish, accompanied by rice, is served on Good Friday and calls for a variety of cooking greens—seven, nine, or eleven types—always an odd number for good luck. Be sure to remove the stems and tough center rib of the turnip tops and of the leaves of hardy greens. I like to wash the greens by soaking them in a big bowl of cold water, changing the water twice, since the leaves tend to trap dirt. I then whirl them dry in a salad spinner.

MAKES ABOUT 6 CUPS/1.4 L; SERVES 6 TO 8

12 cups/300 g lightly packed chopped turnip greens (from about 3 bunches baby turnips)

3 cups/720 ml water

Kosher or fine sea salt

¼ cup/60 ml canola or other neutral oil

¼ cup/30 g all-purpose flour

1 medium yellow onion, diced

1½ cups/90 g thinly sliced green onions, including green tops

1 medium green bell pepper, seeded, deribbed, and diced

2 celery ribs, diced

2 large garlic cloves, minced

1 tbsp Cajun seasoning

¼ tsp freshly ground pepper

½ tbsp minced fresh thyme

½ tbsp minced fresh marjoram or oregano

Tabasco or other hot-pepper sauce

Cooked white rice for serving

1 Place the turnip greens, water, and 1 tsp salt in a large pot with a tight-fitting lid. Bring the water to a simmer over medium-high heat, cover, and reduce the heat to medium-low. Simmer the greens, stirring occasionally, until they are just tender, about 15 minutes. Drain the greens in a colander set over a large heatproof bowl. Reserve the cooking liquid and the greens separately. (There should be about 3½ cups/840 ml liquid.) Set aside.

2 In a Dutch oven or other heavy pot, heat the oil over medium heat and swirl to coat the pan bottom. When the oil is hot, vigorously whisk in the flour to prevent lumps from forming. Reduce the heat to medium-low and continue to cook the mixture, stirring constantly with a wooden spoon or a heat-resistant rubber spatula, until it is the color of peanut butter, 10 to 15 minutes. (This is called a brown roux.) Be sure to stir around the corners of the pan to prevent the flour from burning.

3 Add the yellow onion, 1 cup/60 g of the green onions, the bell pepper, celery, garlic, Cajun seasoning, 1 tsp salt, and the pepper to the pot and cook, stirring often, until the vegetables are crisp-tender, about 5 minutes. Add the reserved cooking liquid, stirring to achieve a smooth, lump-free mixture. Increase the heat to medium-high and bring the mixture to a boil. Reduce the heat to a simmer and cook, stirring frequently, until the gumbo base is thick and the vegetables are tender, about 15 minutes.

4 Stir in the turnips greens, thyme, and marjoram and cook until heated through. Season the gumbo with the Tabasco and with a little more salt if needed. Scoop the rice into warmed individual bowls and spoon the gumbo over the top. Garnish with the remaining ½ cup/30 g green onions. Serve immediately.

PANCETTA-WRAPPED BABY TURNIPS

I like to serve these pancetta-wrapped turnips as appetizers, though they work well as a side dish, too. Look for baby turnips about 2½ inches/6 centimeters in diameter with their greens or at least a little of the stem end still intact. The stems make great "handles" for picking up the appetizers. (Trim the bushy tops and reserve them for the Turnip Greens Gumbo Z'Herbes on facing page.)

Ideally, you want to cook the turnips on a wire rack set on a rimmed baking sheet. If you do not have a rack, the wrapped turnips can be roasted directly on the baking sheet, but the bottoms will get very dark and crusty. I like the contrast between the silky turnips and the crunchy pancetta, but a wire rack will ensure more even browning. If you opt to roast them without the rack, they will roast more quickly, so keep an eye on them. For a deliciously sweet and tart finish to these savory appetizers, drizzle a little aged balsamic vinegar over the top or serve them with peach chutney.

MAKES 12 APPETIZERS

12 baby turnips, preferably with greens attached (about 2 bunches)

12 paper-thin slices pancetta

1 Position a rack in the center of the oven and preheat to 375°F/190°C/gas 5. Place a flat wire roasting rack in a large rimmed baking sheet.

2 If the greens are still attached to the turnips, trim them off, leaving at least ½ in/12 mm of the stem intact. Reserve the greens for another use. Trim the root tends of the turnips flat so they will stand upright. Gently scrub the turnips under cool running water to remove any dirt from the skins and between the stems and then pat dry.

3 Wrap each turnip with 1 slice of pancetta, covering the skin and bottom and leaving the stem exposed. The pancetta should cling tightly to the turnip skins. If not, use toothpicks to secure. Arrange the turnips on the rack in the pan, spacing them at least 1 in/2.5 cm apart.

4 Roast until the turnips are tender when pierced with a paring knife and the pancetta is crisp and golden, 25 to 35 minutes, depending on the size of the turnips. Remove the toothpicks if used. Serve immediately, or let cool and serve at room temperature.

HERB-ROASTED CHICKEN WITH TURNIPS AND CHANTERELLES

The chicken, heady with fresh herbs and lemon, goes into the oven first. Once it has released some of its fat and juices, you add the turnip wedges to the pan, tucking them around the bird, and leave them to roast in the flavorful drippings. While the chicken rests before carving, chanterelles are added to the pan and cooked along with the turnips. This crisp-skinned, golden brown chicken, surrounded by the earthy tastes of autumn, is fall entertaining at its best.

SERVES 4

One 4-lb/1.8-kg whole chicken, preferably free-range

Kosher or fine sea salt

Freshly ground pepper

1 lemon, halved

5 fresh thyme sprigs

2 fresh rosemary sprigs

2 fresh sage sprigs

2 tbsp canola or other neutral oil, plus more if needed

1 lb/455 g medium purple-topped turnips, trimmed, peeled, and cut into wedges 1 in/2.5 cm thick

1 lb/455 g chanterelle or other wild mushrooms, stems trimmed

1 tbsp chopped mixed fresh herbs such as thyme, rosemary, sage, and parsley

1 Remove the chicken from the refrigerator at least 45 minutes before roasting to take the chill off the bird. Position a rack in the center of the oven and preheat to 425°F/220°C/gas 7. Have ready a roasting pan with a roasting rack, preferably V shaped, in the pan.

2 Remove the neck and giblets and any excess fat from the bird's cavity. Reserve the neck and giblets for another use. Trim any excess skin. Rinse the chicken under cool running water and pat dry inside and out with paper towels. Season the inside of the cavity with salt and pepper. Slip a lemon half and all of the herb sprigs into the cavity. Use the remaining lemon half to cap the cavity.

3 Tuck the wing tips under the body and then bring the legs together and wrap kitchen twine around the ends (knobs), securing the twine with a knot. Trim any extra length of twine. Rub the entire surface of the chicken with the oil and sprinkle generously with salt and pepper. Set the chicken, breast-side up, on the roasting rack.

4 Roast the chicken for 25 minutes. Remove the pan from the oven and scatter the turnips around the bottom of the pan, tossing them in the rendered chicken fat to coat. Add a little canola oil if there is not enough rendered fat to coat evenly. Season the turnips with salt and pepper. Lower the oven temperature to 400°F/200°C/gas 6 and return the pan to the oven. Continue to roast until the chicken is deep golden brown and crisp and the juices run clear when the thigh joint is pierced with a fork, or an instant-read thermometer inserted into the thickest part of the thigh away from bone registers 165°F/75°C, 25 to 35 minutes more.

5 Remove the pan from the oven and transfer the chicken to a carving board, ideally one that has a moat and well to catch the delicious poultry juices. Cover the breast loosely with aluminum foil and let rest for 15 minutes before carving to let the juices set.

6 While the chicken rests, add the chanterelles to the roasting pan with the turnips and toss to combine. Return the pan to the oven and roast until the turnips are very tender when pierced with a fork and the chanterelles are tender and beginning to brown, 12 to 15 minutes.

7 Snip and remove the twine from the chicken. Using a sharp carving knife, cut down between the thigh and body until you reach bone. Twist the leg and thigh a little until you see the thigh joint. Now cut through the joint to separate the thigh from the body. Cut the joint where the leg meets the thigh. Repeat on the other side. Transfer the legs and thighs to a warmed platter. To carve the breast meat, start at the keel bone that runs along the top of the breast. Angle the knife and follow the bone line to remove the breast meat from each side of the bird. Either carve the breast meat into thin slices or leave the breasts whole. Transfer the slices or breasts to the warmed platter.

8 Arrange the turnips and mushrooms around the chicken. Scatter the chopped herbs over the chicken and vegetables and serve immediately.

FARFALLE PASTA WITH TURNIPS AND THEIR GREENS

I like to have recipes like this one up my sleeve so I can put one together with a fresh vegetable that I purchase and pantry staples that I have on hand, such as dried pasta, olive oil, garlic, and anchovies. Look for snowy white baby turnips with bushy fresh greens at the farmers' market or pluck them from your garden and make this dish on a harried weeknight. The sauce comes together in the time it takes to cook the pasta.

SERVES 4 TO 6

2 bunches baby turnips with greens attached, about 1½ lb/680 g

Kosher or fine sea salt

1 lb/455 g farfalle (bow-tie pasta)

¼ cup extra-virgin olive oil

8 olive oil–packed anchovy fillets, rinsed, blotted dry, and minced

4 large garlic cloves, minced

2 tbsp chopped fresh flat-leaf parsley

Freshly grated Parmesan cheese, preferably Parmigiano-Reggiano, for serving

1 Trim off the turnip greens. Trim the turnips and cut into wedges ½ in/ 12 mm thick; set aside. Trim away the thick, fibrous portion of the stems from the greens and remove any wilted or spotted leaves. Stack the greens and chop crosswise into pieces about 2 in/5 cm wide. Rinse the greens in a couple of changes of cold water and dry in a salad spinner or blot dry with paper towels. Set aside.

2 Fill a large stockpot two-thirds full with water, add 1 tbsp salt, and bring to a boil over high heat. Add the pasta and stir. Cook the pasta until al dente (cooked through but still slightly chewy), 11 to 12 minutes.

3 While the pasta is cooking, heat the oil in a large sauté pan over medium heat and swirl to coat the pan bottom. Add the turnips (roots only) and ½ tsp salt and sauté until the turnips are tender, 6 to 8 minutes. Add the anchovies and garlic and sauté for 1 to 2 minutes longer.

4 When the pasta is ready, drain it in a colander, reserving 1 cup/240 ml of the cooking water. Add the pasta and turnip greens to the sauté pan and toss to combine. Add just enough of the reserved pasta water, a little at a time, as needed to moisten. Divide the pasta among warmed individual bowls and shower with the parsley and Parmesan cheese. Serve immediately.

SHANGHAI BRAISED BEEF WITH TURNIPS

Here is a stew that makes you hope for leftovers. Chunks of well-marbled beef are browned along with green onions, garlic, chile, and ginger and then slowly simmered in an aromatic broth flavored with star anise, cinnamon, and five-spice powder. When the meat is meltingly tender, wedges of turnip are added, submerged in the sauce, and cooked until they soften and absorb the deep rich flavors.

SERVES 4

3 tbsp canola or peanut oil

1⅓ cups/85 g thinly sliced green onions, including green tops

4 garlic cloves, thinly sliced

1 jalapeño chile, stemmed, halved lengthwise, seeded, deribbed, and minced (see Cook's Note, page 40)

1-in/2.5-cm piece fresh ginger, peeled and thinly sliced

2 lb/910 g boneless beef chuck, trimmed of excess fat and cut into 2-in/5-cm chunks

Kosher or fine sea salt

Freshly ground pepper

3 tbsp all-purpose flour

1 tbsp firmly packed light brown sugar

2 star anise pods

1½-in/4-cm piece cinnamon stick

1 tsp five-spice powder

⅓ cup/75 ml Chinese rice wine or pale dry sherry

2 cups/480 ml homemade beef stock or canned low-sodium beef broth

3 tbsp dark soy sauce

1 lb/455 g medium purple-topped turnips, peeled and cut into wedges 1-in/2.5-cm thick

Steamed white or brown rice or cooked rice noodles for serving

¼ cup/15 g coarsely chopped fresh cilantro

1 Position a rack in the lower third of the oven and preheat to 325°F/165°C/gas 3.

2 In a large Dutch oven or other heavy ovenproof pot, heat 2 tbsp of the oil over medium heat and swirl to coat the pot bottom. Add 1 cup/60 g of the green onions, the garlic, jalapeño, and ginger and cook, stirring, until tender and fragrant, about 3 minutes. Do not allow the garlic to burn. Using a slotted spoon, transfer the onion mixture to a plate. Reserve the pot off the heat.

3 Season the beef generously with salt and pepper and toss it in the flour until evenly coated. Return the pot to medium-high heat and add the remaining 1 tbsp oil. Working in batches to avoid crowding the pan, add the beef and cook, turning occasionally, until browned on all sides, 6 to 8 minutes per batch. Using tongs, transfer the meat to a rimmed baking sheet. Continue until all of the meat is browned.

4 Pour off all but 2 tbsp of the fat from the pot and return the pot to medium-low heat. Add the brown sugar, star anise, cinnamon stick, and five-spice powder and stir until fragrant and the sugar is dissolved, about 1 minute. Add the wine and stir to loosen the brown bits stuck to the pot bottom. Bring to a simmer and reduce the liquid by half.

5 Return the onion mixture and browned meat and any accumulated juices on the baking sheet to the pot. Add the stock and soy sauce and bring to a boil over medium-high heat. Cover with a tight-fitting lid, transfer to the oven, and braise for 2 hours, stirring the meat once after 1 hour. After 2 hours, add the turnips to the pot, stirring to submerge them in the liquid, re-cover, return to the oven, and cook until the turnips are tender when pierced with a fork, about 30 minutes longer. At this point, the meat should be very tender. Taste and adjust the seasoning.

6 Spoon the rice into shallow bowls and ladle the stew over the top. Garnish with the cilantro and the remaining ⅓ cup/25 g green onions. Serve immediately.

WASABI

Wasabia japonica

HISTORY AND LORE Even though wasabi resembles horseradish in flavor and is often called Japanese horseradish, the popular condiment plants are unrelated to each other except for both being members of the sprawling family Brassicaceae. Valued for its finger-thick green rhizomes, wasabi, one of the rarer and more difficult food plants to grow, has been cultivated in Japan for over a millennium. It was found wild from Sakhalin, the first major island to the north of Japan, all the way south to Kyushu, the third largest and most southwestern island in the Japanese archipelago. Early texts on Japanese medicinal herbs praised wasabi as an antidote to food poisoning and a disease preventative. Although the plant is still harvested in the wild, several cultivars are grown commercially in Japan, and, in more recent times, in North America and New Zealand.

VARIETIES A semiaquatic perennial, wasabi grows wild in wet, cool mountain river valleys, along streambeds, and on river sandbars in Japan. The pungent rhizomes grow up to 7 inches/18 centimeters long. The wild species is *Wasabia tenuis*. The cultivated species is *W. japonica,* and the two cultivars most commonly found in markets are Daruma and Mazuma.

NUTRITION Wasabi is consumed in such small quantities that the nutritional value is unimportant. However, scientists are currently studying the ability of wasabi to enhance the natural detoxifying enzymes in our bodies, reduce the risk factors for certain forms of cancer, and inhibit the formation of blood clots.

AVAILABILITY AND SELECTION With a little diligence, fresh wasabi can be found! Although it is expensive, I have found sources for fresh and fresh-frozen wasabi online (see Sources), and it is available in some Japanese grocery stores in big cities. Uwajimaya, a large Japanese market with branches in Seattle, Washington, and Portland, Oregon, carries fresh wasabi. Typically sold with the stems and leaves removed, the roots should be moist and firm and the little nodules along their sides should look fresh. Trimmed of their top leaves, fresh wasabi roots can range in length from 2 to 7 inches/5 to 17 centimeters. Commercially harvested wasabi is typically 2½ to 4 inches/6 to 10 centimeters long and about ½ inch/12 millimeters wide. In the produce aisle, wasabi is often put in a shallow pan of water and misted frequently to keep it fresh.

Wasabi is also available in other forms. Fresh-frozen grated wasabi is sold in airtight packages in the freezer section of Japanese markets. To prepare it, fresh wasabi is grated at an extremely low temperature and then immediately packaged and frozen to maintain its freshness. Wasabi paste (reconstituted powder sold in a tube) is available in the refrigerator section. Wasabi powder (the dried and pulverized root) is available, too, though much flavor and color are lost in this form. Beware of inexpensive powders or pastes that are a mixture of horseradish, mustard powder, or cornstarch and green food coloring. Both the paste and the powder can be found in well-stocked supermarkets.

(If you cannot find fresh wasabi, substitute an equal quantity of prepared wasabi or use wasabi powder following the package directions. Typically, 1½ tsp wasabi powder is mixed with 1 tbsp water to form a paste.)

STORAGE Wrap fresh wasabi in damp paper towels, place in a loosely sealed plastic bag, and refrigerate. Rinse the wasabi in cold water every few days, trim any soft spots, and replace the paper towels. Fresh wasabi will keep for 2 or 3 weeks. Do not remove it from the refrigerator until just before use. You can also freeze whole fresh roots for up to 6 months. Do not thaw before grating.

BASIC USE AND PREPARATION Wasabi is typically served as a condiment with sushi and sashimi, noodles, tempura, tofu, and other dishes and as seasoning for snack foods such as dried peas. Contemporary Japanese chefs are adding wasabi to salad dressings, crackers, and even ice cream. To prepare wasabi, use a vegetable brush to scrub the root and then pat dry with paper towels. Trim the top (thick end) of the root and then trim off the nodules along the root's length to expose the green flesh. Trim only as much of the root as you plan on grating. Using a fine-tooth Japanese grater, grate the flesh, always moving the grater in a circular motion. Finally, press the grated flesh with the flat side of a chef's knife. This step will release more flavor. Form the wasabi into a ball and let stand for 5 to 10 minutes to allow the flavor and heat to develop before serving. Rewrap the unused portion of the root and return it to the refrigerator. (For a more detailed description of how to grate wasabi and of traditional Japanese graters, see Fresh Wasabi Paste on page 352.)

YIELDS

2½ in/6 cm wasabi root = scant 1 oz/30 g

7½ in/19 cm wasabi root = about 2½ oz/70 g

7½ in/19 cm wasabi root, grated = 3 tbsp paste

WASABI MAYONNAISE

Slather this on a burger, especially the Asian Turkey Burgers on page 361, or on a salmon or tuna burger. I've used it as a sauce for steamed baby bok choy and asparagus spears, crisp-tender cooked sugar snap peas, and grilled vegetables, chicken, and pork. You can also add a generous spoonful to a simple baked potato and top it with some freshly snipped chives. It is perfect for French fries, too.

MAKES ABOUT 1⅓ CUPS/315 ML

1 large egg

1 tbsp Dijon mustard

1 tbsp unseasoned rice vinegar

1 tsp kosher or sea salt

1 tsp granulated sugar

1 cup/240 ml canola or other neutral oil

3 tbsp Fresh Wasabi Paste (page 352)

In a blender or food processor, combine the egg, mustard, vinegar, salt, and sugar and process until combined. With the machine running, pour in the oil in a slow, steady stream and continue to process until all of the oil has been absorbed, the mixture has emulsified, and the mayonnaise is thick. Add the wasabi paste and process for 1 minute longer. Transfer to a bowl, cover, and refrigerate until ready to use. The mayonnaise will keep for up to 5 days.

FRESH WASABI PASTE

Because fresh wasabi is expensive, you will want to take special care when handling it and you will want to have the proper tools. Only then will you be able to produce an authentic wasabi paste.

Top Japanese chefs grate fresh wasabi on a sharkskin grater (*samekawa oroshi ki*), which is simply a piece sharkskin mounted on a wooden or ceramic paddle. It is the ideal abrasive surface for grating the densely textured rhizome. Alternatively, you can use a small-toothed ceramic, copper, or stainless-steel grater. The teeth should be as fine as possible to produce a paste that delivers the full heat and flavor of the rhizome. Once I started working with the fresh root, I decided to invest in a sharkskin grater. I tried using a Microplane grater, but the result was not nearly as satisfactory as what is possible with even the small Japanese stainless-steel graters sold at Asian markets that carry housewares.

Pacific Coast Wasabi (www.wasabia.com) explains the importance of proper grating this way: "Grating [wasabi] releases volatile compounds called isothiocyanates that gradually dissipate with exposure to the air. These compounds are not found in wasabi until after the cells of the plant are broken up and turned into a paste. The finer the paste the more chemical reactions take place. Using a wasabi grater and keeping the rhizome perpendicular to the grating surface minimizes exposure to the air. In this way, the volatile compounds are allowed to develop with minimal dissipation. This combination of natural volatiles, consistency, and texture distinguishes fresh wasabi from the imitation products of powdered and paste horseradish, which have been mixed with Chinese mustard and green food coloring."

MAKES 3 TBSP PASTE

2½ oz/70 g fresh wasabi root (about 3 roots, each 2½ in/6 cm long)

1 Rinse the wasabi under cool running water. Use a vegetable brush to scrub the root and then pat dry with paper towels. If the stems are still attached, trim them off just below their base. Use a paring knife rather than a peeler to trim the top (thick end) of the root and then trim off the nodules along the root's length to expose the green flesh. Trim only as much of the root as you plan on grating.

2 With the thick end of the wasabi held perpendicular to the grater, press tightly and use a small circular motion to grate the wasabi, producing a small pile of the mashed plant. (If you have sensitive eyes, you might want to invest in a pair of onion goggles, available at cookware stores.) Once the wasabi is grated, press on the paste with the flat side of a chef's knife to further release the flavors and maximize the taste. By hand, gather and press the grated wasabi into a small ball and let it breathe at room temperature for a few minutes, allowing it to further maximize its flavors. The wasabi paste is now ready to use.

> **COOK'S NOTE**
> According to top sushi chefs, 10 minutes after preparation is the optimal time to serve freshly grated wasabi and the flavor will "peak" after 20 to 30 minutes. The flavors can be reinvigorated by remixing it and forming a new ball, or even adding a pinch of sugar to reactivate the enzymes.

WASABI AVOCADO DIP

Luscious and creamy, this pale green dip is addictively good. The richness of the avocado is balanced with the heat from the fresh wasabi. Serve the dip with sea salt–flavored rice chips, with tortilla chips, or with crisp-cooked vegetables, such as blanched asparagus spears, snow peas, or broccoli florets. Raw jicama spears, celery sticks, or even radishes would be great, too. It is so good I sometimes eat it with a spoon.

MAKES 1¼ CUPS/300 ML

2 large, ripe Hass avocados, halved, pitted, peeled, and diced

2 tbsp Fresh Wasabi Paste (facing page)

2 tbsp crème fraîche

1 tbsp fresh lime juice

1 tsp kosher or fine sea salt

1½ tbsp finely snipped fresh chives

In a medium bowl, combine the avocados, wasabi, crème fraîche, lime juice, and salt. Using a rubber spatula, mix the ingredients to create a creamy dip with some small chunks of avocado still visible. Transfer to a serving bowl and garnish with the chives. Serve immediately.

COOK'S NOTE

The dip can be made up to 4 hours in advance. Do not garnish until just before serving. To store, place a piece of plastic wrap directly on the surface of the dip, pressing gently to eliminate any air pockets, and refrigerate. (This will keep the dip from turning brown.)

WASABI MASHED POTATOES

The fresh wasabi not only delivers a subtle taste of heat but also colors the potatoes a lovely pale sage green. It might seem over the top to serve the potatoes with the Wasabi-Crusted Roast Beef Tenderloin on page 362, but I found the pairing perfect.

SERVES 4

1½ lb/680 g russet or other floury potatoes, peeled and cut into 2-in/5-cm chunks

1½ tsp kosher or fine sea salt

4 tbsp/55 g unsalted butter, melted

½ cup/120 ml crème fraîche

⅓ cup/75 ml heavy whipping cream

2 tbsp Fresh Wasabi Paste (page 352)

1 Put the potatoes in a large saucepan and add cold water to cover. Place over high heat, cover partially, and bring to a boil. Add 1 tsp of the salt and reduce the heat so the water boils gently. Cook until the potatoes are very tender when pierced with a knife, 10 to 12 minutes.

2 Drain the potatoes in a colander or sieve. Return them to the pot and set over medium heat for just a few seconds to remove any moisture from the pan. Turn off the heat. Using a potato masher, mash the potatoes. Add the melted butter and continue to stir and mash until the butter is absorbed. Stir in the crème fraîche, cream, wasabi, and the remaining ½ tsp salt. Serve immediately, or cover and keep warm until ready to serve.

OYSTER SHOOTERS WITH WASABI

You'll need twelve to twenty-four ¼ cup/60 ml oversize shot glasses for serving this appetizer. I bought inexpensive contemporary shot glasses at a restaurant-supply house near where I live. They make a festive statement when passed on a tray at a cocktail party, and if your guests are anything like mine, they'll come into the kitchen looking for refills. I've found many other ways to use these glasses for entertaining, such as filling them with cold soup in the summer for appetizer "soup shots," serving miniature portions of chocolate pudding topped with a whipped cream rosette for dessert, or turning my brunch oyster shooters into Bloody Mary shooters with oysters and a tiny stick of celery.

MAKES 24 SHOOTERS

One ½-pt /240-ml jar yearling-size fresh oysters (about 24)

2 tbsp Fresh Wasabi Paste (page 352)

2 tbsp finely snipped fresh chives

⅓ cup/40 g very finely diced English cucumber

One 750-ml bottle sake, ice-cold

For each shooter, put 1 oyster in a shot glass and top with ⅛ tsp of the wasabi, ¼ tsp of the chives, and ¾ tsp of the cucumber. Pour 2 tbsp sake over the top. Serve immediately.

TUNA TARTARE WITH WASABI

Serve this tuna tartare as an elegant appetizer or first course. Place the tuna center stage on an oversize plate with an artful flourish of paper-thin cucumber slices strewn around it. A drizzle of extra-virgin olive oil, a scattering of minced chives, and a dusting of fleur de sel make this a showstopper for a sophisticated dinner party. Buy your tuna from a reputable fishmonger to ensure that it is very fresh.

SERVES 6 AS AN APPETIZER OR FIRST COURSE

One 8-oz/225-g ahi (yellowfin) tuna fillet, skin and pin bones removed

1 tbsp finely snipped fresh chives, plus more for garnish

1 tbsp minced shallot

1 tbsp minced fresh cilantro

1½ tsp fresh lemon juice

1 tbsp extra-virgin olive oil, plus more for drizzling

¾ tsp kosher or sea salt

1 or 2 pinches of freshly ground white pepper

1 English cucumber

½ cup/120 ml Wasabi Mayonnaise (page 351)

Fleur de sel for sprinkling

1 Using a very sharp knife, cut the tuna into ¼-in/6-mm dice. (Do not use a food processor. It will damage the texture of the fish, making it coarse and mushy.) Place the tuna in a medium bowl. Gently fold in the chives, shallot, cilantro, and lemon juice. Stir in the oil and season with the salt and pepper. Cover and refrigerate for at least 30 minutes or up to 8 hours. Remove from the refrigerator 20 minutes before serving.

2 Cut the cucumber in half crosswise. Cut each half lengthwise into paper-thin slices. Set aside on a plate, covered, until ready to serve.

3 Have ready large salad or dinner plates. Scatter several slices of cucumber around each plate in a random, artful way. Leave the center of each plate open. Spoon one-sixth of the tartare into a mound in the center of each plate. Place a rounded 1 tbsp of the mayonnaise on top of the tartare. Drizzle oil over the cucumber slices, garnish the tartare with chives, and lightly sprinkle fleur de sel on both the tartare and cucumbers. Serve immediately.

SEARED SCALLOPS WITH WASABI-DAIKON RELISH

This recipe may look like top-chef cuisine, but it is simple enough to prepare, especially since the relish can be made a few hours in advance. The secret to beautifully crusted scallops is a heavy cast-iron pan, oil hot enough to give an instant sear, and a cook who is patient enough to leave the scallops untouched for the few minutes it takes to brown them.

SERVES 3 OR 4 AS A MAIN COURSE, OR 6 TO 8 AS AN APPETIZER

RELISH

2½ oz/70 g daikon radish, peeled and cut into ⅛-in/3-mm dice

2 tbsp finely minced shallot

1½ tbsp Fresh Wasabi Paste (page 352)

1 tbsp fresh lime juice

2 tsp extra-virgin olive oil

1 tsp mirin (Japanese sweet cooking wine)

½ tsp granulated sugar

½ tsp kosher or fine sea salt

12 to 16 large sea scallops, 1 to 1½ lb/455 to 680 g

Kosher or fine sea salt

Canola or other neutral oil for frying

1 To make the relish, in a medium bowl, stir together the daikon, shallot, wasabi, lime juice, oil, mirin, sugar, and salt, mixing gently. Set aside until ready to serve.

2 Remove the small, tough connective tissue at the side of each scallop. Blot the scallops dry with paper towels. Just before searing the scallops, season them lightly with salt.

3 When ready to sear the scallops, pour in just enough oil to film the bottom of a heavy 12-in/30.5-cm frying pan, preferably cast iron. Place the pan over high heat and heat the oil until hot but not smoking. Carefully arrange the scallops in the pan so they aren't touching. (You should have enough room to sear all of the scallops at one time.) Sear until a nice brown crust forms on the bottom, about 3 minutes. Turn them over, reduce the heat to medium, and continue to cook the scallops until they are lightly crusted brown on the bottom and just cooked through without being rubbery, about 2 minutes longer.

4 Arrange two scallops on each warmed appetizer plate or four scallops on each warmed dinner plate. Top each scallop with a small spoonful of the relish and serve immediately.

SALMON HAND ROLLS WITH FRESH WASABI

I'm a huge fan of sushi and hand rolls, especially salmon hand rolls that include the contrasting texture of crisp salmon skin. The recipe looks long because I've tried to include detailed instructions, but making the rolls is actually quite easy. One of my favorite things to do for casual entertaining is to have all of the ingredients ready to assemble, invite my guests to watch me as I make a roll, and then let them make their own hand rolls.

MAKES 8 HAND ROLLS; SERVES 4 TO 8 AS AN APPETIZER

1 cup/215 g Japanese short-grain rice

1½ cups/360 ml water

¼ cup/60 ml mirin (Japanese sweet cooking wine)

2 tbsp seasoned rice vinegar

One 6-oz/170-g salmon fillet from tail end, skin and pin bones removed and skin reserved

2½ tbsp *kecap manis* (see Cook's Note)

4 sheets toasted nori, each 7¼ by 8 in/18 by 20 cm

1 tbsp Fresh Wasabi Paste (page 352)

16 fresh chive stems, 4 in/10 cm long

1 small cucumber, peeled, halved lengthwise, seeded, and cut into thin strips about 4 in/10 cm long

16 fresh cilantro sprigs

Soy sauce for serving

1 Place the rice in a medium bowl, cover with cold water, swish the rice around with your hand, and drain the cloudy water. Repeat two or three times until the water runs clear. This removes the residual starch. Drain in a sieve. Place the rice in a heavy 2-qt/2-L saucepan and add the water. Cover the pan and bring to a boil over high heat, about 5 minutes. Reduce the heat to low and cook the rice at a bare simmer for 15 minutes. As tempting as it might be, don't remove the lid and peek at any point or all of the steam will escape. Remove from the heat and let stand for 15 minutes. (Alternatively, use a rice cooker and follow the manufacturer's instructions.)

2 Meanwhile, combine the mirin and vinegar in a heatproof glass measuring cup and microwave on high power until warm, about 20 seconds. Alternatively, place the cup in a small pan of simmering water and heat until warm. Transfer the rice to a large, shallow bowl. Drizzle half of the mirin mixture over the rice and, using a wooden spoon or rubber spatula, gently fold in the liquid, using a light lifting and folding motion to avoid mashing the rice. As you fold, fan the rice with a fan or rolled-up section of newspaper to cool the rice. Add the remaining mirin mixture and continue folding and fanning, about 5 minutes total. The rice should glisten. Cover the rice with a clean, damp dish towel and set aside until ready to make the hand rolls. The prepared rice can be made several hours ahead and left standing at room temperature.

3 Position an oven rack or broiler pan about 4 in/10 cm from the heat source and preheat the broiler. Line a rimmed baking sheet with aluminum foil. Cut the salmon into eight long strips and brush each strip with some of the *kecap manis*. Arrange the strips on the prepared baking sheet. Cut the salmon skin into eight long strips and brush each strip with some of the *kecap manis*. Add to the baking sheet. Broil the salmon and salmon skin until the skin begins to crackle and the salmon is bronzed, 3 minutes. Use a spatula or tongs to transfer the salmon to a plate. Turn the salmon skin over and broil until the skin is crackly and crisp, 2 to 3 minutes longer. Transfer to a separate plate and set aside.

4 Cut each piece of nori in half lengthwise to form eight 7¼-by-4-in/ 18-by-10-cm rectangles. Have ready a small bowl with lukewarm water and a clean, dry linen tea towel. Working with one nori rectangle at a time, place it vertically, shiny-side down, on the towel. Dampen your fingertips lightly. Spread about ⅓ cup/75 ml rice on the lower half of the nori, patting it down lightly. Dampen your fingertips a bit more if the rice is sticking to them. Use your finger or the back of a teaspoon to smear a diagonal line of wasabi paste across the rice. Stacking them together, place 1 piece salmon, 1 piece salmon skin, 2 chive stems, 2 or 3 cucumber strips, and 2 cilantro sprigs across the rice from the upper left corner to the bottom right.

5 Fold the lower left-hand corner of the nori over the filling toward the right side. Keep rolling the nori, now rolling over toward the left side to form a cone. Just before you get to the end, moisten your finger with a little water and moisten the top end of the nori to seal the edge of the cone. Place on a serving tray. Repeat to form eight hand rolls total. With a little practice, you'll be able to assemble two at a time. Serve the rolls with little bowls of soy sauce for dipping. (The hand rolls can be made up to 2 hours ahead. Arrange on a serving platter and cover tightly with plastic wrap to keep them from drying out.)

COOK'S NOTE

Kecap manis is an Indonesian sweet soy sauce flavored with palm sugar, garlic, star anise, and other spices. It is sweeter, more complex, and thicker than soy sauce and is used as a marinade, glaze, and condiment in Indonesian dishes. Look for *kecap manis* in bottles at Asian grocery stores or, occasionally, in a well-stocked supermarket with a large Asian clientele. Once opened, store in a cool, dry place.

GRILLED WASABI SALMON

I have adapted this recipe from Tori Ritchie's Web site, www.tuesdayrecipe.com. She named it Brita's Wasabi Salmon, after her friend Brita Gemmo, who lives in Rome and hungers for Asian food every time she visits Tori in San Francisco. It's one of those easy-breezy grill recipes that every cook ought to have in the repertoire, because the fish marinates in the time it takes the grill to get hot. I chose to grate fresh wasabi for this recipe to get a nice kick of heat, increasing the quantities over the original recipe that calls for 1 teaspoon prepared wasabi. If you can find fresh wasabi, by all means use it, but prepared wasabi will work well, too. It is available in little tubes in the Asian foods section of many supermarkets.

SERVES 4 TO 6

MARINADE

¼ cup/60 ml fresh lime juice

2 tbsp soy sauce

1 tbsp canola or other neutral oil

1 tsp granulated sugar

1½ tbsp peeled and finely minced fresh ginger

1 tbsp Fresh Wasabi Paste (page 352)

½ tsp freshly ground pepper

Four to six 6-oz/170-g center-cut wild king salmon fillets, skin on and pin bones removed

Vegetable oil for brushing the grill grate

1 To make the marinade, in a small bowl, combine the lime juice, soy sauce, oil, sugar, ginger, wasabi, and pepper and stir to dissolve the sugar.

2 Place the fillets, flesh-side down, in a baking dish just large enough to hold them in a single layer. Pour the marinade over the top. Slosh the salmon around and flip it over once or twice to make sure all sides are well coated with the marinade. Set aside at room temperature for 20 minutes.

3 Meanwhile, prepare a medium-hot fire in a charcoal grill or preheat a gas grill to medium-high.

4 When ready to grill, generously brush the grill grate with vegetable oil to prevent the salmon from sticking. (Fish tends to stick and is trickier to grill than poultry or meat, so slicking the grate thoroughly really helps.) Lift the salmon from the marinade but do not discard the marinade. Place the salmon, skin-side up, directly over the fire. Cover the grill and cook on one side until beautiful grill marks are etched across the fillets, about 3 minutes. Turn the fish, baste with the marinade, and then cover the grill. Cook until the salmon is almost opaque throughout but still very moist, about 5 minutes more. An instant-read thermometer inserted into the center should register 125°F/52°C. Serve immediately.

ASIAN TURKEY BURGERS WITH WASABI MAYONNAISE

Lean turkey burgers are a healthful alternative to traditional beef burgers, but I find them to be pretty bland without additional ingredients to pump up the flavor. I've chosen Asian flavors, loading these burgers with ginger, garlic, cilantro, green onions, and soy sauce. I have also kicked up the heat, adding a little wasabi paste to the burgers and serving them with Wasabi Mayonnaise slathered on the bun.

SERVES 4

1½ lb/680 g ground turkey

3 tbsp chopped fresh cilantro

2 green onions, including 2 in/5 cm of green tops, very thinly sliced

2 tbsp peeled and minced fresh ginger

1 tbsp freshly grated wasabi

3 tbsp soy sauce

2 tsp fresh lemon juice

Vegetable oil for brushing the grill grate

2 tbsp canola or other neutral oil

4 sesame-seed hamburger buns, split

4 lettuce leaves

½ cup/120 ml Wasabi Mayonnaise (page 351)

1 Prepare a hot fire in a charcoal grill or preheat a gas grill to high.

2 In a large bowl, combine the turkey, cilantro, green onions, ginger, wasabi, soy sauce, and lemon juice and mix well. Divide into four equal portions and shape each portion into a patty 1 in/2.5 cm thick. Refrigerate the patties while the grill heats.

3 Brush the grill grate with vegetable oil. Brush the burgers on both sides with the canola oil. Place the burgers directly over the hot fire and sear on one side, about 5 minutes. Turn and sear on the other side until almost cooked through, about 4 minutes longer. Place the buns, cut-side down, on the grill to toast during the last minute of grilling.

4 Serve the turkey burgers on the toasted buns with the lettuce and mayonnaise.

WASABI-CRUSTED ROAST BEEF TENDERLOIN

Elegance is the word for this main course, especially with the nut butter and wasabi-crusted top. Beef tenderloin is the cut from which filets mignons are portioned, so you and your lucky guests will be eating a tender, great-flavored cut. Armed with an instant-read thermometer and an accurately calibrated oven, any cook can succeed with this recipe—even a novice. Freeze the extra flavored butter and cut slices to top grilled or pan-seared steaks, lamb, or pork.

SERVES 4

CURRIED PISTACHIO BUTTER

3 tbsp unsalted butter, at room temperature, plus ½ cup/115 g

1 cup/55 g fresh bread crumbs (see Cook's Note, page 136)

3 tbsp black sesame seeds

3 tbsp unsalted roasted shelled pistachio nuts

1 tbsp curry powder

1 tsp kosher or fine sea salt

1 egg yolk

One 1¾-to-2-lb/800-to-910-g beef tenderloin

Kosher or fine sea salt

Freshly ground pepper

3 tbsp canola or other neutral oil

3 tbsp Fresh Wasabi Paste (page 352)

1 To make the pistachio butter, in a medium frying pan, melt the 3 tbsp butter over medium-high heat. Add the bread crumbs and sauté, stirring constantly, until crisp and golden brown, about 2 minutes. Transfer to a plate to cool. Put the sesame seeds on a small microwave-safe plate and microwave the seeds on high power until lightly toasted, about 4 minutes. Set aside to cool. (It is hard to tell with black sesame seeds when they are toasted because they are black! In my microwave oven, at 2 minutes they felt hot but not crisp, so I toasted them 1 minute longer, checked to make sure they weren't burning, and then toasted 1 minute longer.)

2 In a food processor, combine the pistachios, sesame seeds, curry, and salt and process until the nuts are finely chopped, about 30 seconds. Cut the remaining ½ cup/115 g butter into thin slices and add to the processor along with the egg yolk. Process for 1 minute, stopping the machine once or twice to scrape down the sides of the work bowl. Scatter the bread crumbs over the top and pulse five or six times until incorporated. Spread a long sheet of plastic wrap on a clean work surface. Using a rubber spatula, form the butter into a log about 1½ in/3 cm in diameter. Wrap the plastic wrap around the butter and roll to form a tight, compact log. Refrigerate until ready to use. (The flavored butter can be refrigerated for up to 5 days or frozen for up to 2 months.)

3 Remove the tenderloin from the refrigerator 1 hour before you plan to roast it. Position a rack in the center of the oven and preheat to 400°F/200°C/gas 6.

4 Rub the meat on all sides with some salt and pepper. Place a heavy, ovenproof 10-in/25-cm frying pan, preferably cast iron, over high heat. When hot, add the oil and swirl to coat the pan bottom. Immediately add the tenderloin, rounded-side (top-side) down. Sear without moving the meat for 4 minutes. Turn and sear the second side for 3 minutes. Immediately transfer the pan to the oven and roast the meat for 15 minutes, and then check the internal temperature using an instant-read thermometer. Remove the meat when the thermometer registers 115° to 120°F/46° to 49°C for rare, 125° to 130°F/52° to 54°C for medium-rare, or 130° to 140°F/54° to 60°C for medium. (Keep in mind that the temperature of the meat will increase a few degrees once it is placed under the broiler.) Remove the pan from the oven and turn on the broiler. Adjust the oven rack if necessary, so the top of the tenderloin will be about 4 in/10 cm from the heat source.

5 Spread the wasabi paste all over the top of the roast. Cut the log of pistachio butter into thin slices and lay the slices over the wasabi. Place the roast under the broiler and broil until the butter is crusted and turns deep brown, 3 to 4 minutes. (The egg yolk in the butter keeps it from melting, forming a lovely crunchy crust.) Carefully transfer the roast to a carving board. Let the meat rest for 5 minutes to allow the juices to set. Carve across the grain into thick slices and serve immediately.

WATER CHESTNUT

Eleocharis dulcis

CHINESE WATER CHESTNUT / MATI *(MANDARIN CHINESE)* / MA TAI *(CANTONESE)* / SOMWANG *(THAI)* / SINGHAGA *(HINDI)*

HISTORY AND LORE A member of the sedge family (Cyperaceae), water chestnuts are the small, crisp, round corms of a perennial water plant native to China. They have been cultivated for thousands of years in flooded paddy fields in southern China and underwater along the muddy banks of streams, ponds, and marshes. Do not confuse *Eleocharis dulcis* with the three species of aquatic plant in the genus *Trapa*: the Asiatic *T. bicornis*, commonly known as water chestnut, caltrop, or ling nut, with shiny black, two-horned "chestnuts" that carry edible seeds; *T. natans,* or European water chestnut, which has a seed with an edible kernel, and *T. bispinosa*, or large-spined singhara nut, which is used primarily in Kashmiri cuisine.

The Cantonese think of water chestnuts first as a medicinal tonic and only secondarily as a crunchy accent to the dishes. They are believed to remedy everything from coughs, nausea, indigestion, and fevers to intestinal tract maladies. Today, water chestnuts are commercially cultivated in China, Japan, Taiwan, Thailand, and Australia and are exported both fresh and canned. Most fresh chestnuts sold in the United States are imported from China.

VARIETIES Fresh Chinese water chestnuts are not distinguished by variety in markets.

NUTRITION Water chestnuts are a good source of dietary fiber, riboflavin, vitamin B_6, potassium, copper, and magnesium. There are 106 calories in a 3½-ounce/100-gram serving.

AVAILABILITY AND SELECTION Fresh water chestnuts are usually available year-round in good-size Chinese and other Asian markets. They have rings of papery leaves at their base, a tufted top, and are often coated with mud. Instead of scooping up a handful, I select each mahogany-colored water chestnut individually, choosing those that are rock hard, have smooth, shiny skin, and feel a bit heavy for their size. Look for larger specimens, as they are easier to peel and produce less waste. Also, buy a few more than you think you'll need. I inevitably find a few bad ones in the bunch, even after carefully selecting them. Canned water chestnuts have none of the sweet, nutty taste of fresh ones. The sweet rewards are worth the effort of peeling them.

STORAGE Refrigerate unwashed, unpeeled water chestnuts in a brown-paper sack for up to 1 week. I have seen recipes that suggest peeling water chestnuts 1 to 2 days in advance and then refrigerating them in a covered jar filled with water. I find they taste waterlogged, however, and their taste is diminished. It works best to peel them right before, or at most a few hours before, you plan to use them.

BASIC USE AND PREPARATION Fresh water chestnuts are prized for their sweet, succulent crispiness and are eaten raw and cooked in both sweet and savory dishes. Street stalls in China sell peeled fresh water chestnuts on a stick as a snack food. They can be used whole, sliced, quartered, diced, or finely minced in salads, soups, stir-fries, sautés, braises, noodle or rice dishes, and even with fruit and can be grilled or pickled whole. Water chestnuts are also dried and ground to a flour that is used as a thickening agent and to make water chestnut cake, a traditional dim sum offering.

To prepare fresh water chestnuts, wash them thoroughly under cool running water to remove any caked-on mud and then blot dry. Use a sharp paring knife to slice off the top and bottom ends. As if peeling an apple, angle your knife and peel around the edge to remove the mahogany skin. The flesh should be pure white. Trim away any brown or yellowish spots, which are an indication of decay. If using immediately, there is no need to soak them in water to prevent discoloration. If prepping them in advance, soak them in a bowl of cool water until ready to use.

YIELDS

1 fresh water chestnut = scant 1 oz/30 g

6 fresh water chestnuts = about 5½ oz/155 g

12 fresh water chestnuts = about 11 oz/310 g

16 fresh water chestnuts = about 1 lb/455 g

8 oz/225 g fresh water chestnuts, peeled and diced = about 1 cup/170 g

12 oz/340 g fresh water chestnuts, peeled and thinly sliced = about 1½ cups/270 g

---

PORCUPINE BALLS

Called either pearl balls or porcupine balls, these Chinese appetizers (or dim sum delights) are amusing—and incredibly tasty and fun—finger foods: when the balls are steamed, the pearly grains of soaked rice swell and look like the quills of a porcupine. The meatball is a savory mix of pork, garlic, ginger, green onions, soy sauce, toasted sesame oil, and Chinese black mushrooms, with the added crunch of diced water chestnuts. If you make meatballs often, or need a small scoop to portion cookie dough, it's worth investing in a 2-tbsp/ 30-ml ice-cream scoop that measures 1½ in/4 cm in diameter.

MAKES 24 MEATBALLS

1 cup/215 g medium- or short-grain white rice

6 medium dried Chinese black mushrooms

1 lb/455 g ground pork

6 fresh water chestnuts, ends trimmed, peeled, and cut into ¼-in/6-mm dice

4 green onions, including green tops, quartered lengthwise and finely diced

1 tbsp peeled and finely minced fresh ginger

1 large garlic clove, minced

2 tsp kosher or sea salt

2 tsp soy sauce

1 tsp Asian sesame oil

Soy sauce or Chinese hot-mustard sauce for serving

1 Soak the rice in a bowl of cold water for at least 4 hours or overnight. Drain well in a sieve and spread on paper towels to dry. Transfer the rice to a medium bowl when ready to shape the meatballs.

2 Soak the mushrooms in a small container of hot water until softened, about 20 minutes. (I like to put them in a small plastic container with a lid so the lid keeps the mushrooms submerged.) Drain and blot the mushrooms dry, remove and discard the stems, and cut into ¼-in/6-mm dice. Set aside.

3 In a large bowl, combine the pork, diced mushrooms, water chestnuts, green onions, ginger, garlic, salt, soy sauce, and sesame oil. Use your hands or a rubber spatula to mix the ingredients until well combined. Line a rimmed baking sheet with parchment paper. Using a 2-tbsp/30-ml ice-cream scoop that measures 1½ in/4 cm, shape 24 meatballs. Alternatively, shape the meatballs between your palms, forming balls about 1½ in/4 cm in diameter. Working with one meatball at a time, gently roll it in the rice until evenly coated with the kernels and then place on the prepared baking sheet. When all of the meatballs are coated with rice kernels, cover and refrigerate until ready to steam the meatballs. They will keep for up to 8 hours. (Alternatively, freeze the meatballs on the baking sheet and transfer them to a covered freezer container, layering them between sheets of parchment paper.)

4 Set up a wok with a large bamboo steamer basket on top, or use a large pot with a steamer insert. Line the basket or insert with parchment paper. Bring 2½ in/6 cm of water to a boil in the wok or pot. Arrange the meatballs in the basket or insert, spacing them about 1 in/2.5 cm apart. Cover and steam the meatballs over the boiling water until the pork is cooked through and the rice has swelled, about 25 minutes. (If you have frozen the meatballs, cook them without thawing, adding an additional 10 minutes to the cooking time.) Serve the meatballs hot with soy sauce for dipping.

ASIAN SHRIMP DIP

Relish the splendors of beautifully pink, delicately cooked shrimp—preferably wild-caught Gulf shrimp—loaded with the heady accents of ginger, garlic, and green onion and the crunch of fresh water chestnuts. The sweet crustacean flavor is complemented by a splash of sesame oil and just enough mayonnaise and sour cream to call this delicious concoction a dip.

MAKES ABOUT 3 CUPS/720 ML

1 tsp kosher or fine sea salt

1 lb/455 g medium shrimp in the shell

6 fresh water chestnuts, ends trimmed, peeled, and cut into ¼-in/6-mm dice

4 green onions, including green tops, finely minced

1 rounded tbsp peeled and finely minced fresh ginger

1 tsp finely minced garlic

⅓ cup/75 ml mayonnaise

2 tbsp sour cream

4 tsp fresh lemon juice

2 tsp Asian sesame oil

½ tsp freshly ground white pepper

Crostini, baked pita chips, or *lahvosh* for serving

1 Fill a 3-qt/3-L saucepan two-thirds full with water, add ½ tsp of the salt, and bring to a boil over high heat. Add the shrimp and cook just until they are pink and firm, about 2 minutes. Drain and rinse under cool running water. Peel and devein the shrimp and then finely chop and place in a medium bowl.

2 Add the water chestnuts, green onions, ginger, garlic, and the remaining ½ tsp salt to the shrimp and mix well. Add the mayonnaise, sour cream, lemon juice, sesame oil, and pepper and stir until the ingredients are well combined. Taste and adjust the seasoning.

3 Transfer to a serving bowl, cover, and refrigerate for at least 1 hour to allow the flavors to meld. (The dip will keep for up to 1 day.) Remove from the refrigerator 20 minutes before serving. Serve with crostini.

SHRIMP TOASTS

Crisp and hot from the deep fryer, these pink shrimp toasts make a spectacular appetizer. They can be assembled several hours ahead, arranged on a baking sheet, and kept tightly covered in the refrigerator until you are ready to deep-fry. Although you can skip the garnish of black sesame seeds, they add a dramatic touch. The shrimp mixture retains a lot of heat right out of the oil, so let the toasts cool for a few minutes before serving.

MAKES 24 TOASTS

8 oz/225 g medium shrimp, peeled and deveined

5 fresh water chestnuts, ends trimmed, peeled, and cut into ¼-in/6-mm dice

2 tbsp finely minced fresh cilantro

2 tsp finely minced fresh ginger

2 tsp mirin (Japanese sweet cooking wine)

½ tsp kosher or fine sea salt

⅛ tsp freshly ground pepper

2 tsp cornstarch

1 egg white, lightly beaten until foamy

6 slices firm white bread, about 7½ oz/215 g, crusts removed and each slice quartered

2 tbsp black sesame seeds

Canola or other neutral oil for deep-frying

1 In a food processor, pulse the shrimp until finely minced. Transfer to a medium bowl and stir in the water chestnuts, cilantro, ginger, mirin, salt, and pepper. Put the cornstarch in a small bowl and slowly whisk in the egg white until the mixture is lump free and the cornstarch is absorbed. Stir into the shrimp mixture. (The shrimp mixture can be prepared up to 1 day in advance, covered, and refrigerated. Remove from the refrigerator 20 minutes before assembling and frying the toasts.)

2 Use a table knife to lightly and evenly spread rounded 2 tsp of the shrimp mixture on each piece of bread. Arrange the toasts on a baking sheet. Sprinkle the top of each toast with a few sesame seeds, just enough for a garnish.

3 Line a baking sheet with a double thickness of paper towels and set it near your stove. Set a slotted spoon or pair of long tongs alongside the baking sheet. Pour the oil to a depth of 3 in/7.5 cm into a deep, heavy pot, a wok, or an electric deep fryer and heat to 350°F/180°C on a deep-frying thermometer. (If using an electric deep fryer, follow the manufacturer's instructions.)

4 Fry the shrimp toasts in small batches. Carefully place them, shrimp-side down, in the oil and fry for 1 minute. Turn and fry until the bread is golden brown, 1 to 1½ minutes longer. Using a slotted spoon or a wire-mesh skimmer, transfer the toasts to the prepared baking sheet to remove excess oil. Continue frying until all of the toasts are fried. Make sure the oil is at 350°F/180°C before you add a new batch. Transfer to a serving plate and serve.

THAI SEAFOOD SALAD WITH FRESH WATER CHESTNUTS

In this light, refreshing salad, a bright-flavored Thai vinaigrette dresses flaked crabmeat and shrimp. Hints of cilantro and a touch of heat from paper-thin slices of serrano chile deliver bite, and thin disks of sweet fresh water chestnuts deliver a contrasting crunch. This fabulous salad makes a great appetizer or light main course.

SERVES 6

GARNISH

¾ cup/180 ml canola or other neutral oil

2 shallots, thinly sliced

8 oz/225 g large (26 to 30 count per lb/455 g) shrimp, peeled, deveined, tail segments removed, and halved lengthwise

2 tsp finely minced garlic

¼ cup/60 ml fresh lemon juice

2 tbsp Asian fish sauce

4 tsp granulated sugar

2 tsp peeled and finely minced fresh ginger

1 tsp freshly grated lemon zest

8 oz/225 g fresh crabmeat, well drained and picked clean of shell

16 fresh water chestnuts, ends trimmed, peeled, and thinly sliced

½ cup/30 g lightly packed fresh cilantro leaves

1 to 2 serrano chiles, stemmed and thinly sliced (see Cook's Note, page 40)

1 To make the garnish, line a small baking sheet with a double thickness of paper towels. In a heavy 8-in/20-cm sauté pan, heat the oil until it is hot but not smoking (360°F/180°C on a deep-frying thermometer). Add half of the shallots to the hot oil and fry until crisp and beautifully browned, 1 to 1½ minutes. Using a slotted spoon, transfer to the paper towels. Fry the remaining shallots in the same way. Pour off all but 2 tbsp of the oil from the pan into a heatproof bowl. (When the frying oil in the bowl has cooled, transfer it to a jar with a tight-fitting lid and refrigerate it for another use, such as sautéing vegetables or potatoes; it will be delicately flavored with shallot.)

2 Return the sauté pan to medium heat and heat the oil. When it is hot, add the shrimp and garlic and sauté, stirring frequently, until the shrimp are opaque, about 3 minutes. Add the lemon juice and use a wooden spatula to scrape up any brown bits stuck to the pan bottom. Transfer the shrimp mixture and any juices from the pan to a large bowl. Add the fish sauce, sugar, ginger, and lemon zest and toss to mix. Fold in the crabmeat, water chestnuts, cilantro, and chiles.

3 Transfer the salad to a serving bowl and garnish with the fried shallots. Serve immediately. (The salad, without the garnish, can be made up to 4 hours in advance, covered, and refrigerated. Remove from the refrigerator 20 minutes before serving. Garnish with the crisped shallots just before serving.)

GINGER CHICKEN SOUP WITH FRESH WATER CHESTNUTS AND NAPA CABBAGE

I think of this aromatic, warming soup as the Chinese version of "chicken soup for the soul." It is what you want on a cold, rainy night or when you feel under the weather and need a bowlful of comfort. Briefly marinating the chicken and then partially cooking it before adding it to the soup yields a more delicate texture than you get if you simmer the raw chicken strips directly in the broth.

SERVES 6

1 tbsp Chinese rice wine or pale dry sherry

1 tbsp cornstarch

1 tsp kosher or fine sea salt

1 egg white

12 oz/340g skinless, boneless chicken breasts

1 lemongrass stalk

7 cups/1.7 L homemade chicken stock or canned low-sodium chicken broth

5 garlic cloves, smashed

3 green onions, including green tops, cut into 2-in/5-cm lengths

½-in/12-mm piece fresh ginger, peeled and thinly sliced

1 serrano chile, stemmed and halved lengthwise (optional)

3 carrots, about 9 oz/255 g, trimmed, peeled, and thinly sliced on a sharp diagonal

4 cups/170 g firmly packed finely sliced napa cabbage

8 fresh water chestnuts, ends trimmed, peeled, and thinly sliced

3 green onions, including green tops, thinly sliced

⅓ cup/20 g firmly packed fresh cilantro leaves

⅛ tsp freshly ground pepper

1 In a medium bowl, whisk together the wine, cornstarch, and salt. Add the egg white and whisk until frothy. Cut the chicken breasts crosswise into slices about ¼ in/6 mm thick. Stir in the chicken and toss to coat all sides. Cover and set aside to marinate for 30 minutes. (The chicken can be refrigerated for up to 1 day before continuing.)

2 Trim off the root end from the lemongrass stalk, then cut off and discard the tough green tops. You should have a bulb about 4 in/10 cm long. Peel away the tough outer leaves, cut into 2-in/5-cm lengths, and then smash the pieces.

3 In a large pot, combine the 1 cup/240 ml water, the stock, garlic, green onions, ginger, chile (if using), and lemongrass and bring to a boil over high heat. Reduce the heat so the liquid simmers gently, cover, and cook for 30 minutes to infuse the broth. Use a skimmer to remove the aromatics.

4 While the soup is simmering, fill a medium saucepan two-thirds full with water and bring to a simmer over medium-high heat. Add the chicken, give it a stir with a spoon to separate the pieces, and cook just until the outside turns white and the chicken is partially cooked through, about 1 minute. Drain in a colander, shaking to remove the excess water. Transfer the chicken to a bowl and set aside.

5 About 10 minutes before serving, add the carrots to the simmering broth and cook until crisp-tender, about 6 minutes. Add the reserved chicken, cabbage, and water chestnuts and simmer until the chicken pieces are opaque and fully cooked, about 3 minutes. Reduce the heat to low and stir in the green onions, cilantro, and pepper. Taste and adjust the seasoning. Ladle the soup into warmed soup bowls. Serve immediately.

PORK SOONG IN LETTUCE CUPS

Years ago, when my husband, Greg, was in graduate school, we lived in Chicago. We would go with friends to a favorite Cantonese restaurant in Chinatown and order this dish. To eat it, you cup a big leaf of butter lettuce in one hand, use your other hand to spoon a mound of the flavorful diced vegetable and pork mixture into the leaf, and then fold it into a burrito-style bundle. It is nonstop deliciousness, because putting the bundle down means it all falls apart. The peas give it color, the mushrooms deliver an earthy richness, and the diced water chestnuts provide a sweet crunch.

SERVES 6 AS A MAIN COURSE, OR 12 AS AN APPETIZER

1 tbsp cornstarch

2 tbsp water

1 tbsp soy sauce

1 tbsp Chinese rice wine or pale dry sherry

1 tbsp canola or other neutral oil

½ tsp kosher or fine sea salt

1 lb/455 g ground pork

SAUCE

1 tbsp soy sauce

2 tbsp Chinese rice wine or pale dry sherry

2 tsp Chinese chile-garlic sauce (preferably Lee Kum Kee brand)

2 tsp Asian sesame oil

¼ tsp granulated sugar

8 medium dried Chinese black mushrooms

12 fresh water chestnuts, ends trimmed, peeled, and cut into ¼-in/6-mm dice

1 cup/140 g frozen green peas, thawed

1 tbsp peeled and minced fresh ginger

1 large garlic clove, minced

3 tbsp canola or other neutral oil

12 butter lettuce leaves

1 In a medium bowl, whisk together the cornstarch and water until the cornstarch is dissolved. Add the soy sauce, wine, oil, and salt and whisk to combine. Add the ground pork and toss to coat the meat evenly. Cover and set aside at room temperature to marinate for 30 to 45 minutes.

2 Meanwhile, make the sauce. In a small bowl, combine the soy sauce, wine, chile-garlic sauce, sesame oil, and sugar and stir until the sugar is dissolved. Set aside.

3 Soak the mushrooms in a small container of hot water until softened, about 20 minutes. (I like to put them in a small plastic container with a lid so the lid keeps the mushrooms submerged.) Drain and blot the mushrooms dry, remove and discard the stems, and cut into ¼-in/6-mm dice. Set aside. Prepare the water chestnuts, ready the peas, and mince the ginger and garlic and have everything near the stove ready to stir-fry.

4 In a wok or a large, deep frying pan, heat 1 tbsp of the oil over high heat and swirl to coat the pan bottom and sides. Add the marinated pork and stir-fry, breaking up any clumps with the side of a spatula, until the pork is cooked through, 2½ to 3 minutes. Transfer to a plate. Add the remaining 2 tbsp oil to the pan. Add the ginger and garlic and stir-fry until fragrant but not brown, about 1 minute. Add the mushrooms, water chestnuts, and peas and stir-fry just until heated through, about 30 seconds. Return the pork to the pan, add the sauce, and stir-fry for 1 minute longer. Transfer the stir-fry to a warmed serving bowl.

5 Arrange the lettuce leaves on a plate. Pass the lettuce leaves and the stir-fry at the table, letting everyone fill a leaf, fold it over into a bundle, and eat it out of hand.

SCALLOP AND WATER CHESTNUT STIR-FRY

Looking at the finished dish, you can't easily discern the scallops from the water chestnuts. Sliced the same way, they mimic each other in color, shape, and thickness. Only when you take a bite does the crunch of the water chestnuts distinguish itself from the soft, luscious texture of the scallops. This delicately flavored stir-fry is elegantly designed to be white on white with dabs of color from the red pepper flakes and barely wilted cilantro leaves. Steamed white rice is the obvious and traditional accompaniment. Serving the stir-fry with steamed black rice is more dramatic and equally good.

SERVES 3 OR 4

1¼ lb/570 g large sea scallops

8 fresh water chestnuts

1½ tbsp fresh lemon juice

1½ tbsp Chinese rice wine or pale dry sherry

1 tsp kosher or fine sea salt

½ tsp granulated sugar

2 tbsp canola or other neutral oil

1½ tbsp peeled and minced fresh ginger

1 tsp freshly grated lemon zest

1 tsp red pepper flakes

½ cup/30 g lightly packed fresh cilantro leaves

1 Remove the small, tough connective tissue at the side of each scallop. Blot the scallops dry with paper towels. Cut the scallops crosswise into rounds, either into halves or thirds depending on their thickness. Set aside.

2 Trim and peel the water chestnuts and then cut into thin rounds to mimic the scallop slices. Set aside.

3 In a small bowl, combine the lemon juice, wine, salt, and sugar and stir to dissolve the salt and sugar.

4 In a wok or a large, deep frying pan, heat the oil over high heat and swirl to coat the pan bottom and sides. Add the ginger, lemon zest, and red pepper flakes and stir-fry just until fragrant, about 30 seconds. Scatter in the scallops and water chestnuts and stir-fry until the scallops are partially cooked through, about 2 minutes. Pour the lemon juice mixture over the top and continue to stir-fry until the sauce is reduced and glazes the scallops and water chestnuts, about 2 minutes longer. Scatter the cilantro over the top and stir-fry just until the leaves are wilted, about 15 seconds. Transfer to a warmed serving dish and serve immediately.

STIR-FRIED WATER CHESTNUTS, SUGAR SNAP PEAS, AND SHIITAKES

What sets this quick-to-make vegetable stir-fry apart is the addition of fresh water chestnuts. For color and additional crunch, I've added sugar snap peas, though you could choose whatever is in season, such as asparagus, green beans, baby zucchini, or even pattypan squash.

SERVES 6

2 tbsp canola or other neutral oil

12 oz/340 g fresh shiitake mushrooms, stems removed and cut in half if large

3 tbsp Chinese rice wine or pale dry sherry

2 tsp peeled and finely minced fresh ginger

12 oz/340 g fresh water chestnuts, ends trimmed, peeled, and thinly sliced

1 lb/455 g sugar snap peas, stem end trimmed and strings removed

1 tsp Asian sesame oil

1 tsp kosher or fine sea salt

In a wok or a large, deep frying pan, heat 1 tbsp of the canola oil over high heat and swirl to coat the pan bottom and sides. Add the mushrooms and stir-fry for 1 minute. Add 1 tbsp of the wine and stir-fry until the mushrooms are browned and softened, about 1 minute longer. Using your spatula, push the mushrooms to one side of the pan and add the remaining 1 tbsp canola oil. When the oil is hot, add the ginger and water chestnuts and stir-fry for 1 minute. Add the peas and the remaining 2 tbsp wine and stir-fry until the peas are bright green and crisp-tender, 1 to 2 minutes longer. Add the sesame oil and salt, give the vegetables a quick stir, and then transfer to a warmed serving dish. Serve immediately.

YAM

Dioscorea species

HISTORY AND LORE The best-known member of the family Dioscoreaceae is the yam, which belongs to the genus *Dioscorea*. Within the genus are some 150 species, of which 5 domesticated species are important agricultural crops: *D. alata* and *D. esculenta* from Southeast Asia; *D. opposita* from China; and *D. rotundata* and *D. cayenensis* from West Africa. The New World also boasts a domesticated species, *D. trifida*, though it is not widely cultivated. All of these yams, regardless of country or region, are grown in tropical and warm temperate zones. The yam was originally cultivated in Africa, Asia, and the Americas and is thought to have been grown in Asia as early as 4500 B.C. But the yam as a gathered wild food is believed to be significantly older than that. Unlike Peruvian tubers, whose fossilized remains have been carbon-dated, African and Southeast Asian yams have less conclusive data on the age of domesticated plants. Instead, the primary evidence on the history of the yam is linguistic. Such research indicates African yams could be as old as 6000 B.C., though they were probably not cultivated until 1000 B.C.

Pursuing the story of the dispersal of yams throughout the world's tropical and temperate regions involves untangling conflicting theories, decoding detailed studies, and sorting through mountains of scholarly research—tasks beyond my ability. But the straightforward part of the history that is relevant here is the value of yams as a pantry staple, sustaining and nourishing populations since antiquity. In *The Oxford Companion to Food*, author Alan Davidson sums up what is important: "Yams existed at least as far back as the beginning of the Jurassic era, when dinosaurs had not yet been succeeded by mammals and [South] America and Asia were still joined. After the continents separated at the end of the Cretaceous era, the evolution of American yams proceeded separately, but they are still not much different from their Old World relatives."

VARIETIES With so many species in the genus *Dioscorea*, it is no surprise that yams come in many shapes, sizes, colors, and textures, with diverse flavor profiles and cooking characteristics to boot! But, as noted previously, only a few species are commonly cultivated for food. In general—if I dare to generalize—yams are an oblong tuber with rough, sometimes barklike skin and a starchy flesh that is hard and brittle when raw but quite tender, even creamy, when cooked. Although most yams are about the size of a sweet potato, some varieties can weigh as much as 100 pounds/45.5 kilograms and many average roughly 30 pounds/13.5 kilograms. The flesh can range from creamy white to orange to reddish orange and even to purple. (See the discussion on sweet potato varieties on page 293 to untangle the confusion over the use of the term *yam* for various types of sweet potato.)

FROM SOUTHEAST ASIA

Lesser Asiatic Yam or Potato Yam *Dióscorea esculenta*
This was one of the first yam species cultivated, but it is seldom found today outside of its native Southeast Asia and Pacific Islands. The flesh is soft with a slightly sweet taste. This is one species that does not store well.

Purple Yam As the name implies, this yam is characterized by its vibrant violet flesh, which makes a statement in desserts and savory dishes in Hawaii, the Philippines, Vietnam, and India.

White Yam *D. alata* Sometimes called greater Asiatic yam or water yam, this white-fleshed yam is the most important species in Southeast Asia and the nearby islands and the yam with the largest global distribution.

FROM AFRICA

African Guinea (Yellow and White) Yam *Dióscorea cayenensis* **and** *D. rotunda* These yellow and white yams, which are native to West Africa, are varieties that have been so hybridized that they are difficult to discern as separate species. These are the most potato-like of the yam family.

FROM CHINA

Chinese Yam/Yamaimo/Nagaimo/Mountain Yam *Dióscorea opposita* (syn. *D. batatas, D. japonica*) Native to China, these yams grow up to 3 feet/1 meter long and are quite different from other cultivated yams. They have hairy, pale beige skin dotted with dark spots. Their unusual flesh is slimy on the surface, yet crisp. When grated, they have a milky and slithery consistency like egg whites. Unlike other yams that must always be cooked before consumption, these can be eaten raw, as they often are in Japan and China.

FROM THE NEW WORLD

Cushcush Yam/Ñame *D. trifida* The cushcush is the only native American yam cultivated as a commercial crop. In comparison to other yams that are generally considered bland and starchy, this species has good flavor and texture. It is grown in tropical Central and South America and in the Caribbean.

NUTRITION Yams, which are typically bland and filling, are a significant source of calories and nutrition for many cultures around the world. They are between 15 and 40 percent starch and have about as much protein as a potato. Most species contain about 110 calories in a 3½-ounce/100-gram serving. Yams are generally high in vitamins C and B$_6$, potassium, manganese, and dietary fiber.

AVAILABILITY AND SELECTION Look for yams year-round in Asian and Latin American markets, though the availability of some types can be sporadic. Select specimens that are very firm with no soft spots, shriveled skin, cracks, or signs of mold. They should also be evenly shaped to ease peeling. I haven't noticed a difference in the quality of big versus smaller yams, but they should feel heavy for their size, which indicates that they are moist inside. Sometimes yams are sold wrapped in plastic wrap with the ends trimmed to reveal the flesh. Check the cut ends to make sure they look fresh and moist and are free of any mold around the cut edge of the skin.

STORAGE Store unwashed yams in a cool, dry spot with good ventilation for up to 2 weeks. Avoid the refrigerator and plastic bags, both of which promote softening and molding. Yams must be kept at temperatures close to 50°F/10°C. During the cool months of the year, I store yams in my basement enclosed in a loose brown-paper sack with the top crumpled over but not tightly sealed. This blocks out light but doesn't trap moisture. During the warmer months, I buy what I need for a recipe and use them right away.

BASIC USE AND PREPARATION With the exception of Chinese yams (*Dióscorea opposita*), yams must always be cooked to remove harmful compounds that may irritate the skin and throat. Preparations, both sweet and savory, are as diverse as the botanical varieties. Boiling is the most common cooking method worldwide, but yams can be grated and panfried, mashed with cream or coconut milk, sautéed, or stewed in a flavorful broth. In Africa, yams are also pounded into a starchy paste or dried in the sun and milled into a powder. Baking is not recommended because the hard, dry texture of the flesh needs moisture to soften it. With a relatively bland flavor and excessive starchiness, yams beg for a robust sauce.

Chinese yams can be sliced, shredded, or grated and eaten raw or cooked. When they are sliced and panfried, they have a slightly crisp exterior and melty-soft interior. When they are grated, they liquefy into a sticky, slimy texture that is surprisingly tasty. Grating the yams is popular in Japanese cuisine, such as in the "Snow" Hot Pot with Mountain Yam on page 384.

When preparing yams, I suggest wearing disposable gloves to protect your hands from possible irritation. Use a vegetable brush to scrub the root under cool running water. Slice off the ends and use a paring knife or vegetable peeler to pare away the skin. Trim until you get to the firm, white flesh. Discard the peel. When working with Chinese yams, apply a firm grip with the aid of a paper towel to manage their slippery texture. Rinse the tuber again and pat dry. In general, yams should be peeled and cut up before cooking.

A CAUTIONARY NOTE There are two cautions: First, raw yams contain compounds that are potentially harmful to the skin. When peeling raw yams, it is important to wear disposable surgical gloves or to coat your hands with cooking oil, especially if you have sensitive skin. Second, never eat yams raw, with the exception of the Chinese yam, as these same compounds can irritate the mouth and throat.

YIELDS

It is challenging to provide generalized yields for yams because each variety varies so much in weight and shape. To complicate matters further, some of the long varieties, such as the Chinese yam, are cut into sections and packaged for sale. Here, I am providing some measurements for cooked or cut up yams that apply to all yams. In each recipe, I have specified the raw, untrimmed weight to make shopping for the yams easier.

¾ cup cooked and mashed yams = 8 oz/225 g

1½ cups cooked and mashed yams = 1 lb/455 g

3 cups trimmed, peeled, and diced yams = 1 lb/455 g

YAMAIMO GREEN ONION PANCAKES

The yam used to make these pancakes is known either as *yamaimo* (mountain tuber) or *nagaimo* (long tuber). In the Chinese market I frequent, it is labeled *nagaimo* (yes, a Japanese name), and at the Japanese market, the very same tuber is labeled *yamaimo*. Have I confused you yet? It is certainly confusing to me. That said, yams traveling under either label will work here. They fry up golden, yet moist and a tad gooey at the center. This is a treasured texture for the Japanese. For me, and all my tasters, these crisp-edged pancakes were appealing and incredibly delicious.

MAKES TWELVE 4-IN/10-CM PANCAKES

1 lb/455 g *yamaimo* or *nagaimo*

1½ tbsp dried shrimp, pulverized (see Cook's Note)

½ tsp kosher or fine sea salt

3 green onions, including green tops, sliced paper-thin

Canola or other neutral oil for frying

1 Trim and peel the yams and then rinse under cool running water and blot dry. Using the small holes on a box grater or a food processor fitted with the fine grating disk, finely grate them. The grated flesh will appear goopy and a bit slimy, which is what you want. (Trust me, it will cook up beautifully and be delicious.)

2 Transfer the grated yams to a bowl and stir in the shrimp, salt, and all but 2 tbsp of the green onions. Reserve the remainder for garnish. (The batter can rest for up to 2 hours before making the pancakes. Cover and set aside at room temperature.)

3 Preheat the oven to 250°F/120°C/gas ½. Line a dinner plate with a double thickness of paper towels. Pour just enough oil into a large nonstick frying pan to film the pan bottom. Heat the oil over medium-low heat until a little ball of the batter sizzles on contact. (You want the pancakes to sizzle lightly but not get too dark at the edges.) For each pancake, ladle about 3 tbsp of the batter into the pan, being careful not to crowd the pan. Fry the pancakes until golden and crisp at the edges, about 4 minutes. Turn and cook until brown on the second side, 2 to 3 minutes longer. Carefully transfer the pancakes to the towel-lined plate to drain briefly and then transfer them to a warmed serving plate. (Do not leave them on the paper towels or they will stick. Just give them a quick blot and move them to a plate.) Keep warm in the oven while you cook additional batches. Repeat until you have used up all of the batter, adding more oil to the pan as needed. Garnish with the remaining green onions and serve immediately.

COOK'S NOTE

Look for dried shrimp at Japanese and Chinese markets. The best brands are packaged and found in the refrigerator section, assuring their freshness. Dried shrimp are typically about the size of a small coin, and the shells are pink to coral. Although they may seem a bit weird to Western palates, they deliver a pleasant briny tang to cooked foods. For these pancakes, pulverize the shrimp to a fluffy dust in a spice grinder or a mortar.

YAM AND SWEET POTATO SESAME PATTIES

This recipe is adapted from *New Thai Cuisine*, by Nathan Hyam. An American who studied extensively in Thailand, he brought his expertise back to Vancouver, British Columbia, where he shares his love for Thai cuisine. He is particularly taken with Thailand's wonderful street foods, such as these hard-to-resist sesame-crusted yam and sweet potato patties. For entertaining, form the patties and coat them with the sesame seeds up to 8 hours in advance. Fry them 30 minutes in advance and keep them warm in a low oven until ready to serve.

MAKES EIGHTEEN 2½-IN/6-CM PATTIES

30 fresh bushy cilantro sprigs

1 lb/455 g white-fleshed yams, trimmed, peeled, and cut into 1-in/2.5-cm chunks

8 oz/225 g Jewel or Garnet sweet potatoes, peeled and cut into 1-in/2.5-cm chunks

2½ tsp kosher or fine sea salt

½ cup/65 g all-purpose flour, plus more for dusting

½ cup/40 g unsweetened medium-shred dried coconut

1 tbsp Asian sesame oil

¼ tsp freshly ground pepper

⅔ cup/60 g sesame seeds, toasted (see Cook's Note, page 64)

Canola or other neutral oil for frying

1 Pluck the leaves from the cilantro sprigs. Reserve the stems, and coarsely chop the leaves.

2 In a large saucepan, combine the yams, sweet potatoes, cilantro stems, and 1 tsp of the salt with water to cover by 2 in/5 cm. Bring to a boil over high heat, reduce the heat so the water simmers, and cook, uncovered, until the yams and sweet potatoes are fork-tender, 10 to 12 minutes. Drain in a colander and discard the cilantro stems. Return the yams and sweet potatoes to the pan and place over medium heat for about 1 minute to evaporate any excess moisture. Transfer to a large bowl and let cool for 10 minutes.

3 Using a potato masher, mash the yams and sweet potatoes. Stir in the cilantro leaves, flour, coconut, sesame oil, pepper, and the remaining 1½ tsp salt until evenly distributed and all of the flour is absorbed.

4 Have ready a baking sheet. Dust your hands lightly with flour. For each patty, scoop up a level 1 tbsp of the yam mixture and form it into a patty about 2½ in/6 cm in diameter and ¼ in/6 mm thick. As each patty is formed, place it on the baking sheet. You should have 18 patties. Place the sesame seeds on a plate. Dip each patty into the sesame seeds, coating both sides, and then return it to the baking sheet.

5 Preheat the oven to 250°F/120°C/gas ½. Line a second baking sheet with a double thickness of paper towels. Pour the oil to a depth of ⅛ in/3 mm into a large, heavy frying pan and heat over medium-low heat until it is hot enough to make a sesame seed sizzle on contact. Working in batches, carefully place the patties in the hot oil and fry, turning once, until golden brown on both sides, about 3 minutes total. Carefully transfer the patties to the towel-lined baking sheet to drain. Keep warm in the oven while you fry the remaining pancakes in batches. Serve hot.

FRITURAS DE ÑAME
(FRIED YAM CAKES FROM THE DOMINICAN REPUBLIC)

After making these crunchy-edged, wickedly addictive cakes, I wondered if anyone would notice if I replaced the traditional potato latkes at Hanukkah with them. I'm certain that in the Dominican Republic these cakes aren't served with sour cream and applesauce, but they could be, and the combination would be amazing. But they are also incredibly delicious unadorned. The recipe uses the native American yam called *ñame*, which is how I have found it labeled at both Latin American and Chinese grocery stores.

MAKES ABOUT TWENTY 2-IN/5-CM CAKES

1 lb/455 g *ñame* (cushcush yams)

¼ small yellow onion

2 egg yolks

1 tbsp unsalted butter, melted

1½ tbsp minced fresh flat-leaf parsley

Kosher or fine sea salt

¼ tsp freshly ground pepper

Canola or other neutral oil for frying

1 Trim and peel the yams, then rinse under cool running water and blot dry. Using the small holes on a box grater or a food processor fitted with the fine grating disk, finely grate them. Grate the onion at the same time.

2 Transfer the grated yams and onion to a bowl. Add the egg yolks and beat vigorously with a wooden spoon until the mixture begins to pull away from the sides of the bowl. Stir in the melted butter, parsley, 1½ tsp salt, and the pepper.

3 Preheat the oven to 250°F/120°C/gas ½. Set a large wire rack in a rimmed baking sheet. Line a second baking sheet with a double thickness of paper towels. Pour just enough oil into a large nonstick frying pan to film the pan bottom and heat the oil over medium-low heat until a little ball of the batter sizzles on contact. (You want the pancakes to sizzle lightly but not get too dark at the edges.) Ladle about 1 tbsp of the batter into the pan, spreading it gently with the bottom of the ladle to form a 2-in/5-cm pancake. Repeat to form more pancakes, being careful not to crowd the pan. Fry the pancakes until golden and crisp at the edges, about 3 minutes. Turn and cook until brown on the second side, 2 to 3 minutes longer. Carefully transfer the pancakes to the towel-lined baking sheet to drain briefly and then transfer them to the wire rack in the second sheet pan and keep warm in the oven. Repeat until you have used up all of the batter, adding more oil to the pan and adjusting the heat as needed to maintain an even temperature.

4 Arrange the cakes on a warmed serving plate and sprinkle with a little salt. Serve immediately.

COOK'S NOTE
The yam cakes can be made 1 day in advance if refrigerating them, or up to 2 weeks in advance if freezing them. Let cool, layer between sheets of waxed paper in a covered container, and refrigerate or freeze. Reheat in a 350°F/180°C/gas 4 oven until hot and crisp, 15 to 20 minutes.

"SNOW" HOT POT WITH MOUNTAIN YAM

The recipe for a "snow" hot pot in *Japanese Hot Pots*, by Tadashi Ono and Harris Salat, intrigued me. It called for mountain yam (*nagaimo*) in a way I had never used it: coarsely chopped and then liquefied in a blender. Here, I pour the blended yam over simmering dashi laced with scallops, napa cabbage, and shiitake and enoki mushrooms, creating a layer of "snow" on top. It's an aesthetic touch that is at once poetic and unfamiliar to the Western palate. Look for the *mitsuba*, an aromatic Japanese herb, and the *naga negi* (see the headnote on page 314) at well-stocked Japanese markets. If you can't find *mitsuba*, substitute 1 tablespoon minced fresh cilantro. Although it is not as tasty as the *mitsuba,* it will deliver a bright, refreshing note. A ceramic hot pot would be traditional, but a medium-size Dutch oven is an excellent substitute.

SERVES 4

1 lb/455 g *nagaimo* or *yamaimo*

4 cups dashi (see Cook's Note, page 71)

¼ cup/60 ml mirin (Japanese sweet cooking wine)

1 tbsp light soy sauce

1 tsp kosher or fine sea salt

8 oz/225 g napa cabbage, cut into 1-in/2.5-cm pieces

1 lb/455 g large sea scallops, small, tough connective tissue removed and halved horizontally

4 oz/115 g fresh shitake mushrooms, stemmed

One 7-oz/200-g package enoki mushrooms, trimmed and pulled apart

1 *naga negi* or large leek, white and light green part only, trimmed and cut on the diagonal into ovals ¼ in/ 6 mm thick

One 1-oz/30-g package *mitsuba*, leaves plucked and stems cut into 1-in/2.5-cm pieces

1　Trim and peel the yams and then rinse under cool running water and blot dry. Cut into small chunks. Working in batches if necessary, transfer to a blender and blend until foamy and liquefied. Set aside.

2　In a large measuring cup or bowl, stir together the dashi, mirin, soy sauce, and salt.

3　Place the cabbage on the bottom of a Dutch oven or hot pot. Top with the scallops, then with the shiitake and enoki mushrooms, and finally with the *naga negi.* Pour the dashi mixture over the top. Cover the pot and bring to a boil over medium-high heat. Reduce the heat so the stock just simmers and cook for 5 minutes. Uncover the pot and pour the liquefied yam over the top, spreading it with chopsticks or the back of a spoon to cover the surface. Re-cover and simmer for 3 minutes longer. Garnish with the *mitsuba* leaves and stems. Serve immediately.

GUJARATI-STYLE STEW WITH PURPLE YAMS

Delightfully colorful, with intriguing, exotic flavors—that describes this Indian-inspired stew. It is a mix of purple-fleshed yams, orange-fleshed sweet potatoes, and bits of tomato, all in a thick green pea and coconut purée. I imagined serving this dish with hot Indian breads, but I didn't have any on hand the day I made it. This recipe is loosely adapted from a root vegetable stew in Raghavan Iyer's *660 Curries*. I used three Thai chiles and they delivered quite a kick; adapt as you like to please your palate. Serve with roti or other Indian bread if possible.

SERVES 6

¼ cup/20 g unsweetened medium-shred dried coconut

¼ cup/60 ml boiling water

1 cup/140 g frozen green peas, partially thawed

½ cup/35 g firmly packed fresh cilantro leaves and tender stems, plus 1 tbsp minced leaves for garnish

2 to 4 green Thai or serrano chiles, stemmed

2 tsp granulated sugar

1½ tsp kosher or fine sea salt

½ tsp garlic powder

Juice of 1 small lime

2 tbsp canola or other neutral oil

1 tsp black or yellow mustard seeds

1½ cups/360 ml cold water

1 lb/455 g purple-fleshed yams, trimmed, peeled, and cut into 1-in/2.5-cm chunks

1 orange-fleshed sweet potato such as Jewel or Garnet, about 8 oz/225 g, peeled and cut into 1-in/2.5-cm chunks

1 tomato, about 3 oz/85 g, cored, seeded, and cut into ½-in/12-mm dice

1 Put the coconut in a small heatproof bowl, add the boiling water, and set aside to rehydrate for 15 minutes. Drain off any excess water.

2 In a food processor, combine the peas, coconut, cilantro leaves and stems, chiles, sugar, salt, garlic powder, and lime juice and process to form a textured purée.

3 In a heavy, deep sauté pan with a tight-fitting lid, heat the oil over medium-high heat and swirl to coat the pan bottom. Add the mustard seeds, cover, and cook, shaking the pan a bit, until the seeds pop (similar to making popcorn), about 30 seconds. Carefully remove the lid, add the pea mixture, and cook until slightly thickened and a bit of the sauce sticks to the pan bottom, about 3 minutes.

4 Add the cold water and bring to a simmer, stirring with a wooden spoon to scrape up the bits sticking to the pan bottom. Add the yams, stir well, cover, and cook for 15 minutes. Add the sweet potatoes, cover the pan, and continue to cook until the potatoes are fork-tender and the sauce is thick, about 10 minutes longer. Stir in the tomato and cook until heated through, about 2 minutes longer. Transfer to a warmed serving bowl, garnish with the minced cilantro, and serve immediately.

YUCA

Manihot esculenta (syn. M. utilissima)

CASSAVA/MANIOC/MANDIOCA/MANIHOT/TAPIOCA-PLANT

HISTORY AND LORE As the only member of the spurge family (Euphorbiaceae) that provides food, yuca, also commonly known as cassava or manioc, is an herbaceous perennial whose starch-rich tuberous root is one of the most important food crops in the tropics. Many scholars agree that the first wild forms of yuca were found and cultivated in west-central Brazil more than three thousand years ago. Others insist it was growing in Mexico as early as 2500 B.C., suggesting that there may be two regions of origin. By around 200 B.C., yuca had become a staple food of native populations throughout much of the tropical and subtropical regions of the Americas.

In the sixteenth and seventeenth centuries, the Portuguese carried yuca, along with maize, from Brazil to their colonies in West Africa. By the late eighteenth century, it had spread to East Africa, where it quickly became a dominant crop. The Spanish also transported the root, carrying it westward across the Pacific to the Philippines, from which it spread into Southeast Asia. Today, yuca is cultivated in nearly every country with a tropical or subtropical climate, and it remains a dominant staple crop (famine food) in Africa because of its trouble-free cultivation and its ability to survive in harsh drought conditions.

VARIETIES First, a clarification: Yuca (pronounced YOO-ka) is not to be confused with yucca (pronounced yuhk-uh), which is the common name for the many species of the genus *Yucca*. Members of the Asparagaceae family, yuccas thrive in warm regions, like yuca, and bear edible parts, including fruits, seeds, flowers, and flowering stems—but not the roots.

Now back to yuca. There are two primary varieties, bitter and sweet, distinguished by the level of the toxic glycoside linamarin present in the root. Have no fear: processing yuca through peeling, washing, boiling, roasting, toasting, or fermentation removes all toxicity. Sweet yuca, which is what we find in the marketplace as an unprocessed root, comes to the United States primarily from Costa Rica and the Dominican Republic. When cooked, it has a nuanced sweet taste and dry, mealy texture and can replace boiled potatoes in many dishes.

Bitter yuca is processed into tapioca or manioc meal (*farinha de mandioca*), which is consumed daily in Brazil and other tropical regions of South America, and into yuca flour (*harina de yuca*), which is used to make breads and cakes. It is also widely eaten in Africa, where it is made into a granular meal.

NUTRITION Yuca has a high starch content, making it a good source of food energy. It also contains significant amounts of calcium, vitamin C, and potassium. It is relatively high in calories and carbohydrates, too, with 120 calories and almost 27 grams carbohydrates in a 3½-ounce/100-gram serving.

AVAILABILITY AND SELECTION Yuca is available year-round in most supermarkets and in Latin American and Asian markets. It looks like an elongated sweet potato and usually measures 8 to 10 inches/20 to 25 centimeters long and about 1½ inches/4 centimeters in diameter. It has a distinct dark brown, coarse, scaly skin that almost looks like bark. The skin is usually waxed to preserve the root, as it is susceptible to mold. Look for roots that are firm and free of soft spots, cracks, or any signs of mold. The flesh should be pure white or cream colored with no black veins.

STORAGE Store the roots in a closed brown-paper bag in a cool, dark spot for up to 10 days. They will soften quickly if left in a plastic bag or refrigerated. Yuca can also be frozen: peel it, cut it into manageable chunks, wrap well, and freeze for up to 2 months. (It is sometimes sold this way in Latin American markets.)

BASIC USE AND PREPARATION Yuca must always be cooked. It can be used in both sweet and savory dishes. The flesh can be cooked and puréed or riced, or it can be prepared like potatoes: boiled and mashed, cooked and sliced as a side dish, or added to a soup or stew. It can also be thinly sliced on a mandoline for making deep-fried chips, or it can be coarsely grated for a sweet dessert filling. The starch in yuca is commercially processed to produce the pearled starch known as tapioca. The roots are ground into flour or meal to make dumplings, bread, and porridge-style dishes.

To prepare yuca, use a heavy chef's knife to trim off the ends and cut the root crosswise into manageable lengths. Stand each section upright and use a paring knife to cut down between the outer bark and the flesh, removing all of the waxy brown skin and the pinkish layer underneath. Halve or quarter the peeled yuca lengthwise and then remove the fibrous, inedible central core that runs the length of the root. Slice or chop as desired or as directed in individual recipes. (I wear disposable gloves when working with fresh yuca to protect my hands from the coarse, scaly skin.)

A CAUTIONARY NOTE Never eat yuca raw! The raw tubers are bitter and contain enough poisonous hydrogen cyanide to be toxic. The toxins are neutralized during cooking.

YIELDS

1 medium yuca = 11 to 13 oz/310 to 370 g

1 large yuca = 1 to 3 lb/455 g to 1.4 kg

1 cup trimmed, peeled, cooked, and mashed yuca = 8 oz/225 g

2¼ cups trimmed, peeled, and diced raw yuca = 1 lb/455 g

3½ cups trimmed, peeled, and finely grated raw yuca = 1⅓ lb/600 g

YUCA CHIPS

Yuca chips are supercrispy and divinely addictive. While deep-frying can be a messy hassle, yuca chips fry cleanly with virtually no splatter because the tuber contains very little water, which is what causes oil to splatter. I suggest using a mandoline, Japanese vegetable slicer, adjustable ceramic mandoline, or very sharp knife to slice the yuca crosswise into paper-thin slices. A dusting of salt is the simple way to enjoy these chips, but I also like to toss them with a favorite BBQ spice rub or with finely grated Parmesan cheese.

MAKES ABOUT 100 CHIPS

14 oz/400 g yuca, ends trimmed, peeled, and cut crosswise into rounds $1/16$ in/2 mm thick

About 5 cups/1.2 L peanut, grape seed, or vegetable oil for deep-frying

Kosher or fine sea salt

1 Slice the yuca just before you are planning to fry the chips.

2 Line two baking sheets with a double thickness of paper towels. Set a slotted spoon or a wire-mesh skimmer alongside the baking sheets. Pour the oil to a depth of about 3 in/7.5 cm into a deep, heavy pot, wok, or an electric deep fryer and heat to 360°F/180°C on a deep-frying thermometer. (If using an electric deep fryer, follow the manufacturer's instructions for heating the oil.)

3 Fry the yuca in small batches. Add a handful of slices to the hot oil and deep-fry, stirring once or twice, until they are golden brown, 2½ to 3 minutes. (The timing will vary slightly, so look for color first and then sample a chip, testing for crispiness.) Using the slotted spoon or skimmer, transfer the chips to a prepared baking sheet to remove excess oil. Sprinkle lightly with salt. Continue frying in small batches until all of the slices are fried. Make sure the oil is at 360°F/180°C before you add a new batch.

4 Warm chips right out of the oil are delicious, but yuca chips keep well and will stay deliciously crisp for several days. Store in an airtight container at room temperature.

YUCA FRIES
WITH CREAMY CILANTRO-LIME DIPPING SAUCE

Put a pile of crisp, golden, salty, hot yuca fries in front of me and they will disappear in a heartbeat. The nutty, sweet flavor of the flaky interior is wonderful—and almost more interesting than a potato fry. Although the dipping sauce is nontraditional, the combination is completely appealing. I like to whirl the sauce in the blender until it turns pale green, with just specks of cilantro showing. To save time, you can whisk the ingredients together in a bowl.

SERVES 4

DIPPING SAUCE

½ cup/120 ml sour cream

½ cup/30 g minced fresh cilantro

2 tsp fresh lime juice

¼ tsp kosher or fine sea salt

1½ lb/680 g yuca

8 cups/2 L water

Kosher or fine sea salt

3 small dried red chiles such as *chile de árbol*

About 5 cups/1.2 L peanut, grape seed, or vegetable oil for deep-frying

1 To make the dipping sauce, in a blender, combine the sour cream, cilantro, lime juice, and salt and process until puréed. The sauce should turn soft green with dark flecks of cilantro. Transfer to a serving bowl, cover, and refrigerate until ready to serve. (The sauce can be made 1 day in advance.)

2 Use a heavy chef's knife to trim off the ends and cut each yuca crosswise into pieces 3 in/7.5 cm long. Stand each piece upright and use a paring knife to cut down between the outer bark and the flesh, removing all of the waxy brown skin and the pinkish layer underneath. Halve the yuca lengthwise. Remove the fibrous central core.

3 In a large saucepan, bring the water to a boil over high heat. Add 2 tbsp salt and the chiles, then add the yuca. Simmer, uncovered, until tender when pierced with a wooden skewer, about 20 minutes. (Check often for tenderness. The yuca should be cooked through without getting mushy. In my experience, the pieces of yuca cook unevenly, with some turning tender before others. Remove the tender ones with a slotted spoon and drain, continuing to cook the other pieces until done.) Drain the yuca and transfer it to a bowl of ice water. When the yuca is cool, lift it out of the ice water and blot dry with paper towels. Cut the yuca into thick fries about ¾ in/2 cm wide.

4 Line two baking sheets with a double thickness of paper towels. Set a slotted spoon or wire-mesh skimmer alongside the baking sheets. Pour the oil to a depth of 3 in/7.5 cm into a deep, heavy pot, a wok, or an electric deep fryer and heat to 360°F/180°C on a deep-frying thermometer. Fry the yuca in small batches. Add a handful of fries to the hot oil and fry, stirring once or twice, until they are golden brown, 2½ to 3 minutes. (The timing will vary slightly, so look for color first and then sample a fry, testing for a crisp exterior and flaky interior.) Using the slotted spoon or skimmer, transfer the chips to a prepared baking sheet to remove excess oil. Sprinkle lightly with salt. Continue frying in small batches until all of the pieces are fried. Make sure the oil is at 360°F/180°C before you add a new batch.

5 Transfer to a basket or serving bowl and serve hot with the dipping sauce.

MASHED YUCA

Infusing the water in which the yuca cooks with garlic, chiles, and spices gives a depth of flavor to yuca's mild and starchy character. I took a traditional approach to the mash, adding melted butter and warmed milk, along with a restrained touch of fresh thyme and a hint of pepper and nutmeg. My favorite way to serve this is with grilled meats, fanning out slices of Caribbean-spiced pork or beef over the yuca so that the meat juices mingle with the mash, delivering big island flavors on the plate.

SERVES 4 TO 6

1½ lb/680 g firm fresh yuca

8 cups/2 L water

Kosher or fine sea salt

4 cloves garlic, smashed with the side of a chef's knife

3 small dried red chiles such as *chile de árbol*, seeded

1 bay leaf

1 tsp whole allspice

5 tbsp/70 g unsalted butter, melted

½ cup/120 ml milk, warmed

1 tsp finely minced fresh thyme

Freshly ground pepper

Freshly grated nutmeg

1 Use a heavy chef's knife to trim off the ends and cut each yuca crosswise into pieces 2 in/5 cm long. Stand each piece upright and use a paring knife to cut down between the outer bark and the flesh, removing all of the waxy brown skin and the pinkish layer underneath. Quarter the yuca lengthwise. Remove the fibrous central core.

2 In a large saucepan, bring the water to a boil over high heat. Add 2 tbsp salt, the garlic, chiles, bay leaf, and allspice. Then add the yuca, reduce the heat so the water barely simmers, and cook, uncovered, until tender when pierced with a wooden skewer, about 20 minutes. (Check often for tenderness. The yuca should be cooked through without getting mushy. In my experience, the pieces of yuca cook unevenly, with some turning tender before others. Remove the tender ones with a slotted spoon and drain, continuing to cook the other pieces until done.) Drain the yuca and transfer to a warmed bowl.

3 Using a potato masher, mash the yuca. Add the melted butter and continue to stir and mash until the butter is absorbed. Stir in the milk and thyme until combined and season with salt, pepper, and nutmeg. Serve immediately, or cover and keep warm until ready to serve.

YUCA WITH TANGERINE-SERRANO MOJO

In Cuba, chunks of boiled yuca are traditionally served with *mojo crillo* (citrus-garlic sauce) spooned over the top. This sauce is a variation on the traditional *mojo*. I have used a combination of fresh tangerine juice and lime juice to approximate the flavor of the sour orange juice used in the original sauce. To keep the herbs tasting fresh, I toss them into the sauce after it comes off the heat. The amount of serrano chile you add is up to you; one chile delivers a subtle kick of heat, two makes it pronounced. This sauce would also be terrific with grilled fish or chicken.

SERVES 4 TO 6

MOJO

2 tbsp canola or other neutral oil

3 shallots, sliced paper-thin

2 garlic cloves, minced

1 to 2 serrano chiles, stemmed, seeded, and finely chopped (see Cook's Note, page 40)

¾ cup/180 ml fresh tangerine juice (from about 5 tangerines)

3 tbsp fresh lime juice

2 tbsp finely snipped fresh chives

1 tbsp finely minced fresh cilantro

Kosher or fine sea salt

2 lb/910 g yuca

8 cups/2 L water

Kosher or fine sea salt

3 small dried red chiles such as *chile de árbol*

1 To prepare the *mojo,* in a medium frying pan, heat the oil over medium heat and swirl to coat the pan bottom. Add the shallots and sauté, stirring frequently, until soft but not brown, about 3 minutes. Add the garlic and serranos and sauté for 1 minute longer. Stir in the tangerine and lime juices and simmer to blend the flavors for 2 minutes longer. Remove from the heat, stir in the chives and cilantro, and season with salt. Set aside until ready to serve.

2 Use a heavy chef's knife to trim off the ends and cut each yuca crosswise into pieces 2 in/5 cm long. Stand each piece upright and use a paring knife to cut down between the outer bark and the flesh, removing all of the waxy brown skin and the pinkish layer underneath. Halve the yuca lengthwise. Remove the fibrous central core.

3 In a large saucepan, bring the water to a boil over high heat. Add 2 tbsp salt and the dried chiles. Add the yuca, reduce the heat so the water barely simmers, and cook, uncovered, until tender when pierced with a wooden skewer, 15 to 20 minutes. (Check often for tenderness. The yuca should be cooked through without getting mushy. In my experience, the pieces of yuca cook unevenly, with some turning tender before others. Remove the tender ones with a slotted spoon and drain, continuing to cook the other pieces until done.) Drain the yuca and blot dry with paper towels. Cut crosswise into slices ½ in/12 mm thick and arrange in a warmed serving bowl. Pour the sauce over the yuca and serve immediately.

BRAZILIAN VACA ATOLADA
(COW STUCK IN THE MUD)

Catherine Manterola, one of my food-writing students and a Texan with Mexican lineage, grew up eating yuca and shared this recipe with me. She laughed when she told me the English translation for the dish and said, "You will see exactly why it's called Cow Stuck in the Mud when you make it." *Cachaça*, a sugarcane-based liquor, is a favorite of Brazilians. This is an absolute stick-to-the-ribs stew full of enticing, deeply rich flavors. It's perfect comfort food for a dark, dreary day in the middle of winter.

SERVES 6

2½ lb/1.2 kg beef short ribs, cut into 2-in/5-cm pieces

¼ cup/60 ml *cachaça* or light rum

2 tbsp fresh lime juice

Kosher or fine sea salt

Freshly ground pepper

2 tbsp unsalted butter or bacon fat

2 medium yellow onions, about 1¼ lb/570 g, chopped

1½ tbsp finely chopped garlic

1 tbsp annatto powder

3 cups/750 ml homemade beef stock or canned low-sodium beef broth

11 cups/2.6 L water

1 bay leaf

2 lb/910 g yuca

1 serrano chile, stemmed, seeded, and finely chopped (see Cook's Note, page 40)

2 tbsp finely chopped fresh flat-leaf parsley

2 tbsp finely chopped green onions, including green tops

Chopped fresh cilantro, for garnish

1 Place the short ribs in a large saucepan, pour the *cachaça* and lime juice over the top, and add just enough water to cover the ribs by 1 in/2.5 cm. Bring to a boil over medium-high heat, reduce the heat so the liquid simmers gently, and cook, uncovered, for 20 minutes to cook the ribs partially. Drain the ribs in a colander and pat dry with paper towels. Place on a rimmed baking sheet and season on all sides with salt and pepper.

2 In a large Dutch oven or other heavy pot, melt the butter over medium heat and swirl to coat the pan bottom. Working in batches if necessary, brown the meat on all sides and then transfer to a clean baking sheet. Set aside. Add the onions to the fat remaining in the pot and sauté, stirring frequently and scraping up the brown bits stuck to the pan bottom, until they begin to brown, about 5 minutes. Add the garlic and cook until fragrant, about 1 minute longer. Stir in the annatto powder and cook for 1 minute longer. Return the beef to the pan. Add the stock, 3 cups/720 ml of the water, and the bay leaf and bring the liquid to a boil. Reduce the heat to a simmer and cook, uncovered, for 40 minutes.

3 Meanwhile, use a heavy chef's knife to trim off the ends and cut each yuca crosswise into pieces 2 in/5 cm long. Stand each piece upright and use a paring knife to cut down between the outer bark and the flesh, removing all of the waxy brown skin and the pinkish layer underneath. Quarter the yuca lengthwise. Remove the fibrous core.

4 In a large saucepan, bring the remaining 8 cups/2 L water to a boil over high heat. Add 2 tbsp salt. Then add the yuca, reduce the heat so the water barely simmers, and cook until tender when pierced with a wooden skewer, about 20 minutes. (Check often for tenderness. The yuca should be cooked through without getting mushy. In my experience, the pieces of yuca cook unevenly, with some turning tender before others. Remove the tender ones with a slotted spoon and drain, continuing to cook the other pieces until done.) Drain the yuca and blot dry with paper towels. Cut crosswise into slices ½ in/12 mm thick.

5 Add the yuca to the short ribs along with the chile, parsley, green onions, and 2 tsp salt. Continue to cook until the ribs are fork-tender and the yuca is melting into the sauce to form a nice, thick gravy and succulent stew, about 30 minutes. If necessary, add a little more water and use the back of a large spoon to mash the yuca against the side of the pan. Taste and adjust the seasoning. Serve immediately, garnished with a generous sprinkling of chopped cilantro, or keep warm until ready to serve.

COLOMBIAN CHICKEN SANCOCHO

This hearty, traditional stew is made with a combination of meat and poultry such as oxtails and chicken, just chicken, or with fish. It is meant for a big family gathering, typically a Sunday lunch. I have cooked it on top of the stove, but it could be made in a large pot over an open fire, letting the smoky flavor enhance the dish. Serve it with sliced avocado and additional chiles. Freeze the extra *sofrito* or use it to make the Alcapurrias on page 200.

SERVES 6

SOFRITO

2 red bell peppers, seeded, and chopped

2 sweet banana peppers, seeded, and chopped

1 medium yellow onion, roughly chopped

2 green onions, including green tops, roughly chopped

5 garlic cloves, crushed

1 serrano chile, stemmed, seeded, and roughly chopped (see Cook's Note, page 40)

One 4-lb/1.8-kg whole chicken, cut into serving pieces

Kosher or fine sea salt

Freshly ground pepper

3 tbsp canola or other neutral oil

8 cups/2 L homemade chicken stock or canned low-sodium chicken broth

2 plantains, about 11 oz/310 g each, ends trimmed, halved lengthwise, peeled, and cut into 1-in/2.5-cm chunks

1½ lb/680 g yuca

3 medium boiling potatoes, peeled and cut into 1-in/2.5-cm chunks

2 ears yellow corn, husks removed and cut crosswise into three pieces

⅔ cup/40 g chopped fresh cilantro

1 To make the *sofrito,* in a food processor, combine the bell and banana peppers, yellow onion, green onions, garlic, and chile and pulse until finely chopped. Transfer to a bowl and set aside.

2 Season the chicken pieces on both sides with salt and pepper. In a large Dutch oven or other heavy pot that will comfortably accommodate the chicken in a single layer, heat the oil over medium-high heat and swirl to coat the pot bottom. Add the chicken, skin-side down, and cook until lightly browned, about 5 minutes. Turn the chicken and brown on the second side, about 5 minutes longer. Transfer the chicken to a plate. Drain off the fat from the pan and then return the chicken to the pot. Add the stock, 1½ cups/360 ml of the *sofrito,* and the plantains. Bring to a boil, reduce the heat so the liquid just simmers, cover, and then braise the chicken for 15 minutes.

3 Meanwhile, use a heavy chef's knife, to trim off the ends and cut each yuca crosswise into pieces 2 in/5 cm long. Stand each piece upright and use a paring knife to cut down between the outer bark and the flesh, removing all of the waxy brown skin and the pinkish layer underneath. Halve the yuca lengthwise. Remove the fibrous central core. Cut the yuca into 1-in/2.5-cm chunks.

4 Add the yuca to the simmering chicken, using a spoon to tuck it down into the simmering liquid. Cover the pot and cook for 10 minutes. Add the potatoes, covering them with the simmering sauce, re-cover, and cook for 10 minutes longer. Add the corn, re-cover, and continue to cook until the yuca and potatoes are fork-tender, about 10 minutes longer. Some of the yuca will have nearly melted down and thickened the sauce. If needed, add a little water to thin the sauce. Taste and adjust the seasoning with salt and pepper. Serve immediately, garnished with the cilantro, or keep warm until ready to serve.

COCONUT CUSTARD CAKE WITH YUCA

I decided to have a little fusion fun with this recipe. The traditional recipe for Southeast Asian coconut-yuca cake uses pandan leaves to infuse the custard with a nutty vanilla scent, and also instructs the cook to line the baking pan with banana leaves. I simplified both of these steps. First, I substituted vanilla extract for the pandan leaves, and then I decided to pat a coconut shortbread crust into the bottom of the baking pan. If you love tapioca pudding or rice pudding, this is the cake for you. There is no doubt it is rich, but lusciously so. I dusted each cake slice with confectioners' sugar and served it with a scoop of mango sorbet. My husband declared it excellent for breakfast, too. The cake can be made the night before you plan to serve it.

SERVES 12 TO 16

CRUST

1½ cups/180 g all-purpose flour

1 cup/85 g unsweetened medium-shred dried coconut

½ cup/50 g confectioners' sugar

½ cup plus 3 tbsp/155 g unsalted butter, at room temperature

FILLING

Two 13½-oz/405-ml cans unsweetened coconut milk

2 tsp pure vanilla extract

3 large eggs

2 cups/400 g granulated sugar

2 tbsp unsalted butter, melted

1 tsp kosher or fine sea salt

1⅓ lb/600 g yuca, ends trimmed, peeled, and finely grated

CUSTARD

1 egg yolk

One 14-oz/300-ml can sweetened condensed milk

½ cup/115 g unsalted butter, melted

1 cup/240 ml coconut cream reserved from making filling

Confectioners' sugar for dusting

1 Position a rack in the center of the oven and preheat to 350°F/180°C/gas 4. Butter a 9-by-13-in/23-by-33-cm baking pan or dish.

2 To make the crust, in a large bowl, stir together the flour, coconut, and confectioners' sugar. Using a pastry blender or a handheld mixer on low speed, cut in the butter until well blended and small clumps form. Press the dough onto the bottom and ½ in/12 mm up the sides of the prepared baking pan. Bake until the crust just begins to turn golden, about 20 minutes. Set aside on a wire rack to cool for 10 minutes.

3 While the crust is baking, make the filling. Open the cans of coconut milk without shaking them. Spoon out the thick cream that has separated out at the top of each can and measure 1 cup/240 ml. (You will have extra coconut cream. Save it for another use, such as making curry. It freezes well.) Measure 2 cups/480 ml of the thin coconut milk into another measuring cup. (If you don't have quite enough, stir in just enough of the extra coconut cream to total 2 cups/480 ml liquid.) Add the vanilla to the thin coconut milk. In a large bowl, whisk together the eggs, sugar, butter, and salt. Stir in the thin coconut milk and then the grated yuca.

4 Pour the filling over the crust. Bake until the filling is almost set, 30 to 40 minutes. (The filling needs to be set enough so the custard doesn't sink into the filling.)

5 While the filling is baking, make the custard. In a medium bowl, whisk together the egg yolk and condensed milk. Stir in the melted butter and the reserved coconut cream and whisk until smooth. Gently pour the custard over the top of the hot filling. Bake until the custard is set and speckled light brown, 20 to 25 minutes longer. Cool on a wire rack.

6 Serve at room temperature, dusted with confectioners' sugar. (The cake can be covered and kept at room temperature for up to 1 day, or covered and refrigerated for up to 2 days.)

OTHER ROOTS

This chapter presents a quick overview of other notable edible roots. In some cases, a root is included here because it is a significant food source for a particular population but is otherwise not broadly distributed. Enset is an example. Others, such as chicory root or ginseng, are interesting but not deserving of a stand-alone chapter because they are primarily used as additives or for their medicinal properties. To leave these roots out altogether would lessen the appreciation of the spectacular underground world of edible foods. Gaining at least a cursory understanding of this select list provides enrichment, just like the roots themselves.

ARROWROOT *Maranta arundinacea*
FAMILY MARANTACEAE

This perennial tropical plant is cultivated for its starch-rich rhizomes. Not to be confused with the bulbous Chinese arrowhead (see page 35), arrowroot is cultivated commercially in the West Indies and Latin America. It grows up to 12 inches/30.5 centimeters long and about 1 inch/2.5 centimeters in diameter and is covered with loose scales. Arrowroot is available almost exclusively as an ultrafine powder, which is made by stripping away the scales, beating the flesh to a milky pulp, and then drying the pulp and pulverizing it.

The neutral-tasting, silky white powder is prized as a thickener for sauces because it does not produce a cloudy sheen like cornstarch, potato starch, or flour does. It also contains stabilizing properties that make it the ideal thickener for highly acidic foods or for foods that will be frozen. To use arrowroot powder, mix it with a cool liquid before adding it to a hot liquid. It thickens at a lower temperature than most other starches, so once it has been added to a sauce, continue cooking just until the sauce thickens sufficiently and then remove it from the heat promptly, as overcooking can diminish the arrowroot's thickening ability. To use arrowroot powder in recipes calling for a cornstarch or flour thickener, substitute 2 teaspoons arrowroot for 1 tablespoon cornstarch or 2 tablespoons all-purpose flour. Arrowroot is also used as a thickener for pie fillings and puddings and in fruit gelatins.

CHICORY ROOT *Cichorium intybus*
FAMILY ASTERACEAE

Grown along the banks of the Nile and across Italy, chicory root is most commonly roasted and ground and used as a caffeine-free alternative (or additive) to coffee. The French began adding chicory root to coffee during the French Revolution, when coffee beans were scarce. The Americans did the same thing during World War II when coffee imports were halted. In many parts of the world, including the Mediterranean region, India, and New Orleans, chicory root is still a common coffee additive. Although slightly bitter itself, the root softens the bitterness of coffee beans and enhances their earthy richness.

Common Italian chicory root varieties, all parsniplike in color and shape, include Soncino, Chiavari, and Magdeburgo, each named for its place of origin (the latter a town in Germany). During the winter months, large conical Soncino roots are available fresh in markets in the Lombardy region. Both bitter and slightly sweet, they are delightful roasted or sautéed and topped with a squeeze of lemon juice. Radice Amare, a variety found around Verona, is boiled and sliced and served as an antipasto. Inulin-rich chicory root has also been used for centuries to improve digestion and liver and blood health, and in the treatment of gout, jaundice, and inflammation.

CORIANDER ROOT *Coriandrum sativum*
FAMILY APIACEAE

Coriander is an annual plant native to southern Europe, North Africa, and southwestern Asia. The root of the plant appears frequently in Thai recipes, including soups and curry pastes. Bunches of the delicately leaved greens are common in most supermarkets in North America, often labeled cilantro, but the roots are hard to come by. If you have a garden, the plants are easy to grow. In cities with a large Southeast Asian population, you can often find plants with the roots still attached at Asian groceries. Or, you may be able to special order them from an Asian market or even from a farmer at your local farmers' market.

To use the roots, trim them, leaving ½ inch/12 millimeters of the stems intact. Before cooking, bruise the root in a mortar to release the full flavor. Coriander roots have a deeper, more intense flavor than the leaves, but the stems can be substituted in recipes when the root is unavailable. If you do get your hands on some fresh roots, they can be frozen for later use.

EARTHNUT/PIGNUT *Conopodium majus*
FAMILY APIACEAE

This perennial herb, with its chestnutlike edible tuber, goes by many names, including earthnut and pignut. The name pignut refers to the apparent fondness pigs have for the root and for their ability to smell it even when the plants are dormant. Historically, these roots were foraged in the British Highlands, but this quote from a Victorian botanist suggests their minor role as a food source: "Better fitted to the digestion of the respectable quadrupeds, whose name they share, than for Christian bipeds of tender years." Earthnuts are rarely cultivated, which makes sourcing them difficult. Avid foragers should watch for a delicate plant with a tall, thin, smooth stem topped with six clusters of small white flowers that branch from the stem. The edible tuber is no larger than 1 inch/2.5 centimeters in diameter and is covered with brown skin. To prepare it, simply peel and discard the skin and then eat the tuber raw or cooked. As the name suggests, the flavor is sweet and nutty, similar to that of chestnuts.

ENSET *Ensete ventricosum*
FAMILY MUSACEAE

The most important staple root crop of Ethiopia, enset is sometimes dubbed "false banana" due to its botanical relationship and physical similarity to the banana plant. The fruit of the enset plant is not edible, however; only the corm and parts of the stem are. Wild enset grows throughout Asia and sub-Saharan Africa, but it is domesticated solely in Ethiopia, where the corm is mashed and fermented for making a steamed flat bread, dried and then boiled to make a hot beverage or porridge, and, more rarely, cut into pieces and cooked over hot stones. A second nickname translates as "the tree against hunger," an acknowledgment of the plant's ability to tolerate drought conditions and to flourish in relatively small spaces. In recent years, however, its value as a food to fight famine has decreased because of continuing drought conditions that have forced farmers to harvest the plants too early, leaving a large gap of time before a new crop can mature.

GINSENG *Panax* species
FAMILY ARALIACEAE

Native to eastern Asia and North America, ginseng encompasses eleven different species of perennial plants grown mostly for the medicinal value of their roots. Each species has its own set of characteristics, but all contain complex ginsenoside compounds responsible for various health effects. According to Chinese medicine, ginseng consumption brings the body's yin and yang into equilibrium, with different effects associated with American and Asian species. In general, the root is believed to boost energy and to promote men's health, and is used in the treatment of type 2 diabetes. Some studies have shown that ginseng can increase the quality of life for cancer patients and may even prevent breast cancer, though research results vary and are somewhat contradictory. Ginseng is usually sold as a dried herbal supplement and taken orally. It is also found in some energy drinks and teas.

GROUNDNUT *Apios americana*
FAMILY FABACEAE/LEGUMINOSAE

Groundnut, also known as Indian potato, hopniss, and American potato bean, as well as a long list of other aliases, is a perennial vine native to eastern North America. The small, crunchy tuber was a staple food of Native Americans, who introduced it to New England colonists. Groundnuts can be eaten raw, cooked, or dried and ground into flour. They are nutrient rich, with about three times as much protein as potatoes, and though they can be gathered throughout the year, they are best when harvested from late fall through early spring. The groundnut is one of many heirloom plant species that is now being developed for domestication.

KONJAC *Amorphophallus konjac*
FAMILY ARACEAE

Konjac, also known as devil's tongue, voodoo lily, snake palm, and elephant yam, is a perennial plant native to India and eastern Asia, including Japan, China, Korea, and Indonesia. Although it is often called a yam, the name is a misnomer. Because the large corm, which grows up to 10 inches/25 centimeters in diameter, has an unremarkable flavor, it is made into flour or into a jellylike substance that can be used as a vegan substitute for gelatin. In Japan, the flour is used to make noodles called *ito konnyaku* or *shirataki* (and devil's tongue noodles in English), which are served in sukiyaki and *oden* (a vegetable and fish cake stew). Low in calories and high in fiber, konjac is also used to make a popular Asian fruit jelly snack.

KUDZU *Pueraria lobata*
FAMILY FABACEAE/LEGUMINOSAE

Kudzu is native to southeast China and to southern Japan, where it is known as *kuzu*. It was introduced to the United States from Japan and adapted so well to the climate of the Southeast, particularly Georgia, that it soon became invasive and was promptly dubbed "mile-a-minute vine" and "the vine that ate the South." In Asia, in contrast, the tuber of this weedlike plant is prized for its starch, which is commonly used in Chinese and Japanese cooking as a thickener in soups and sauces, producing a luminous sheen. It is also used as a coating for deep-fried foods, yielding a light, crisp texture and translucent appearance. Look for kudzu starch in Asian markets, particularly those that specialize in Japanese ingredients (it may be labeled *kuzu*). The small crystal-like chunks (they look like little white rocks), which are sold in cellophane packets, dissolve easily in water or can be crushed into a fine powder.

LICORICE *Glycyrrhiza glabra*
FAMILY FABACEAE/LEGUMINOSAE

A perennial, licorice is cultivated extensively and found wild throughout the Mediterranean region, Russia, the Middle East, and central Asia. The roots, really a network of woody rhizomes, are used for their aniselike flavor and as a sweetener (they contain a chemical compound that is fifty times sweeter than glucose). In some countries, the roots are dried and then chewed as a sweet snack. More commonly, juice extracted from the roots is reduced to a black syrup or concentrate and used in confections such as licorice sticks, candy, and chewing gum. On occasion, licorice is used to flavor dark beers like Guinness stout. As a cautionary note, licorice should be eaten in moderation, as large doses have been linked to high blood pressure, headaches, fatigue, and other ailments. In small doses, however, licorice is used as a gentle laxative, to treat heartburn, to heal stomach ulcers, and as a sweetener by diabetics.

MACA *Lepidium meyenii*
FAMILY BRASSICACEAE

Maca is native to the Andean region of Bolivia and Peru. The portion of the plant that is consumed as a "root vegetable" is the taproot. Maca flourishes at high elevations despite cold temperatures, adverse soil conditions, and pests, a resilience that accounts for its role as a pantry staple for over two thousand years. It is botanically related to radishes and turnips, but its shape varies widely from triangular to spherical and every profile in between. It comes in a variety of colors, as well. The sweet flavor of the cream-colored root is favored in Peru, though blue, black, and red varieties are all increasing in popularity due to the various flavor and nutritional benefits each offers. In Peru, maca is roasted; mashed and boiled to produce a sweet, thick liquid; fermented to make a rustic beer; and dried and ground into flour or reconstituted in milk for porridge.

MASHUA *Tropaeolum tuberosum*
FAMILY TROPAEOLACEAE

A perennial tuber grown in the Andes, mashua is the fourth most important root vegetable in the region, behind potatoes, oca (see following), and ulluco (see page 21). Also known as *añu, isanu, ysaño,* and *cubio,* mashua has a peppery bite similar to radishes when raw, but the pungency mellows and sweetens when cooked. Preparations vary among the Andean cultures in which mashua is consumed, but stewing the tubers with meat, herbs, and other vegetables, such as corn and potatoes, is common. In Bolivia and Peru, mashua is cooked with molasses for dessert or coated in molasses and frozen for a traditional sweet treat.

MAUKA *Mirabilis expansa*
FAMILY NYCTAGINACEAE

Mauka, also known as chago, was an important root crop of the Inca empire. After being relatively forgotten for centuries, it was rediscovered in the mid-twentieth century in Ecuador, Peru, and Bolivia and is now widely cultivated throughout the Andes from Venezuela to Chile. It is a valuable root crop in part because it thrives at high altitudes. The leaves of the plant are tender like spinach and can be eaten raw in salads. The hardy tuberous root grows up to 16 inches/40.5 centimeters long, with several fingers (perhaps arms is more descriptive) shooting out from the stem. The tubers are often sun dried, which enhances their sweet flavor and eliminates their natural bitterness. They must always be eaten cooked because they contain a compound that will irritate the mouth's mucous membranes if eaten raw. Drying enhances the tuber's sweet flavor and eliminates bitterness. In Bolivia, mauka is commonly boiled and then tossed with honey, molasses, or sugar. The cooking liquid is then consumed as a sweet soft drink.

OCA *Oxalis tuberosa*
FAMILY OXALIDACEAE

This member of the wood sorrel family is a perennial tuber of the Andes and second only to potatoes in the roster of staple food crops of the region. It is now commonly consumed in Mexico and in New Zealand, where it is known as New Zealand yam, but is only rarely available elsewhere. Oca is eaten raw, pickled, or cooked like potatoes: boiled, fried, mashed, or roasted. Its texture is crunchy when raw and starchy and mealy when cooked. In Mexico and South America, oca comes in various shades of purple to tan; the New Zealand variety is a pretty pink.

PERUVIAN PARSNIPS *Arracacia xanthorrhiza*
FAMILY APIACEAE

Peruvian parsnip, sometimes called Peruvian carrot, is a perennial taproot native to South America and may be one of the oldest cultivated plants in the region. It is an important commercial crop in Brazil, where it is known as *batata baroa.* Its flavor has been likened to a mix of potato, celery, and carrots, with a slight nuttiness reminiscent of macadamia nuts. Under the creamy white skin you may find purple, white, or yellow flesh. Peruvian parsnips can be prepared in many of the same ways as potatoes are cooked, including boiled, fried, roasted, simmered in soups, or braised in stews. They are inedible raw.

PRAIRIE TURNIPS *Psoralea esculenta*
FAMILY FABACEAE/LEGUMINOSAE

Prairie turnip is the edible tuberous root of an herbaceous perennial plant native to the central plains of North America. It boasts many English and Native American names, including breadroot, tipsin, teepsenee, pomme blanche (as it was known by early European settlers), and *timpsula* (its Lakota name). The plant's hairy stems support clusters of purple and blue flowers in the summertime. The dark brown roots grow up to 4 inches/10 centimeters long and 1 inch/2.5 centimeters in diameter. The sweet turnip flavor of the root is most apparent when it is eaten raw. It can be cooked like most other starchy root vegetables—boiled, roasted, mashed, or sautéed—and it can be dried and ground into flour. At this point, the prairie turnip is not cultivated commercially, so foraging or planting are the only options for sourcing.

SKIRRET *Sium sisarum*
FAMILY APIACEAE

This perennial plant has roots that grow in clusters, unlike other family members with a single taproot. The roots, about the size of a skinny, small carrot, are gray on the outside concealing white flesh. The flavor resembles celery root but sweeter. Others describe the flavor as a cross between a carrot and a parsnip, with a subtle nutty flavor. Although the roots can be eaten raw or cooked, they are traditionally simmered in soups and stews. The plant is native to China and has been eaten in China and Japan for centuries. According to nineteenth-century French-born botanist Alphonse de Candolle, the cultivation of skirret spread westward from Siberia to Russia and then to Germany. Several references to skirret appear in British cookery books from the eighteenth century, but the root appears to have disappeared by the beginning of the nineteenth century. *Sium cicutaefolium,* a close relative, is found in North America with the common name water parsnip. While there is renewed interest in this root, at this point it is not being grown commercially.

TIGERNUT *Cyperus esculentus*
FAMILY CYPERACEAE

Tigernuts are also known as *chufa* (Spanish) and earth almonds. They are the edible tubers of a weedlike grass native to warmer regions of the Northern Hemisphere. A popular culinary ingredient in ancient Egypt, tigernuts were later brought to Spain and are now cultivated in the province of Valencia, where they are the key ingredient in the locally popular milky beverage called *horchata de chufas*. The sweet, nutty tubers are dried after harvesting, resulting in a hard texture that can be ground into flour, as is done for *horchata*, or soaked in water and eaten as a snack. Tigernuts are rich in healthful unsaturated fats and packed with nutrients, including phosphorus, potassium, and vitamins C and E. Their high fat content makes them a viable source for oil production. Spanish company Tigernuts Traders, S.L. (www.tigernuts.com), is Europe's largest exporter of tigernuts, and its Web site is a good source of information on the tuber.

TURNIP-ROOTED CHERVIL
Chaerophyllum bulbosum
FAMILY APIACEAE

Turnip-rooted chervil is an annual herb grown for its large edible taproot. It should not be confused with the herb chervil (*Anthriscus cerefolium*), a different species in the carrot family that is grown for its delicate feathery leaves and is prized in French cuisine. The roots of turnip-rooted chervil are stubby, growing up to just 4 inches/10 centimeters long and weighing 7 ounces/200 grams. With a starchy, floury texture and sweet herbaceous flavor, they are wonderful roasted or boiled, and the French include them in soups and stews. It is difficult to source turnip-rooted chervil outside of France, but gardeners may be able to purchase seeds online from sites like B & T World Seeds (www.b-and-t-world-seeds.com).

YACÓN *Smallanthus sonchifolius*
FAMILY ASTERACEAE

Also known as "Peruvian ground apple" or "apple of the earth," yacón is a perennial herb grown for its edible roots and leaves. Cultivated in the Andes from Argentina to Venezuela, the tuberous root resembles the Jerusalem artichoke in appearance but is sweet, crunchy, and fruity, like jicama, with which it is often confused. Yacón root can be eaten raw or partially dried. (Its leaves are traditionally used for medicinal purposes.) It is a good source of fructooligosaccharide (FOS), which nourishes friendly bacteria in the digestive system that aid fat metabolism and vitamin absorption. Yacón has recently begun appearing in farmers' markets and natural foods stores in the United States, but your best bet for sourcing it is to buy seeds and grow it in your home garden (see www.seedsofchange.com).

SELECTED BIBLIOGRAPHY

BOOKS CONSULTED

Alford, Jeffrey, and Naomi Duguid. *Hot Sour Salty Sweet: A Culinary Journey Through Southeast Asia.* New York: Artisan, 2000.

Andoh, Elizabeth. *Kansha: Celebrating Japan's Vegan and Vegetarian Traditions.* Berkeley, CA: Ten Speed Press, 2010.

———. *Washoku: Recipes from the Japanese Home Kitchen.* Berkeley, CA: Ten Speed Press, 2005.

Arcaya de Deliot, Flor. *The Food & Cooking of Peru.* London: Aquamarine, 2009.

Bauer, Michael. *The Secrets of Success Cookbook: Signature Recipes and Insider Tips from San Francisco's Best Restaurants.* San Francisco: Chronicle Books, 2000.

Beard, James. *James Beard's American Cookery.* Boston: Little Brown, 1972.

Belleme, Jan, and John Belleme. *Japanese Foods That Heal: Using Traditional Japanese Ingredients to Promote Health, Longevity & Well-Being.* North Clarendon, VT: Tuttle, 2007.

Biggs, Matthew, Jekka McVicar, and Bob Flowerdew. *Vegetables, Herbs & Fruit: An Illustrated Encyclopedia.* Buffalo, NY: Firefly Books, 2006.

Bishop, Jack. *Vegetables Every Day: The Definitive Guide to Buying and Cooking Today's Produce, with More Than 350 Recipes.* New York: HarperCollins, 2001.

Brennan, Georgeanne. *Down to Earth: Great Recipes for Root Vegetables.* San Francisco: Chronicle Books, 1996.

Bubel, Mike, and Nancy Bubel. *Root Cellaring: Natural Cold Storage of Fruits and Vegetables*, 2nd ed. North Adams, MA: Storey, 1991.

Burpee Lois. *Lois Burpee's Gardener's Companion and Cookbook.* New York: Harper & Row, 1983.

Chang, David, and Peter Meehan. *Momofuku.* New York: Clarkson Potter, 2008.

Chesman, Andrea. *Recipes from the Root Cellar: 270 Fresh Ways to Enjoy Winter Vegetables.* North Adams, MA: Storey, 2010.

Dahlen, Martha. *A Cook's Guide to Chinese Vegetables.* New York: Workman, 2000.

Davidson, Alan. *The Oxford Companion to Food.* New York: Oxford University Press, 1999.

Escoffier, A. *The Escoffier Cook Book: A Guide to the Fine Art of Cookery.* New York: Crown, 1941.

Evenden, Karen. *A Taste of Croatia: Savoring the Food, People and Traditions of Croatia's Adriatic Coast.* Ojai, CA: New Oak Press, 2008.

Fortin, François. *The Visual Food Encyclopedia.* Hoboken, NJ: John Wiley & Sons, 1996.

Fulwiler, Kyle D. *Roots & Tubers: A Vegetable Cookbook.* Seattle: Pacific Search Press, 1982.

Goldstein, Joyce. *Cucina Ebraica: Flavors of the Italian Jewish Kitchen.* San Francisco: Chronicle Books, 1998.

Hahn, Jennifer. *Pacific Feast: A Cook's Guide to West Coast Foraging and Cuisine.* Seattle: Skipstone, an imprint of The Mountaineers, 2010.

Hisamatsu, Ikuko. *Tsukemono: Japanese Pickling Recipes.* Tokyo: Joie, 2005.

Hyam, Nathan. *New Thai Cuisine.* North Vancouver, BC: Whitecap Books, 2005.

Iyer, Raghavan. *660 Curries.* New York: Workman, 2008.

Joseph, James A., M.D., Daniel A. Nadeau, M.D., and Anne Underwood. *The Color Code: A Revolutionary Eating Plan for Optimum Health.* New York: Hyperion, 2002.

Kafka, Barbara. *Vegetable Love: Vegetables Delicious, Alone or with Pasta, Seafood, Poultry, Meat and More.* New York: Artisan, 2005.

Kavasch, Barrie. *Native Harvest: Recipes and Botanicals of the American Indian.* New York: Vintage Books, 1979.

Kazuko, Emi. *Japanese Cooking: The Traditions, Techniques, Ingredients, and Recipes.* London: Hermes House, 2002.

Kijac, Maria Baez. *The South American Table: The Flavor and Soul of Authentic Home Cooking from Patagonia to Rio de Janeiro, with 450 Recipes.* Boston: Harvard Common Press, 2003.

Kiple, Kenneth F., and Kriemhild Coneè Ornelas. *The Cambridge World History of Food Vol. I & II.* Cambridge, UK: Cambridge University Press, 2000.

Kitchen, Leanne. *The Produce Bible: Essential Ingredient Information and More Than 200 Recipes for Fruits, Vegetables, Herbs & Nuts.* New York: Stewart, Tabori, & Chang, 2007.

Ko, Masaki. *Taste of Japan.* London: Anness, 1997.

Kuo, Irene. *The Key to Chinese Cooking.* New York: Alfred A. Knopf, 1977.

La Puma, John, M.D., and Rebecca Powell Marx. *Chef MD's Big Book of Culinary Medicine.* New York: Three Rivers Press, 2008.

Lach, Alma. *Hows and Whys of French Cooking.* Chicago: University of Chicago Press, 1974.

Larkcom, Joy. *Oriental Vegetables: The Complete Guide for Garden and Kitchen.* New York: Kodansha International, 1991.

MacKenzie, Jennifer, and Steve Maxwell. *The Complete Root Cellar Book: Building Plans, Uses and 100 Recipes.* Toronto: Robert Rose, 2010.

Marks, Copeland. *The Exotic Kitchens of Peru: The Land of the Incas.* New York: M. Evans, 1999.

Mathiot, Ginette. *I Know How to Cook.* New York: Phaidon Press, 2009.

National Geographic Society. *Edible: An Illustrated Guide to the World's Food Plants.* Washington, DC: National Geographic Society, 2008.

Nguyen, Andrea. *Into the Vietnamese Kitchen: Treasured Foodways, Modern Flavors.* Berkeley, CA: Ten Speed Press, 2006.

Oliver, Raymond. *La Cuisine: Secrets of Modern French Cooking.* New York: Tudor, 1969.

Olney, Richard, chief series consultant. *The Good Cook: Vegetables.* Chicago: Time-Life Books, 1979.

Ono, Tadashi, and Harris Salat. *Japanese Hot Pots: Comforting One-Pot Meals.* Berkeley, CA: Ten Speed Press, 2009.

Oseland, James. *Cradle of Flavor: Home Cooking from the Spice Islands of Indonesia, Malaysia, and Singapore.* New York: W.W. Norton, 2006.

Pratt, Steven, M.D., and Kathy Matthews. *Super Foods: Fourteen Foods that Will Change Your Life.* New York: William Morrow, 2004.

Robinson, Mark. *Izakaya: The Japanese Pub Cookbook.* Tokyo: Kodansha International, 2008.

Ross, Rosa Lo San. *Beyond Bok Choy: A Cook's Guide to Asian Vegetables with 70 Recipes.* New York: Artisan, 1996.

Routhier, Nicole. *The Foods of Vietnam.* New York: Stewart, Tabori, & Chang, 1989.

Schlesinger, Chris, John Willoughby, and Dan George. *Quick Pickles: Easy Recipes with Big Flavor.* San Francisco: Chronicle Books, 2001.

———. *Vegetables from Amaranth to Zucchini: The Essential Reference.* New York: William Morrow, 2001.

Schneider, Elizabeth. *Uncommon Fruits & Vegetables: A Commonsense Guide.* New York: Harper & Row, 1986.

Shimbo, Hiroko. *The Japanese Kitchen: 250 Recipes in a Traditional Spirit.* Boston: Harvard Common Press, 2000.

Shimizu, Shinko. *New Salads: Quick, Healthy Recipes from Japan.* Tokyo: Kodansha International, 1986.

Solomon, Charmaine. *The Complete Asian Cookbook.* Dee Why West, NSW: Paul Hamlyn, 1976.

Stone, Martin, and Sally Stone. *The Essential Root Vegetable Cookbook: A Primer for Choosing and Serving Nature's Buried Treasures.* New York: Clarkson N. Potter, 1991.

Teubner, Christian. *The Vegetable Bible.* New York: Chartwell Books, 2010.

Thomas, Cathy. *Melissa's Great Book of Produce: Everything You Need to Know About Fresh Fruits and Vegetables.* Hoboken, NJ: John Wiley & Sons, 2006.

Thompson, David. *Thai Street Food: Authentic Recipes, Vibrant Traditions.* Berkeley, CA: Ten Speed Press, 2009.

Tsuji, Shizuo. *Japanese Cooking: A Simple Art.* New York: Kodansha International, 1980.

Trang, Corinne. *Essentials of Asian Cuisine: Fundamentals and Favorite Recipes.* New York: Simon & Schuster, 2003.

Tropp, Barbara. *China Moon Cookbook: 250 Homestyle Recipes from the Chef of San Francisco's Acclaimed Chinese Bistro.* New York: Workman, 1992.

Van Wyk, Ben–Erik. *Food Plants of the World.* Singapore: Times Editions–Marshall Cavendish, 2005.

Vassallo, Jody. *Basic Japanese Cooking: Including Sushi, Sashimi and Yakitori.* North Vancouver, BC: Whitecap Books, 2009.

Vaswani, Suneeta. *Complete Book of Indian Cooking: 350 Recipes from the Regions of India.* Toronto: Robert Rose, 2007.

Vaughan, J. G., and C. A. Geissler. *The New Oxford Book of Food Plants*, 2nd ed. New York: Oxford University Press, 2009.

Waters, Alice. *Chez Panisse Vegetables.* New York: William Morrow, 1996.

Yu, Su-Mei. *Cracking the Coconut: Classic Thai Home Cooking.* New York: William Morrow, 2000.

ARTICLES AND WEB SITES CONSULTED

Gush, Rick, "Produce Bound Underground," *Hobby Farms* magazine, June/July 2003 (www.HobbyFarms.com).

Tortorello, Michael, "Food Storage as Grandma Knew It," *New York Times,* November 6, 2008.

"The History of Root Cellars," www.ehow.com

www.africanfoods.co.uk

www.food.oregonstate.edu

www.kew.org/plant-cultures

www.seedsofchange.com

www.sweetpotatoes.com

SOURCES

GENERAL ROOT VEGETABLE AND SEED SOURCES

FRIEDA'S: www.friedas.com
Over 600 varieties of fruits, vegetables, and companion products.

HEIRLOOM SEEDS: www.heirloomseeds.com
Large selection of root vegetable seeds.

LOCAL HARVEST: www.localharvest.org
National source for organic foods from local farmers' markets and family farms.

MELISSA'S: www.melissas.com
Extensive variety of seasonal produce from around the world.

PACIFIC FARMS USA: www.freshwasabi.com
Wasabi paste from roots grown in Oregon.

REAL WASABI: www.realwasabi.com
Fresh wasabi roots shipped directly to your door.

SEEDS OF CHANGE: www.seedsofchange.com
Certified-organic plant seeds.

ASIAN / JAPANESE FOODS AND TOOLS

KATAGIRI: www.katagiri.com
New York–based Japanese grocer that ships root vegetables and Japanese ingredients.

PACIFIC RIM GOURMET: www.pacificrimgourmet.com
Offers a broad selection of Asian ingredients.

UWAJIMAYA: www.uwajimaya.com
Asian grocery retailer in the Pacific Northwest.

THE WOK SHOP: www.wokshop.com
Excellent selection of Asian cooking equipment and tools.

THAI FOODS

GROCERY THAI: www.grocerythai.com
Fresh produce and packaged Thai food products.

TEMPLE OF THAI: www.templeofthai.com
Online Thai grocery store.

THAI GROCER: www.importfood.com
Offers fresh Thai groceries and cookware.

CARIBBEAN AND SOUTH AMERICAN INGREDIENTS

AMIGO FOODS: www.amigofoods.com
Food products from fifteen different Latin American nations.

BROOKS TROPICALS: www.brookstropicals.com
Supplier of tropical fruits and vegetables.

INDIAN FOODS

I SHOP INDIAN: www.ishopindian.com
Large selection of packaged curries, chutneys, and dals.

INDIAN BLEND: www.indianblend.com
Wide variety of fresh and packaged Indian foods.

SPICES AND SPECIALTY FOODS

E FOOD DEPOT: www.efooddepot.com
Importers of specialty foods and supplies from around the world.

KALUSTYAN'S: www.kalustyan.com
Global importer and processor of spices and herbs.

PENZEYS SPICES: www.penzeys.com
Wonderful resource for spices, with retail locations in select cities.

JR MUSHROOMS AND SPECIALTIES: www.jrmushroomsandspecialties.com
Large selection of specialty foods, including black truffle tapenade.

INDEX

ACKNOWLEDGMENTS

On a farm, it takes many hands to produce a bounty of vegetables—backbreaking work that's a labor of love. So, too, for a book, except it is more like butt-breaking work, with hours spent just sitting and writing. On many days, I would have preferred the glow of the morning sun to the glow of my computer screen. But the image of a solo writer hunkered down in an isolated place creating flowing text is all wrong—at least for me. Many hands helped create this book, and I have much gratitude to express.

This is my seventeenth book, and my fourteenth with Chronicle Books. During that long history some constants have existed, and Bill LeBlond is one of them. He has shaped me as a writer, encouraged me, supported my projects, and, best of all, has been a dear friend. I am profoundly grateful.

Chronicle Books has a great team filled with creative minds and incredible talent. A big thank-you to editor Amy Treadwell, who has attentively supported this project and kept it on track. To Sarah Billingsley, Doug Ogan, Claire Fletcher, Sara Schneider, Sarah Pulver, and Tera Killip. Special thanks also to Peter Perez and David Hawk, who work tirelessly and joyfully to promote and publicize my books.

To Lisa Ekus, my agent, for her amazing advice, enthusiasm, and friendship. To the entire staff at The Lisa Ekus Group for their dedicated support and work on my behalf.

To Andrea Slonecker, my fabulous assistant, a big hug and thanks. We've developed, tested, and retested so many recipes that I can hardly keep track—but you can, and that's what makes you such a gift in my life. Your generosity and spirit are a delight, making it a joy to work in the kitchen together.

This book has been improved immeasurably by the creative input from my Portland chef-friends. I am grateful to Vitaly and Kimberly Paley of Paley's Place; Kevin Ludwig, owner of Beaker & Flask; Ben Bettinger of Imperial; Gabe Rosen of Biwa; Matt Lightner, now in New York City at Atera; Greg Denton of Ox Restaurant; Chris Israel of Grüner; Pascal Sauton; and Doris Rodriguez de Platt of Andina Restaurant.

My sincerest thanks to the farmers who grow all of these wonderful roots: Alex Weiser of Weiser Family Farms in Lucerne Valley, California, for cultivating crosnes and mailing them to me; Leslie and Manuel Recio of Viridian Farms in Grand Island, Oregon, for sharing their crosne harvest with me; John Eveland and Sally Brewer of Gathering Together Farms in Philomath, Oregon; all of the folks at Spring Hill Farm in Albany, Oregon; Gene and Patrick Thiel of Prairie Creek Farm in Joseph, Oregon; and the staff and board of the Portland Farmers' Market, who make our thriving markets the best in the nation.

I would like to extend a special thank you to Elizabeth Andoh, who generously helped me understand Asian roots, and to Domenica Marchetti, who didn't hesitate for a second when I asked her if she wanted to contribute a recipe. Laura Byrne Russell not only provided a delicious recipe for sweet potatoes but also generously spent many hours reading the manuscript, ferreting out typos and inconsistencies that only an experienced food writer would recognize. Jolene George deserves special mention for her enthusiastic support in so many ways. She dug up detailed information and recipes on many of the less common roots in the book. We had great fun cooking together with Peruvian tubers, malanga, and yuca. I owe her many glasses of wine.

Many thanks to my friends who brighten my day— every day. Harriet and Peter Watson are always there to support me, providing unswerving support and laughter— it is a friendship beyond compare. To David Watson and to Paola Gentry and Eric Watson and their children, Aracely and Oliver, thank you for being such enthusiastic friends. I am grateful to be surrounded by wonderful friends and family: Richard, Barb, Abe, and Ellen LevKoy; Larry LevKoy; Barbara and Emil Trellis; Roxane, Austin, Joey, and Tommy Huang; Priscilla and John Longfield; Charlie and Jeanne Sosland; Margie Miller; Steve and Marci Taylor; Ann and Brijesh Anand; Cheryl Russell; Sherry Gable; Josie Jimenez; Summer Jameson; Karen Fong; Tori Ritchie; Laura Werlin; Karen and Bill Evenden; Susie Middleton; Suneeta Vaswani; Raghavan Iyer; Deb and Ron Adams; Braiden Rex-Johnson and Spencer Johnson; and my dear mentor, Alma Lach.

And especially to my family, Greg, Eric, Molly, and now Casey, for sharing in all that I do. Thank you for all of the love, nurturing, humor, caring, and music! With your love, I feel deeply rooted.